The Spirit of the New Testament

The SPIRIT of the NEW TESTAMENT

John Christopher Thomas

BLANDFORD FORUM

Published by Deo Publishing
P.O. Box 6284, Blandford Forum, Dorset DT11 1AQ, UK

Copyright © 2005, 2011 Deo Publishing

Printed in the United Kingdom by Henry Ling Limited, at the Dorset Press, Dorchester DT1 1HD

All rights reserved. No part of this publication may be reproduced, translated, stored in a retrieval system, or transmitted in any form or by any means, electronic, mechanical, photocopying, recording or otherwise, without prior written permission from the publisher.

The Odyssea Greek font used in the publication of this work is available from Linguist's Software, Inc., www.linguistsoftware.com, PO Box 580, Edmonds, WA 98020-0580 USA, tel. (425) 775-1130.

British Library Cataloguing-in-Publication data
A catalogue record for this book is available from the British Library

ISBN 978-905854-0294

Contents

Preface vii
Acknowledgements.. x
Abbreviations xii

Introduction.. 1

Chapter 1
Pentecostal Theology in the Twenty-First Century 3

Chapter 2
The Spirit, Healing, and Mission: A Survey of the Biblical Canon............... 23

Chapter 3
The Kingdom of God in the Gospel according to Matthew 48

Chapter 4
Discipleship in Mark's Gospel 62

Chapter 5
A Reconsideration of the Ending of Mark.. 77

Chapter 6
(With Kimberly Ervin Alexander) "And the Signs Are Following":
Mark 16.9-20 – A Journey into Pentecostal Hermeneutics......................... 93

Chapter 7
The Composition of the Fourth Gospel... 116

Chapter 8
The Fourth Gospel and Rabbinic Judaism 130

Chapter 9
The Spirit in the Fourth Gospel: Narrative Explorations 157

Chapter 10
Healing in the Atonement: A Johannine Perspective................................. 175

Chapter 11
A Note on the Text of John 13:10 190

Chapter 12
Footwashing in the Context of the Lord's Supper 197

Chapter 13
Footwashing: A Bibliographic Essay 213

Chapter 14
The Charismatic Structure of Acts 223

Chapter 15
Women, Pentecostals, and the Bible:
An Experiment in Pentecostal Hermeneutics 233

Chapter 16
The Order of the Composition of the Johannine Epistles 248

Chapter 17
The Literary Structure of 1 John 255

Index of Names 267
Index of Biblical and Other Ancient References 273

Preface

The road one travels in life is marked by specific points, the significance of which occasions a certain taking stock of and personal reflection about one's journey. As with a number of other colleagues, the approach of my fiftieth birthday has presented such an opportunity for me. Unlike some of my companions, this occasion does not generate within me a sense of dread or fear, as if the arrival of a certain age carries with it ominous signs of one's demise. Perhaps this missing component in my own journey has something to do with the fact that I never really thought about living this long. It is not that I have had a premonition of an early death nor a desire for an early demise. I really just have not thought much about living a long life. Consequently, I suppose that part of my response to the arrival of this half-century mark in my life is a certain amount of relief that I made it this far and a sense of anticipation as to where any bonus years might take me.

One result of this milestone, and the reflection it has generated, is the decision to publish this book of essays. While I have given some thought to such a project over the last several years, there was either not enough time to devote to the project, given other commitments that parish and seminary life necessitated, or when I decided to move forward with the project I simply did not feel that the time was right. However, as the years have gone by, the contexts in which I live and work have made it clear that the time is now right to proceed with this project. Specifically, the needs of my students to have in one volume a number of the essays I have generated over the years convinced me to approach a publisher about this book. In addition to this, I finally settled upon a title for the book – one suggested by my friend David E. Orton.

As with any journey traveling companions determine to one extent or another how one experiences the journey and sometimes even the direction of the journey. When one is joined by enjoyable companions even an unforeseen delay is treated with joy as it provides additional time to be in their company. Conversely, other companions can make a potentially pleasurable and productive trip seem tedious and painful.

In my case, the journey has been shared with numerous individuals and groups whose influence, ideas, and support may be detected by the discerning reader in the studies that make up this collection. They include family and friends, teachers and colleagues, brothers and sisters in the Lord. They are North American and South American, African and Asian, European and Australian.

When making a long journey with others, one has opportunity not only to learn about one's companions but also to learn much about oneself. This has certainly been the case with my journey. The longer I live, the more I come to realize how intertwined my own existence (and thought) is with my companions and how difficult it is to disentangle my own ideas and discoveries from those with whom I travel. This is particularly true of my relationship(s) with several colleagues: my former teacher R. Hollis Gause, my fellow editors Rick D. Moore and Steven J. Land, Cheryl Bridges Johns, and more recently Kimberly Ervin Alexander and Lee Roy Martin. These and other colleagues, past and present, have made their own unique contributions to my pathway, making the Church of God Theological Seminary an ideal place for the work of constructive Pentecostal Theology. Without the influence and support of this community, my life and work would be all the poorer.

In addition to these, there are other traveling companions who merit mention. I should very much like to thank David E. Orton for agreeing to the publication of this volume and for his many sensitive and valuable suggestions. His life and work have crossed paths with my own at very strategic moments and it only seems proper that we wound up working together on this project. My former graduate assistant, Richard Hicks, is also to be thanked for his help on a number of manuscript related items. I should like to offer my heartfelt appreciation and thanks to Ethan Everts, my current graduate assistant, who prepared the indices and read the proofs.

One of the communities of faith that regularly informs and transforms my life and theology is the Woodward Ave Church of God in Athens, TN. The resiliency and strength of this community continues to amaze and inspire me. I am grateful for their abiding spiritual support.

My parents' contribution to me and my various pursuits cannot be measured by any instrument or means. I could never repay the debt I owe them for their undying support of me and my family. They are models of spirituality, encouragement and empowerment.

My wife, Barbara, is without question the hardest-working person I have ever known. Despite the ways in which my research, writing, and teaching duties complicate her own very busy schedule, over these years she has never complained nor failed to provide the stable context that is our home. My gratitude cannot adequately be expressed in words. My daughters, Paige and Lori, who both 'reach for the stars' in their own distinct ways, continue to blossom into the wonderful individuals they were born to be. They have no idea how proud their mother and I are of them. They are their parents' delights.

It is with a profound sense of gratitude for my journey and those who have traveled with me that I offer these studies to those who may have reason to look to them as they make their own journeys.

Acknowledgements

The following publishers and journals kindly granted permission to include versions of the following in this volume:

'Pentecostal Theology in the Twenty-First Century', *Pneuma* 20 (1998), pp. 3-19.

'The Spirit, Healing, and Mission: A Survey of the Biblical Canon', *International Review of Mission* 93 (2004), pp. 421-42.

'The Kingdom of God in the Gospel according to Matthew', *New Testament Studies* 39 (1993), pp. 136-146.

'Discipleship in Mark's Gospel', in *Faces of Renewal* (Stanley Horton FS; ed. Paul Elbert; Peabody: Hendrickson Publishers, 1988), pp. 64-80.

'A Reconsideration of the Ending of Mark', *Journal of the Evangelical Theological Society* 26 (1983), pp. 405-419.

(With Kimberly Ervin Alexander) '"And the Signs Are Following": Mark 16.9-20 – A Journey into Pentecostal Hermeneutics', *Journal of Pentecostal Theology* 11.2 (2003), pp. 147-70.

'The Fourth Gospel and Rabbinic Judaism', *Zeitschrift für die neutestamentliche Wissenschaft* 82 (1991), pp. 159-182.

'The Spirit in the Fourth Gospel: Narrative Explorations', *The Spirit and the Mind: Essays in Informed Pentecostalism* (Donald N. Bowdle FS; ed. T.L. Cross and E. Powery; Lanham, MD: University Press of America, 2000), pp. 87-104.

'Healing in the Atonement: A Johannine Perspective', *Journal of Pentecostal Theology* (forthcoming).

'A Note on the Text of John 13:10', *Novum Testamentum* 29 (1987), pp. 46-52.

'Footwashing in the Context of the Lord's Supper', *The Lord's Supper: Believers' Church Perspectives* (ed. Dale Stoffer; Scottdale, PA: Herald Press, 1997), pp. 169-84.

'The Charismatic Structure of Acts', *Journal of Pentecostal Theology* 31.1 (2004), pp. 19-30.

'Women, Pentecostals, and the Bible: An Experiment in Pentecostal Hermeneutics', *Journal of Pentecostal Theology* 5 (1994), pp. 41-56.

'The Order of the Composition of the Johannine Epistles', *Novum Testamentum* 37 (1995), pp. 68-75.

'The Literary Structure of 1 John', *Novum Testamentum* 40 (1998), pp. 369-81.

Abbreviations

Bib	*Biblica*
BibSac	*Bibliotheca Sacra*
BJRL	*Bulletin of the John Rylands Library*
BO	*Bibliotheca orientalis*
BZ	*Biblische Zeitschrift*
CBQ	*Catholic Biblical Quarterly*
CTM	*Currents in Theology and Mission*
DNTT	*New International Dictionary of New Testament Theology*
EDNT	*Exegetical Dictionary of the New Testament*
ETPA	*European Theological Pentecostal Association*
EvT	*Evangelische Theologie*
ExpTim	*The Expository Times*
HTR	*Harvard Theological Review*
Int	*Interpretation*
JBL	*Journal of Biblical Literature*
JETS	*Journal of the Evangelical Theological Society*
JSNT	*Journal for the Study of the New Testament*
JSNTS	Journal for the Study of the New Testament Supplement Series
JSOT	*Journal for the Study of the Old Testament*
JSOTS	Journal for the Study of the Old Testament Supplement Series
JPT	*Journal of Pentecostal Theology*
JPTS	Journal of Pentecostal Theology Supplement Series
JTS	*Journal of Theological Studies*
Neot	Neotestamentica
NTS	New Testament Studies
NovT	*Novum Testamentum*
RB	*Revue biblique*
RSR	*Recherches de science religieuse*
SJT	*Scottish Journal of Theology*
SPS	Society for Pentecostal Studies
TD	*Theology Digest*
TDNT	*Theological Dictionary of the New Testament*

TDOT	*Theological Dictionary of the Old Testament*
ThS	*Teologiese Studies/Theological Studies*
TWOT	*Theological Wordbook of the Old Testament*
TynB	*Tyndale Bulletin*
TZ	*Theologische Zeitschrift*
ZNW	*Zeitschrift für die neutestamentliche Wissenschaft*
ZTK	*Zeitschrift für Theologie und Kirche*

Introduction

This collection of studies has taken shape over the last quarter century. They represent markers along the way of my own academic, theological, and spiritual journeys. The road has certainly been long and winding, often taking me in new and exciting directions that I had not envisioned nor even thought possible. These studies represent a variety of approaches, methods, and subject matter. Within these chapters one can discern the methodological shifts in my thinking and the extent of the integration of my discipline and my Pentecostal identity.

These essays have in common the fact that for the most part they were written within the context of my work at the Church of God Theological Seminary. The significance of this Pentecostal context, which has been discussed briefly in the Preface of this volume, is hard to underestimate as its impact upon these essays is felt at every level.

As the word 'Spirit' in the title of this collection suggests, several of these studies are devoted to some aspect of Pentecostal Theology. Specifically, many of these studies contribute to the emerging field of Pentecostal Theology by addressing a number of issues significant for the discipline or by examining certain topics utilizing a distinctively Pentecostal methodology. As a corollary to these overt contributions, the attentive reader will discover within a number of these essays the extent to which the role of the Holy Spirit is explored, whether the topic be pneumatology, theology, hermeneutics, healing, discipleship, or even structure. Even the other, less overtly Pentecostal, essays also fit well within the volume, for the title is *The Spirit of the New Testament*, not *The Spirit in the New Testament*. In this broader sense, whether literary, historical, or text critical in nature, each of these studies makes its own distinctive contribution to understanding something of the Spirit *of* the New Testament.

1

Pentecostal Theology in the Twenty-First Century

Pentecostalism is a relatively recent phenomenon in comparison to its Christian siblings, given that its formal origins go back about a hundred years. By any means of calculation it continues to grow very rapidly in many places around the globe and accounts for a significant percentage of the world's Christians. As Pentecostal theology continues to come of age there appears to be an emerging consensus that despite the enormous cultural, ethnic, linguistic, and theological diversity of those who make up the movement, certain defining characteristics may be identified that many in Pentecostalism share.

If it is true that Pentecostalism is still in its adolescence as a movement,[1] with the many resulting conflicts which that stage brings, then one would think that the tradition will at some point in the not too distant future enter its period of adulthood. Normally adulthood brings with it a growing sense of one's own identity and *raison d'être*, an independence, and a host of responsibilities, especially with regard to various dependants – some daughters and sons, others inherited. The nature and significance of Pentecostal theology in the twenty-first century will be determined in large part by how we as a movement make the transition from adolescence to adulthood.

In the editorial of the inaugural issue of the *Journal of Pentecostal Theology*, the history of Pentecostal scholarship was sketched in terms of three distinct phases.

> First there came a generation of Pentecostal scholars who completed graduate theological programs in an environment which did not encourage nor even perceive the viability of interaction between Pentecostal faith and critical theological scholarship.[2]

---

[1] For this analysis cf. the SPS presidential address of C. Bridges Johns, 'The Adolescence of Pentecostalism: In Search of a Legitimate Sectarian Identity', *Pneuma* 17 (1995), pp. 3-17.

[2] R.D. Moore, J.C. Thomas, S.J. Land, 'Editorial', *JPT* 1 (1992), p. 3.

One could say that these scholars received their theological training *despite* being Pentecostal! The most one could do in that environment was to undertake research on a topic or issue of some relevance to the tradition. But more times than not, even this luxury was denied with the unspoken suspicion that the individual scholar in question could not be objective enough.

> A second generation of Pentecostal scholars found opportunity for the first time to bring their Pentecostalism to bear upon their graduate research, but only in the area of descriptive historical study or social scientific analysis of the Pentecostal movement.[3]

One of the best known and earliest of such studies was that of Vinson Synan on the history of the holiness Pentecostal movement in the United States.[4] But a variety of such works could be cited here as well.

> Now Pentecostalism is witnessing the rise of a third generation of theological scholarship, in which the distinctives of Pentecostal faith are informing critical theological research across the entire range of theological subdisciplines.[5]

Among the earliest such attempts were Ronald Kydd's *Charismatic Gifts in the Early Church*,[6] Roger Stronstad's *The Charismatic Theology of St. Luke*,[7] and Harold Hunter's *Spirit Baptism: A Pentecostal Alternative*.[8] Now, it is difficult to keep up with the many theses and dissertations which either address Pentecostal topics or take a Pentecostal approach to a given topic.

If the assessment of that inaugural editorial was anywhere near the mark, the last few years have perhaps witnessed the emergence of still another generation of Pentecostal theological scholarship. Given the growing numbers of Pentecostals pursuing graduate theological training, the landscape at many seminaries is changing, if not always on the faculties, at least in a new freedom with regard to research options for Pentecostal research students. This generation (which includes boomers, busters, and Xers) not only benefits from the demographic shift which has resulted in Pentecostals being the largest student constitu-

---

[3] Moore, Thomas, and Land, 'Editorial', p. 3.
[4] V. Synan, *The Holiness-Pentecostal Movement in the United States* (Grand Rapids: Eerdmans, 1971).
[5] Moore, Thomas, and Land, 'Editorial', pp. 3-4.
[6] R.A.N. Kydd, *Charismatic Gifts in the Early Church* (Peabody, MA: Hendrickson, 1984).
[7] R. Stronstad, *The Charismatic Theology of St. Luke* (Peabody, MA: Hendrickson, 1984).
[8] H.D. Hunter, *Spirit Baptism: A Pentecostal Alternative* (Lanham, MD: University Press of America, 1983).

ency at many institutions, but also from the paradigm shift from modernity to post-modernity, as a variety of methodologies and participants are finding a place at the academic table. In addition, this fourth generation has the opportunity to read, assess, and critique academic works by Pentecostal scholars, an opportunity largely impossible just a few short years ago. Being able to pursue theological training in constructive Pentecostal contexts, to learn from the attempts of those who have ventured into the academic study of Pentecostal theology, and to enter into dialogue with a growing number of interested outsiders, many members of this most recent generation are exhibiting a confidence that suggests the inferiority complex of previous generations is beginning to disappear and with it the courage to construct Pentecostal theological paradigms from the ground up; paradigms that are faithful to the ethos and world view of the tradition, rather than simply settling for ill-fitting paradigms which often are greater hindrances than helps in the articulation of a Pentecostal theology.

It is, of course, true that this generation faces a variety of dangers, some from outside, others from inside the tradition. Although welcomed for their numbers, enthusiasm, and vigor, Pentecostals continue to receive mixed signals from the academy. Despite numerous recent initiatives, with rare exceptions funding agencies have still not demonstrated a willingness to allow Pentecostal scholars a piece of the funding pie. Despite the official denials and explanations, inadvertent comments from 'blind reviewers' and unofficial comments from sympathetic development officers reveal the existence of surprisingly deep-seated prejudices. Even the AAR, that organization which seems to have a tent big enough for everyone, apparently does not believe that Pentecostals can be trusted with their own section or group, despite the fact that their Evangelical counterparts seem to have gotten on quite well for a number of years now. Simply put, the academy at large, like Evangelical associations before it, wants to make a place officially for this large demographic group, but is still reluctant to entrust or empower with any sort of ongoing leadership roles to those who continue to be openly identified as Pentecostal. Thus, while many in this fourth generation have the opportunity to interact with the best of scholarship in a variety of places, the 'glass ceiling' continues to be a factor in everything from employment to research funding. It remains to be seen whether this generation will have the courage to remain Pentecostal despite the concrete liabilities such a decision entails.

This fourth generation also faces a variety of dangers from inside the tradition, dangers that while quite different are no less real. Specifically, this generation faces the twin dangers of suspicion and jealousy. Several things account for this situation. First, opportunity to study at leading centers for biblical and theological enquiry around the world has been cause for concern on the part of those who have been guardians of the theological tradition. Sometimes this suspicion is the result of anxiety about new methodologies or fears about contamination from 'liberal theology'. Unfortunately, this fear is compounded by the fact that within certain parts of our movement, the tradition's theological positions have become fossilized so that much more effort is spent rehearsing long-held opinions than the work of constructive Pentecostal theology. Efforts to rethink certain issues, even when the rethinking results in stronger, more articulate and better-nuanced understandings of extraordinarily important doctrines, often are simply ignored if not met with criticism for complicating the issue.

In addition to suspicion, this and other generations face the danger of jealousy. Part of the problem here results from the competitive spirit which has often been the hallmark not only of Pentecostal educational institutions but also denominations within the tradition. It is this jealousy which so often makes it difficult to dialogue or support one another for fear of losing one's own place. What has often been absent in these situations is a leadership or, to use more biblical terminology, an eldership which seeks to nurture and empower those whom the Lord is raising up rather than protecting professional and ministerial turf. Sadly, these obstacles combine in ways that result in the loss of many of the tradition's best, brightest, and most dedicated individuals. In order to avoid the repetition of such a tragic situation with yet another generation, leaders within the tradition must be intentional about their role as cultivators of those who are coming on the scene. Thus, most of the responsibility lies with those of us entrusted with leadership roles. At the same time, those within this new generation can contribute to the process in at least two ways. First, gratitude needs to be expressed for those of previous generations upon whose shoulders the most recent generation stands. The current opportunities would not be possible without those who have gone before. Second, passion for the theological heart of Pentecostalism needs to be demonstrated. Such a passion for what God has done and will do through Pentecostalism can go a long way toward undermining the caricature, commonplace at various levels in the church, that equates academic pursuits with a loss of spirituality.

If these are some of the dangers, what of Pentecostal theology's future? Without any illusions on my part of being able to predict the future of Pentecostal theology or to offer a comprehensive prescription, the remainder of this essay will seek to describe certain characteristics of Pentecostal theology in the twenty-first century and offer two attempts at constructive Pentecostal theology in different academic disciplines.

Characteristics of Pentecostal Theology in the Twenty-First Century

Given the recent history and developments within academic circles of the tradition, the following aspects would appear to be some of the more prominent and important characteristics of Pentecostal theology in the next century.

Community

It would seem safe to suggest that it is extraordinarily difficult to be a Pentecostal theologian or do constructive Pentecostal theology if one is not part of a believing, worshipping Pentecostal community. Given the dynamics of the Pentecostal church, with its emphasis upon our corporate life together and an appreciation for the spiritual and scriptural phenomenon of unity and diversity within the body, such an observation should surprise few. It should be obvious to most that to argue the need for Pentecostal theology to be informed and shaped by the Pentecostal community is more than an acknowledgment that Pentecostal theologians should be church attendees or conversant with the theology of the tradition. Rather, it is a confession of the extremely tight interplay that must exist between the ethos of the tradition and the work of those called to discover, construct, and articulate its theology. If the intent of the Pentecostal theologian is to speak to, as well as for, the tradition, there can be no substitute for a very intense engagement with the Pentecostal community in ways that go beyond guest speaking or somewhat 'detached' observation.

Sadly, some scholars working within the tradition have been characterized more by isolation from and an antagonistic position over against the community than critical active engagement with it. This isolation is, in part, the result of (a) the academy's influence, which has at times projected the view of the scholar as one who works in isolation from others, (b) a lack of appreciation for the distinctive way in which Pentecostals do theology, often within the context of worship,

(c) insecurity on the part of those in leadership positions within local churches which sometimes results in rejection of the theologian's gifts, (d) a lack of sufficient role models who combine rigorous academic enquiry with an intense spirituality, and (e) time constraints that many of us feel given other responsibilities. Whatever the reasons, it is sufficiently clear that some of the more recent encouraging contributions to constructive Pentecostal theology have come from those whose theological enquiries are pursued within the context of a worshipping Pentecostal community that informs and sustains it. My guess is that the best of Pentecostal theology in the twenty-first century will be characterized by a strong commitment to community.

Integration
Another defining characteristic of Pentecostal theology in the twenty-first century, I would suggest, is integration. Specifically, integration would appear to be crucial in three particular aspects of the constructive theological task. As each of these aspects is surveyed, it should become apparent how the issue of integration is closely associated with doing theology within the context of a worshipping Pentecostal community.

The integration of heart and head is clearly one of the most significant challenges to the formation of those involved in the theological task. Pentecostals, perhaps more than most, should understand that doing theology is more than an exercise in rationalism. Unfortunately, often within our tradition theology has been pursued in just this fashion, resulting in a bifurcation of theology and ethics – a division that is both without scriptural support and out of keeping with the very heart of the tradition. The integration of heart and head means that theologians within the tradition do not have the luxury of simply focusing on 'pure' theology while leaving for the so-called 'practitioners' the task of working out its implications. Such an approach would seem to miss the point completely. Doing theology in a way that is intentional about the integration of heart and head should not only lead to a transformation of the theologian, but also make clear that the work of Pentecostal theology is not simply concerned with orthodoxy (right doctrine), but orthopraxy (right practice) and orthopathy (right passions/affections) as well.[9] It hardly needs to be noted that the community context for the pursuit of such integration is essential.

---

[9] For these designations cf. S.J. Land, *Pentecostal Spirituality: A Passion for the Kingdom* (JPTS 1; Sheffield: Sheffield Academic Press, 1993), pp. 41-42. On orthopathos cf.

A second aspect of the integrative element of Pentecostal theology in the next century concerns relationships outside the tradition. The term which might best describe this dimension in dialogical. How one relates to those outside one's own theological tradition is, of course, a perennial challenge. While most of us would want to believe that God has done and is doing something special within this particular branch of the Christian tree, it seems to me that few of us would want to suggest that what is taking place outside our movement is without merit or God's blessing. In order for Pentecostal theology to function as it should in the new century, we must be willing to dialogue with a wide variety of theological dialogue partners. What is called for is not the kind of 'emperor worship' that on occasion results when Pentecostals receive the attention of a major figure within the circle of academic theology. There has sometimes been a tendency for Pentecostals to turn such opportunities into times of affirmation for the views of the scholar in question, whether or not they accurately represent the views and ethos of the movement. Nor is this a call for the accommodating 'house-servant' attitude that on occasion is exhibited when those in wider ecumenical circles invite this or that Pentecostal to participate in some consultation. Who of us involved in such work has not had the experience at one time or another of eventually understanding that the purpose of our presence was simply to sign off on the work of others rather than be given or take the opportunity to play an active role in the deliberations? Rather, what is needed is honest, sometimes even hard-hitting exchanges where theological differences and similarities may be fully appreciated. The goal, it would seem, is to testify to others about what we know to be true and to reexamine our faith in the light of the testimony of fellow travelers who have a genuine desire for dialogue. Sadly, not all who claim such a desire for dialogue live up to their promise. However, it is only through such honest exchanges that we can hope to draw nearer to a more perfect understanding of the Kingdom, while at the same time avoiding the trap of letting other groups and their agenda (both stated and hidden) define who we are and what we are about.

Given the incredible magnitude of the theological task that lies before us, integration is also needed in approaching our work together within the tradition. The word which might best convey this aspect of integration is interdisciplinary. For too long academic institutions have been characterized by more and more specialization resulting in a sense

---

also S. Solivan, *The Spirit, Pathos and Liberation: Toward an Hispanic Pentecostal Theology* (JPTS 14: Sheffield: Sheffield Academic Press, 1998).

of isolation with little or no opportunity for interdisciplinary dialogue. As my colleague, Steve Land, is fond of saying, the university has plenty of "(di-)versity" but little "uni(-ty)". The Pentecostal theology which emerges in the next century will likely be characterized by a rejection of such artificial isolation and the construction of more holistic approaches. Granted, this process takes more energies than those which stand within only one theological discipline. But the fruit of such efforts is well worth the labor. For through collaboration in this fashion, creative new constructions emerge which would otherwise be out of the reach of scholars working on their own. The need for a healthy community in which to pursue such theologizing should be apparent.

Accountability

Pentecostal theology in the twenty-first century will likely be characterized by a greater degree of accountability than currently exists among scholars working within the movement. The accountability here envisioned is not to be seen as a form of censorship, but rather as an example of the biblical view of the Body of Christ at work. For Pentecostal theologians, there is more at stake in our work than making a name, professional advancement, or development. Our children are at stake, and there are right ways and wrong ways of disagreeing in front of the children. Unfortunately, given the maverick attitude and insecurities of many in academia, often the children are used as pawns where the welfare of the teacher rather than the student is primary.

This is not to say that there is no room for honest, vigorous, and hard-hitting disagreements. Passionate disagreements are to be expected where so much is at stake. Nor is this to be heard as a call for monolithic uniformity on all interpretive issues. The lack of a healthy diversity would be a denial of the kind of diversity modeled in the canon itself. Rather, this accountability entails a rejection of carnal ways of relating to one another and assessing our own importance. Perhaps an example from the local church would be helpful at this point. If one fancies oneself as having this or that particular spiritual gift, but no one else in the community confirms such a charism in that individual, it may well be that the person needs to take seriously the lack of affirmation from the community. Likewise, it would appear that Pentecostal theologians need to be attentive to confirmation or the lack of it in our theological constructions. The point, after all, is not to be able to claim exclusive rights to the truth, but together to draw nearer to it.

Contextual
The emerging Pentecostal theology will also be contextual in nature. The diverse voices from all parts of the world which make up the Pentecostal family must not only be encouraged to find a voice, but also be encouraged and expected to speak their own theological language, making their own contributions to the larger Pentecostal family. Modernity has long embraced the idea that one theological size fits all. On this view the challenge is to articulate an a-cultural or 'pure' theology that may be applied to any and every context. Fortunately, such a position is beginning to show signs of deconstruction. The diversity of Scripture undermines this view when it reveals that uniformity is not to be confused with (spiritual) unity. In addition, the rich theological and experiential variety manifest in global Pentecostalism suggests that we as a movement are not faced with the task of re-paving a highway; rather, we stand at the edge of a wood with machete in hand, seeking to clear a path.

Clearly, one of the great strengths of contextual approaches to Scripture and theology is the empowerment that takes place for those within specific contexts which engenders the confidence necessary to enter into the difficult work of theological construction. This approach also reveals dimensions of the text and theology that have gone unnoticed, at best, or have been ignored or down-played by those in other contexts. Of course, it is always possible for contextual approaches to distort as well as clarify. But it should be noted that distortions are part of all approaches and that specific contexts determine which aspects of the faith call for emphasis. Accountability to and for the larger Pentecostal community should go a long way toward ensuring that contextual theological contributions (and it should be noted that all theological contributions are contextual!) do not become too idiosyncratic and that the larger community is not allowed to ignore the implications of the work of sisters and brothers located in contexts unlike our own. Thus, it falls to those who find themselves in leadership positions within the tradition to partner with sisters and brothers across the great cultural, ethnic, and national expanse of the movement in order that the distinctive contributions of the whole body are not only heard but also engaged. Such a task clearly involves more than tokenism or the parroting by those at the margins of more established positions. What is called for is much more difficult to achieve. On the one hand, it necessitates the development of a mechanism by which the multitude of Pentecostal voices may be identified and the various modes of discourse both appreciated and engaged. On the other hand, it necessitates the cultivation of individuals and communities within a variety of contexts capable of the articulation of constructive Pentecostal theologies. By such active engagement the entire community may be strengthened and critiqued.

Confessional

A final characteristic of Pentecostal theology in the twenty-first century is that it will be more avowedly confessional in nature. With the rise of post-modernity, the metanarratives of modernity are beginning to crumble, for their somewhat one-dimensional emphasis/basis no longer satisfies many of those in the academic arena, among others. In scholarly circles, the rules of modernity called for an approach to any and every topic that was neutral and objective. It was an approach that valued the renunciation of all presuppositional baggage that might distort or color one's work and results. Unfortunately, the effect upon many Pentecostal scholars has been to hide, if not renounce outright, their Pentecostal identity in order to do scholarly work that is respected in the guild. But if Pentecostal scholarship is to be more than a joining of ranks with the last defenders of modernity (an ironic twist if ever there was!), there must be a willingness to engage the postmodern world with the Gospel in new and creative ways. For those willing to accept such a challenge, the confessional stakes have never been higher.

The call for a more self-consciously confessional approach should not be understood as advocating the defense of every aspect of the tradition at any and all costs. Rather, it is a conscious decision to allow the implications of what we know to be true from the way in which God deals with us to have a place in the way we approach Scripture, theology, and ministry. For one thing, this means not being content with the research agenda of others but allowing our confessional context to help define the contours of our research both with regard to subject and approach. Such a move would not only help to preserve the testimony of the tradition's ambivalent relationship to modernity, where we have been para-modern at best,[10] but also to help construct and sustain 'the havens of the masses', 'the little outposts of the Kingdom', the zones of liberation and freedom, 'the tents of meeting' so

---

[10] For this terminology I am indebted to my colleague Jackie Johns. For a helpful analysis of Pentecostalism's place in a postmodern world cf. J.D. Johns, 'Pentecostalism and the Postmodern Worldview', *JPT* 7 (1995), pp. 73-96.

essential in ministering in a postmodern world.[11] This is the context for a testimony from the margins to a world desperately seeking meaning and comfort. As the modern world view begins to resemble that of the world at the time of the early church, Pentecostals seem to be in a unique position to offer an 'apology' from the margins which relies on both word and deed. No doubt some in the tradition will find this to be too much of a challenge. For those who have the strength to take it up, I believe the rewards will be great.

Two Modest Attempts at Pentecostal Theology

While it is perhaps presumptuous to attempt to lay out anything thought to be paradigms for Pentecostal theology in the twenty-first century, for integrity's sake it seems that I should at least send up a couple of trial balloons to illustrate my own limited thinking on such issues. Although I do not intend to delineate the ways in which each of these proposals are related to the characteristics described in the previous section, let me mention at the outset that they have been conceived and developed within the context of a worshipping Pentecostal community which is confessional in nature, they aim for integration at several levels and are offered here in an attempt to be accountable to a wider audience, or should I say audiences.[12]

In what follows I shall make two specific and very different proposals. One seeks to reflect upon the way a Pentecostal might approach the New Testament in an introductory or survey course. The other attempts to gain some leverage on the difficult question of a Pentecostal ecclesiology by means of a clearly Pentecostal paradigm. The latter proposal will no doubt be regarded as much more hubristic, as I am daring to make a proposal in a discipline to which I am a stranger: theology proper.

---

[11] Cf. esp. the work of C. Bridges Johns, 'Meeting God in the Margins: Ministry among Modernity's Refugees,' in *The Papers of the Henry Luce Fellows in Theology, Vol. III* (ed. M. Zyniewicz; Atlanta: Scholars Press, 1999), pp. 7-31.

[12] While a large number of dialogue partners have contributed to these proposals, special mention should be made of my colleague and friend Kimberly E. Alexander with whom both these ideas were conceived and who has field-tested them in Lee University courses offered in an extension at the Woodward Avenue Church of God in Athens, TN, where I serve as a part-time Associate Pastor. Our consultations have constantly focused upon the ways in which our courses address the formational needs of those in our Pentecostal community and have been intentional about a Pentecostal process. I am happy to offer my thanks publicly to such a valuable colleague.

A Pentecostal Approach to the New Testament

Anyone familiar with the contemporary study of the New Testament appreciates the paradigm shifts that have recently been felt with regard to methodological questions. Currently, a plethora of approaches to the New Testament are advocated, either as stand-alone methods or in combination with other methods. The dominant approach for most of the last couple of centuries has been that of historical criticism. But recently other approaches have sought to claim their share of the methodological market. Some of the more prominent include: narrative analysis, canonical criticism, contextual and ideological readings, deconstruction, intertextuality, and history of effects, to name a few. For a variety of reasons, in most cases individual interpreters simply opt for one of the several available options. For the most part, Pentecostals have been indistinguishable from many of their New Testament colleagues with regard to method, although their results have often resembled those of Evangelicalism more than others.

But what would happen if Pentecostals rethought the task of teaching New Testament Introduction or New Testament Survey from the ground up? Anyone faced with the prospects of having to teach an introductory course on the New Testament understands very well the struggle of deciding what a beginning student needs to be exposed to in their initial encounter with the New Testament. My suggestion is that the nature of the Pentecostal tradition itself can offer some assistance in making these decisions.

It would appear that from a Pentecostal perspective the New Testament documents would fall rather naturally into four categories: Stories of Jesus' Life, Story of the Early Church, Epistles and Sermons of the Early Church, and Vision of the Early Church. One of the things immediately evident from this simple division is how much connection there is between the New Testament documents themselves and the Pentecostal world-view. First, the sheer amount of narrative contained in this part of the canon is quite impressive and resonates with the place of story and testimony in Pentecostalism. Second, it is significant that one of the categories, the Apocalypse, has a very deep connection with a particular stream of the movement, ecstasy, dream, and visionary experience. Third, the role of sermon and epistle within Pentecostalism (both past and present) hardly needs to be documented. The other thing that is immediately recognizable is how different this division is from most introductory courses on the New Testament, where pride of place is often given to things that are extra-textual. Obviously these categories could be supplemented by a variety of excurses (e.g. on The World of Jesus – Judaism; The World of the Early Church – The Greco-Roman Environment; which might be effectively located after the sections devoted to The Stories of Jesus' Life and the Story of the Early Church, respectively), but the heart of the outline would focus on these four categories.

With regard to the specific methodological approach to the individual New Testament books, the following proposal seeks to keep the focus of study upon content and a variety of contexts.

1. Content, Structure, and Theological Emphases

Owing to the Pentecostal view of Scripture,[13] primary emphasis is given to the content of the New Testament itself. Consequently, close attention should be focused upon the actual content of each individual book. Given the fact that the structure and shape of a document often reveal much about the text's meaning, issues of structure are not reduced to the role of an addendum at the end of other discussions but serve as a means of entry into the world of the text itself. The particular theological emphases of the given book are also identified in this initial and largest part of the approach to Scripture.

In this section attention should be given to the literary markers in the text in order to discern the book's structure. An example drawn from the book of Acts will illustrate this point. After noting that the book can be divided into eight panels, each ending with a summary statement (2.47; 6.7; 9.31; 11.21; 12.24; 16.5; 19.20; 28.31), one discovers that each of the sections contains a description of a charismatic anointing or reference to those so anointed (2.1-4; 4.30-31; 8.14-17; 10.44-48; 11.24-28; 13.9; 19.1-17; 20.22-21.11). Such structural emphasis indicates the extraordinarily important role given to the Holy Spirit in the theology of the book, an emphasis even greater than most Pentecostals realize.[14]

This initial discussion of the content of the book is followed by discussions of the text's various contexts.

2. Canonical Context

The first such context to which attention should be paid is the book's context within the canon. Whatever the historical events that resulted in the current New Testament canon, it is clear that the structure of the canon is not without significance with regard to a particular book's

---

[13] Cf. J.C. Thomas, 'The Word and the Spirit', *Ministry and Theology* (Cleveland, TN: Pathway, 1996), pp. 13-20.

[14] Cf. Chapter 14 below.

interpretation and interpretive influence. The primary goal of this section is to determine as near as possible the role and function of a given book in the New Testament canon.[15] Here, the ways in which a book picks up on previous emphases, prepares for later developments, or acts as a transition from one section to another are all very much at issue.

Examples of the Fourth Gospel's canonical function illustrate this dimension of the approach. First, given the unique and independent nature of the Fourth Gospel's story, the Fourth Gospel serves to offer a rich theological complement to the other stories of Jesus read to this point. Whether this was intentional on the author's part or not, one of the canonical functions of the Fourth Gospel is not far removed from Clement of Alexandria's suggestion that the Fourth Gospel was written to supplement the others. Thus, the distinctive contribution of the Fourth Gospel in all its richness is part of its canonical contribution.

Second, part of the Fourth Gospel's contribution is that it presents a larger stage than do the other canonical Gospels, serving as the backdrop for understanding the story of Jesus. While Mark pushes Jesus' origin back to the baptism of John, and Matthew and Luke push back to his virginal conception by the Holy Spirit, John goes all the way back before the creation of the world as he explains Jesus' unique person and work. Therefore, before leaving the Gospels, one has some appreciation for the remarkable theological assessments of Jesus found later in the New Testament.

Third, the Fourth Gospel also prepares one for the Acts narrative which follows, in at least two ways. In ways absent from the Synoptics, the Fourth Gospel includes an explicit rehabilitation of Peter, by allowing for his triple declaration of love for Jesus to match his triple denial recorded earlier. In this way, the reader is prepared for the prominent role that Peter is to play in Acts. By focusing more attention upon Jesus' teaching about the Holy Spirit, the Fourth Gospel anticipates one of the dominant themes in Acts and other New Testament documents to follow.

3. Original Context

Although many approaches to the New Testament begin with questions of original *Sitz im Leben*, it is only after considering the book's content and canonical context that attention is given to first readers.

---

[15] Cf. esp. the helpful work of R.W. Wall and E.E. Lemcio (eds.), *The New Testament as Canon: A Reader in Canonical Criticism* (JSNTS 76; Sheffield: Sheffield Academic Press, 1992).

Part of the justification for such a methodological move is due to the fact that we know less about these issues than many of the others. How odd, then, that many of us spend most of our time on the things we are least certain about![16] This is not to say that behind-the-text concerns are unimportant nor is it to say that they are without their own distinctive contributions. It is to acknowledge, however, the provisional and hypothetical nature of much historical critical work on New Testament documents.

While a number of the traditional issues of New Testament Introduction are covered in the section devoted to the Original Context of a given book, as far as possible, literary approaches are used to gain leverage on historical issues. For example, it is after a literary analysis of the Johannine Epistles that a proposal is put forward as to the order of the composition of these documents. Owing, in part, to the absence of concern with false teaching in 3 John it is argued that this is the first of the letters to have been written, followed by 2 John, which appears to be somewhat of a knee-jerk reaction to the outbreak of false teaching. For its part, 1 John appears to be a more reflective and deliberative response to the false teaching, which has now rather clearly (been) separated from the community.[17]

4. Context in the Church

The next area of emphasis concerns the book's context within the church. Here, the primary goal is to discover something of the book's effects in the history of the church. The history of effects method is an attempt to trace the effects a given text has had since its writing. In this approach, the text is likened to a source of water that may flow in a variety of directions.[18] In one sense, to hear voices from the church with regard to a given book is like hearing testimonies of the effect this or that book has had in the church.

By way of example, one thinks immediately of the impact Romans has had upon Augustine, Luther, Wesley, and Barth, the Sermon on the Mount upon Wesley, Tolstoy, Bonhoeffer, and King, or Jas 5.16 upon Dr. Charles Cullis and Sarah Mix, a black woman who was the first itinerant healing evangelist. But there are also more mixed testi-

---

[16] As my good friend Blaine Charette once observed to me.

[17] Cf. Chapter 16 below.

[18] On this method cf. U. Luz, *Matthew in History* (Minneapolis: Fortress, 1994). For a Pentecostal critique cf. E.B. Powery, 'Ulrich Luz's *Matthew in History*: Contribution to Pentecostal Hermeneutics?' *JPT* 14 (1999), pp. 3-17. Cf. also U. Luz, 'A Response to Emerson B. Powery', *JPT* 14 (1999), pp. 19-26.

monies, as for example those related to Philemon, where both slave and slave-holder have appealed to the support of the text,[19] or the way in which Matthew 23 was utilized in Nazi Germany's anti-Semitic propaganda, or Charles Manson's interpretation of the four angels of Revelation 9, who would kill a third of humankind, as having reference to the Beatles, resulting in the Tate-LaBianca murders.[20] Discernment is required as one hears these testimonies no less than in testimonies offered in the context of Pentecostal worship. However, the history of effects has an enormous contribution to make to a Pentecostal study of the New Testament.

5. Pentecostal Context

The final component in this approach is to say something about the context of a given book within Pentecostalism. This section seeks to combine both testimonies of the book's effect with implications this book may have for the movement.

One of the greatest examples of such Pentecostal contextualization involves how Mark 16.9-20 functioned within early Pentecostalism. The magnitude of the influence of this 'longer ending' was nearly unparalleled in the biblical teaching of the movement for this text combined so many of the elements of great significance for the movement; healing, signs following believers, tongues speech, and missionary activity.[21] Its influence was enormous despite the text-critical problems, which those in the tradition addressed in a variety of ways. Another example of Pentecostal contextualization may be offered from the book of Jude. In the first place, the importance of Jude is testified to by the fact that Jude 3 ('"Earnestly contend for the faith which was once delivered unto the saints." – Jude 3') was used on the masthead of a publication no less important to Pentecostalism than *The Apostolic Faith* published by William Seymour in the heyday of the Azusa Street revival. Furthermore, few within the tradition would deny that Jude's hard-hitting words about false teachers (and their characteristics) find application within a movement that has had to contend with false teachers from the beginning.

---

[19] Cf. the provocative work by A. Callahan, *Embassy of Onesimus: The Letter of Paul to Philemon* (Valley Forge, PA: Trinity, 1997).

[20] Barry Miles, *Paul McCartney: Many Years from Now* (New York: Henry Holt and Co., 1997), pp. 488-90.

[21] On this cf. esp. K.E. Alexander, *Pentecostal Healing: Theology and Practice* (JPTS 30; Blandford Forum: Deo Publishing, forthcoming). Cf. also Chapter 6 below.

A Pentecostal Approach to Ecclesiology

One of the areas within the tradition where theological reflection may remain in its infancy is ecclesiology. While bitter debates have taken place over this or that particular ecclesiological understanding, largely pertaining to matters of polity, theologians of the movement appear to be taking their first small steps toward the discovery and articulation of a Pentecostal ecclesiology. It is to this disputed area that I focus my last comments of this study.

By means of the work of Don Dayton[22] and Steve Land[23], among others, I have come to be convinced that standing at the theological heart of Pentecostalism is the five-fold Gospel: Jesus is Savior, Sanctifier, Holy Ghost Baptizer, Healer, and Coming King. It is my belief that when a Pentecostal theology is written from the ground up, it will be structured around these central tenets of Pentecostal faith and preaching. In fact, I have to admit to a great deal of surprise at my colleagues in theology proper that this approach has not been taken up formally, for it seems like such a natural place to begin and appears to have so much promise for the articulation of a theology that is distinctively Pentecostal. One of the very helpful things about this paradigm is that it immediately reveals the ways in which Pentecostalism as a movement is both similar to and dissimilar from others within Christendom. To mention but two examples, when the five-fold Gospel paradigm is used as the main point of reference the near kinship to the holiness tradition is obvious, as is the fundamental difference with many of those within the evangelical tradition.

Perhaps the time has come for those within the tradition to ask what contribution the five-fold Gospel paradigm can make to an understanding of Pentecostal ecclesiology. Rather than simply modifying one of the competing views of the church currently being advocated or opting for one of the several New Testament models, while ignoring or conflating the others, perhaps the time is right for a construction which is not only conscious but intentional about its connection with the movement. In the brief observations that follow, I shall highlight a few of the salient features of such an attempt.

One of the first questions raised by this approach has to do with where in the development of the theology one would place a discussion of ecclesiology. In contrast to many theological constructions,

---

[22]D.W. Dayton, *The Theological Roots of Pentecostalism* (Peabody, MA: Hendrickson, 1991).

[23]Land, *Pentecostal Spirituality*.

where this discussion is located near the end, often in a somewhat detached fashion, a five-fold method would necessitate a much more integrated approach. Therefore, reflection about the nature, mission, and identity of the church would constitute a portion of the discussion in each of the five elements making up the whole. Thus, each of the five major divisions would conclude with a section devoted to the church, where the implications of each element for the community and its life are explored.

Specifically, discussions would focus on the church and salvation (or the Church as Redeemed Community), the church and sanctification (or the Church as Holy Community), the church and Spirit Baptism (or the Church as Empowered Missionary Community), the church and healing (or the Church as Healing Community), and the church and the return of Christ (or the Church as Eschatological Community). Such an approach would make clear the integral connection between the theological heart of Pentecostalism as revealed in the fivefold Gospel and the nature of its community life. Obviously, the biblical metaphors used for the church would find a prominent place in these discussions.

Finally, this method would also go some way toward reclaiming and re-appropriating the sacraments for a tradition which has been a bit uncertain about them and their place in the community's worship. Just as discussion of the church would no longer be artificially separated from the doctrines which give it meaning, so discussion of the sacraments would become grounded both in the relevant discussions of the church and in the larger discussion of a particular aspect of the fivefold Gospel. Thus, this approach to the church would help make clear for Pentecostals the dynamic relationship that should exist between these Signs and the experience of salvation itself. In addition, it might also lead Pentecostals to a reconsideration of the nature and number of sacraments and the discovery that there is in our life and practice a Sign to accompany each element of the five-fold Gospel! What are these five sacraments and how do they relate to the five-fold Gospel? With regard to *Salvation*, most would agree that Water Baptism is an appropriate sign. With regard to *Sanctification*, my own work[24] and that more recently of Frank Macchia[25] suggests that Footwashing is the sign of sanctification, a practice present in various streams of our tradition

---

[24]J.C. Thomas, *Footwashing in John 13 and the Johannine Community* (JSNTS 61; Sheffield: JSOT Press, 1991).

[25]F.D. Macchia, 'Is Footwashing the Neglected Sacrament?', *Pneuma* 19 (1997), pp. 239-49.

including Azusa Street.[26] With regard to *Spirit Baptism*, Frank Macchia has argued persuasively that for Pentecostals glossolalia is the visible sign of God's presence *par excellence*.[27] The relationship of glossolalia to Spirit Baptism for most Pentecostals is quite well known. With regard to *Healing*, anointing the sick with oil, a practice based upon Jesus' implicit command in Mark 6.13 and the practice of the church in James 5, has long functioned sacramentally for Pentecostals despite the

---

[26] The practice of footwashing in early Pentecostal circles was remarkably widespread. The emerging Church of God practiced footwashing from the beginning. For Richard Spurling, one of the founders of the Christian Union (1886), the practice of footwashing predates his involvement with the Christian Union as footwashing was regularly practiced at the Holly Springs Baptist Church where he was a member.

The experience of A.J. Tomlinson with the practice of footwashing also predates his involvement with the Church of God and a precise date can be established for his initial experience with the practice. According to his diary, Tomlinson first practiced footwashing on 25 March 1901. His entry for that day reads:

"The day and week began with a special burden and prayer on my heart for $5,000 [for the orphanage work], after a special outpouring of the Spirit in our Sunday meeting yesterday. I could not take my breakfast as usual. At night we had special prayer and after prayer I read the words of Jesus that we received the petitions we desired because we keep his commandments. I then turned, guided by the Spirit and read where Jesus washed the disciples' feet and said, 'ye ought to wash one another's feet'. I had never obeyed this commandment. I at once laid aside my coat, girded myself with a towel, poured water into a basin and washed the feet of the brethren present. Praise God."

There is also evidence for the practice of footwashing among other early Pentecostals. The practice of footwashing is found to be part of the life and ministry of C.H. Mason and the Church of God in Christ, which he founded. According to the September 1907 issue of The Apostolic Faith, footwashing was practiced at the Azusa Street revival as an ordinance along with Water Baptism and the Lord's Supper. E.N. Bell, editor of *The Weekly Evangel*, an early Assemblies of God publication, advocates the practice of footwashing among believers (only) and gives instructions for how the rite is to be observed. There are several other references to the practice of footwashing in the January 8, 1916 issue of *The Weekly Evangel*. The 1917 edition of The Pentecostal Holiness Church book of discipline (p. 9) states, 'Each individual member of The Pentecostal Holiness Church shall have liberty of conscience in the matter of footwashing' indicating that a not insignificant number in this body made a place for this practice in their worship.

For the practice of footwashing at Azusa Street cf. D.T. Irvin, '"Drawing All Together in One Bond of Love": The Ecumenical Vision of William J. Seymour and the Azusa Street Revival', *JPT* 6 (1995), p. 35 esp. n. 23. I am indebted to David Roebuck for the information on Spurling.

[27] F.D. Macchia, 'Tongues as a Sign: Towards a Sacramental Understanding of the Pentecostal Experience', *Pneuma* 15 (1993), pp. 61-76.

fact that we have not used that language to describe the practice.[28] With regard to *Coming King*, the sacramental sign of the Lord's return is appropriately, the eschatological banquet, the Lord's Supper, a meal in which past, present, and future converge[29] as we long for his appearing.

My desire in this study is not necessarily to be right in all that I have here said, but rather to serve as a catalyst for theological reflection that is wholly Pentecostal. Reflection that is more concerned about its rightness for the tradition than its acceptance in the guild. May the Lord grant us the courage to be what he has called us to be.

---

[28] Cf. J.C. Thomas, 'The Devil, Disease, and Deliverance: James 5:14-16', *JPT* 2 (1993), pp. 34-40.

[29] Land, *Pentecostal Spirituality*, p. 98.

2

The Spirit, Healing, and Mission: An Overview of the Biblical Canon[*]

Anyone familiar with Pentecostalism knows that the doctrine and practice of divine healing is a particularly important part of the Pentecostal movement's life and beliefs. As has been documented by various students of the movement, the theological heart of Pentecostalism is the five-fold Gospel: the conviction that Jesus is our Savior, our Sanctifier, our Holy Ghost Baptizer, our Healer, and our Soon Coming King.[1] Thus, for Pentecostals divine healing does not function as a peripheral element or a theological addendum to the proclamation of the Gospel, but is part and parcel of such Gospel proclamation.

The issue of healing intersects with my life at many points. As a student of the New Testament, I have sought to explore certain dimensions of the subject in an academic monograph on the topic[2] and on a yearly basis I teach graduate level seminars devoted to healing. As a member of a vibrant Pentecostal worshiping community, I participate in prayer for the sick several times a week. The occasion for this study offers me the opportunity to think intentionally about the relationship between the Spirit, healing, and the mission of the church in an ecumenical context.

Having said something about my contextual identity, I should like to offer a very brief orientation to the chapter that follows. First, like most Pentecostals, I am convinced of the Spirit's activity both in the

---

[*] Earlier versions of this chapter were presented to the WCC Consultation on Healing and Mission in Santiago, Chile and the Post-Graduate Seminar at the Church of God Theological Seminary in Cleveland, TN. I am grateful for the many helpful suggestions made by the participants of these two forums.

[1] Cf. esp. D.W. Dayton, *The Theological Roots of Pentecostalism* (Peabody, MA: Hendrickson, 1991) and S.J. Land, *Pentecostal Spirituality: A Passion for the Kingdom* (JPTS 1; Sheffield: Sheffield Academic Press, 1993).

[2] J.C. Thomas, *The Devil, Disease, and Deliverance: The Origins of Illness in New Testament Thought* (JPTS 13; Sheffield: Sheffield Academic Press, 1998).

inspiration³ and interpretation⁴ of Scripture. This means, in part, that one should not shrink from what is found within Scripture, but that the unity and diversity present must be allowed to stand and not be hammered into an artificial unity. I would like to suggest that Scripture be likened to a choir – not just any choir but a black gospel choir.⁵ Those familiar with this musical style and tradition will immediately recognize why I have chosen this metaphor. If you have ever been to a black gospel choir practice and heard the individual notes which are rehearsed you come away with the firm belief that there is simply too much dissonance for all these notes to be sung together. The end result, one is certain, will be a horribly offensive noise. But when the music starts, unbelievably the dissonance is extraordinarily beautiful. The temptations in the choir practice to make the notes sound more similar, or change the music to suppress artificially the dissonance are based on a misunderstanding of the music's intent and function. One of the many other aspects of this metaphor worthy of comment is the moment in a black gospel song when the choir goes silent and the person, seemingly with the smallest, softest voice takes the lead for a stanza or chorus. In some choirs this person would not even find a place, but in this choir this small voice is occasionally given the lead. The lessons for a view of Scripture are not hard to see. Temptations to force the diversity of Scripture into an artificial unity are illegitimate and do the canon a disservice. It is only through allowing the dissonance to be heard in all its intensity that the Scripture can have its full impact. In addition, this approach to Scripture makes it possible for even the smallest and seemingly most insignificant voice to take the lead at the appropriate moment.

Second, one of the many hermeneutical questions facing interpreters is to determine as nearly as possible the location of meaning. Is the location of meaning to be found behind the text, so that the meaning of Scripture is not in the words themselves but in the events and words which lie behind the text and, consequently, must be discov-

---

³ J.C. Thomas, 'The Word and the Spirit', in *Ministry and Theology: Studies for the Church and Its Leaders* (Cleveland, TN: Pathway, 1996), pp. 13-20.

⁴ For my own thoughts on the role of the Spirit in the interpretive process cf. Chapter 13 below.

⁵ As the attentive reader may already have discovered, a hint in the direction of this metaphor is reflected in the subtitle of this chapter, as the term 'canon' can also have reference to a musical 'piece with different parts taking up the same theme successively, either at the same or a different pitch' (*The Oxford Encyclopedic English Dictionary* [New York: Oxford University Press, 1996], p. 214). I am indebted to my colleague, R.D. Moore, for this and other suggestions.

ered through a variety of historical critical procedures? Is the location of meaning in the text itself, so that whatever redactional history may lie behind a portion of Scripture, its meaning is available for those attentive to its literary structure and the clues the readers are given? Or is the location of meaning found in front of the text in the context of the reader? The answer to all three questions, of course, is Yes! But how does one work that out methodologically? My own approach will be to rely primarily upon a literary approach to the text, realizing that my own context both enables me to recognize certain clues in the text and at the same time makes me less aware of and even oblivious to other interpretive clues. In addition, it is the nature of texts that certain gaps exist within them which may sometimes be helpfully supplied by information that comes from behind the text.

Third, while oceans of ink have been devoted to the defining of terms like Spirit, healing, and mission, in this study they will primarily be understood as having reference to the Holy Spirit (the Spirit of God), the healing of individuals with physical and/or emotional infirmities, and the missionary activity to which the church is called in a variety of Scriptural texts.

Fourth, owing to the limitations of space there appear to be two options open with regard to how one should approach this task. Either one can attempt to offer a survey of the relevant Biblical materials in order to offer a general orientation to the topic or one can offer a detailed analysis of an individual case. For a variety of reasons I have chosen the former approach.

Voices from the Old Testament

In the Old Testament the healing activity of God is connected to the issue of Israel's mission among the nations in two primary ways. There are a variety of texts where divine healing occurs in order to preserve God's redemptive purposes and texts that reveal God's activity in afflicting and healing in order that the nations might 'know' (ידע) him.[6] Each of these themes is briefly treated.

In the Torah the healing activity of God is most often associated with the fulfillment of the promise God makes to Abram with regard to Abram's descendants in Gen. 12.1-3 (v. 3 - 'and in you all the fami-

---

[6] For the theological idea of 'knowing' God in the Old Testament cf. J. Bergman & G.J. Botterweck, 'ידע', *TDOT*, V (ed. G.J. Botterweck & H. Ringgren; trans. D.E. Green; Grand Rapids: Eerdmans, 1986), pp. 448-81.

lies of the earth will be blessed'). Specifically, by means of divine intervention, the barren Sarah conceives and gives birth to Isaac, the son of the promise (Gen. 18–21). Enveloped within this stretch of text is the closing and subsequent healing of the wombs of King Abimelech's wife and female servants, for Abimelech had taken Sarah to be his wife, not knowing that she was indeed Abram's wife (Genesis 20). God's intervention in the closing of the wombs and the subsequent healing of those involved appears to be directly related to his purpose for Abraham and Sarah's descendants. This motif continues later in Isaac's prayer for his barren wife Rebekah, whom the Lord heals so that she conceives (Gen. 25.21), and in God's remembering Rachel by opening her womb and removing her reproach (Gen. 30.22-24). Though not explicitly stated, in both cases God's promise to Abraham and plan to bless all families of the earth are the reasons for such intervention. Two of the other miracles of healing found within the Torah involve the affliction and healing of an individual (Miriam's leprosy – Num. 12) or group (the bites of poisonous snakes – Num. 21) who oppose God and/or his servant (Moses). These stories stand in some continuity with the preceding ones in that the afflictions and healing occur to further God's purpose in Abraham and his descendants

In the Prophets one finds the continuation of the barren woman motif, where in each case, the offspring of the formerly barren women, Samson's mother (Judg. 13) and Hannah (1 Sam. 1), play a significant role in the life of the community. The conception and resurrection of the Shunammite woman's son through Elisha's intervention (2 Kgs 4) appears to be connected to the vindication of God's servant. The connection between healing and the deliverance of the nation appears to be present in the healing of Hezekiah and the subsequent deliverance of Israel from the king of Assyria (Isa. 38).

As noted earlier, there are also texts that describe God's healing activity as being a witness to the nations. **In the Torah** the smiting of Moses' hand with leprosy and its subsequent healing by God is given as a sign to Moses to be shown before the Egyptians so that they might believe or give heed to him (Exod. 4.6-8). Moses later performs the signs before the Israelites, who believe that God had heard their cries (4.29-31). Somewhat surprisingly, the reader is never told that this sign is actually performed before the Egyptians. Later in the book, God promises that if Israel is faithful in keeping his commands and decrees, 'I will not bring on you any of the diseases I brought on the Egyptians, for I am the Lord who heals you' (Exod. 15.26). Given the context, it might be appropriate to ask if the signs given earlier were provided so that the Egyptians might 'know' the God of Israel? Is it possible that God's healing activity among Israel is to be seen as a testimony to the nations? Another text from the Torah indicates that God's power to wound and heal reveals his unique identity among the gods:

> See now that I myself am He!
> There is no god besides me.
> I put to death and I bring to life,
> I have wounded and I will heal,
> and no one can deliver from my hand (Deut. 32.39).

The implications of such claims for mission would appear to be clear.

In the Prophets the connection between healing miracles and 'knowledge of' the God of Israel is also found. The first example of such a relationship occurs in the story of the widow of Zarephath who supports the prophet Elijah (1 Kgs 17). When her son dies, through Elijah's intervention, he is brought back to life, resulting in the Gentile woman's confession:

> Now I know that you are a man of God, and that the word of the Lord in your mouth is truth (17.24). [7]

Such an understanding would appear to cohere well with Jesus' appeal to the significance of this event in Lk. 4.25-26. Perhaps the best example of this relationship is found in the story of Naaman (2 Kgs 5). By means of the testimony of a young Israelite servant girl and the intervention of Elisha, this Syrian army commander is not only healed of leprosy but also acknowledges his knowledge of (v. 15) and worship of the God of Israel (v. 17).[8] Similarly, the idea of affliction followed by healing, as a means of bringing people to knowledge of Yahweh, is found in Isaiah:

> The Lord will strike Egypt with a plague; he will strike them and heal them. They will turn to the Lord, and he will respond to their plea and heal them (Isa. 19.22).

---

[7] On this text cf. the comments of R.G. Branch, 'Evangelism via Power and Lifestyle: Elijah's Method in 1 Kings 17', A Paper Presented to the 2001 Annual Meeting of the Society for Pentecostal Studies, Tulsa, OK, and R.D. Moore, 'Response to Robin Branch's Look at the Evangelism of Elijah', 2001 Annual Meeting of the Society for Pentecostal Studies, Tulsa, OK.

[8] On the Naaman story cf. esp. R.D. Moore, *God Saves: Lessons from the Elisha Stories* (JSOTS 95; Sheffield: JSOT Press, 1990), pp. 69-84.

Again the missiological implications are apparent.

In the **Writings** the well-known warning from 2 Chron. 7.13-14 occurs:

> When I shut up the heavens so that there is no rain, or command locusts to devour the land or send a plague among my people, if my people, who are called by my name, will humble themselves and pray and seek my face and turn from their wicked ways, then I will hear from heaven and will forgive their sin and will heal their land.

This passage may contain an implicit promise that the healing of their land will draw attention to the God of Israel, for if Israel is disobedient, they will suffer at the hand of God and become a byword among all people (v. 20).

Voices from the New Testament

When one turns to the New Testament, one hears a number of voices that testify to the relationship between the ministry of healing and the mission of the church.

Matthew

The Gospel according to Matthew, the first voice heard in the New Testament canon, makes explicit the connection between healing and mission. The Gospel itself is structured around the five major sermons/discourses it contains: the Sermon on the Mount (5-7), the missionary discourse (10), the parables of the Kingdom (13), discipline within the community (18), and the great eschatological discourse (24-25). Whether or not Jesus is to be viewed as the new Moses, the strategic location of these sermons makes clear the significance of the content of Jesus' teaching.[9]

Just before the initial major sermon begins, there is a brief description of Jesus' ministry as he travels the whole of Galilee, which focuses upon his healing and exorcistic ministry (4.23-25). This gives way to the Sermon on the Mount, where for all practical purposes, the readers are given 'The Words of the Messiah'. Significantly, this major sermon is immediately followed by two chapters which focus on 'The Deeds of the Messiah' (8-9). Here, miracle story is followed by miracle story as the readers learn of the intricate connection between word and deed

---

[9] On the structure of Matthew's Gospel cf. D.R. Bauer, *The Structure of Matthew's Gospel: A Study in Literary Design* (BLS 15: Sheffield: Almond Press, 1989).

as Gospel proclamation. With the exception of the Stilling of the Storm in 8.23-27, all of the miracle stories in this section are accounts of Jesus' healing and exorcistic activity. Within this section devoted to the deeds of the Messiah, the readers learn that Jesus' healing and exorcistic ministry is closely connected to his atoning life (8.16-17). Owing to the way in which the life of Israel is recapitulated in the life of Jesus to this point within the Gospel according to Matthew, the reader is not surprised at this connection. In this passage, one might say that Jesus' healing and exorcistic ministry is viewed as standing in the shadow of the cross, for such activity is seen as a direct fulfillment of Scripture (Isa. 53.4). The connection between healing and the mission of Jesus could hardly be clearer.

At this point in the narrative, the conclusion of the two chapters devoted to the deeds of the Messiah, one finds the second major sermon in the Gospel according to Matthew: the missionary discourse. Here the readers learn that the missionary activity of the disciples, which is at this point restricted to the house of Israel, is to mirror that of their Lord - for their Gospel proclamation also consists of word and deed. In point of fact, just as the initial major sermon of Jesus (5-7) is bordered or surrounded by accounts of his healing activity (4.23-25; 8-9), so Jesus' commands to the disciples to go preach are surrounded by references to their own healing and exorcistic activity. In Mt. 10.1, Jesus calls his Twelve disciples and gives them authority to cast out unclean spirits and to heal every disease and every sickness. He then tells them to go and preach, 'The Kingdom of Heaven is near' (10.7). Following immediately on this command are the words, 'Heal the sick, raise the dead, cleanse the lepers, cast out demons' (10.8). While the missionary activity of the Twelve is not described within the narrative itself, the implication from v. 5 is that not only were they sent, but that they went, proclaiming the Gospel in word and deed.

The emphasis upon Jesus' healing ministry is not limited to the contents of Matthew 8-10, for a number of healing accounts occur later in the narrative.[10] By this means, the Gospel proclamation in deed continues alongside the proclamation in word.

The connection between healing and mission is underscored further by the so-called 'Great Commission' (Mt. 28.16-20). Here, Jesus gives his eleven disciples the following instructions:

> All authority in heaven and upon earth has been given to me. Therefore, going, disciple all the nations, baptizing them in the name of the Father

[10] Cf. esp. Mt. 12.9-14; 22-32; 14:35-36; 15.21-28; 17.14-20; 20.29-34.

and of the Son and of the Holy Spirit, teaching them to keep all the things I have commanded to you; and behold I am with you all the days until the end of the age.

Rather clearly, Jesus' instruction to teach them to keep all things he has commanded has reference to the five major sermons found within the Gospel.[11] Consequently, the Gospel's concluding commission, which appeals to all that has gone before, includes reference to the healing ministry of the disciples within the narrative, the readers implied by the text, and later readers of the text as well. It would seem appropriate to conclude that within the Matthean community, healing and mission are intimately connected.[12]

Mark

The next canonical voice found within the New Testament, the Gospel according to Mark, also testifies to the close connection between healing and mission. In this Gospel, the reader finds that miracles of healing play a significant role in Jesus' ministry. The intimate connection between healing and mission is revealed in several ways.

The first thing to indicate the importance of the miraculous in the mission of Jesus is the sheer amount of narrative space devoted to recounting the miracle stories. Nearly one third of the Gospel according to Mark (31%) consists of miracle stories. This, along with the fact that there is little teaching of Jesus in discourse form (as compared to the other Gospel accounts), indicates that for Mark, the miraculous events hold a special place in the mission of Jesus. In other words, it would not be going too far to say that the miraculous activity of Jesus in the Gospel according to Mark is the proclamation of the Gospel, perhaps even surpassing Matthew in this regard.

A second way in which this emphasis is conveyed to the reader is the attention given to this theme near the beginning of the Gospel. After the title is given (1.1) and a section devoted to John the Baptist and Jesus in the wilderness (1.2-13) occurs, Jesus appears preaching the nearness of the Kingdom of God (1.14-15) and calls his first four disciples (1.16-20). At this point, after a mere two sentences devoted to the

---

[11] Cf. A.T. Lincoln, 'Matthew – A Story for Teachers?' in *The Bible in Three Dimensions: Essays in Celebration of Forty Years of Biblical Studies in the University of Sheffield* (ed. D.J.A. Clines, S.E. Fowl, S.E. Porter; JSOTS 87; Sheffield: JSOT Press, 1990), pp. 103-25.

[12] On the relationship between the Spirit, healing, and mission in Matthew cf. the very helpful discussion in B.B. Charette, *Restoring Presence: The Spirit in Matthew's Gospel* (JPTS 18; Sheffield: Sheffield Academic Press, 2000), esp. pp. 126-35.

'words' of Jesus, the narrative gives way to a string of miracle stories. These include: an exorcism (1.21-28), the healing of Simon's mother-in-law along with the healing and exorcism of numerous others (1.29-34), the preaching and exorcistic activity of Jesus (1.35-39), and the cleansing of a leper (1.40-45). This emphasis on the healing and miraculous activity of Jesus continues throughout the first portion of the Gospel narrative. In point of fact, the next section, which is devoted to the growing hostility of the religious leaders to Jesus (2.1-3.6) - note how the unspoken opposition in the first pericope (2.7-8) grows into a plot to kill Jesus in the final one (3.6) - , is framed on either side by stories of Jesus' healing ministry (2.1-12; 3.1-6). In the next pericope (3.7-12), which provides transition from this section of the Gospel to the call, training, and sending of the Twelve (3.13-6.13), the healing and exorcistic activity of Jesus is again highlighted (3.10-11). Consequently, by this point in the narrative, the reader has no doubt as to the close relationship between Jesus' healing ministry and his mission.

A third means by which the connection between healing and mission is underscored is found within the section of the narrative devoted to the call, training, and sending of the Twelve (3.13-6.13). In this stretch of text it becomes clear that the Twelve are to share in the ministry of Jesus.[13] Going up on a mountain, 'Jesus chooses those whom he desires and makes them Twelve' (3.13-14a). The purpose of such choosing is conveyed by means of two purpose (ἵνα) clauses: 'in order that they might be with him and in order that he might send them to preach and have authority to cast out demons' (3.14b-15). Significantly, the next three chapters are devoted to the fulfillment of the first purpose clause 'that they might be with him', for the disciples are constantly by his side. It is within this context of their 'being with Jesus' that the disciples undergo preparation 'to be sent to preach and have authority to cast out demons'. Here the Twelve learn about the demonic (3.20-30; 5.1-20), the nature of the Kingdom - by means of parables of the Kingdom (4.1-34), miraculous authority over nature (4.35-41), miracles of healing (5.21-43), and the rejection which the ministry of the Kingdom brings (3.31-34; 6.1-6a). It is at this point that Jesus calls and begins to send the Twelve, two by two, giving them authority over unclean spirits (6.7). The succeeding narrative makes clear the success of the Twelve's mission by twice mentioning

---

[13] For more on this theme cf. Chapter 4 below.

its results. The first mention occurs at the end of this pericope (6.12-13) where the text says:

> And they went out preaching in order that 'they might convert' and casting out many demons, and anointing many sick individuals with oil and healing them.

Though anointing with oil and healing the sick are not specifically mentioned in their commission, it is clear that in this activity they share in the ministry of their Lord. The second mention of the results of their mission comes immediately after the story recounting the death of John the Baptist (6.14-29). Here (6.30), the apostles gather and report to Jesus all the things that they had done and taught. Such focus makes clear the tight connection between healing and mission for the Twelve.

A fourth indication of the close relationship between healing and mission within the text of Mark's Gospel is the fact that not only are healing and preaching a part of the Gospel proclamation, but also on more than one occasion healing results in preaching. In other words, the ministry of healing as part of Gospel proclamation generates additional Gospel proclamation in the form of preaching and perhaps additional healing activity, as reference to such is no doubt part of the content of the preaching. On at least three occasions preaching results from a miracle of healing and/or exorcism. Near the end of the first chapter, after Jesus cleanses a leper he instructs the healed man not to tell anyone about what has happened but to show himself to the priest and offer the sacrifices commanded by Moses. However, the texts states, 'But he went out and began to preach (κηρύσσειν) many things and to spread abroad the word' (1.45). Later in the narrative, Jesus casts out the many unclean spirits from the Gerasene Demoniac, who desires to go with Jesus. However, Jesus refuses the man and instructs him to return to his family and tell them about the things the Lord has done for him and the mercy bestowed upon him. At this point the text reads, 'And he departed and began to preach (κηρύσσειν) in the Decapolis whatsoever Jesus had done for him, and all were amazed' (5.20). A final example of the preaching which sometimes results from the healing activity of Jesus in Mark's Gospel occurs near the end of the account of the healing of a deaf and mute man (7.31-37). Having healed the man, Jesus instructs the crowds not to say anything about the miracle. But the more he instructed them, 'all the greater they were preaching' (αὐτοὶ μᾶλλον περισσότερον ἐκήρυσσον).

A final way in which the Gospel according to Mark reveals the connection between healing and mission is by making explicit the holistic nature of various healing miracles. In addition to those places where a miracle of healing results in preaching, appeal could also be made to certain passages that point to the salvific nature of healing. Though no explicit connection is drawn between the forgiveness of sins and the healing of the paralytic (2.1-12), the fact that both forgiveness and healing are found in such close proximity to one another suggests to the reader that the forgiveness of sin and healing may be connected at a deeper level. However, the reader does not have to wait long for an explicit connection between healing and salvation to be made in the text itself. For in the account devoted to the healing of the woman with the issue of blood, Jesus knows that power has gone out from him after being touched by the woman. When the woman comes to him and tells him 'the whole truth', he responds, 'Daughter, your faith has saved (σέσωκέν) you; go in peace, and be made whole from your illness' (5.34). In the last healing miracle in the Gospel according to Mark, in response to the cries and request of Blind Bartimaeus Jesus says, 'Your faith has saved (σέσωκέν) you' (10.52). As if to underscore the connection between this healing miracle and salvation the text goes on to state, 'And immediately he received his sight, and followed him in the way'.

It would seem safe to conclude that within the Markan community, there is a very close connection between healing and mission.

Mark 16.9-20

The next voice in the canonical choir to be heard is that of Mk 16.9-20. Though rather clearly non-Markan in origin, owing to the antiquity of this 'longer ending', the way a variety of Gospel traditions have been integrated into it, and the fact that with few exceptions the 'longer ending' was regarded to be and functioned as part of the canon of Scripture confessed by the church, these twelve verses should be included in any canonical discussion of this topic.[14]

Mk 16.9-20 is structured around three resurrection appearances of Jesus to various followers (vv. 9-14), an extended discourse in which the disciples are commissioned to take the Gospel to all creation (vv.

---

[14] For a more detailed discussion of the nature and purpose of Mk 16.9-20 cf. Chapter 6 below (J.C. Thomas & K.E. Alexander, '"And the Signs Are Following": Mark 16.9-20 – A Journey into Pentecostal Hermeneutics', *JPT* 11.2 [2003], pp. 147-70). Cf. also R.W. Wall, 'A Response to Thomas/Alexander, "And the Signs Are Following" (Mark 16.9-20)', *JPT* 11.2 (2003), pp. 171-83.

15-18), and a concluding section that describes Jesus' actions of ascension to heaven and being seated at the right hand of God, as well as his actions of accompanying those who went out to preach everywhere (vv. 19-20).

It is the third resurrection appearance (v. 14) that provides the context for the commission of the disciples by the resurrected Jesus to go into all the world and preach the Gospel to every creature. The commission to go and preach is followed by a promise and warning: each one who believes and is baptized will be saved while the one who does not believe will be condemned. On the heels of this promise and warning is the promise of signs following believers. The words which follow have an almost formulaic or creedal feel. In the Greek text, in each instance the noun is followed by the verb, reading somewhat literally: 'demons they will cast out' (δαιμόνια ἐκβαλοῦσιν), '(with) new tongues they will speak' (γλώσσαις λαλήσουσιν καιναις), 'serpents they will take up' (ὄφεις ἀροῦσιν), 'deadly poison ... will not hurt them' (θανάσιμόν ... μὴ αὐτοὺς βλάψῃ), 'upon the sick hands will be laid' (ἐπὶ ἀρρώστους χεῖρας ἐπιθήσουσιν). It is clear from the context that these signs are expected to accompany the disciples as they preach the Gospel, an expectation fulfilled in the 'longer ending' itself (v. 20).

The final section (vv. 19-20) is structured around a (μὲν ... δέ) grammatical construction, best translated 'on the one hand' and 'on the other hand', indicating that these verses stand together around the actions of Jesus. These include his 'heavenly' actions (ascension to heaven and being seated at the right hand of God), on the one hand, and his earthly ones (working with them and confirming his word by the signs which accompanied them), on the other hand. Two aspects of v. 20 should be mentioned. First, the commission to go and preach (v. 15) and the promise of signs following the believers (vv. 17-18) are treated as being fulfilled in this verse. Second, it is very clear that despite his physical absence Jesus continues to be present with his disciples, working with them in their mission. Thus, the relationship between healing and the mission of the church appears to be a very important one in this canonical voice as well.

Luke

The next voice in the canonical choir, the Gospel according to Luke, describes the relationship between the Spirit, healing, and mission in even clearer terms. Such is perhaps not surprising in a Gospel that is literally filled with accounts of and references to healing. Not only is the sheer volume of miracle stories an indication of their significance in this document, but also the fact that a miracle of healing occurs as late as the passion of Jesus (Lk. 22.51), a unique phenomenon among the canonical Gospels.

One does not have to read very far into the Gospel before finding words of Jesus which go some way toward explaining the relationship between his anointing by the Spirit, his mission, and his ministry of healing. Returning to Galilee from the Wilderness Temptations full of the Holy Spirit, Jesus reads from the Isaiah scroll in a synagogue in Nazareth:

> The Spirit of the Lord is upon me;
> therefore he has anointed me
> to preach good news to the poor.
> He has sent me to preach release for the captives
> and recovery of sight to the blind
> to release the oppressed
> to preach the year of the Lord's favor (Lk. 4.18-19).

This programmatic text not only sets the agenda for Jesus' ministry as it unfolds within the Gospel,[15] but it also contains in embryonic form many of the issues related to the topic of this study. Therefore, several of the observations that follow find their foundation in this text.

First, the strategic location of this passage is revealed in part by the fact that there are no miracles attributed to Jesus before this pericope in Luke's Gospel. However, from this point on Jesus' ministry of healing is a regular part of the Gospel narrative. The importance of this programmatic statement is further underscored by the fact that portions of it are repeated at various points in the narrative. For example, in responding to John's question to Jesus, 'Are you the coming one or should we expect another?', Jesus, who at that moment (ἐν ἐκείνῃ τῇ ὥρᾳ) is involved in healing many from various diseases, illnesses, unclean spirits, and blindness, harks back to the words of Luke 4:

> Go tell John that which you have seen and heard; the blind receive their sight, the lame walk, the lepers are cleansed and the deaf hear, the dead are being raised, and the poor are receiving the good news (Lk. 7.22).

---

[15] On this point cf. J.B. Green, *The Theology of the Gospel of Luke* (Cambridge: Cambridge University Press, 1995), pp. 95-97.

Still later in the narrative, echoes of this activity are heard in Jesus' response to word brought by the Pharisees that Herod was trying to kill him. On this occasion Jesus says:

> Go tell that fox, 'Behold I cast out demons and accomplish healings today and tomorrow, and on the third day I will complete (my work /goal)' (13.32).

Therefore, in addition to his healing activity, Jesus continues to speak of its significance in his mission.

A second, related point in this programmatic text is the way in which Jesus puts the reader on notice that healing is a not insignificant aspect of his Gospel proclamation, but rather is itself Gospel proclamation. As the Gospel according to Luke unfolds, it becomes clear that the relationship between word and deed in Luke leaves neither in a position of primacy but both are a testimony to the in-breaking Kingdom of God.

It is also significant that Jesus' healing activity is tied to his anointing by the Spirit. It is clear that he takes the action he does in the synagogue in Luke 4 owing to the fact that he is full of the Holy Spirit, as a result of the Spirit's anointing at his baptism. Apparently, the anointing by the Spirit empowers his healing ministry throughout the Gospel,[16] and is at times made explicit by reference to healing power present and/or leaving his body. For example, Lk. 5.17 notes that the power of the Lord was present to heal the sick. Similarly, in a text devoted to his ministry to the crowds which came from Judea and Jerusalem, and as far away as Tyre and Sidon, one reads:

> These came to hear him and to be healed from their diseases; and those troubled by unclean spirits were being healed. And the whole crowd was seeking to touch him, because power was coming out from him and healing all (6.18-19).

Significantly, this text is the preamble to Luke's Sermon on the Plain (6.17-49). This theme is developed later in the Gospel when Jesus himself says, in response to the woman with an issue of blood who 'touches' him, 'Who touched me? For I know that power has gone out from me' (8.46).

Still another important aspect of the Luke 4 text is the intimate connection between physical healing and salvation in the ministry of Jesus. While there may be a sense in which all the healing activity that

---

[16] Cf. J.B. Shelton, *Mighty in Word and Deed: The Role of the Holy Spirit in Luke-Acts* (Peabody, MA: Hendrickson, 1991), pp. 74-84.

follows conveys salvation to their recipients, this connection is made explicit at several points in the following narrative. At the conclusion of the story of the healing of the woman with the issue of blood Jesus says, 'Daughter, your faith has saved (σέσωκέν) you; go in peace' (8.48). Later in the Gospel one finds the story of the ten lepers whom Jesus makes clean (17.11-19). After they had been cleansed (v. 14), one of them finds that he has been healed, returns glorifying God with a loud voice, falls at the feet of Jesus, and thanks him. To this cleansed and healed Samaritan Jesus says, 'Raising, go; your faith has saved (σέσωκέν) you' (v. 19). Finally, in the Lukan version of the healing of the blind man (18.35-43), the text reads:

> And Jesus said to him, 'Receive your sight; your faith has saved (σέσωκέν) you. And at once he received his sight and followed him, glorifying God (vv. 42-43a).

Before leaving the Gospel according to Luke, two additional points should be made. The role of the Twelve as participants in Jesus' healing and preaching ministry is even more explicit in Luke than in Matthew and Mark. For the story devoted to their call, commission, and sending (Lk. 9.1-6) contains three separate references to their healing activity, as a reading of the text makes clear:

> And calling the Twelve together he gave them power and authority over all demons and to heal diseases, and he sent them to preach the Kingdom of God and to heal (vv.1-2) ... And going out they went from village to village preaching the good news and healing everywhere (v. 6).

Returning, the Apostles reported to Jesus everything they had done (v. 10). However, participation in the healing ministry of Jesus is not limited to the Twelve in the Gospel according to Luke, for a mere one chapter later (10.1-24) Jesus sends out the Seventy[-Two], instructing them to heal the sick and to preach that the Kingdom of God is near you (v. 9). Upon their return, they report that even the demons were subject to them in Jesus' name (v. 17). By this means, the reader of these Lukan texts is prepared for the activity of the disciples in the Acts narrative.

A final note about the relationship between miracles of healing and mission is related to the response that these miracles generate. Often a miracle of healing leads to amazement, faith or praise of God on the part of the one healed or those who witness the healing (5.25-26;

7.16, 17; 9.43; 13.17; 18.43). This emphasis is also a dominant one in Luke's second volume.[17]

John[18]

In the Gospel according to John, Jesus' miracles of healing are part of the Fourth Gospel's use of 'signs'. Briefly put, signs in the Fourth Gospel are miraculous events that point beyond themselves to faith in Jesus as the Son of God. Often the signs give way to an extended discourse where part of the sign's significance is made more explicit. Though they are part of the revelation of the Father through the Son, the signs are not to be understood in a mechanical fashion. For the same set of signs can produce genuine belief evidenced by a full commitment to Jesus (2.11; 4.42), faith in Jesus which is private owing to 'the fear of the Jews' (19.38), faith in Jesus which Jesus himself does not have faith in (2.24), lack of belief in Jesus (12.37), and an outright hostility to Jesus which remains constant throughout much of the Fourth Gospel. The purpose of the signs is succinctly stated near the conclusion of the Gospel:

> Therefore, there are many other signs which Jesus also did before the disciples, which are not written in this book; but these have been written in order that you might believe that Jesus is the Christ, the Son of God, and in order that believing you might have eternal life in his name (20.30-31).

Therefore, from the outset of this section devoted to hearing the voice of John, it is clear that the relationship between the signs and mission is an especially close one in the Fourth Gospel. As will be seen, the relationship between the accounts of healing, within the signs, and mission is made explicit.

Among the signs described in the Fourth Gospel one finds four specific signs of healing along with a general reference to Jesus' signs of healing. These include: the healing of the nobleman's son (4.46-54), the healing of the man at the pool (5.1-18), the general statement with regard to the signs Jesus did upon the sick (6.2), the healing of the man born blind (9.1-41), and the resurrection of Lazarus from the dead (11.1-57). When examined closely, each of the signs of healing reveal

---

[17] One also finds a few examples of such an effect in Mt. 9.8, 33; 15.31; Mk 2.12; 5.20; and Jn 7.21.

[18] This section becomes the basis for the more extensive discussion in Chapter 9 below.

the holistic nature of healing and salvation within the Fourth Gospel, for each of the individual signs of healing conveys this very message.

The healing of the nobleman's son is described as the second sign that Jesus did when going out of Judea into Galilee, following the turning of water into wine, called the first or beginning of signs which Jesus did in Cana of Galilee. In that text it is clear that through this sign Jesus manifested his glory and his disciples believed in him (2.11). The first healing in the Fourth Gospel is strategically located near the end of the portion of the Gospel that describes the early mostly positive responses to Jesus. In this story it is clear that the nobleman seeks out Jesus for the healing of his son who is near death. The text says, hearing that Jesus had come back into Cana of Galilee where he had made the water into water, the man came to Jesus. Despite words of rebuke, the man makes his request. Jesus instructs the man to return home and speaks words of healing. The man believes Jesus' word and obeys his command (in conformity to the words of Mary 'whatever he says to you, do it' – 2.5). When learning of his son's healing the nobleman and his whole house believe in Jesus. These details would be enough on their own to reveal the close relationship that exists between healing and mission in the Fourth Gospel, however, there is more. For what the attentive reader learns is that a refrain runs throughout the passage that highlights the kind of (eternal) 'life' which Jesus brings (cf. 1.4; 3.15-16, 36; 4.14, 36). Jesus' response to the nobleman in v. 50 is, 'Go, your son lives'. On his journey back to his home, the nobleman's servants meet him with the news that 'His son lives' (v. 51). If that emphasis is not sufficient to speak to the reader, the text states that after the man heard the news from his servants and discovered the hour of his son's recovery, he knew it was the hour that Jesus said, 'Your son lives' (v. 53). The relationship between this sign of healing, belief in Jesus, and the life which Jesus brings is quite clear in this first sign of healing in the Fourth Gospel.

The second sign of healing occurs in the very next pericope (5.1-18). In this episode, Jesus seeks out the man who for thirty-eight years has been lying at the pool. Several things in this passage are important for the purposes of this study. First, the vocabulary used to describe this man's transformation is not the ordinary terminology used for healing. In other words, Jesus does not ask the man if he wants to be healed, but 'Do you desire to be whole (ὑγιής)?' (v. 6). The significance of this term is revealed in part by the fact that it is used only six times in the Fourth Gospel, each occurrence having reference to this particular man. In addition, just as Nicodemus had earlier misunderstood Jesus' use of the word ἄνωθεν (which can mean 'from above' or 'again'), and the Samaritan woman had misunderstood Jesus' reference to ὕδωρ ζῶν (which can mean 'running water' or 'living water'), so the man at the pool misunderstands ὑγιής (which can mean 'well' or 'whole'), indicating that there is more to this Johannine term than meets the eye. A second, related issue is the fact that apparently, the transformation that led to the man being made whole, includes the forgiveness of sin, for he is later warned, 'See you have become whole! Stop sinning, in order that something worse does not come upon you' (v. 14). A third significant aspect of this text is found in the man's response to the enquiries of the Jews as to the identity of the one who instructed him to carry his mat on the Sabbath. After discovering the identity of the one who healed him, the man proclaims to them that 'Jesus is the one who made him whole' (v. 15). Two things indicate the positive nature of the man's proclamation. On the one hand, he does not respond to their question with regard to the identity of the one who instructed him to carry his mat on the Sabbath, but rather he says that Jesus made him whole. On the other hand, the word used to describe the man's proclamation (ἀνήγγειλεν), is the same term used elsewhere in the Johannine literature to describe the activity of the Messiah (4.25), the activity of the Paraclete (16.13-15), and the authoritative proclamation of the Johannine church (1 Jn 1.5). Thus, in this passage the holistic nature of the healing is in full view.[19]

The next sign of healing, after the more general reference to Jesus' healing ministry connected to the signs (6.2), involves the man born blind. A number of aspects of this passage indicate that there is a close connection between the healing, salvation, and mission in the giving of sight to the man born blind. One of the first things to alert the reader to the significance of the ensuing sign is Jesus' words that the man was born blind so that the 'works of God might be manifested in him' (9.3). Attention is also drawn to the way in which Jesus' identity, his mission, and this healing converge in v. 7. Here, Jesus (the One Sent by God) sends the blind man to wash ('Go and wash') in a pool called Siloam, the name of which, according to the following parenthetical statement, means 'Sent'. The effect of the healing upon the formerly blind man is immediate, and not confined to his physical recovery. For he immediately identifies the one who restores his sight as 'the man called Jesus' (v. 11), repeats the details of the healing two

---

[19] For a more detailed discussion of this text cf. Thomas, *The Devil, Disease, and Deliverance*, pp. 92-109.

times, and whilst being interrogated by the Pharisees calls Jesus a prophet (v. 17). Eventually, he asks the Pharisees, 'Do you also wish to become his disciples?' (v. 27), prompting the Pharisees to identify him as 'a disciple of that one' (v. 28). Later in the narrative his belief in Jesus is made explicit when he is given opportunity to confess, 'I believe, Lord' and to worship Jesus, in keeping with the true worship of which Jesus spoke in his words to the Samaritan woman (4.23).[20] Another related emphasis is the preoccupation in the passage with the question, who is a sinner? Despite the fact that Jesus clearly denies that culpability is at the root of the man's blind condition (v. 3), the Pharisees end up accusing the man of being a sinner (v. 34). They also accuse Jesus of being a sinner in the story (v. 24), a charge against which the formerly blind man defends Jesus (vv. 25-33). The other major relevant theme concerns the broader issue of who sees and who is blind. Clearly, the man's encounter with Jesus results in more than physical sight. Yet, the Pharisees, though physically sighted, remain in their spiritual blindness. The themes of sin and blindness converge as the passage concludes (vv. 39-41), offering additional evidence of the holistic nature of this sign.[21]

The final sign of healing in the Fourth Gospel is the well-known account of the resurrection of Lazarus. Given the obvious ways in which John 11 testifies to the relationship between healing and mission, the following comments are minimal. However, several aspects of this text should be highlighted. Like the story in John 9, the event to follow is 'in order that the Son of God might be glorified through him' (v. 4). Upon learning that Lazarus is asleep, the disciples almost prophetically observe, 'Lord, if he has fallen asleep, he will be saved (σωθήσεται)' (v. 12).[22] The relationship of Lazarus' death and the belief of the disciples is underscored (v. 15). The dialogue with Martha not only highlights the fact that her confession is perhaps the most significant one in the Fourth Gospel, but also the fact that Jesus is the resurrection and the life – a point made clear in the resurrection of Lazarus (vv. 20-27). In the ensuing dialogue, Mary invites Jesus to the place of Lazarus' burial by use of a formula, 'Come and See' (v. 34),

---

[20] For this suggestion cf. J.-M. Sevrin, 'L'intrigue du quatrième évangile, ou la christologie mise en récit', A Paper Presented to the 2003 Annual Meeting of the Studiorum Novi Testamenti Societas in Bonn, Germany.

[21] For a more detailed discussion of this text cf. Thomas, *The Devil, Disease, and Deliverance*, pp. 110-23.

[22] I am indebted to Patrick Jensen, a member of my Gospel of John seminar, for first drawing my attention to this detail.

that has appeared upon the lips of Jesus (1.39), Philip (1.46), and the Samaritan Woman (4.29). In each case, it invites deeper exploration with regard to Jesus' person and identity. The prayer of Jesus (vv. 41b-42), which focuses upon the belief of the crowds more than the resurrection of Lazarus, is answered later in the narrative when many of the Jews behold the sign which he did and believe in him (v. 45). Suffice it to say that this sign contains overt references to Jesus' resurrection and life giving powers which culminate in the belief of many who see this sign.

A final observation with regard to the holistic nature of the Johannine signs of healing is related to the structure of the Fourth Gospel. In the Gospel according to John the signs of healing are framed by two references to Jesus' exaltation upon the cross. In the discourse that develops from the dialogue with Nicodemus, Jesus says:

> And just as Moses lifted up the serpent in the wilderness, so it is necessary for the Son of Man to be lifted up, in order that each one who believes in him might have eternal life (3.14-15).

It is significant that this first unambiguous reference to Jesus' exaltation on the cross, which precedes all the miracles of healing, is explicitly tied to this Old Testament sign that afforded physical healing. Not only this, but the mention of the cross in 3.14 also points forward by means of anticipation to Jesus' exaltation on the cross in the passion narrative proper, culminating in the blood and water that come forth from his side in 19.34. Thus, all the signs of healing occur between these two references to the cross. Another aspect of Jesus' words in 3.14-15 worthy of comment is the way in which this event, well known from the Jewish Scriptures, is taken up and reinterpreted in the process. While the event recorded in Num. 21.9 focuses upon physical healing which preserves life and points toward spiritual healing/salvation, John's use of the text focuses upon the salvific dimension of the event, pointing in a subtle fashion toward the implications for physical healing.[23] The emphasis upon eternal life in v. 15 underscores this primary meaning of the text and at the same time

---

[23] Cf. the following assessment from early Pentecostalism. 'Now we see clearly that the Srpent (*sic*) was a type of Jesus; and if a look at the type healed the sick and dying, how much more will Jesus Himself heal our diseases' (*Pentecostal Holiness Advocate* 2.59 [3 April 1919], p. 5). For more on healing within early Pentecostalism cf. K.E. Alexander, *Pentecostal Healing: Theology and Practice* (JPTS 30; Blandford Forum: Deo Publishing, forthcoming).

serves as a sign of the holistic nature of salvation and the signs of healing in the Fourth Gospel.

Although the commission of the disciples takes different forms in the Fourth Gospel (cf. esp. 4.31-38; 15.26-16.4; 17.13-21; 20.19-23) than in the Synoptics, there is still reason to believe that the disciples will themselves be involved in the same works of the Father as Jesus. In the Farewell Discourse, Jesus promises:

> Truly, truly I say to you, the one who believes in me, the works which I work that one will also work, and greater than these will he do, because I go to the Father. And whatever you ask in my name I will do this, in order that the Father might be glorified in the Son; if you ask anything in my name I will do it (14.12-13).

It appears safe to conclude that members of the Johannine community would see themselves as heirs to these words, highlighting the connection between healing and mission.

Acts

The final dominant voice in the canonical choir relevant to the issue of healing and mission is the Book of Acts. A number of indicators in the text reveal that this relationship is an important one.[24] One of the first hints about such an emphasis is found in the book's prologue where the author informs the recipient that in his first work he wrote about 'what Jesus began to do and to teach' until the ascension (1.1). One of the implications of this statement is that in the account that follows, the reader will encounter those things Jesus continued to do and to teach through the ministry of the church. This expectation on the reader's part is literally fulfilled at various points in the Acts narrative. For example, Jesus appears to Stephen during his martyrdom (7.56), to Saul at his conversion (9.1-19; 22.6-16; 26:12-18), and the Spirit of Jesus is present in the missionary activity of the church (16.7). Perhaps the best example of this understanding is reflected in Peter's words to a paralytic, infirm for eight years, 'Jesus Christ heals you' (9.34).

More than the other voices, Acts makes explicit the relationship between the Spirit and mission, in ways that make clear the significant role miracles, generally, and healing, more specifically, play. This theme is developed by means of the charismatic anointing that a variety of individuals and groups receive in the narrative, enabling them to

---

[24] Given the acknowledged connection between healing and mission in the Acts narrative, this treatment is less extensive than that offered in the other sections of this chapter.

minister as had Jesus. In point of fact, Luke seems careful to include either a description of charismatic anointing (Spirit Baptism) or a reference to individuals so anointed within each of the major panels of the narrative: Acts 2:1-4; 4:30-31; 8:14-17; 10:44-48; 11:24-28; 13:9; 19:1-7; 20:22-21:11.[25] Thus, the theme of charismatic anointing is part of the very fabric of the narrative, which goes some way toward making clear the connection between healing and the mission of the church.[26]

According to the text of Acts (1.8), the purpose of Holy Spirit Baptism is empowerment for missionary activity.[27] One of the characteristics of such empowerment is the fact that 'signs and wonders' are regularly part of Gospel proclamation in the Acts narrative. This phrase appears in a variety of places to describe the results of the Day of Pentecost (2.19), the ministry of Jesus (2.22), the Apostles (2.43; 4.30; 5.12), Stephen (6.8), Paul and Barnabas (14.3; 15.12), and God's activity on behalf of the church (ἐκκλησία) in the wilderness (7.38).[28] These events which accompany the preaching of the word often produce awe, fear, and/or praise of God resulting in belief in God in many of the people who witness them.

The healing activity of a variety of Spirit empowered individuals and groups appears to be closely related to the ministry of signs and wonders. Such activity includes the healing ministry of Peter and the Apostles (3.1-10; 4.30; 5.15-16; 9.33-34, 36-42), Philip (8.6-7), and Paul (14.8-10; 19.11-12; 20.7-12; 28.3-9). It is obvious in the Acts narrative that the proclamation of the Gospel includes the public proclamation of the word (cf. esp. the disciples' prayer in 4.29-30). At the same time, it is also evident that healing and signs and wonders accompany such proclamation and can themselves be regarded as part of

---

[25] For a detailed discussion of the structure of Acts cf. Chapter 12 below.

[26] In some ways it is possible to subsume all other major theological themes in Acts under this one for it includes the activity of God, Jesus, the church, evangelization, and individuals within the narrative.

[27] A number of helpful works explore the significance of Lukan pneumatology. These include R. Stronstad, *The Charismatic Theology of St. Luke* (Peabody, MA: Hendrickson, 1984); Shelton, *Mighty in Word and Deed*; R.P. Menzies, *Empowered for Witness* (JPTS 6; Sheffield: Sheffield Academic Press, 1994); and M. Turner, *Power from on High* (JPTS 9; Sheffield: Sheffield Academic Press, 1996). On the relationship between the Spirit and mission cf. esp. J.M. Penney, *The Missionary Emphasis of Lukan Pneumatology* (JPTS12; Sheffield: Sheffield Academic Press, 1997).

[28] On this Lukan theme cf. L. O'Reilly, *Word and Sign in the Acts of the Apostles: A Study in Lucan Theology* (Rome: Editrice Pontificia Universita Gregoriana, 1987), esp. pp. 161-90.

this Gospel proclamation. Several texts indicate that as a result of God's activity among these Spirit empowered figures, numerous individuals come to faith (5.14; 9.42; 13.12; 19.17-18).

A corollary point to the above discussion is the fact that in the book of Acts God is depicted, in the working of miracles (including healing), as being more powerful than any rivals.[29] Such an attitude has clear implications for the relationship between healing and mission. According to one historian of early Christianity, it is precisely this dimension of the early church's activity that accounts for its triumph over all competitors in Greco-Roman antiquity.[30]

It almost goes without saying that the readers of Acts would have every reason to believe that such miraculous activity was to be an on-going part of the church's Gospel proclamation.

Paul

The next voice in the canonical choir is that of Paul. At one level, this voice has already been encountered as reflected in Luke's Acts narrative, where a close connection exists between healing and mission. Thus, as the canonical choir assembles one is prepared for additional evidence of this theme in the Pauline literature. Although not expressed in as explicit a fashion as in the other voices, a variety of hints in the Pauline texts suggest that in this literature too there is a connection between healing and mission. The phenomenon of healing appears prominently in 1 Corinthians (12.9, 28, 30) where 'the gifts of healings' (χαρίσματα ἰαμάτων) are regarded as an on-going part of the ministry of the church. While it might be possible to argue hypothetically that such phenomenon are part of the internal dynamics of the community and not an explicit part of its missionary activity, such a conclusion would be premature. For a number of Pauline texts reveal that Pauline Gospel proclamation also takes place in word and deed. Such evidence is found at several places in the Pauline corpus. For example, Paul informs his Roman readers that his preaching takes place

> in word and deed, in the power of signs and wonders, in the power of the Spirit (Rom 15.19).

To the Corinthians Paul writes:

---

[29] J.D.G. Dunn, *Jesus and the Spirit* (Philadelphia: Westminster Press, 1975), p. 168.
[30] On this point cf. esp. R. MacMullen, *Christianizing the Roman Empire A.D. 100-400* (New Haven: Yale University Press, 1984).

Both my word and my preaching were not with persuasive words but with a demonstration of the Spirit and power, in order that your faith would not be in the wisdom of men but in the power of God (1 Cor. 2.4-5).

Similarly, in what was perhaps his first epistle Paul states:

... because our Gospel did not come to you in word only but also in power and in the Holy Spirit and in deep conviction, just as you know we lived among you (1 Thess. 1.5).

Therefore, when the canonical choir sings about the relationship between word and deed in Gospel proclamation, Paul's voice is heard in that chorus. Given the prominence of this relationship in Paul's own Gospel proclamation, the presence of healing activity in his community, and the relationship that exists between healing and the miraculous generally in various forms of early Christianity, it would appear safe to conclude that a close connection also exists in the Pauline communities between healing and mission.

Revelation

The final faint voice on this topic in the canonical choir comes from the Apocalypse. It is clear from this book that the Beast gains a following owing to the fact that he suffers a fatal wound to his head, which is healed. This results in the whole world following him (13.3, 12). While it is evident that the wounding (ἐσφαγμένην) and healing of the beast is a parody of Jesus' own wounding (ἐσφαγμένον) and healing, it is also evident that there is a warning here to the readers about the need for discernment when faced with the phenomenon of healing.[31] Healing imagery is also used to describe the promises given to the innumerable multitude (7.17) and in the description of the new heaven and new earth (21.4). Such imagery is based in the fact that in the New Jerusalem there exists a tree of life, the leaves of which are for the healing of the nations. Such a notation is consistent with the missiological optimism found throughout the Apocalypse.[32]

Putting the Choir Together

While a great deal could be said at this point about the texture and richness of the song this biblical choir sings about healing and mission,

---

[31] A similar idea might be present in Mt. 7.15-20, though healing as such is not mentioned.

[32] On the missiological optimism of the Apocalypse cf. R. Bauckham, *The Climax of Prophecy: Studies on the Book of Revelation* (Edinburgh: T&T Clark, 1993), pp. 238-337.

given the space constraints and nature of the voices heard to this point, perhaps all that is needed is a brief word of summary. It appears from the biblical voices heard that there is an intricate and significant connection between the ministry of healing and the mission of the church. If one expands the definition of the church's mission to include its internal dynamics as well, there are many additional texts to be consulted.[33] However, perhaps enough has been offered to facilitate dialogue among those interested in this topic.

---

[33] For example, nothing has been said in this study of the content of Jas 5.14-18 – a most important healing text.

3

The Kingdom of God in the Gospel according to Matthew

One of the better-known characteristics of the Gospel according to Matthew is its extensive use of the phrase 'kingdom of heaven', which occurs over thirty times in the gospel. Due to Matthew's decided preference for this phrase, and the fact that he alone of the canonical evangelists uses it,[1] scholars have sought to explain this unique phenomenon, concluding generally that Matthew uses 'kingdom of heaven' as a synonym for the Synoptic 'kingdom of God'. One dimension of this discussion, however, has not yet received adequate attention, the fact that on at least four occasions Matthew uses the term 'kingdom of God' rather than the more frequent 'kingdom of heaven' (Mt. 12.28; 19.24;[2] 21.31, 43).

This study seeks (1) to survey the different scholarly explanations that distinguish between the two terms, (2) to survey the different scholarly explanations that view the terms as synonyms, (3) to offer a modest proposal for Matthew's use of the kingdom of God, and (4) to discover the relevance of these texts for research on the Matthean community.

I

A few scholars have argued that for Matthew the 'kingdom of heaven' and the 'kingdom of God' have two distinct meanings. These views are diverse both in the definitions they assign to the respective kingdoms and in the variety of theological schools of thought which they represent.

---

[1] The only exception is the textually uncertain Jn 3.5, where kingdom of heaven appears in a handful of witnesses, including ℵ*.

[2] For a discussion of the textual uncertainty regarding ἡ βασιλεία τοῦ θεοῦ in 19.24 cf. J. O'Callaghan, 'Examen critic de Mt. 19:24', *Bib* 69 (1988), pp. 404-405.

W.C. Allen proposed that Matthew intended to emphasize two different aspects of the kingdom by the use of these terms. On the one hand, the kingdom of God usually implies that the kingdom is present (albeit only by anticipation) because the Messiah is present. In fact, '"the kingdom of God" might well be used to sum up that whole revelation of God to the Jewish people which was to be transferred to others.'[3] On the other hand, Allen claims that Matthew 'everywhere uses ἡ βασιλεία τῶν οὐρανῶν of the kingdom which Christ announced as at hand, to be inaugurated when the Son of Man came on the clouds of heaven.'[4] Although he makes such claims about the differences between the terms, Allen concedes that in 12.28 and 21.43 Matthew uses 'kingdom of God' because it occurs in his source.[5]

Following the lead of Allen, Margaret Pamment has sought to demonstrate, through an examination of the many passages where the terms occur, that Matthew assigns different meanings to the kingdom of heaven and the kingdom of God.[6] Pamment concludes that for Matthew:

> the term ἡ βασιλεία τῶν οὐρανῶν refers to a wholly future reality which is imminent but other-worldly in the sense that the world as it is experienced now will no longer exist. He uses the term ἡ βασιλεία τοῦ θεοῦ to refer to God's sovereignty, actualized and recognized in the past and present here on earth, especially in the covenant relationship with Israel in the past, and more generally wherever a response is made to the call to righteousness or wherever evil is overcome by good.[7]

For Pamment, the kingdom of God is a present reality which prepares individuals for the eschatological kingdom of heaven, a wholly future phenomenon in Matthew.

W.F. Albright and C.S. Mann have argued for still another understanding. According to these scholars, Matthew is very careful to distinguish between the kingdom of heaven (i.e. the continuing community of The Man) and the kingdom of God (i.e. the reign of the Father). The former is identified as the community which exists with Jesus until the time of the final judgment, while the latter will be es-

---

[3] W.C. Allen, *The Gospel according to S. Matthew* (Edinburgh: T. & T. Clark, 1912), pp. lxviii.

[4] Allen, *Matthew*, p. lxvii.

[5] Allen, *Matthew*, p. 135. Cf. also Allen's discussion on pp. lxvii-lxviii and 232.

[6] M. Pamment, 'The Kingdom of Heaven According to the First Gospel', *NTS* 27 (1981), pp. 211-232.

[7] Pamment, 'Kingdom of God', p. 232.

tablished at the final judgment.[8] Although the two are not synonyms, in some ways it could be said that the kingdom of heaven prepares the way for the kingdom of God. For, while one may rather easily enter into the kingdom of heaven, far stricter demands will be placed upon those who seek to enter the kingdom of God.[9] In a later publication, Mann again affirms this understanding of the terms in Matthew, while noting that Mark does not make the same fine distinction between God's Reign and the Son's mission.[10]

The most recent attempt to distinguish between these terms is made by Daniel Patte. Although he regards kingdom of heaven and kingdom of God as complementary in that they have the same ultimate goal of gathering individuals into the people or household of God, Patte proposes that each term stands for a particular manifestation of the kingdom. The kingdom of God 'refers to the aggressive manifestation of the *power of God* which asserts itself against satanic and demonic powers.'[11] For Patte, this liberation from demonic powers is an essential preparatory step so that people might be favorably inclined toward the kingdom of heaven. Patte argues that the kingdom of heaven has reference to the authority of God which, at present, is not imposed upon people but must be accepted without coercion.[12]

II

Despite such attempts to discern a difference in the meaning of these terms, most scholars remain convinced that Matthew used the kingdom of heaven and the kingdom of God interchangeably. A rather high percentage of scholars who view these terms as synonyms believe that 'the kingdom of heaven' is a concession on Matthew's part to the sensitivities of his Jewish-Christian audience. On this view, heaven serves as a circumlocution for the divine name.[13] But even if this point

---

[8] W.F. Albright and C.S. Mann, *Matthew* (Garden City: Doubleday, 1971), pp. c-cv and 155.

[9] Albright and Mann, *Matthew*, p. 233.

[10] C.S. Mann, *Mark* (Garden City: Doubleday, 1986), pp. 153 and 206.

[11] D. Patte, *The Gospel According to Matthew: A Structural Commentary on Matthew's Faith* (Philadelphia: Fortress Press, 1987), p. 177.

[12] Patte, *Matthew*, p. 177.

[13] For this position cf. the following: A. Schlatter, *Der Evangelist Matthäus: Seine Sprache, sein Ziel, seine Selbständigkeit* (Stuttgart: Calwer, 1929), p. 57; J. Schniewind, *Das Evangelium nach Matthäus* (Göttingen: Vandenhoeck & Ruprecht, 1936), p. 23; W. Michaelis, *Das Evangelium nach Matthäus* (Zurich: Zwingli, 1948), pp. 109-10; F.V. Filson, *A Commentary on the Gospel according to St. Matthew* (New York: Harper &

3. The Kingdom of God in Matthew

be granted, one must still explain why Matthew uses kingdom of God on certain occasions. Consequently, several explanations have been set forth.

One rather common proposal suggests that when kingdom of God appears rather than kingdom of heaven Matthew is simply following his source.[14] In fact, James D.G. Dunn goes so far as to say that in 12.28 '... Matthew has hurried over the Q version of Matt. 12:28 without stopping to modify it as he would naturally have done.'[15] In other words, sometimes kingdom of God appears in Matthew due to an editorial error.

W.D. Davies and Dale C. Allison have argued that the use of 'kingdom of heaven' and 'kingdom of God' by Matthew is nothing more than a stylistic variation which is not peculiar to Matthew but is found in other writings of the era. As evidence they cite the *Testament of Jacob* (2.25; 7.11, 19-20, 23, 27; 8.3) and the *Testament of Isaac* (1.7; 2.8; 8.5-6), where both phrases occur, as well as the variation of the kingdom language in the other Synoptics. They conclude that for the most part, Matthew and Jesus used periphrasis, but did not shy away from using the divine name. Consequently, the terms have reference to the same thing, God's rule, both present and future. This variation is not deemed to be significant.[16]

However, a number of scholars suggest that Matthew's use of the kingdom of God is intentional, appearing in contexts where the evan-

---

Brothers, 1960), p. 32; W.O. Walker, 'The Kingdom of the Son of Man and the Kingdom of the Father in Matthew', *CBQ* 30 (1968), p. 574; L. Goppelt, *Theology of the New Testament*, I (Grand Rapids: Eerdmans, 1981), p. 44; R. Schnackenburg, *Matthäusevangelium* 1,1-16,20 (Würzburg: Echter Verlag, 1985), p. 41; F.W. Beare, *The Gospel according to Matthew* (Peabody, MA: Hendrickson, 1987), p. 33 and many others.

[14] For this suggestion cf. the following: F.C. Grant, *The Gospel of Matthew*, I (New York: Harper & Brothers, 1955), p. 23; P. Gaechter, *Das Matthäus-Evangelium* (Innsbruck: Tyrolia-Verlag, 1962), pp. 678 and 686; P. Bonnard, *L'Évangile selon Saint Matthieu* (Neuchatel: Delachaux et Niestlé, 1963), p. 181 n. 2; W. Grundmann, *Das Evangelium nach Matthäus* (Berlin: Evangelische Verlagsanstalt, 1968), p. 463; D. Hill, *The Gospel of Matthew* (Grand Rapids: Eerdmans, 1972), p. 301; E. Schweizer, *The Good News according to Matthew* (trans. D.E. Green; Atlanta: John Knox Press, 1975), pp. 287, 410; D.A. Carson, 'Matthew', *The Expositor's Bible Commentary*, XIII (Grand Rapids: Zondervan, 1984), p. 289; R. Mounce, *Matthew* (San Francisco: Harper & Row, 1985), p. 117.

[15] J.D.G. Dunn, *Jesus and the Spirit* (Philadelphia: Westminster, 1975), p. 45. For similar suggestions cf. A.H. McNeile, *The Gospel According to St. Matthew* (Grand Rapids: Baker, 1980), pp. 280 and 306.

[16] W.D. Davies and D.C. Allison, *The Gospel According to Saint Matthew*, I (Edinburgh: T. & T. Clark, 1988), pp. 390-92.

gelist desires a greater contrast than is possible through the utilization of kingdom of heaven. For example, it is proposed that in 12.28 kingdom of God appears, rather than the usual kingdom of heaven, because it is a better parallel to 'the spirit of God' and because it serves as a better contrast to Satan's kingdom, which occurs earlier in the passage.[17] In a similar vein, a few commentators believe that literary reasons are responsible for the use of kingdom of God in 19.24,[18] 21.31,[19] and 21.43.[20] M.D. Goulder offers one of the most concise statements regarding explanations of this sort:

> Matthew always uses the standard rabbinic 'kingdom of heaven' unless he has a reason. At Matthew 21.43; he inserts the phrase ἡ βασιλεία τοῦ θεοῦ editorially into Mark's vineyard parable: just as the owner will kill those wretches and let out his vineyard to other tenants, so God's kingdom will be taken from the Jews and given to the Church. In exactly the same way, just before (Matt. 21.31;), just as the initially recalcitrant son did the will of his father, so do the publicans do God's will and go into God's kingdom before the Pharisees ... In each case the word 'God' is used with emphasis to represent the owner or the father of the parables, or to contrast with Satan and his kingdom, as here: the phrase should be translated 'God's kingdom', and not 'the kingdom of God'.[21]

---

[17] Cf. McNeile, *Matthew* 176; Grundmann, *Matthäus,* p. 329 n. 5; F. Stagg, 'Matthew', *Broadman Bible Commentary* (Nashville: Broadman Press, 1969), p. 149; G. Maier, *Matthäus-Evangelium* I (Stuttgart: Hänssler-Verlag, 1979), p. 48; J.P. Meier, *Matthew* (Wilmington: Michael Glazier, 1980), p. 135; Carson, 'Matthew', p. 289; J. Gnilka, *Das Matthäusevangelium,* I (Freiburg: Herder, 1986), pp. 458-59; R. Smith, *Matthew* (Minneapolis: Augsburg, 1989), p. 165.

[18] R. Gundry [*Matthew: A Commentary on his Literary and Theological Art* (Grand Rapids: Eerdmans, 1982), pp. 389-90] states that Matthew uses the rarer term for the sake of variation, while J.C. Fenton [*Saint Matthew* (Baltimore: Penguin, 1966), p. 316] remarks that the substitution is designed to place emphasis on God's power in v. 26.

[19] Gundry [*Matthew*, p. 423] assigns this change to 'the need for the personal emphasis in God's name', while R.T. France [*Matthew* (Grand Rapids: Eerdmans, 1985), p. 307] notes that perhaps it was 'to emphasize the personal nature of ... [the religious leaders'] response to and relationship with God in which they had failed.' In contrast, M.-J. Lagrange [*Évangile selon Saint Matthieu* (Paris: Gabalda, 1948), p. 412] notes that one finds 'τοῦ θεοῦ et non, "des cieux" comme à l'ordinaire, parce que le royaume est déjà commencé.' Lagrange (p. 418) makes similar comments on 21.43.

[20] Gundry [*Matthew*, p. 430] observes, 'As in v 31, the use of God's name is determined by the contextual need for the personal term'.

[21] M.D. Goulder, *Midrash and Lection in Matthew* (London: SPCK, 1974), p. 332 n. 64.

Of the four occurrences of kingdom of God in Matthew, 21.43 in particular has prompted a variety of explanations. In his comments on 21.43, McNeile argues, 'τοῦ θεοῦ and not τῶν οὐρανῶν is used ... because the meaning is different from that of the "Kingdom of Heaven".'[22] For McNeile, in this context the kingdom of God is to be equated with the vineyard of the parable, i.e. the community of Israel. Therefore on this one occasion, McNeile seems to detect a difference in kingdom of heaven and kingdom of God. David Hill suggests that, if the evangelist is not merely preserving traditional material in 21.43, perhaps:

> Matthew intentionally differentiates between the eschatological Kingdom (which the Jews never possessed, in any case) and the 'sovereignty of God' over Israel, expressed in terms of the special covenantal relationship. The Jewish nation, as a corporate entity, had now forfeited its elect status.[23]

Thus, Matthew may use kingdom of God to make a theological distinction in this passage. Another view is suggested by Trilling, '"Reich Gottes" wurde in 21,43 interpretiert als die Gegenwart, die *Anwesenheit Gottes* in der Geschichte des Volkes und seiner gnädigen Heilsführung.'[24]

One final proposal concerning Matthew's use of kingdom of God should be mentioned before concluding this little survey. Julius J. Scott, Jr. conjectures that Matthew avoids kingdom of God, except 'in contexts in which the other-worldly or spiritual character of that kingdom is evident...' due to the politico-military connotations Scott believes the term to have had in first century Jewish circles.[25]

III

This survey has revealed that (1) while most scholars regard kingdom of heaven and kingdom of God as synonyms for Matthew, and (2) while many scholars believe that Matthew's general preference for kingdom of heaven is an accommodation to Jewish sensitivities, there is as of yet no consensus concerning Matthew's occasional use of king-

---

[22] McNeile, *Matthew*, p. 312.

[23] Hill, *Matthew*, p. 301.

[24] W. Trilling, *Das wahre Israel: Studien zur Theologie das Matthaüs-Evangeliums* (München: Kösel-Verlag, 1964), p. 85.

[25] J.J. Scott, Jr., 'The Synoptic Gospels', *The Expositors Bible Commentary*, I (Grand Rapids: Zondervan, 1979), p. 508.

dom of God. Although this overview of scholarly thinking might justly discourage one from being so bold as to enter the discussion, perhaps there is still room for one rather modest proposal.

A comparison of the Matthean occurrences of kingdom of God with their Synoptic counterparts reveals a couple of interesting points. First, Matthew's use of kingdom of God is represented rather equally in each of his sources, with 12.28 coming from Q, 19.24 from Mark, and 21.31, 43 from 'M'.[26] Such a distribution would seem to imply that if the use of kingdom of God is due to careless editorial work on Matthew's part,[27] it appears that Matthew is remarkably non-discriminatory in his editorial slips.

Second, a comparison of Matthew's use of kingdom of heaven with their Synoptic counterparts shows that in places Matthew seems to substitute kingdom of heaven for the Synoptic kingdom of God. Taken by itself, this evidence suggests that indeed the terms are synonyms for Matthew. Yet, over sixty percent of the time Matthew's kingdom of heaven finds no Synoptic parallels. It is theoretically possible, therefore, to argue that in those occurrences of kingdom of heaven peculiar to Matthew, one is dealing with a concept different from that disclosed in occurrences of kingdom of God as documented in Matthew and/or the Synoptics. But an examination of this special 'M' material reveals that the content of these passages defines the kingdom of heaven in ways that are not unlike that revealed in the kingdom of God materials.[28] Thus, attempts to discern a difference between the kingdom of heaven and the kingdom of God on the basis of so-called 'M' material appear to be ill-founded.

If, then, it may be assumed that, (1) the kingdom of heaven and kingdom of God serve as synonyms for Matthew, and (2) if heaven is a circumlocution for the divine name, and (3) if the occurrences of kingdom of God are intentional on the part of the evangelist, then one must wonder if the many proposals have been comprehensive enough in their scope. This observation is not intended to deny the validity of particular points within the explanations offered for Matthew's use of the kingdom of God, but to suggest that if an explanation can be offered which takes seriously each of the above premises, then that theory should merit serious consideration.

---

[26] Of course, if Matthew were the first gospel written, then it would be extremely difficult to demonstrate that Matthew's occasional use of kingdom of God is attributable to his sources.

[27] As McNeile (*Matthew*) and Dunn (*Jesus*) state.

[28] Cf. J.F. Walvoord, 'The Kingdom of Heaven', *BibSac* 124 (1967), pp. 198-99.

It is rather odd that in spite of the proliferation of literary approaches to the New Testament, no one has yet examined this issue via literary analysis (in particular, narrative analysis and/or rhetorical analysis). Yet, literary analysis, along with traditional historical critical approaches, might hold the key that unlocks this little mystery. Therefore, in the proposal which follows, these texts will be approached in order to discern their function for the gospel as a whole and after this determination, an attempt will be made to discover the relevance of these texts for the Matthean community.

This modest proposal may be set forth as follows: If the majority of scholars are correct in their view that kingdom of heaven and kingdom of God are synonyms, that heaven serves as a circumlocution for God, and that occasionally Matthew has intentionally used kingdom of God in the place of kingdom of heaven, then the most plausible explanation for the substitution of kingdom of God for kingdom of heaven in 12.28, 19.24, 21.31, and 43 is that for Matthew kingdom of God is a literary device used to draw the readers' attention to passages of special significance. More specifically, if the use of heaven is a means of avoiding the offense caused by use of the divine name, then Matthew's intentional use of the divine name in this formula is no doubt a most graphic means of emphasis.

This suggestion is supported by the exceptional nature of the passages in which kingdom of God occurs. For example, 12.28 is located within the pericope devoted to Jesus' words regarding exorcism and his warning concerning the blasphemy of the Spirit, while 19.24 is part of Jesus' warning about the dangers wealth poses to those who desire entry into the kingdom. In a discussion with the chief priests in the temple (21.23-46), Jesus makes two extraordinarily sharp statements. First, he tells the religious leaders of Israel that tax-collectors and prostitutes will enter the kingdom of God before them. Second, Jesus charges that the kingdom of God will be taken from these religious leaders and 'given to a people who will produce its fruit'. Each of these texts is forceful enough without the substitution of God for heaven, however when the divine name is used it is difficult not to be impressed with the attention the phrase focuses upon its topic.

Two dimensions of this evidence are noteworthy. On the one hand, it is clear that Matthew does not use kingdom of God in every context where he records stern words of Jesus. For example, in the scathing denunciations of the scribes and Pharisees found in Matthew 23, only the phrase kingdom of heaven is found. Therefore, it would be wrong to conclude that this phrase is simply Matthew's way of emphasizing a point. On the other hand, although each of the Matthean occurrences of kingdom of God are in contexts which carefully address obstacles to entrance into the kingdom, the evangelist also uses kingdom of heaven in passages which describe entrance into the kingdom (5.20; 7.21; 18.3; 19.23; and 23.14). All of this implies that the use of kingdom of God in 12.28; 19.24; and 21.31, 43 is deliberate and is intended to emphasize the specific teaching of these passages.

This evidence suggests that the readers of Matthew, who were accustomed to seeing kingdom of heaven, would at the very least pause at the sight of kingdom of God and ponder the content of these passages. It is difficult to believe that such use of the divine name would not have drawn the attention of first century Jewish Christian readers.

IV

While the proposal offered above for the use of kingdom of God may explain the literary function of the phrase, one may still ask, But why these four uses and no more? In all likelihood the answer to this question has to do with the context of the Matthean community. That is to say, perhaps the occurrences of Kingdom of God reveal significant issues with which the Matthean church struggled. In order to gauge the plausibility of such an hypothesis it will be necessary to compare the themes identified in these passages with their development in the rest of the gospel and their prominence in the scholarly discussions on important dimensions of the Matthean community.

The use of kingdom of God in 12.28 suggests that exorcism is one of the major issues with which the community struggled. The occurrence of the phrase at this point in the gospel is significant for at least two reasons. First, kingdom of God is used in response to the charge that Jesus casts out demons because of Beelzebul. Instead of being a sign of collusion with Satan, Jesus states that exorcisms are evidence that the kingdom of God has arrived. Second, the phrase appears just before Jesus' warning regarding blasphemy of the Spirit. Apparently, such blasphemy is directly linked to the assigning of the works of the Spirit (exorcisms) to Satan (Beelzebul).

An examination of the rest of the gospel bears out the prominence of demon possession and/or exorcism in Matthean thought. On several occasions, Jesus is described as casting out demons and/or healing those who were afflicted by a demon (4.24; 8.16, 28-34; 9.32-34; 12.22; 15.21-28; 17.14-18). When accused of casting out demons by the authority of Beelzebul (12.22-37), a charge the disciples are instructed to expect as well, Jesus warns his opponents regarding blasphemy of the Spirit and later cautions them (12.43-45) about the sevenfold return of an unclean spirit which had previously been cast out.

Interestingly enough, Jesus' first and last words concerning exorcism in Matthew are devoted, on the one hand, to those (false prophets?) who claim to have cast out demons in the name of Jesus but never knew the Lord (7.22) and, on the other hand, to the disciples who, despite their commission for such activity (10.5-15), are unable to cast out demons owing to their lack of faith (17.19-22).

Several scholars working on the historical reconstruction of the Matthean community have come to believe that this community was familiar with a variety of charismatic activities.[29] This conclusion is based in part on the fact that the ministry of Jesus exhibits charismatic activity[30] (such as exorcisms, healings, prophetic utterances, etc.), but is also based on the fact that such characteristics are an expected part of the disciples' ministry as well. In addition, the stern denunciations of false prophets (7.15-23; 24.23-28) indicate that in all probability the Matthean church knew of their presence, while the existence of genuine prophets is also presupposed (10.41).

If both the text of Matthew and the scholarly reflection on the Matthean community lend support to the idea that exorcism was an important issue within the Matthean church, then the question that remains is, what exactly is at stake for Matthew in his use of kingdom of God in 12.28?

Perhaps the use of kingdom of God in the place of kingdom of heaven in 12.28 was a warning to the community about the danger of attributing exorcisms to Satan. If, as the text seems to indicate, false prophets were able to cast out demons in the name of Jesus (7.22),

---

[29] Cf. E. Schweizer, 'Observance of the Law and Charismatic Activity in Matthew', *NTS* 16 (1969/70), pp. 213-30; E. Schweizer, 'Matthew's Church', in *The Interpretation of Matthew* (ed. G. Stanton; Philadelphia: Fortress Press, 1983), pp. 129-55; J.P. Martin, 'The Church in Matthew', *Int* 29 (1975), pp. 41-56; G.T. Montague, *The Holy Spirit: Growth of a Biblical Tradition* (New York: Paulist Press, 1976), pp. 302-10; J.D.G. Dunn, *Unity and Diversity in the New Testament* (London: SCM Press, 1990), p. 249; C. Holman, 'A Lesson from Matthew's Gospel for Charismatic Renewal', in *Faces of Renewal* (ed. P. Elbert; Peabody, MA: Hendrickson, 1988), pp. 48-63; R.T. France, *Matthew: Evangelist and Teacher* (Grand Rapids: Zondervan, 1989), pp. 118-19; R.H. Smith, 'Matthew's Message for Insiders: Charisma and Commandment in a First-Century Community', *Int* 46 (1992), pp. 229-39.

[30] Cf. M. Hengel, *The Charismatic Leader and his Followers* (trans. James Grieg; New York: Crossroad, 1981).

while those within Matthew's church were not always as successful in such endeavors (17.19-22), then there may have been a growing tendency to attribute such activity to Satan as a way of discrediting the false prophets. In contrast to this attitude, Matthew insists that not only was charismatic activity such as exorcism a genuine part of Jesus' ministry, but that it was also to be normative in the ministry of the disciples.[31] As for the legitimate criteria by which to assess 'charismatic activity', Matthew points to the ethical character of the 'prophet'.

The appearance of kingdom of God in 19.24 suggests that wealth posed a not insignificant problem for the community. Here, more than anywhere else in Matthew, it becomes clear that kingdom of God serves as a synonym for kingdom of heaven, for the latter phrase appears in the previous verse (19.23) with an identical meaning. The proverbial nature of 19.24, coupled with the appearance of kingdom of God so close on the heels of kingdom of heaven, appear to indicate that the Evangelist desires to emphasize the dangers of wealth for his community.

Issues of wealth and/or money appear in many passages throughout the Gospel.[32] These passages may broadly be categorized as describing: the misuse of money (21.12-17; 26.14-16; 27.1-10; 27.38-44; 28.11-15); Jesus' relationship with wealth (4.8-10; 8.18-22; 17.24-27); the disciples and money (4.18-22; 9.9-13; 10.9-10; 19.23-30); an example of the proper use of wealth (26.6-13); proper attitudes toward wealth (6.1-4, 19-24, 25-34; 13.44-46; 19.16-22; 22.15-22; 24.45-51; 25.14-30, 37-46); and incidental comments pertaining to wealth (16.24-28; 18.21-35; 20.1-16; 27.57-61).

Two of the more recent examinations of wealth in Matthew, while differing in emphases and detail, tend to confirm that wealth was a concern for the community.[33] Generally speaking, David L. Mealand argues that the Matthean church exhibits signs of growing affluence and accommodation toward wealth,[34] while Thomas E. Schmidt maintains that Matthew reflects a fair amount of hostility toward wealth.

---

[31] Since the Gospel nowhere describes the disciples as fulfilling the charismatic dimensions of their commission given in chapter ten, one must assume that at the least such a commission was fulfilled later.

[32] Cf. W.G. Marx, 'Money Matters in Matthew', *BibSac* 136 (1979), pp. 148-57.

[33] Cf. D.L. Mealand, *Poverty and Expectation in the Gospels* (London: SPCK, 1980) and T.E. Schmidt, *Hostility to Wealth in the Synoptic Gospels* (Sheffield: JSOT Press, 1987), pp. 121-34.

[34] Cf. also the discussion of R. H. Smith, 'Were the Early Christians Middle Class? A Sociological Analysis of the New Testament', *Currents in Theology and Mission* 7 (1980), pp. 260-76.

However, despite the differing emphases of these studies, their conclusions are not necessarily mutually exclusive.

If wealth was an important issue for the Matthean church, what exactly is at stake for Matthew in his use of kingdom of God in 19.24? Perhaps the use of kingdom of God in 19.24 serves as a warning to the community regarding the dangers of wealth. If, as Mealand observes, '... the economic circumstances of Matthew's church seem to have been less harsh than those of the earlier Christian communities',[35] then in all probability Matthew's church was a settled community of believers which had made some accommodation toward possessions and the use of wealth.[36] If such were the case, Matthew's hostile attitude toward and/or critique of wealth would be easy to understand.[37]

Although the appearance of kingdom of God in 21.31 is a bit more difficult to contextualize than the other occurrences of the phrase, it is still possible to gain some leverage on its significance for the community. In this passage, Jesus informs the chief priests and the elders that tax collectors and prostitutes would enter the kingdom of God before them. More than likely, tax collectors and prostitutes are not the most important aspect of this text, as tax collectors appear in a few other contexts in Matthew[38] and prostitutes appear only in this context. Rather, the emphasis is upon who qualifies to enter the kingdom and how one enters.

In Matthew, Jesus makes very clear that not everyone who cries 'Lord, Lord' will enter the kingdom (7.21), that it is nearly impossible for a rich person to enter (19.23), and that some scribes and Pharisees do not themselves enter and actually prevent others from entering the kingdom (23.14). It is made equally clear how one must enter the kingdom; with a righteousness that exceeds that of the scribes and Pharisees (5.20) and through a change which makes one like a little child (18.3). The point is that one must enter the kingdom through faith (21.32), not by reliance upon charismatic activity (7.21), wealth (19.23), or religious position (23.14).

---

[35] Mealand, *Poverty*, p. 16.

[36] Mealand, *Poverty*, p. 92.

[37] Therefore, rather than regarding Mealand's argument as overly subtle, as Schmidt [*Hostility to Wealth*, p. 122] charges, the hostile attitude toward wealth exhibited by Matthew might very well be a sign of the church's growing affluence.

[38] It is noteworthy that in three of the six passages where tax collectors are mentioned, they are either in the company of Jesus (9.9-13; 11.18-19) or they are described as having believed in John the Baptist (21.32), while one of the other texts states that a tax collector was one of the Twelve (10.3).

If this analysis is at all accurate, then perhaps the use of kingdom of God in the place of kingdom of heaven in 21.31 was a warning to the community about the dangers of presuming on one's place in the kingdom. If, as the church settled, it became institutionalized[39] and enamored with positions (note the strong denunciations of titles in 23.5-12), there may have been a tendency to exclude the disenfranchised from the community and to marginalize specific groups or segments of society. A stern warning such as the one in 21.31 would serve to remind the community of how one enters the kingdom and lives in it.

The final appearance of kingdom of God in Matthew occurs within the parable of the vineyard and the tenants (21.43). The context is apparently the same as that described in 21.23, where Jesus is in dialogue with the chief priests and elders. Having completed the parable, Jesus states that the kingdom of God will be taken from the leaders of Israel (cf. 21.43) and given to a people (ἔθνει) who would bring forth the fruit of the kingdom.

It would indeed seem pointless to cite the many passages and/or scholars who support the conviction that the Matthean community was divided over the question of the mission to the gentiles. Suffice it to say that this issue has been one of the major points of discussion in Matthean studies and that numerous passages reflect just this tension.[40]

Given this background and the emphasis Matthew places upon bringing forth good fruit (3.7-11; 5.3-10; 7.15-23; 12.33-37; 21.18-22; and 25.31-46), more than likely the use of kingdom of God in 21.43 is a warning to those who would challenge the legitimacy of the Gentile mission and an admonition concerning the unequivocal nature of bringing forth good fruit.

V

This study has proposed that kingdom of God is a literary device which Matthew used to draw attention to significant issues for his community. Therefore, its appearance should be taken as a sign that the concerns reflected in those passages are essential for the community to address. This proposal has been supported by the development of

---

[39] Cf. R.E. Brown & J.P. Meier, *Antioch & Rome* (New York: Paulist Press, 1983), pp. 65-72.

[40] Of the many works that discuss this issue cf. Meier's discussion in *Antioch & Rome*, pp. 45-72 and S. Brown, 'The Matthean Community and the Gentile Mission', *NovT* 22 (1980), pp. 193-221.

these themes within the rest of the gospel and by the thought of many of those scholars doing research on the Matthean community.

If this proposal is correct, then not only is kingdom of God a significant phrase for Matthew, but also future studies on the Matthean community should give more attention to the issues emphasized here. Perhaps this study will contribute in a small way to a better understanding of both Matthew and his community.

4

Discipleship in the Gospel according to Mark

A proper understanding of biblical discipleship is essential if spiritual renewal is to be productive and continual. But what does it mean to be a disciple? Is there any one way of making disciples, or are there a number of options available? This study examines the issue of discipleship in order to discover a biblical paradigm for discipleship which might be used by those interested in renewal. This necessitates an entrance into the debate concerning Jesus' role as teacher, which leads to a consideration of the relationship Jesus had with the disciples. The results of this investigation are then tested by examining a few significant passages in the Gospel according to Mark that are particularly pertinent for understanding discipleship. Finally, a section is devoted to applying these conclusions to the contemporary situation.

Jesus as Charismatic Leader

Without a doubt, the Gospels testify to the fact that Jesus was looked upon as a teacher by his contemporaries. διδάσκειν (to teach) appears over 90 times in the New Testament, with about two thirds of those occurrences being in the Gospels and the early parts of Acts.[1] Jesus is frequently referred to as *rabbi* and διδάσκαλος (teacher). Traditionally, scholars have understood this to imply that Jesus was a rabbi. Bultmann's comments are representative of this view.

> The title (*rabbi*), which in the Greek gospels is usually rendered by the ordinary Greek form of address (Lord, Sir), marks Jesus as belonging to the class of scribes. And that implies, if it is to be taken seriously, that Je-

---

[1] K. Rengstorf, 'διδάσκω', *TDNT*, I, p. 138. R.T. France, 'Mark and the Teaching of Jesus', *Gospel Perspectives I: Studies of History and Tradition in the Four Gospels* (eds. R.T. France and D. Wenham; Sheffield: JSOT, 1980), pp. 118, 120, argues that 50% of Mark's Gospel is devoted to presenting Jesus' teaching and that 35% of this teaching material is devoted to the theory and practice of discipleship.

sus, being a scribe had received the necessary scribal training and had passed the requisite scribal tests ... But if the gospel record is worthy of credence, it is at least clear that *Jesus actually lived as a Jewish rabbi*. As such he gathers around him a circle of pupils. As such he disputes over questions of the Law with pupils and opponents or with people seeking knowledge who turn to him as the celebrated rabbi, so also it is significant that his adherents (not the twelve) are called pupils (disciples). That too is a technical term, and designates the pupils of a rabbi, not the members of a religious fellowship.... We cannot doubt that the characteristics of a rabbi appeared plainly in Jesus' ministry and way of teaching, unless the tradition has radically distorted the picture.[2]

As Bultmann observes, there are a number of similarities between Jesus and the rabbis. He is called rabbi (cf. 9.5; 11.21; 14.45; Jn 1.39, 49; 3.2: 4.31; 6.25; 9.2; 11.8). He teaches in the synagogues (Mk 6.1; Lk. 4.16-30). He sits when he teaches (Mt. 5.1). He has a group of followers (μαθηταί), and he is asked to render decisions on points of Torah. Despite these similarities, a number of real differences between Jesus and the rabbis have also been emphasized. Even Birger Gerhardsson, an advocate of using rabbinic methods of oral transmission as the paradigm for explaining early Christian transmission of tradition, criticizes Bultmann for not placing enough emphasis on the differences.[3]

The number of significant differences between Jesus and the rabbis are far reaching. (1) Jesus speaks on the basis of his own authority (ἐξουσία). He was not like the scribes, who tended to cite other teachers as authorization for their message. (2) He does not recite the introductory quote from the Hebrew Scriptures, 'Thus says the Lord', he replaces it with 'truly I say to you'. In doing that he speaks as God, at least implicitly. (3) Jesus seems less concerned with the letter of the Law than do the rabbis, for at many points he appears to move beyond it to the Torah's original intent (cf. Mk 10.1-12). (4) Ordinarily, he resorts to rabbinic exegesis only when drawn into debates. This does not necessarily imply that he normally approached Scripture in this manner.[4] (5) Jesus holds a position above the Torah for his disciples, which certainly distinguishes him from the rabbis. (6) One of the most characteristic differences between Jesus and the rabbis lies in the

---

[2] R. Bultmann, *Jesus and the Word* (trans. L.P. Smith, E.H. Lantero; New York: Scribner's, 1958), pp. 57-61 (italics mine).

[3] B. Gerhardsson, *Memory and Manuscript: Oral Tradition and Written Transmission in Rabbinic Judaism and Early Christianity* (trans. E.J. Sharpe; Copenhagen: Munsgaard, 1961) n. 4.

[4] Cf. E.E. Ellis, *Prophecy and Hermeneutic in Early Christianity* (Grand Rapids: Eerdmans, 1978), pp. 237-53.

method of discipleship. Ordinarily, prospective students would join themselves to a rabbi of their own choosing. However, Jesus' disciples responded to *his* call. The disciples' commitment to him far transcends that expected of a rabbinic pupil. Rabbinic students are trained to replace their masters, yet Jesus is indispensable to his disciples, even after his death. The rabbis seem reluctant to teach in the open, but Jesus teaches wherever an appropriate situation arises. Finally, Jesus teaches certain individuals who would in no respect qualify as rabbinic students: sinners, tax collectors, women, prostitutes, and even children.[5] Consequently, while he may have borne an outward similarity to the rabbis, Jesus was different from them in many respects.

The question remains, was Jesus a rabbi? After all, Jesus is addressed as rabbi. However, several scholars are concluding that the term rabbi would have had different nuances in 30 CE than during the latter part of the first century. Hengel observes that 'as an established title-- despite the rabbinical tendency to date back the forms of their own period into the past – "Rabbi" only appears from the time of Johanan ben Zakkai and his disciples, i.e., very probably only after 70 A.D.'[6] Jacob Neusner would be in basic agreement with this assessment.[7] It seems better to view ῥαββι, διδάσκαλος, and κύριος as synonymous during the time of Jesus.[8] If this is true, then Jesus would not have to be trained as a rabbi to be called teacher. Even if an ordained rabbinate existed at his time, there were other individuals in close temporal proximity who also served as teachers, but were not rabbinic figures. First-century sources suggest that no groups of consequence existed very long without a teacher.[9] Additionally, Jesus' prophetic role need not be emphasized to the exclusion of his teaching role. (These roles seem to have been combined at Qumran.) Even at the end of the first

---

[5] I am indebted to Bruce M. Metzger for several of these observations on the difference between Jesus and the rabbis. I also acknowledge his helpful contemporary analogue on discipleship quoted near the end of this study.

[6] M. Hengel, *The Charismatic Leader and His Followers* (ed. J. Riches; trans. J. Greig; Edinburgh: T. & T. Clark, 1981) n. 22.

[7] J. Neusner, *From Politics to Piety: The Emergence of Pharisaic Judaism* (New York: Ktav, 1979); *The Pharisees: Rabbinic Perspectives* (New York: Ktav, 1985); cf. M. Hengel, *Judaism and Hellenism*, I (trans. J. Bowden; London: SCM, 1974), pp. 81-83.

[8] This should not be taken to imply that κύριος is never used as a christological title. It certainly has this implication in Mark 2.28. Cf. C.F.D. Moule, *The Origins of Christology* (Cambridge: Cambridge University, 1977), pp. 35-46; H. Bietenhard, 'Lord', *DNTT*, II, p. 514.

[9] Most certainly the Essenes had a teacher or teachers and it is probable that the Zealots did as well.

century a prophetic figure like John the Baptist can be referred to as rabbi (Jn 3.26).[10] This also demonstrates that a prophet could, at the same time, be a teacher. The Samaritan Taheb seems to have combined these two roles as well. Consequently, to speak of Jesus as teacher is a necessity. Yet, despite the similarities, it may do more harm than good to identify him as rabbi, specially with its later Mishnaic meaning.[11]

A much more probable explanation of Jesus' role would be the identification as prophet. Most scholars agree that there are 'indubitably authentic materials' present in the canonical Gospels which identify Jesus as prophet.[12] Not only is Jesus regarded as prophet by the people at large (cf. Mk 6.15; 8.27, 28), but he implicitly accepts the title at Nazareth (Mk 6.4). Not only is he 'a prophet like one of the prophets' (Mk 6.15), but eventually 'the prophet' (Mt. 21.11). Oscar Cullmann concludes, 'The application of the concept of *the* prophet to Jesus explains perfectly, then, both his preaching activity and the unique authority of his eschatological vocation and appearance in the end time.'[13] But, even this designation does not go far enough in understanding Jesus,[14] for he transcends the jurisdiction of the prophets. He forgives sins. He casts out demons. He speaks on God's behalf, as God (in some real sense). He has authority over the Sabbath. He goes behind the Law to its original intention. These considerations lead Hengel to the conclusion that Jesus was an eschatological figure who acted on the basis of 'a charismatic authority which wholly transcended

---

[10] If, as L. Goppelt, *Theology of the New Testament*, I (ed. J. Roloff; trans. J.E. Alsup; Grand Rapids: Eerdmans, 1975), pp. 16-17, suggests, the Fourth Gospel was written to a community familiar with the Synoptic tradition, then a reference to the prophetic Baptist as rabbi indicates that the term was still somewhat fluid.

[11] G. Friedrich, 'Προφήτης', *TDNT*, VI, pp. 841-48 and E. Lohse, 'Ῥαββί', *TDNT*, VI, p. 965.

[12] R. Fuller, *The Foundations of New Testament Christology* (New York: Scribner's, 1965), pp. 125-31; G. Vermes, *Jesus the Jew* (London: Collins, 1976), pp. 86-102. Backgrounds to this Jesus material are well set out by G. Dautzenberg, *Urchristliche Prophetie* (BWANT 104; Stuttgart: Kohlhammer, 1975), pp. 43-97. Jesus' prophetic status is also argued by D. Aune, *Prophecy in Early Christianity and the Ancient Mediterranean World* (Grand Rapids: Eerdmans, 1983).

[13] O. Cullmann, *The Christology of the New Testament* (trans. S.C. Guthrie & C.A.M. Hall; Philadelphia: Westminster, 1963), p. 44. Jesus was surely well aware of this unique prophetic status, cf. J.D.G. Dunn, *Jesus and the Spirit* (Philadelphia: Fortress, 1975), p. 84.

[14] This is demonstrated in the fact that προφήτης seems to have fallen quickly out of usage as a conceptually adequate title, cf. Cullmann, *Christology*, pp. 44-50; Aune, *Prophecy*, p. 189.

that of contemporary apocalyptic prophets'.[15] This is best explained as messianic authority.

The Disciples as Charismatic Followers

If rabbi is not the best descriptive title for Jesus, then the disciples are probably not best understood as rabbinic students.[16] How are the disciples of Jesus to be understood? Hengel suggests that the best parallels to Jesus' disciples are to be found in charismatic-prophetic-eschatological contexts. Beginning with the call of Elisha by Elijah, Hengel surveys the uses of 'following' and 'call' in various eschatological texts. Of particular interest is Mattathias' call in 1 Macc. 2.27, 28:

> Mattathias cried out throughout the town in a loud voice, 'all who are zealous for the sake of the Torah, who uphold the covenant, march out after me (ἐξελθέτω ὀπίσω μου)!' Thereupon he and his sons fled to the mountains, leaving behind all their possessions in the town (ἐγκατέλιπον ὅσα εἶχον ἐν τῇ πόλει).[17]

Others considered are Ehud and Barak following Deborah (Judg. 3.28) and Josephus' list of 'prophets' - particularly Judas the Galilean. He concludes with an examination of the followers of John the Baptist.[18] The context of the majority of these cases includes the disintegrating of society. Out of this matrix comes a charismatic figure who calls for radical obedience, a forsaking of possessions, a breaking away from family, and so complete an identification with the leader or master than even the death of the follower on the master's behalf was not out of the ordinary. These examples come closer to explaining the relationship of Jesus and his disciples than the rabbinic model. Yet, owing to Jesus' unique messianic authority, even these analogies are far transcended by Jesus' call of the disciples. Hengel concludes:

---

[15] Hengel, *Charismatic Leader*, p. 64; cf. J. Jeremias, *New Testament Theology* (trans. J. Bowden; Philadelphia: Fortress, 1971), p. 77, who observes that 'Jesus, then, was regarded as a *charismatic* rather than a professional theologian' (italics his).

[16] Hengel (*Charismatic Leader*, pp. 50-51) notes that there are no stories of calling and following in rabbinic literature comparable to those found in Mark and Q. In addition, the events of joining and learning were described by 'learning Torah', never by 'following after'. When the latter thought does occur it is used solely to express the natural subordination of pupil to teacher.

[17] Cited according to the translation of Jonathan A. Goldstein, *1 Maccabees* (AB 41; Garden City: Doubleday, 1976), p. 234. Cf. also the RSV's rendering.

[18] Cf. Hengel, *Charismatic Leader*, pp. 16-37.

Just as in the Old Testament God himself called individual prophets from work and family – 'and Yahweh took Me from the flock and said to me "Go and prophesy against my people Israel"' (Amos 8:15) – so Jesus also calls individuals away from all human ties to follow him ... 'Following' means in the first place unconditional *sharing of the master's identity*, which does not stop even at deprivation and suffering in the train of the master, and is possible only on the basis of complete trust on the part of the person who 'follows'; he has placed his destiny and his future in his master's hands.[19]

Consequently, Jesus is best understood as a charismatic leader and his disciples as charismatic followers.[20]

An Examination of Pertinent Markan Texts

At this point some New Testament texts are consulted, in an effort to determine if the proposed hypothesis concerning discipleship is well founded. Several passages from the second Gospel are examined.

Two passages specifically describe a calling of disciples: Mk 1.16-20 and 2.13-14. δεῦτε ὀπίσω μου, ἀφέντες, and ἠκολούθησαν are prominent terms found in these passages. In Mk 1.16-20 Simon and Andrew respond in a way reminiscent of those discussed previously (cf. Mattathias). Mark describes their decision to follow as immediate (καὶ εὐθύς) with far-reaching implications (ἀφέντες τὰ δίκτυα). The radical nature of the acceptance of this call is further heightened in the response of the sons of Zebedee. Simon and Andrew leave their livelihood, but James and John leave both their business and their father. The sudden decision of Levi (Mk 2.13, 14) is no different. Just as the fishermen left their means of support, so does the tax-collector. Without hesitation, Levi responds and follows Jesus.[21]

These two passages tend to indicate that the call of the disciples is a unique invitation rooted in the authority of Jesus himself. His charismatic authority evokes positive decisions to follow him. As Martin observes:

---

[19] Hengel, *Charismatic Leader*, pp. 71-72 (italics his).

[20] G. Theissen (*Sociology of Early Palestinian Christianity* [trans J. Bowden; Philadelphia: Fortress, 1978]), observes that not only was Jesus a charismatic wanderer, but also that the role of charismatic wanderer had a prominent place in the early church for a number of years.

[21] E. Schweizer (*Lordship and Discipleship* [London: SCM, 1960], pp. 11-12) finds that 'There can be no doubt about the fact that Jesus called disciples to follow him'.

The closeness of the bond between Jesus and his chosen followers is a matter of unusual significance ... He boldly innovates a new type relationship, of which the rabbinic 'master-pupil' model is only dimly adequate as a precedent ... The disciples respond to this relationship by their acceptance of his sovereign call and their yielding to his claims.[22]

The Purpose of Discipleship

Mark 3.13-19 is devoted to the choosing of the Twelve. This passage, more than others in Mark, discusses the purpose of Jesus in choosing disciples. Consequently, this pericope deserves somewhat closer attention than the two call-passages discussed above.

The evangelist describes Jesus as going up into the mountain. As the text does not identify this site, it does not appear that the geographical identification was as important for Mark as was the theological significance. More than likely, the evangelist is emphasizing the traditional setting for divine revelatory acts.[23] The use in v. 13 of προσκαλεῖται (he called) indicates that this call was no mere invitation, but a command. In the LXX such a summons depicts a high-ranking person calling subordinate individuals or groups. These include: parents calling children (Gen. 24.58), rulers calling subjects (Exod. 1.18; Judg. 12.1), and Moses calling the elders (Exod. 12.21; 19.7).[24] The use of ἤθελεν αὐτός (he desired) puts additional emphasis upon Jesus' initiative in the call.[25] Mark simply states that the disciples' response was affirmative.

Not only did he call them, but he appointed (ἐποίησεν, 3.14, 16) the Twelve. As Taylor observes, ἐποίησεν probably means 'appoints', reflecting the LXX rendering of as עשה when it is used for appointing priests (1 Kgs 12.21; 13.33; 2 Chron. 2.18) and for appointing Moses and Aaron (1 Sam. 12.6).[26] In the light of the earlier actions of the Markan Jesus, it is probable that divine appointment is in mind here.[27]

---

[22] R.P. Martin, *Mark: Evangelist and Theologian* (Grand Rapids: Zondervan, 1973), pp. 132-133.

[23] W. Lane, *The Gospel According to Mark* (NICNT; Grand Rapids: Eerdmans, 1974), p. 132 and C. Brown, 'Wilderness', *DNTT*, III, pp. 1009-10.

[24] L. Coenen, 'Call', *DNTT*, I, p. 272.

[25] Cf. C.E.B. Cranfield, *The Gospel According to St. Mark* (Cambridge: Cambridge University, 1979), p. 126.

[26] V. Taylor, *The Gospel According to St. Mark* (Grand Rapids: Baker, 1966), p. 230. It should be observed that עשה is used in emphasizing God's acts in the sphere of history. It is also used interchangeably with ברא *bara*; cf. Thomas McComisky,

Central to the present inquiry is the reminder of v.14 and the whole of v.15. Here, the purpose of discipleship is made clear. Mark employs two ἵνα clauses. Both clauses denote purpose, with the second clause growing out of the first. The first reason given for the disciples' call is 'in order that they might be with him'. If Jesus' call is understood as a charismatic one, then the disciples' 'being with' Jesus would demonstrate their solidarity with his identity. In the Marcan narrative world, the disciples spend time with him and observe his teaching and miraculous works before they are sent out (Mk 6.6b-13). Not only do they identify with him, but during this time they are equipped to share in his work. In other words, the disciples' later service is a direct result of the 'being with' Jesus. The tense of ὦσιν (present) indicates that a continuous communion is described.[28] However, the disciples' call was not for them to become an introverted group glorying in their religious experiences. The next ἵνα clause spells out that they were to share in the mission of their leader. There is a double emphasis in the next clause, 'in order that he might send them to preach and to have authority to cast out demons'. The disciples' task is to participate actively in the work of Jesus. They were to do the things that he was doing. Previously, Mark has described Jesus as preaching and driving out unclean spirits. In the next three chapters both of these characteristics are explicitly emphasized. The following part of the Markan narrative includes several parables (with space devoted to an explanation of the purpose of parables), a pericope devoted to the question of the basis of Jesus' authority (3.20-30), the deliverance of a Gerasene demoniac (5.1-20), the healing of a woman with an issue of blood and the resurrection of Jairus's daughter (5.21-43), and teaching about the rejection of a prophet in his hometown (6.1-6a). The disciples were to be Jesus' fellow workers. No doubt they were to proclaim the same message that Jesus proclaimed: the kingdom of God. Having learned about the authority to cast out demons (3.20-30), they are given such authority by Jesus (6.7). Their authority was in actuality the authority of Jesus transferred to the disciples. His authority is the unique authority of the Messiah. More than likely, ἐξουσία technically denotes

'Asa', 'Asah', *TWAT*, II, p. 701. In light of this, Mark's use of ἐποίησεν might be more than coincidence.

[27] Mark's description of the purpose of the Twelve – to be with Jesus and to be sent out to preach and exorcise – is consistent with the concept of divine appointment.

[28] S. Freyne (*The Twelve: Disciples and Apostles* [London: Sheed & Ward, 1968], pp. 119-38) argues that the whole of the second Gospel describes the process of 'being with him'.

power granted by a higher norm, which confers 'the right to do something or the right over something'.[29] This higher power is Jesus, in whom ἐξουσία (authority) and δύναμις (power) are combined. Consequently, the disciples are equipped by Jesus to perform the very things that he is doing, which includes having authority over Satan. According to 6.30 the disciples were able to accomplish their assigned tasks.[30]

It appears that this understanding of the purpose of discipleship coheres better with the charismatic leader-follower analogies than the rabbinic model. In the majority of places where a charismatic call has been issued, the followers participated in the work of their leader (e.g. Elisha, Ehud and Barak, Maccabees, Essenes, and Zealots.)

The Conditions of Discipleship

It should surprise few that attention is now given to Mark 8. The emphasis of the present examination falls upon vv. 34-38. The full implications of this passage become apparent only when this pericope is viewed in its proper location in the Markan narrative. Until this point, a number of deeds and incidents from the life of Jesus have been raising the question, who is Jesus? The first eight chapters of this Gospel seem devoted to setting the reader in the proper frame of mind for this passage. In Peter's confession, placed near the center of the gospel, a number of themes are brought together. Both the confession and ensuing discussion set the stage for much of the remainder of the Gospel.

Not only are passages located in a strategic position in the Gospel narrative, but they also have a significant immediate context. Both Best[31] and Achtemeier[32] have identified Mk 8.22–10.52, the central section in the Gospel, as being wholly devoted to discipleship. This is highlighted by the fact that the section begins (8.22-26) and ends (10.46-52) with the story of blind men receiving their sight.

---

[29] W. Foerster, 'ἐξουσία', *TDNT*, II, p. 562.

[30] R.P. Meyer (*Jesus and the Twelve* [Grand Rapids: Eerdmans, 1968], p. 107) notes how Mark develops his material in that 'Mark 1:17 is in fact to be linked to the appointment of the Twelve in 3:13-19 and the sending of the Twelve on mission in 6:7-13, 30'. Cf. his entire discussion, pp. 106-10.

[31] E. Best, 'Discipleship in Mark: Mark 8:22-10:52', *SJT* 23 (1970), pp. 323-37.

[32] P.J. Achtemeier, '"And he followed him": Miracles and Discipleship in Mark 10:46-52', *Semeia* 11 (1978), pp. 115-42.

With Peter's confession drawing attention to Jesus' true identity, the Lord begins to discuss the major part suffering plays in his own mission. Peter is totally unprepared for this disclosure and promptly began to rebuke him. With his disciples in view, Jesus places Peter's admonitions in the same category as Satan's. Peter is advocating a kingdom without a cross. (Matthew and Luke record that Satan made a similar offer in the wilderness temptations.) It is not without significance that the discussion of the conditions of discipleship so closely follows Jesus' teaching about his own suffering.[33]

According to Mk 8.34, Jesus and the Twelve are joined by the crowd (τὸν ὄχλον). The presence of the crowd is theologically significant. Its appearance indicates that the conditions of discipleship are the same for everyone. This universal note suggests that the Twelve are no different than others. These conditions are for all.

Jesus prefaces three conditions for discipleship by the general call, 'If anyone desires to come after me'. This call is reminiscent of Mattathias' call. Here, in the clearest possible language, is the charismatic leader calling potential followers. As Best concludes:

> 'Come after me' is a general command which specifically links discipleship of Jesus ... The call is not to accept a certain system of teaching, live by it, continue faithfully to interpret it and pass it on, which was in essence the call of a rabbi to his disciples; nor is it a call to accept a philosophical position which will express itself in a certain type behavior, as in Stoicism; nor is it a call to devote life to the alleviation of suffering for others; nor is it the call to pass through certain rites as in the Mysteries so as to become an initiate of God, his companion – the carrying of the cross is no rite! It is a call to fall in behind Jesus and go with him.[34]

Jesus calls disciples to identify with his mission, which involves suffering and death. It appears that Mark is trying to communicate a vision of the Christian message which states: discipleship is the way of the cross with Jesus.[35]

---

[33] The fact that 32% of the sayings in the Markan Jesus material is concerned with elucidating the mission and passion of Jesus relates directly to Mark's understanding of suffering as a condition for discipleship, cf. France, 'Mark and the Teaching of Jesus', p. 121.

[34] Best, 'Discipleship', p. 329.

[35] R. Busemann, *Die Jüngergemeinde nach Markus 10: Eine redaktionsgeschichtliche Untersuchung des 10. Kapitels im Markus-evangelium* (BBB 57; Bonn: Hanstein, 1983). Perhaps a focal point of Mark's understanding of discipleship is in 8.34-38 which encapsulates his 'discipleship of the cross', cf. M. Hengel, 'Entstehungszeit und Situation des Markusevangeliums',*Markus-Philologie. Historische, literargeschichtliche und stilistische Unter-*

The meaning of what it costs to follow Jesus is spelled out in 8.34. First, it involves self-denial (ἀπαρνησάσθω ἑαυτόν). The tense and mood of the verb (aorist imperative), together with the context, suggest[36] that this denial involves a definite decision or ongoing set of decisions. The disciple, who here is the object of the verbal idea, must say no to making self the goal of life. Such denial involves turning 'away from the idolatry of self-centeredness'.[37] It consists of making Jesus and his mission the object of life and learning so as to serve a new leader. Denial, then, is a forgetting of self in order to be at the full disposal of Jesus. Next, the disciple must take up the cross (ἀράτω τὸν σταυρὸν αὐτοῦ). Jesus was quite possibly referring to the gruesome sight that had become common in first-century Palestine.[38] More exactly, what did bearing a literal cross entail in the ancient world?[39] Crucifixion was a political and military punishment inflicted primarily on the lower classes and was remarkably widespread in antiquity. Serving as a deterrent, it was carried out publicly and usually included flogging. This humiliating penalty involved a naked victim publicly displayed at a prominent place. Quite a few of the victims were never buried which further aggravated the humiliation. There is no suitable contemporary analogy for the cross. It appears to have been the most excruciating death possible. The horror of crucifixion for Jews was heightened by Deut. 21.23, 'Anyone who is hung on a tree is under God's curse'. The imperative ἀράτω conveys intense metaphorical feelings of urgency and mission in the midst of suffering. The final command is to follow (καὶ ἀκολουθείτω μοι). That the rabbi-student analogy does not adequately define 'following' is explicit here. 'Fol-

---

suchungen zum zweiten Evangelium (WUNT 33; ed. H. Cancik; Tübingen: Mohr, 1984) p. 136.

[36] Cf. F. Stagg, 'The Abused Aorist', JBL 91 (1972), p. 231; M.L. McKay, 'Syntax in Exegesis', TynB 23 (1972), p. 46.

[37] Cranfield, Mark, p. 281.

[38] H. Ruddi-Weber (The Cross: Tradition and Interpretation [trans. E. Jessett; Grand Rapids: Eerdmans, 1979], p. 9) suggests that hundreds, possibly thousands, had been crucified by the time of Jesus' birth. Another factor latent in this saying is that Jesus probably understood his unique prophetic status as one which would inevitably involve suffering and rejection, cf. Aune, Prophecy, pp. 156-59, 187. This suggests that disciples who might prophesy or preach in his name could be expected to carry a similar, but much lesser, burden.

[39] The following comments are based upon M. Hengel, Crucifixion in the Ancient World and the Folly of the Cross (trans. J. Bowden; Philadelphia: Fortress, 1977), pp. 86-88.

lowing' entails a radical identification of the Lord and follower. As Schweizer concludes:

> Following Jesus means togetherness with Jesus and service to him. It entails giving up all other ties, to boat and tax-office, to father and mother, in short, to one's own life, to oneself. As Jesus' own way, by divine necessity, leads to rejection, suffering and death, and only so to glory, so also the way of those who follow him.[40]

Best's thoughts are in basic agreement:

> The way of the cross can only be a lonely way; as the disciple sees Jesus tread to the cry of dereliction he cannot but be frightened, and Mark depicts him as frightened, not only by the possibility of physical suffering, which for Mark's readers was a real possibility, but by the equally real possibility of mental and spiritual suffering. In responding to his call he has left behind everything and everyone and at the end of the road there may stand only a lonely cross ... Christians go the same way as their Lord but are always in the position of those who follow, never of those who have arrived. But if they are those who follow they are also those who are accompanied – by their Lord and by their fellow disciples. As long as their journey lasts Christians are never alone; the Lord is there to deliver and feed; they are together in the house, the ship and temple as brothers and sisters.[41]

However, the paradox of the suffering Messiah was not the only dilemma for the disciples. Verses 35-38 explain that life itself is attainable only through the sacrifice of life. True life comes through following Jesus, even if it entails shame, humiliation, and/or death. For if life is lost, nothing can be exchanged for it. The loss is irrevocable.

Conclusions

1. To view Jesus primarily as a rabbi serves as a stumbling block in attempting to understand the biblical model of discipleship. A better analogy for Jesus and the disciples is that of charismatic

---

[40] Schweizer, *Lordship and Discipleship*, p. 20. Achtemeier ('Miracles and Discipleship', p. 136) detects as well that one can reach no other conclusion except that 'Mark clearly thinks of discipleship primarily in relation to the passion of Jesus'.

[41] E. Best, *Following Jesus: Discipleship in the Gospel of Mark* (JSNTS 4; Sheffield, JSOT, 1981), pp. 162, 248. For Best, discipleship and Christology are thematically linked. Jesus lays down his life; so do the disciples. Jesus is a servant; so are his followers. What Jesus is and does - that is what the disciples are to be and do. However, even in teaching this, Jesus remains distinct; his person and work are unique.

leader and his followers. Yet even this is not a true analogy, for Jesus is more than a charismatic leader. He has messianic authority.
2. Discipleship is to be understood as issuing out of a call by Jesus. This call is no mere invitation but is more of a command, which is based in the authority of Jesus himself.
3. Radical identification of the disciple with the Lord is one purpose of discipleship. This communion, or 'being with', is a time of fellowship with Jesus, but is also a time of intense learning.
4. The disciple's communion with Jesus will result in a sharing in the work of Jesus. Proclaiming the kingdom of God and having authority over the demons are ways in which the disciples become Jesus' fellow-workers.
5. The conditions of discipleship involve both a denial of self and a sharing the fate of the master on the cross.

Contemporary Implications

At the present a plethora of models for advancing the kingdom are advocated. At this time evidence of success is being interpreted as affluence, numerical strength, social influence, and possession of motivational abilities. Western society reinforces a concentration on the protection and development of the self. Ecclesiastical bodies seek to control internal as well as external situations by resorting to the world's power structures. Consequently, compromise and accommodation appear to be necessary evils.

The Markan admonitions on discipleship indeed sound strange to the present situation. However, despite their foreign ring, these statements can be of genuine use to those interested in renewal through discipleship.
1. There must be a continued emphasis upon the charismatic nature of Jesus' call. Never should this aspect be down-played. There is an authority in the person of Jesus that must be encountered for a true call to take place.
2. The purpose of discipleship must be constantly remembered. Spirit-movements have long emphasized a personal communion with the Lord. This fellowship is essential to discipleship. In the period of time between the call of the disciples and their being sent on a mission, Jesus taught them through parables and demonstrated his authority though exorcisms. They not only observed him, they also experienced him. Those presently wishing to make

disciples would do well to emphasize the importance of integrating information and experience. The gifts and graces of the Holy Spirit cannot be presumptuously and artificially uncoupled from the informational realm of the gospel. Discipleship may be choked in static liturgical soil, but it thrives on a dynamic relationship with the risen Jesus though Scripture, community, prayer, and the sacraments.[42]

3. In addition to communion, the believer must be acquainted with another purpose of discipleship. Jesus' call was for others to join his work. Whether announcing the kingdom of God or exercising authority over demons, the disciple is to be Jesus' fellow worker. Both the message of the kingdom and the exercising of authority come through 'being with' Jesus. Those familiar with charismatic experience(s) should seek humility so as to develop the spiritual sensitivity required for these tasks. The call of discipleship is for service.

4. The conditions for discipleship must be held in their proper place. To follow Jesus entails self-denial and cross-bearing. Only in suffering does the Markan Jesus manifest his true messianic status in the fullest sense and, for Mark, a reflective comprehension of this fact must lead to taking up the cross in authentic discipleship.[43] This might be the most difficult aspect of discipleship to translate into 21st-century secular society with its strong emphasis on instant wealth and health. A radical identification with the suffering and death of Jesus must stand at the heart of a commitment to discipleship. In all likelihood it will be God's will for a disciple to endure suffering in some way. God may allow a disciple to suffer physically and/or mentally from illness or persecution.[44] Today the cross is an ornament, worn around the neck, sometimes casually placed in churches, and printed on bumper stickers. The horrible reality of the cross must be translated to the point that its essence (or dynamic equivalence) speaks to modern believers. Bruce Metzger suggests that one should perhaps say, 'In the elec-

---

[42] Re these latter categories, cf. P. Hinnebusch, 'Using the Scriptures for Prayer', *Scripture and the Charismatic Renewal* (ed. G. Martin; Ann Arbor: Servant, 1979), pp. 59-75.

[43] Cf. M. Hengel, 'Probleme des Markusevangeliums', *Das Evangelium und die Evangelien* (WUNT 26; ed. P. Stuhlmacher: Tübingen: Mohr, 1983), p. 237; 'The Expiatory Sacrifice of Christ', *BJRL* 62 (1980), p. 461.

[44] Such suffering, when it comes and in whatever form it comes, should be viewed christocentrically, i.e. from the perspective of the cross and resurrection.

tric chair or gas chamber of Christ do I glory'. Discipleship embraces a death to self. This aspect of the gospel must not be allowed to be interpreted away in an affluent culture, but must experientially be a constant reminder of the transitory nature of discipleship.
5. Authentic Christian existence is only available through a life given fully to Jesus. The total trust and confidence placed in the leader allows the follower to follow anywhere at any time.
6. In all points of discipleship the inevitable tension between Jesus' continuing call of discipleship and the call of self will always be present. This tension must never be resolved in favor of settling down in an affluent world. There may be some flexibility by the way in which particulars are worked out, but the heart of discipleship, and indeed of the gospel itself, is the message of the cross.

5

The Ending of Mark's Gospel

The problems surrounding the ending of the Gospel according to Mark are rather well known to students of the New Testament. Whilst the vast majority of manuscripts include 16.9-20, the so-called 'Longer Ending', several early manuscripts end the Gospel at 16.8 with the words, 'for they were afraid' (ἐφοβοῦντο γάρ). In addition, an alternate ending to either 16.8 or 16.9-20 is found in a few manuscripts. This study seeks to determine the place where Mark originally ended his gospel, to explain the rise of various textual variants, and to discuss the possible hermeneutical implications of these variants.

Most serious New Testament students are aware of the various problems posed by the ending of Mark. The Greek MSS suggest six different endings.[1]

1. The following MSS of Mark end at 16.8: ℵ B 304 (2386 and 1420 have a page missing at this point); syr^s arm^{8mss} eth^{3mss} geo^{1,A}; Clement, Origen, Eusebius mss$^{according\ to\ Eusebius}$, Jerome mss$^{according\ to\ Jerome}$.

2. The longer ending (Mk 16.9-20) is included in the following MSS: A C D E H K M S U X Y Γ Δ Θ Π Σ Φ Ω 047 055 0211 f^{13} 28 33 274 (text) 565 700 892 1009 1010 1071 1195 1230 1242 1253 1344 1365 1546 1646 2148 2174, etc.; lectionaries 60 69 70 185 547 833; Latin^{vt} aur c d$^{suppff^2}$ l n o q vg syr^c p h pal cop^{sah} boh fay goth arm^{mss} geo^8; Diat$^{arabic,\ Italian,\ Old\ Dutch}$; Justin (?), Irenaeus, Tertullian, Aphraates, Apostolic Constitutions, Didymus, Hippolytus, Marinus (as quoted by Eusebius), Epiphanius.

3. Codex W (also known as the Freer Logion) expands the longer ending at v. 14, 'and they excused themselves, saying, "This age of lawlessness and unbelief is under Satan, who does not allow the

---

[1] The following information is from the Institut für neutestamentliche Textforschung in Munster as given in J.K. Elliot, 'The Text and Language of the Endings to Mark's Gospel', *TZ* 27 (1971), pp. 255-62.

truth and power of God to prevail over the unclean things of the spirits. Therefore reveal thy righteousness now" – thus they spoke to Christ. And Christ replied to them, "The term of years for Satan's power has been fulfilled, but other terrible things draw near. And for those who have sinned I was delivered over to death, that they may return to the truth and sin no more; that they may inherit the spiritual and incorruptible glory of righteousness which is in heaven."'[2]

4. The longer ending is included in the following MSS marked with asterisks, or obeli, or with a critical note added: f[1] 137 138 1110 1210 1215 1216 1217 1221 1241vid 1582.

5. Latin (vt. k) reads, 'But they reported briefly to Peter and those with him all that they had been told. And after this Jesus himself sent out by means of them, from east to west, the sacred and imperishable proclamation of eternal salvation.'[3]

6. The following MSS add the shorter ending (number 5 above) before the longer ending: L Ψ 099 (incomplete up to συντόμως) 0112 (omits πᾶν ... μετὰ δέ) 579 274mg; lectionary 1602; syrhmg coptsahmss bohmss ethmss.

Of these options, reading 3 can be dismissed as an expanded form of the longer ending. Metzger notes, 'The obvious and pervasive apocryphal flavor of the expansion, as well as the extremely limited basis of evidence supporting it, condemns it as a totally secondary accretion.'[4] Reading 5 can be disregarded as the original due to its scanty MS support.[5] Reading 4 obviously reflects a view of the longer ending as somewhat questionable. Reading 6 appears to be an intentional confla-

---

[2] Metzger, *A Textual Commentary on the Greek New Testament* (United Bible Societies, 1971), p. 124.

[3] B.M. Metzger, *A Textual Commentary on the Greek New Testament*, pp. 123-24.

[4] B.M. Metzger, *The Text of the New Testament* (New York and Oxford: Oxford University Press, 1968), p. 227.

[5] H.B. Swete observes, 'As to the origin of this ending there can be little doubt. It has been written by someone whose copy of the Gospel ended at ἐφοβοῦντο γάρ, and who desired to soften the harshness of so abrupt a conclusion, and at the same time to remove the impression which it leaves of a failure on the part of Mary of Magdala and her friends to deliver the message with which they had been charged. Terrified as they were, he adds, they recovered themselves sufficiently to report to Peter the substance of the Angel's words. After this the Lord Himself appeared to the Apostles and gave them orders to carry the Gospel from East to West; and these orders, with his assistance, were loyally fulfilled' (*The Gospel According to St. Mark* [London: Macmillan, 1898], p. ci).

tion of the shorter reading with the longer one and as such offers some support for both readings.

In 1920 Caspar Rene Gregory remarked, 'Mark 16.9-20 is neither part nor parcel of that Gospel'.[6] For years nearly all New Testament textual critics were unanimous in their support of Gregory's position. Recently, however, a few scholars have differed with the consensus position in part or in whole. Consequently a close examination of readings 1 and 3 is necessary.

The external evidence for the longer reading is old and has good family representation. The Byzantine witnesses include A E H K S Π. The Caesarean witnesses include W f[13] 28 565 700 arm geo. The Western witnesses include D and Tatian's Diatessaron. The Alexandrian texts are represented by C 892 Coptic (Sahidic and Bohairic). A C D W arm and geo all date from the third and fourth centuries respectively, with Tatian's Diatessaron ultimately going back to ca. 170. Such weight is quite impressive and should – by mere bulk, variety and date – be cause for further consideration.

The two oldest and most valuable uncial MSS available, however, support the abrupt ending of Mk 16.8. ℵ and B, both fourth-century compositions, are representatives of the Alexandrian witnesses, and except for Syriac[s], Eusebius and Origen, which are Caesarean witnesses, support from other families is lacking. However, due to the stature of the text found in ℵ and B and the fact that original readings are sometimes preserved in only a few MSS, most scholars believe Mark ended at 16.8.

William Farmer is one of the few scholars who attempts to defend 16.9-20 as the original reading.[7] In discussing Origen's somewhat negative estimation of 16.9-20, Farmer suggests that Origen might have been influenced by Celsus's accusation of contradictions in the resurrection accounts given by Matthew and Mark. The question about the legitimacy of 16.9-20 could be used in defense of this charge of inconsistency. Farmer also examines another Alexandrian MS in favor of omission, B, which by the fourth century ended with ἐφοβοῦντο γάρ. Yet it appears that there was some amount of uncertainty about the gospel's original ending. For after 16.8, and the subscription **KATA MAPKON**, the remainder of the column and the

---

[6] C.R. Gregory, *The Canon and Text of the New Testament* (New York and Oxford: Oxford University Press, 1920), p. 227.

[7] Although Farmer might not admit this as his thesis, his conclusions clearly imply his preference for the longer reading. The following discussion is based on W. Farmer, *The Last Twelve Verses of Mark* (London: Cambridge University Press, 1974).

whole of the next column are left blank. The scribe, Farmer notes, 'only knew that the text he was copying up to 16:8 was a matter of dispute. By not copying anything beyond 16:8 he met the essential requirement of those who felt that the Gospel needed either an ending or some word of explanation following 16:8.'[8] The scribe therefore allowed the future owner of the MS the opportunity to make any modification deemed necessary.

Farmer also appeals to a possible allusion to 16.20 in Justin (*Apology* I.45.5) as grounds for an early date of 16.9-20. Irenaeus is referred to as a witness to 16.9 and is cited as additional weight in arguing for the possibility of originality.[9]

One of the more interesting arguments posed by Farmer is the text-critical rule of preferring the more difficult reading. The argument is this: If the last twelve verses of Mark are not original, in what context could they have been accepted and in turn produced? The teachings of these verses pose such problems as 'taking up serpents' and 'drinking deadly poisons'. As Farmer points out, there has been no evidence produced to demonstrate an area in Christendom that would either condone these actions or be powerful enough to impose them on the church at large through an addition to the text of the second gospel.

As difficult as it might be to explain the origin of this ending, it is just as difficult to explain why ℵ and B omit the entire passage instead of simply omitting a couple of lines in the column, thus eliminating the difficult admonition while salvaging the resurrection appearances. The fact remains that while external evidence is not conclusive two of the most important MSS omit these verses. Therefore internal evidence must be consulted in order to decide which reading is original.

Various scholars have appealed to the internal evidence as proof of the non-Markan origin of 16.9-20, yet relatively few have done an exhaustive study. Conversely, a handful of scholars have argued, on the basis of internal evidence, that part or all of 16.9-20 is Markan.

Robert Morgenthaler uses 'word-statistical research' in an attempt to disprove conclusively Markan authorship of the last twelve verses.[10] For instance, Morgenthaler argues that the number of times καί ap-

---

[8] Farmer, *The Last Twelve Verses of Mark*, p. 57.

[9] This much is clear: the longer ending is quite old, dating at least to the middle of the second century.

[10] R. Morgenthaler, *Statistik des neutestamentlichen Wortschatzes* (Zurich, 1958), pp. 58-60. For critiques of Morgenthaler's work cf. Farmer, *The Last Twelve Verses of Mark*, pp. 79-83, and Elliot, 'The Text and Language of the Endings to Mark's Gospel'.

pears in the longer ending is lower than the average in Mk 1.1-16.8, while the number of times δέ appears in the longer reading is greater than in the rest of Mark. Recently these arguments have been called into question. In fact Eta Linnemann[11] and William Farmer have both demonstrated the problems involved in this analysis.

In analyzing Morgenthaler's methodology, Linnemann attempts to demonstrate that 16.15-20 is Markan while Farmer argues that no good reason exists to dismiss 16.9-20 as non-Markan. Consequently, the distinctive features of 16.9-20 must be examined in order to see if either Linnemann or Farmer is on firm ground.

Verse 9. The first peculiar aspect of v. 9 is the fact that the subject changes from v. 8 without being named. Farmer suggests that since Mark uses the name Jesus sparingly in other places (1.21, 1.30-2.4) its absence here is not so unusual.[12] Although these examples do support Farmer's point, the fact remains that the transition is not as smooth here as in other places. πρωΐ, a favorite Markan linking word, is found here (cf. Mk 1.35; 11.30; 13.35; 15.1; 16.2). This is the only place in the New Testament that the verb ἐφάνη is used of a resurrection appearance. While this verb is used with reference to Elijah in Lk. 9.8, this does not seem to be a resurrection appearance. In considering παρ' ἧς ἐκβεβλήκει, Farmer points out that while παρά plus the genitive is found in several other places in Mark (3.31; 5.20; 8.11; 12.2; 14.43) the phrase in question is found nowhere else in the NT. Gould comments, 'This is the only case of the use of this preposition in describing the casting out of demons, and it is as strange as it is unexampled.'[13]

Verse 10. ἐκείνη is not characteristic of Markan style, although it occurs three times in the longer ending (vv. 10, 11, 20). The pronoun is common in the Johannine writings. Although πορεύομαι is quite a common verb in the New Testament, it occurs only once in Mark (9.30), and there in a compound form. It occurs three times, however, in the Longer Ending (vv. 10, 12, 15). Further, the expression τοῖς μετ' αὐτοὺς γενομένοις occurs nowhere else in the New Testament and is an unusual way of referring to the disciples.[14] Although πενθοῦσι does not appear anywhere else in Mark, as Gould observes, 'that

---

[11] E. Linnemann, 'Der wiedergefundene Markusschluss', *ZTK* 66 (1969), pp. 255-287.

[12] Farmer, *The Last Twelve Verses of Mark*, pp. 83-84.

[13] E.P. Gould, *A Critical and Exegetical Commentary on the Gospel According to St. Mark* (Edinburgh: T. & T. Clark, 1896), p. 305.

[14] Elliott, 'The Text and Language of the Endings to Mark's Gospel', p. 259.

does not count, as it is about the rate of its use in the other books of the New Testament'.[15]

Verse 11. Farmer suggests that Mark's use of κἀκεῖνοι is a syntactical peculiarity since κἀκεῖνον is also found in Mk 12.4-5 and provides a syntactical parallel.[16] The verbs ἐθεάθη and ἠπίστησαν occur twice in the longer ending but nowhere else in Mark.

Verse 12. While both Luke and John often employ the expression μετὰ δὲ ταῦτα, this is its only occurrence in Mark. However, twice Mark does employ μετά plus the accusative (1.4; 14.28).[17] ἐφανερώθη occurs elsewhere in Mark, but of course only here in reference to a resurrection appearance of Jesus. As for the use of ἑτέρᾳ in 16.12, Mark seems to have a clear preference for ἄλλος. In addition, there is no firm example of ἕτερος anywhere in Mark.[18] Except for its appearance here, μορφή is used in the NT only by Paul (Phil. 2.6-7).

Verse 14. Though ὕστερον is found in other gospels, Mark does not use it. ἕνδεκα is a technical word used to describe the eleven remaining disciples. It occurs only in post-resurrection situations, which might explain why Mark did not use it before.[19] This is the only place in the New Testament where ὠνείδισεν is used of Jesus rebuking the disciples.[20] Similarly, this is the only place in the New Testament where the faults ἀπιστίαν ... καὶ σκληροκαρδίαν are leveled at the disciples.[21]

Verse 15. Since Mark begins his Gospel with εὐαγγέλιον, Farmer states that the occurrence of the word lends more credence to possible Markan authorship of these verses.[22] It is only here that κτίσει means the sum of creation rather than the creative act.[23]

Verses 16-17. Although κατακρίνω occurs in 10.33 and 14.64, this is the only place that γλώσσαις ... καιναῖς ('new tongues') are mentioned in the New Testament.

Verse 18. ὄφεις does not occur in Mk 1.1-16.8. θανάσιμόν, a rare word, does not appear anywhere else in the whole of the Greek Bible

---

[15] Gould, *A Critical and Exegetical Commentary on the Gospel According to St. Mark*, p. 306.

[16] Farmer, *The Last Twelve Verses of Mark*, p. 89.

[17] Farmer, *The Last Twelve Verses of Mark*, p. 90.

[18] Elliott, 'The Text and Language of the Endings to Mark's Gospel', p. 259.

[19] Farmer, *The Last Twelve Verses of Mark*, p. 93.

[20] Elliott, 'The Text and Language of the Endings to Mark's Gospel', p. 259.

[21] Elliott, 'The Text and Language of the Endings to Mark's Gospel', p. 259.

[22] Farmer, *The Last Twelve Verses of Mark*, p. 94.

[23] Elliott, 'The Text and Language of the Endings to Mark's Gospel', p. 260.

except in the apocryphal Acts of John. βλάψη only occurs in Lk. 4.35 in the New Testament. Even though Mark uses καλῶς in other passages, the combination καλῶς ἕξουσιν appears only here in the New Testament.

Verse 19. The combination μὲν οὖν occurs nowhere in Mark, with οὖν itself being rare.[24] Jesus is never given the Christological title (κύριος) in Mark's Gospel.

Verse 20. While ἐκήρυξαν πανταχοῦ is found only here in the gospels, the verbs συνεργοῦντος, βεβαιοῦντος and ἐπακολουθούντων are found only here in the New Testament.

In drawing some conclusions about the internal evidence, Farmer remarks that 'evidence for non-Markan authorship seems to be preponderant in v. 10. Verses 12, 14, 16, 17, 18, and 19 seem to be either basically, or in balance, neutral. Evidence for Markan authorship seems to be preponderant in vv. 9, 11, 13, 15, and 20.'[25]

Given the difference in the subject matter of the gospel of Mark and the last twelve verses, it is possible to see some reason for a small change in vocabulary. Linnemann, however, seems to be mistaken in separating vv. 9-14 from vv. 15-20. The last verses belong together since several words appear in both sections that are not in Mk 1.1-16.8. Farmer attempts to explain the non-Markan elements present in 16.9-20 by attributing them to the redactional use of older material by the evangelist and suggests that the last twelve verses belong to the autograph.[26] This suggestion is possible but not probable. It seems that Mark uses tradition as his own and modifies it more than Farmer would like to say. Mark's treatment of the passion is an example of this.

Therefore, what does the internal evidence suggest about the ending of Mark? The tentative conclusion about the problem of the place of the last twelve verses would seem to demand one to acknowledge that the Markan text ends at 16.8, despite Farmer's ingenious presentation. Yet it does appear that the last twelve verses are quite old. It appears that these resurrection appearances were added to Mark's Gospel at an extremely early stage to soften the abrupt ending found at 16.8.[27] In the light of this fact, Metzger observes:

---

[24] Elliott, 'The Text and Language of the Endings to Mark's Gospel', p. 261.

[25] Farmer, *The Last Twelve Verses of Mark*, p. 103.

[26] Farmer, *The Last Twelve Verses of Mark*, p. 107.

[27] On the basis of an Armenian manuscript of the gospels, copied A.D. 989, C.R. Gregory adamantly suggests that the last twelve verses were added by the Presbyter Ariston. As intriguing as this suggestion is, it is doubtful that this valuable piece of

> Since Mark was not responsible for the composition of the last twelve verses of the generally current form of his gospel, and since they undoubtedly had been attached to the Gospel before the Church recognized the fourfold Gospels as canonical, it follows that the New Testament contains not four but five evangelistic accounts of events subsequent to the resurrection of Christ.[28]

If the external and internal evidence suggest that 16.8 is the point at which Mark's Gospel concludes, and owing to the abrupt nature of this ending, the question must be raised: Did Mark originally end his gospel at 16.8? Three possible solutions are often suggested: (1) Mark was physically unable to finish his gospel due to death or persecution; (2) at one time there existed an ending to his gospel, but somehow it was separated and lost; and (3) Mark ended his gospel at 16.8 for a specific reason. As is easy to imagine, each of these theories has many supporters.

It is often argued that the gospel could not possibly end at 16.8 since the final word of the text is γάρ. This ending would be strange indeed, for only a handful of sentences can be offered in support of this unconventional ending. W.L. Knox writes:

> To suppose that Mark originally intended to end his Gospel in this way implies both that he was totally indifferent to the canons of popular story-telling, and that by a pure accident he happened to hit on a conclusion which suits the technique of a highly sophisticated type of modern literature. The odds against such a coincidence (even if we could for a moment entertain the idea that Mark was indifferent to canons which he observes scrupulously elsewhere in his Gospel) seem to me to be so enormous as not be worth considering.[29]

Recently, however, P.W. van der Horst has sought to prove once and for all that a book can end with γάρ.[30] Noting the examples of scholars such as R.H. Lightfoot, S.E. Johnson and Walter Bauer, van der Horst seeks to add one final, convincing example. Plotinus ends his thirty-second treatise as follows: τελειότερον γάρ. Even though it is now agreed that treatises 30, 31, 32 and 33 were formerly one ex-

---

information could have eluded all the manuscripts until the end of the tenth century (C.R. Gregory, *The Canon and Text of the New Testament* [New York and Oxford: Oxford University Press, 1920], p. 511).

[28] Metzger, *The Text of the New Testament*, p. 229.

[29] W.L. Knox, 'The Ending of St. Mark's Gospel', *HTR* 35 (1942), pp. 21-22.

[30] P.W. van der Horst, 'Can a Book End with *gar*? A Note on Mark XVI. 8', *JTS* 23 (1972), p. 123.

tended treatise, Richard Harder, a distinguished Plotinus scholar, maintains that Porphyry divided these treatises where he did intentionally.[31] Consequently van der Horst contends that since a philosophical discourse can end with γάρ so can any other work. This proposal certainly casts new light on this long discussed problem, but one must wonder if van der Horst is completely justified in claiming that 'the argument that a book cannot end with the word γάρ is absolutely invalid'.[32]

Others who attempt to deal with the problem of a book ending with γάρ propose a variety of solutions. J. Luzarraga thinks that an oral or written Semitic tradition was adopted by Mark in v. 8 and that Mark, confused the emphasis in a Semitic word בהל, that connotes both fear and haste. Instead of using the Greek word for 'haste', which was intended in the original Semitic tradition, he translated it as 'fear'.[33] Fredrick W. Danker explains that Mark ends with γάρ because of a haplographic omission that took place during the copying process.[34]

C.F.D. Moule suggests that the γάρ-clause was originally parenthetic and that the main sentence continued after it. If the words καὶ εὐθὺς λέγουσιν τοῖς μαθηταῖς περὶ πάντα τοῦτον were added after ἐφοβοῦντο γάρ, the problem would be cleared up.[35]

G.W. Trompf argues that if Mark ended at 16.8 he abandoned his pattern of always ending a pericope with Jesus' comforting words. Mark's usual pattern (cf. 1.27; 2.12b; 4.41; 5.42, 43; 6.2, 52; 7.37; 9.6, 7; 10.32, 33; 11.18; 15.44; 16.5, 6) would indicate that Jesus should appear and dispel the women's fears. Jesus does not appear, and therefore the original ending should be reconstructed on the basis of Matthew. Furthermore, Trompf argues, the ending would need a di-

---

[31] Van der Horst, 'Can a Book End with *gar*? A Note on Mark XVI. 8', p. 123.

[32] Van der Horst, 'Can a Book End with *gar*? A Note on Mark XVI. 8', p. 124.

[33] J. Luzarrage, 'Retraduccion Semetica de phobeomia en Mc 16, 8', *Bib* 50 (1969), pp. 497-510. I am indebted to Dr W.M. Clemmer for this reference.

[34] F.W. Danker, 'Post-script to the Markan Secrecy Motif', *CTM* 38 (1967), p. 26.

[35] Moule comments, 'in that case, I dare to question whether any commentator would have puzzled long over the parentheses. Would it not obviously mean that their trembling and amazement made them run straight back to the disciples, uttering not a syllable either to the young man at the tomb or to anybody they may have met on the way? The refusal to linger over the normal eastern exchange of greetings is a familiar mark of haste or urgency: II Kings IV. 29, Luke X.4 are obvious examples from Scripture' (C.F.D. Moule, 'St. Mark XVI. 8 Once More', *NTS* 2 [1955], pp. 58-59).

vine action.[36] The absence of this ending might have a 'simple' explanation. It is possible that vv. 9-20 belong to a 'second edition' of Mark.

> The answer may well have a good deal to do with the coming of the four Gospels into one corpus – another mid-second century phenomenon. If the four-Gospel canon was sponsored so early both in the West and East, then it was apparently the revised edition of Mark which was sponsored with it, Mark's text now conforming to those of the other (more dominant) evangelists. In view of heretical attempts to corrupt gospel texts in the second century, an authoritative Markan text had to be established. The longer ending thus acquired official support. For largely following the recent and reliable-looking Lukan account, it compromised the earlier traditions by presenting both an appearance to one woman (Magdalene) and to the eleven, whilst putting old 'political' problems into forgotten oblivion by specifying neither a first appearance to Jesus' mother, nor to Peter.[37]

The other endings would easily have fallen under the category of unauthorized and fallen out of use. Trompf's argument is an intricate one based on redaction criticism, but it leaves one wondering about its feasibility. For even if Trompf has discovered the original ending of Mark, his explanation about the absence of such an ending in all of the available manuscripts may be a difficult one to accept.

Another argument advocating a lost ending is that proposed by Charles J. Reedy, who seeks to resolve the problem by making a textual analysis of Mark's gospel. In Mk 8.31-11.10 Reedy claims to have found a pattern that the passion predictions follow while unfolding the messianic secret. The five-part structure is as follows: (A) the Son of Man is betrayed to the authorities; (B) the authorities kill the Son of Man; (C) the Son of Man will rise from the dead; (D) the Son of Man will teach the true meaning of discipleship; and (E) the Son of Man will be given messianic authority. Reedy points out that Mark's passion-resurrection narrative follows this structure consistently through

---

[36] G.W. Trompf, 'The First Resurrection Appearance and the Ending of Mark's Gospel', NTS 18 (1972), pp. 308-330.

[37] Trompf, 'The First Resurrection Appearance and the Ending of Mark's Gospel', pp. 328-329. Trompf continues: 'for those writers (Origen, Eusebius, Gregory of Nyssa, or Jerome) age was not the crucial question, and by "accuracy" they did not mean the application of modern scientific principles of form and textual criticism. The simple facts of manuscript divergence and the integrity of tradition are their key concerns, and nothing they say excludes the possibility of our "original ending," nor leads one to put great store by their critical acumen.'

part (C) but does not describe the last two parts of the fulfillment of the messianic secret. Consequently Reddy concludes:

> On the basis of the textual evidence delineated in this study, it would not seem rash to suggest that the original Marcan Gospel went beyond 16:8, including points D and E, that is depicting the risen Jesus teaching his disciples, in some sort of Farewell Discourse, the nature of true discipleship and openly displaying his Messianic authority in fulfillment of 9:9. For in the words of Anton Chekhov, 'If you hang a pistol on the wall in the first Act, you must fire it by the third.' We must hold Mark accountable to this literary principle.[38]

Rudolf Bultmann can also be added to the list of those who suspect that Mark originally went beyond 16.8. For Bultmann, it seems that an appearance of the risen Jesus in Galilee has been lost.[39]

Two other reasons may be offered in support of a lost ending. First, φοβέομαι is used with an object about half the times it appears in Mark. Second, if Mark ends at 16.8, this gospel would begin with 'good news' and end with 'fear'. It seems that something more is expected.

Is it possible to conceive that the last page of a manuscript could be lost? One obstacle to this view is that nearly all the documents from the first century are scrolls. Since the scroll would expose the beginning of the text it is difficult to comprehend how this would be conducive to a theory that the end of Mark was accidentally lost. However, Peter Katz has suggested that the Gentile Christians early adopted the codex-form for their Scriptures instead of the roll-form, in a deliberate attempt to differentiate the usage of the church from that of the synagogue.[40] Metzger points out the advantages of the codex-form over the scroll-form:

> (a) It permitted all four Gospels or all the Epistles of Paul to be bound into one book, a format which was impossible so long as the roll was used; (b) it facilitated the consultation of proof-texts; (c) it was better adapted to receiving writing on both sides of the page, thus keeping the cost of production down.[41]

---

[38] C.J. Reedy, 'Mk 8:31-11:10 and the gospel Ending: A Redaction Study', *CBQ* 34 (1972), pp. 196-97.

[39] R. Bultmann, *The History of the Synoptic Tradition* (trans. J. Marsh; New York: Harper, 1968), p. 285.

[40] P. Katz, 'The Early Christians' Use of Codices instead of Rolls', *JTS* 44 (1945), pp. 63-65.

[41] Metzger, *The Text of the New Testament*, p. 6.

If the only copy of Mark was in codex form, it is possible that during the time in which Matthew and Luke were dominant Mark was not recopied and the only existing codex became worn, consequently losing the last page.

Another explanation of Mark's ending concerns a deliberate alteration. If the 'original' ending of Mark was not harmonious with the other gospel accounts, it is possible, for the sake of consistency, that the ending was intentionally omitted. J. Jeremias has suggested that Mark stopped where he did in order to keep from pagan readers what was to follow.[42] While such conjectures are possible, their probability is difficult to establish.

Consequently a growing number of scholars assert that Mk 16.8 is the point at which the author originally intended to end his gospel. One of the first to propose that Mark intentionally ended at 16.8 was W.C. Allen. Contrary to those who would later follow this thesis, Allen had a rather low estimate of Mark's literary abilities. Allen claims, 'It is not a literary work planned by a skilled writer; but is a collection of incidents and sayings from the life of Jesus based upon reminiscences of an eye-witness.'[43] By appealing to the transfiguration as a literary parallel, Allen attempts to explain the significance of ἐφοβοῦντο γάρ. The parallelism is set forth as follows:

In the resurrection account, (1) the disciples see a vision of the supernatural, and (2) the women receive what they deemed to be an angelic assurance that Jesus had proved himself to be conqueror of death and was alive. In the transfiguration account, (1) Peter bursts into speech not knowing what to say (or what he was saying) for he is afraid, and (2) the disciples are stunned into silence for they are afraid.[44] The fear was the result of reverential awe. Therefore, Allen suggests, the book ends on a high note. The γάρ is explained as the logical place to finish the sentence since an Aramaic idiom is being reflected (the Aramaic conjunction not coming at the end of the sentence).

Robert Meye argues that the fear in v. 8 is a characteristic Markan reaction to God's power and that Markan theology emphasizes the 'Word of Jesus'. The resurrection was so well known that it is its own ending (or, rather, new beginnings), so there is nothing wrong with Mark ending at v. 8 on the 'Word of Jesus' through an angel with the

---

[42] J. Jeremias, *The Eucharistic Words of Jesus* (trans. N. Perrin; London: Scribners, 1966), p. 132.

[43] W.C. Allen, 'St. Mark XVI.8 "They Were Afraid." Why?', *JTS* 47 (1946), p. 46.

[44] Allen, 'St. Mark XVI.8 "They Were Afraid." Why?', p. 46.

fearful women. The gospel begins abruptly; abruptness is characteristic of Mark's writing; therefore the abrupt ending should be expected.[45]

Danker speculates that the silence and the nature of the messianic secret in Markan theology demand revelation only at the proper time (i.e. after the resurrection). Verses 1-8 are the report of the message through the women to the apostles that it is time to break the silence and to reveal the secret – there is no more than that to the chapter.[46]

Theodore Weeden approaches the problem from a different angle. Presupposing that Mark was written as a severe rebuke of the disciples, Weeden asserts that Mark's ending is more important than often realized:

> The crowning evidence for attributing the programmatic, denigrated picture of the disciples in Mark to the evangelist himself lies in his treatment of, or rather his failure to treat, the disciples after the denial of Peter. Following Peter's denial the disciples do not reappear again in the narrative ... What is even more startling, following their total renunciation of Jesus, not only are the disciples conspicuously absent from all subsequent events – even the kerygmatic event upon which any claim for apostleship must be based: the resurrection – but there is no indication by Mark that the disciples were rehabilitated, that apostolicity was conferred upon them after their apostasy, as the other evangelists clearly record.[47]

Probably one of Weeden's most damaging statements to those who propose a lost ending involves the unsound methodology involved in basing an argument 'on the one-time existence of material for which absolutely no extant trace has been found'.[48] In the light of this charge one does not necessarily have to accept Weeden's thesis about the disciples to discern the strength of his case against a lost ending. But for Weeden this polemic against the disciples is closely tied to the ending, for he comments, 'Mark 16:8b must be read at full face value with all its sundry ramifications'.[49]

---

[45] R.P. Meye, 'Mark's Special Easter Emphasis', *Christianity Today* (1971), pp. 584-86. W. Lane observes, 'Fear is a constant reaction to the disclosure of Jesus' transcendent dignity in the gospel of Mark (cf. Chs. 4:41; 5:15, 33, 36; 6:50; 9:6, 32)... In point of fact, the present ending of Mark is thoroughly consistent with the motifs of astonishment and fear developed throughout the Gospel' (*The Gospel of Mark* [Grand Rapids: Eerdmans, 1974], p. 591).

[46] Danker, 'Post-script to the Markan Secrecy Motif', p. 26.

[47] T. Weeden, *Mark: Traditions in Conflict* (Philadelphia: Fortress, 1971), p. 44.

[48] Weeden, *Mark: Traditions in Conflict*, p. 46.

[49] Weeden, *Mark: Traditions in Conflict*, p. 50.

Norman Petersen presses Weeden's thesis to its logical conclusion. 'In literary terms Weeden's argument is that the narrator has established the character of the twelve disciples as unreliable.'[50] The reader has been led to believe that Jesus is God's Son and that whatever he predicts will come to pass. When the reader comes to 16.8, however, having expected the disciples to meet Jesus in Galilee, he realizes that a cruel thing has taken place: Jesus is unreliable, God has made a mistake. But Petersen states that Mark does not mean what he says in 16.8. Petersen explains:

> In an ironic reading of the narrator's closing sentence we have a bona fide closure and a prism through which the reader must re-view what has been read in order to complete the imaginative work required by the narrator ... First, the reader recognizes irony in 16:8 because a literal ending of it makes nonsense of the narrator's previous generation of expectations and satisfactions ... The ironic equivocation of the meaning of 16:8 redirects the reader's attention back to the immediately preceding words of the young man – he has risen; he is going before the twelve to Galilee; there they will see him, as he told them. These words restore the community interrupted by 16:8 and begin the reader's experience of the second effect of the irony. They tell the reader that even while the women are muddled about (Mark 14-15), Jesus, having risen, is on his way to Galilee where the disciples will soon see him.[51]

By explaining Mark's intention in this way Petersen maintains a 'proper' end to a gospel and yet deals only with what the text actually says.

Still another point of view is J.D. Crossan's contention that the empty tomb was created to avoid and oppose the idea of a resurrection. The women's silence at the end of Mark demonstrates that the 'Jerusalem community led by the disciples, and especially Peter, has never accepted the call of the exalted Lord communicated to it from the Markan community.'[52]

Robert Tannehill argues that 16.8 should really cause no problem at all. Throughout the Gospel, Mark uses various means to convey his point, but one thing is always evident: Whatever Jesus foretells comes to pass. On the basis of Jesus' past performances, the reader of Mark grows to expect fulfillment of 'prophecy'. Consequently, when the reader is faced with Mk 16.8 he or she naturally concludes that Jesus

---

[50] N. Petersen, 'When is the End not the End?', *Int* 34 (1980), p. 160.

[51] N. Petersen, 'When is the End not the End?', pp. 162-163.

[52] J.D. Crossan, 'Empty Tomb and Absent Lord', *The Passion in Mark* (ed. W. Kelber; Philadelphia: Fortress, 1976), p. 149.

will indeed see his disciples in Galilee. Thus, the gospel ends on a high note.[53]

What is one to conclude from this investigation concerning the ending of Mark's Gospel? Several summary statements will draw this inquiry to a close.

1. Although Mk 16.9-20 has much old and good MS support, it appears that this longer reading is quite old but, still, only secondary. Even with the peculiarities of Codex Vaticanus, the variety of family representation of 16.9-20, and the problem of the content of the Longer Ending, the abrupt ending at 16.8 is to be preferred as the original Markan conclusion.

2. Owing to a large number of words that appear in 16.9-20 but nowhere else in Mark, in some cases the whole of the New Testament, the strange syntactical constructions, and the abrupt transition between vv. 8 and 9, it seems that this section does not stand as part of Mark's composition. Even though it is possible to argue that Mk 16.9-20 may have been an ancient collection of resurrection appearances reworked by Mark, it is more probable to assume that those Markan peculiarities that occur in 16.9-20 are due to the compiler's attempt to imitate Markan style.

3. Owing to the problems caused by a document ending with γάρ, the many passion predictions, and the mounting expectation of a resurrection appearance in Galilee, the reader is not totally unjustified in expecting a different ending than what exists (16.8). Since it is not probable that a codex would lose its last page (although some did), it is not absurd to believe that one or more words may have accidentally been omitted after γάρ, in 16:8, if the word(s) was at the top of an 'extra' page. If there were any more words to the Gospel, then Moule's suggestion is probably the best.

4. Owing to the fact that conjectural emendation is not the norm in text criticism, one is compelled to regard 16.8 as the last words penned by Mark. This reading explains the origin of the other readings, which seek to smooth the abrupt ending, and must be considered the more difficult reading (although snake handling and drinking poison are quite difficult in themselves).

5. Several scholars have attempted to interpret Mark on the basis of 16.8 as the end. The most responsible means of dealing with this problem is, as Weeden suggests, to make sense of what exists, not conjecture. Of the several proposed solutions, those of Petersen and

---

[53] R.C. Tannehill, 'The Gospel of Mark as Narrative Christology', *Semeia* 16 (1979), pp. 57-95.

Tannehill seem to have the most to commend them. For the reader is allowed to believe that fear was a natural response for the women, but despite this fact the predictions of Jesus will be fulfilled. The reader is assured that Jesus did go to Galilee, fulfilling his own predictions. Thus the gospel ends with hope, not despair. If not originally part of the Gospel, Mk 16.9-20 is then a fifth witness to the resurrection recorded in the gospels.

Where will future research lead in the discussion of this problem? Farmer's work will probably inspire more research among those who for theological reasons feel compelled to cling to 16.9-20 as Markan. For those scholars incapable of believing a gospel can end with fear, not to mention γάρ, other attempts can be made in conjecturing a conclusion. Yet one profitable area for further inquiry will be with those who view 16.8 as Mark's ending. Petersen and Tannehill have initiated a fruitful area to explore, demonstrating that the Gospel ends on a positive note.

6

'And the Signs are Following': Mark 16.9-20 – A Journey into Pentecostal Hermeneutics[*]

The previous chapter focused upon the textual problems surrounding Mk 16.9-20. There I concluded that the so-called longer ending did not originate from the author of the Gospel according to Mark and, consequently, was to be regarded as a later addition. At the time I originally completed that study,[1] it seemed that researchers were interested primarily in two issues. Either individual scholars were committed to proving the Markan character of Mk 16.9-20, and thus preserving the content of these verses, or they dismissed vv. 9-20 as secondary and devoted their efforts to making some sense of the ending preserved in 16.8. Three things highlighted in my concluding observations continued to intrigue me over the years. (1) It seemed to me that given the age of the longer ending, these verses represented a fifth early 'Gospel' account of the resurrection of Jesus. (2) At the same time, owing to the obvious non-Markan character of these verses it was clear to me that only those with a theological agenda would be motivated to undertake a defense of these verses as originally Markan in some sense, in order to maintain them as part of the Markan text. (3) Rather than attempts to defend 16.9-20 as Markan, or attempts to identify the content of the original 'lost' reading, it seemed to me that the best way forward would be with approaches which sought to make sense of the text as it now stood, ending at 16.8.

It never occurred to me at the time that these somewhat disparate observations might actually be related to one another, for I, as many of my peers in biblical studies, could only read the text through historical

---

[*] This study was co-authored with Kimberly Ervin Alexander (PhD Open University – St John's College, Nottingham), Assistant Professor of Historical Theology, Church of God Theological Seminary.

[1] J.C. Thomas, 'A Reconsideration of the Ending of Mark', *JETS* 26 (1983), pp. 405-19.

critical glasses. But, as Dr Suess said so long ago in that classic title ... 'Oh the Places You'll Go'. My own methodological journey took me from the somewhat narrow confines of historical criticism to the worlds of narrative readings, reader-response criticism, canonical approaches, as well as a somewhat mysterious approach to the text known as the history of effects or *Wirkungsgeschichte*.[2] It was through this growing openness to a variety of approaches to the New Testament that I began to envision the way in which my earlier seemingly disparate observations might possibly fit together.

However, the clear catalyst for my own revisiting Mk 16.9-20 was the emerging results of my colleague's PhD research on a Pentecostal Theology of Healing.[3] Kimberly Ervin Alexander has long been a fruitful dialogue partner for me, as I have sought to rethink a variety of issues from a decidedly Pentecostal perspective. One aspect of her thesis research was particularly significant for my thinking about Mk 16.9-20. As she scoured the early Pentecostal literature with reference to healing, it began to become clear that the place of Mk 16.9-20 was unrivaled within the early Pentecostal literature in position and significance!

This chapter is a tentative step toward a collaborative, interdisciplinary, theological approach to Mk 16.9-20. Limitations of space necessitate that it take the form of a survey and outline of what we hope will one day result in a more comprehensive study.

Mark 16.9-20 in the Pentecostal Tradition

An examination of the nineteenth century Divine Healing Movement reveals that the writings of A.B. Simpson, Charles Cullis, Andrew Murray, A.J. Gordon and Carrie Judd Montgomery were replete with biblical references cited as warrant for the zealous preaching of the message and practice of Divine Healing. Having formulated the doctrinal tenet, which Pentecostals inherited, 'Divine Healing is provided for all in the atonement', these proponents substantiated their claims with multiple references to Isaiah 53, Matthew 8, Psalm 103, Exodus 15 and, predominantly, the miracle stories of the Gospels. They saw themselves as continuing, actually restoring to the church, the 'parallel'

---

[2] For some of my thoughts on the way these methods can inform a Pentecostal approach to the New Testament cf. chapter one above.

[3] Cf. K.E. Alexander, 'Models of Pentecostal Healing and Practice in Light of Early Twentieth Century Pentecostalism' (PhD thesis, St John's College, Nottingham/Open University, 2002).

or 'two-fold' ministry of Jesus: forgiveness of sins and healing of sicknesses.[4]

An examination of *The Apostolic Faith* and *The Church of God Evangel* reveals that for these early Pentecostals there was an addition to the 'canon within a canon'. In the examination of these and other periodicals, such as *The Whole Truth*, *The Pentecostal Evangel*, *The Pentecostal Advocate*, *The Bridegroom's Messenger* and *Triumphs of Faith* one would, of course, expect to see numerous references to Acts, which are indeed plenteous. But, often in banner headlines, the earliest Pentecostals declared that 'the signs were following'! When an inductive approach is utilized in the study of early Pentecostal periodical literature, 'signs following' language emerges from each of the periodicals as one of the dominant beliefs and practices.

The presence of this language makes sense, after all. These Pentecostals, who understood themselves to be *apostolic*, restoring the faith of the New Testament church, were experiencing manifestations and phenomena delineated in the Mk 16.9-20 passage. In addition, they were urgently preaching the Pentecostal message everywhere they went. It should be expected, then, that they would identify with this particular commissioning text, which included preaching, speaking in tongues, healing and exorcising demons.

To illustrate, a comparison of the references in some of these early periodicals to Mk 16.9-20 and those to Mt. 28.20 and Acts 1.8, reveals that the Mark 16 text was decidedly favored over the other commissions. A Scripture index of *The Church of God Evangel* (1910-1919)[5] lists twenty-six references to Mt. 28.18-20, sixteen references to Acts 1.8, and seventy-five to Mk 16.9-20.[6] A similar comparison of those texts cited in *The Apostolic Faith* from September 1906-May 1908 reveals that there were three references to the Matthew text, five to the Acts text, and twenty references to the Mark text.[7] These indices do

---

[4] Gordon interpreted the parallel mention of sin and sickness as having reference to the 'two-fold ministry' of Christ 'affecting constantly the souls and the bodies of men'. He cites Isa. 53.4 and Mt. 8.17 which refer to Christ bearing our infirmities and our sicknesses. He further illustrates this two-fold nature of Christ's ministry by citing Jesus' words, '"Thy sins are forgiven thee" and "Be whole of thy plague"' (A.J. Gordon, *The Ministry of Healing – Miracles of Cure in All Ages* [Harrisburg, PA: Christian Publications, n.d.], p. 19).

[5] There are no extant copies of the issues published in the years 1911-1914.

[6] A Scripture index for *The Church of God Evangel* may be accessed at the Dixon Pentecostal Research Center.

[7] A Scripture index for *The Apostolic Faith*, prepared by Church of God Theological Seminary graduate Brian M. Hunter, may be accessed on the web page for the Dixon

not include reference to the many allusions to the text in the language of the testimonies of Pentecostals.

Invariably, the earliest Pentecostals saw the Mark 16 text as a kind of litmus test for the authenticity of their experience. In the inaugural issue of *The Apostolic Faith*, the text is quoted as support for the phenomena appearing at Azusa Street. The signs confirmed the Word and confirmed what was happening in Los Angeles.[8] Issue number 3 of that same year reports that all the signs had followed at Azusa except raising the dead. The issue reports that they were waiting on that sign, because it would prove God to be true and would 'result in the salvation of many souls'.[9] *The Apostolic Faith* boldly proclaimed in headlines that these signs were following at Azusa.[10] These signs were even the subject of songs given by the Holy Spirit[11] and of messages in tongues interpreted by the Holy Spirit.[12] 'Signs following' became the litmus test for a movement of God.

C.H. Mason's testimony in *The Apostolic Faith* began with a quotation of Mk 16.17, 18. Mason explains that prior to his Pentecostal experience at Azusa Street, he had taken the command to lay hands on the sick literally, but had not taken the reference to speaking in tongues literally. He saw this as his failure to consent to the Word. As a result, he began to seek a Pentecostal experience and found that experience, singing in tongues and preaching in tongues at the Azusa Street Mission.[13]

The commission given to the disciples in Mk 16.15-18 was adopted as the commission of Mason's periodical, *The Whole Truth*. These verses were reprinted in the publishing information found on page two of the October 1911 edition. Following this quotation one finds the words of Mk 16.20, 'And they went forth and preached everywhere, the Lord working with them and confirming the words with signs following.' It was this confirmed *truth* which Elder Mason, Editor Bowe, and others would publish. Mason would later preach that the signs were 'witness of His glory and return'.[14]

Pentecostal Research Center [www.leeuniversity.edu/library/dixon/Resources/Scripture_Index/scripture_index.htm/].

[8] *Apostolic Faith* 1.1 (September, 1906), p. 2.
[9] *Apostolic Faith* 1.3 (November, 1906), p. 4.
[10] *Apostolic Faith* 1.4 (December, 1906), p. 1.
[11] *Apostolic Faith* 1.8 (May, 1907), p. 2.
[12] *Apostolic Faith* 1.4 (December, 1906), p. 3.
[13] *Apostolic Faith* 1.6 (Feb.-March, 1907), p. 7.
[14] C.H. Mason, 'Friday, December 5, 1919 – His Invocation in the Holy Convocation', Elnora L. Lee, *A Life Fully Dedicated to God* (No publisher, 1967), p. 62.

Spirit baptism and glossolalia moved the readers and writers of *The Bridegroom's Messenger* to read Mark 16 with new eyes and understanding, typical of Pentecostals generally. They had spoken in tongues and had heard others speaking in tongues. Now, they expected all of the other signs to follow. A.H. Butler notes that before the resurrection and Pentecost, 'The apostles had power over all devils to cast them out, to heal the sick, raise the dead, tread on serpents, but could not yet speak with other tongues as the Spirit gave the utterance. Jesus imparted to them every thing it was possible for them to receive before His crucifixion.'[15] In Acts, after Pentecost, all of these things were witnessed. J.E. Sawders notes this and calls it 'The Pentecostal Standard'. He exhorts, 'Demons must be cast out, those of all tongues must be addressed in their own language, sick must be healed, the unbelieving must see signs and know of a truth "this is that".'[16]

With this new 'Pentecostal' reading of the Mark 16 text, evangelists, pastors, and newly baptized Pentecostals sought to fulfill this commission. Elizabeth Sexton writes,

> As a result of our contending for this same faith once delivered to the saints, we are beginning to be enlarged in expectation, we are now expecting these signs to follow the ministry of the saints, and even to learn that the dead are being raised, which so thrills our grateful hearts and humbles us at His dear feet, no longer seems in the realm of impossibility, but rather that which we might confidently expect, knowing our Lord has power also over the enemy of death. [sic][17]

What they witnessed were surely these signs.

Similarly, Hattie M. Barth, contributor to *The Bridegroom's Messenger*, understood the signs to be signs of the age to come. In a brief article in March 1909, she describes the signs which followed believers in relation to the Kingdom of God. She discusses the cessationist view and that of those who see these signs as only belonging to 'the next dispensation'. But she proposes a third view: 'It is true that these marvelous things belong, in a sense, to the next dispensation, but also it is true that God has provided a way for us to receive them now.' She goes on to define the Kingdom as 'that time when Jesus is to reign on the earth, destroy sin, sickness, death, all the curse, bring all things back to a perfect state.' But for those who 'receive the King, "the Kingdom of heaven is within".' She declares that where he is received

---

[15] *The Bridegroom's Messenger* 1.5 (January 1, 1908), p. 4.
[16] *The Bridegroom's Messenger* 1.4 (December 15, 1907), p. 4.
[17] *The Bridegroom's Messenger* 3.67 (August 1, 1910), p. 1.

as King, he reigns and there 'the blessed signs of this kingdom, life and peace and healing and the removal of the curse, begin to appear'.[18]

Barth perceives that there is an 'overlap', what later theologians and New Testament scholars would call a 'tension between the ages'. She writes, 'The ages overlap like links in a chain. From the time of Pentecost till now there have been some living by faith a few thousands, or hundreds of years ahead. Pentecost itself really belongs to the next dispensation. The prophecy in Joel 2.28, "I will pour out My Spirit upon all flesh," only began to be fulfilled on the day of Pentecost (Acts 2:17), the complete fulfillment, as the context shows, is in the next dispensation.'[19]

The signs, as given in Mark 16, are a 'foretaste of that coming Age'. She explains their function in this way:

> Are we to cast out devils in His name? Satan will be bound the thousand years. Are we to drink deadly poison without hurt? Thorns, weeds, poisonous plants shall no more infest the ground. Are we to take up serpents? The suckling child shall play on the hole of the asp and the weaned child shall put his hand on the cockatrice den. Are we to heal the sick? When Jesus comes, 'The inhabitant shall not say, 'I am sick.' Are we to overcome this age, all sin, sickness, death, and be caught up to meet him in the air without dying? He must reign, till he hath put all enemies under His feet. The last enemy that shall be destroyed is death. Do we begin now to speak with other tongues of men and of angels, and have gifts of interpretation? The time is coming when that old curse given at Babel shall be lifted, and the inhabitants of the earth shall be no more divided, but shall have knowledge of His power, and be one people with God. Do we have knowledge of His power and taste of the glories of the age to come? 'The earth shall be filled with the knowledge of the glory of the Lord, as the waters cover the sea.'[20]

If these are things of the age to come, how then does one see them now? She answers that one sees them now by living 'in advance of our time'. This will result in being 'misunderstood and persecuted by the world'. But if one is to be salt of the earth, one must live according to this next age.

One cannot read the early issues of *The Church of God Evangel* without being struck by the prominence of the Mark 16 text in the healing theology and eschatology of these early Pentecostals. Headlines exhort and affirm that signs [driving out demons, speaking in tongues, taking

---

[18] *The Bridegroom's Messenger* 2.34 (March 15, 1909), p. 4.
[19] *The Bridegroom's Messenger* 2.34 (March 15, 1909), p. 4.
[20] *The Bridegroom's Messenger* 2.34 (March 15, 1909), p. 4.

up serpents, laying hands on the sick] will follow believers.[21] Lead articles explained the text and attempted to demolish all doubt concerning its viability. Testimonies offered proof that these signs did follow.

Tomlinson offers an apologetic for The Church of God position on the text and chides other Pentecostals for quoting and practicing only part of the text.[22] He held that the clauses beginning with 'they shall' constituted commands of Jesus. By this he endorsed and encouraged casting out demons, speaking in tongues, handling serpents and laying hands on the sick. He interpreted the clause, 'If they drink any deadly thing' to mean that it was not to be a normal occurrence, 'to be displayed as frequent as the others'.[23] He would not allow that it was just a promise that one who was accidentally poisoned[24] or poisoned as a result of persecution would be spared, but that it was a demonstration of God's power which called for a 'special anointing'.[25] Tomlinson appeals to an instance reported in Eusebius' *Ecclesiastical History* in which it is said that 'Justus, surnamed Barsabas' drank poison and was not harmed.[26] Partial evidence for the actual practice of drinking deadly poison in the Church of God comes in the sad report from 1921, that an evangelist in Texas, V.A. Bishop, died in a revival service about one hour after having ingested 'strychnine or arsenic'. The incident was reported on the front page of *The Church of God Evangel*.[27]

In like fashion Tomlinson also rejects the interpretation that 'taking up serpents' referred to an accidental occurrence such as is found in Acts 28.3-6, where Paul accidentally picked up a piece of firewood on which was a poisonous snake. He rebuts, 'Paul did not aim to take his serpent up. He did not know he was about him till he was fastened on his hand, and then he shook him off as quickly as possible. Applying the same analogy, we are not to lay our hands on the sick intentionally, and when we do get our hands on them accidentally we must shake them loose as quickly as possible, as if it is dangerous to keep

---

[21] See *Church of God Evangel* 9.26 (June 29, 1918), p. 1 and 11.15 (April 10, 1920), p. 1, for example.

[22] *Church of God Evangel* 11.15 (April 10, 1920), p. 1. However, Sam C. Perry, a leader in the Church of God, does just this in an article on 'Healing for the Body' in 8.3 (January 20, 1917), p. 3. This is interesting because, Tomlinson as the editor of the periodical has apparently allowed this selective quotation on Perry's part.

[23] *Church of God Evangel* 8.14 (April 14, 1917), p. 1.

[24] The text was appealed to in a testimony of a baby healed after poison ingestion in *Church of God Evangel* 11.25 (June 19, 1920), p. 4.

[25] *Church of God Evangel* 8.14 (April 14, 1917), p. 1.

[26] *Church of God Evangel* 8.14 (April 14, 1917), p. 1.

[27] *Church of God Evangel* 12.19 (May 7, 1921), p. 1.

them there.'[28] Clearly, for Tomlinson, taking up serpents was commanded as a sign.[29]

The words of Jesus in Mark 16 proved that the ministry of Jesus was to continue after Jesus' earthly life. Sam C. Perry writes that it is 'a sign given to holiness in general and for all time and with no particular limitations or restrictions.'[30] If the signs were not present, one should examine oneself, and, couched in military terminology, 'see if we have disobeyed orders'.[31] Again, as at Azusa Street, 'signs following' becomes the litmus test. They were also the proof that God was blessing the Church, that 'The great Church of God is moving onward. The gifts, graces, fruits and signs are being manifested.'[32]

For Carrie Judd Montgomery signs function as confirmation of a work already done. In fact, she goes so far as to instruct the sick to make a faith claim regarding the sign. They are instructed to pray: 'Thou has said the sign of recovery shall follow (literal, accompany). Lord, I believe Thy word alone. I believe the sign of healing now follows or accompanies the laying on of hands in Thy Name.'[33]

E.N. Bell, as early as 1912, justified tongues speech by identifying it as a sign following believers. In specifying the benefits of speaking in tongues, he defines a 'sign' as pointing to belief or faith, as confirmation that the Holy Spirit has been poured out and that Jesus is at the right hand of the Father.[34] Likewise, healing is a sign of the same[35] and a demonstration of the Gospel.[36] To support this claim, missionaries reported that Mk 16.18 was being fulfilled in India,[37] China,[38] and Japan.[39] The text appeared on the masthead of *The Weekly Evangel* in 1918.

---

[28] *Church of God Evangel* 9.26 (June 29,1918), p. 1.

[29] *Church of God Evangel* 9.26 (June 29, 1918), p. 1. There are 94 articles referring to serpent handling in the *Church of God Evangel* appearing between 1910 and 1923. Many of these are testimonies or reports of actual incidences where snakes were handled. An index of articles referring to serpent handling has been prepared by W.P. Williamson of the University of Tennessee at Knoxville.

[30] *Church of God Evangel* 8.5 (February 3, 1917), p. 3.

[31] *Church of God Evangel* 10.6 (February 8, 1919), p. 2.

[32] *Church of God Evangel* 10.9 (March 1, 1919), p. 1.

[33] *Triumphs of Faith* 28.5 (May, 1908), p. 99.

[34] *Word and Witness* (August 20, 1912), p. 4.

[35] *Word and Witness* (Oct. 20, 1912), p. 1.

[36] *Christian Evangel* (August 8, 1914), p. 1.

[37] *Christian Evangel* (August 22, 1914), p. 4.

[38] *Weekly Evangel* (February 3, 1917), p. 12.

[39] *Weekly Evangel* (May 26, 1917), p. p. 2.

One of the more interesting interpretations of the text is found in an article titled 'The Restoration of All Things'. The signs designated by Jesus in Mark 16 are here understood to be a reversal of the curse: Adam's tongue had been 'tainted'; Satan came in the form of a serpent and was cursed to crawl on his belly; Satan's venom (poison) had been 'put into the minds of men'; and sickness was in the earth.[40] A later article, 'The Pentecostal Commission' emphasizes this reversal: 'The resurrected Christ commenced the new work of restoration by giving a commission to His disciples, and one of the first items of the commission was to cast out the devils, the intruders who came into the Paradise, the Eden of God.'[41]

As might be expected, a survey of early Oneness Pentecostal sermons and tracts reveals that these preachers connected *signs* with *the Name*. Andrew Urshan cites the commissions of Jesus to his disciples, offering commentary along the way: '"Go ye into all the world, and preach the Gospel (of the Kingdom) [sic] to every creature (every Person). He that believeth, AND IS BAPTIZED, shall be saved, but he that believeth not (of course needs not to be baptised [sic]) shall be damned; and these signs (the wonderful operations of the Holy Spirit) shall follow them that believe (of course being baptised [sic] also) IN MY NAME, etc". ' He concludes, 'Here again, the Water of Baptism and the Holy Spirit's Power casting out Devils, causing believers to speak with other Tongues, healing the sick, etc., etc., are in connection, and that in the Name of the Lord Jesus.'[42] Urshan points to Philip in Samaria as an example of the connection of these signs to the Name. Urshan notes that Philip, who, among other things, is able to 'heal the lame and blind, turning the whole town toward the Lord and baptising [sic] hundreds into the Name of Christ Jesus.'[43]

A clue to the significance of the Name for Oneness adherents may be found in G.T. Haywood's chorus 'Do All in Jesus Name':

---

[40] *Weekly Evangel* (August 11, 1917), p. 8.

[41] *Pentecostal Evangel* (January 26, 1924), pp. 4-5.

[42] Andrew Urshan, 'The New Testament Teaching on the New Birth', *Seven 'Jesus Only' Tracts* in D.W. Dayton, ed., *The Higher Christian Life* (Sources for the Study of the Holiness, Pentecostal, and Keswick Movements series; New York and London: Garland Publishing, Inc., 1985), p. 22.

[43] Urshan, 'The New Testament Teaching on the New Birth' in Dayton, p. 24. He goes on, however, to explain that Philip was not able to 'get his Samaritan converts through the baptism of the Holy Spirit' because 'the keys of the kingdom to enter in were in the hands of Peter.' Therefore, Peter and John had to lay hands on the Samaritan believers.

Preach in Jesus' Name, Teach in Jesus' Name
Heal the sick in His Name
And always proclaim, it was Jesus' Name
In which the power cam; [sic]
Baptize in His Name, enduring the shame,
For there is victory in Jesus' Name.[44]

In another song, 'These Signs Shall Follow Them', Haywood sees the signs of Mark 16 as being confirmation of the gospel that is preached by those who believe upon the name.[45]

Pentecostal Responses to the Text Critical Problem

An examination of the literature reveals that these early Pentecostals were neither unaware of the textual problems associated with Mk 16.9-20 nor unprepared to respond to these problems.

An unsigned article (apparently by Florence Crawford?) in *The Apostolic Faith*[46] gives some attention to the questions surrounding the longer ending of Mark. Two points are made in this short article. (1) It is observed that the reason for the omission of Mk 16.9-20 is owing to the fact that Dr Godbey leaves them out of his commentary on account of their absence from Codex Sinaiticus, the Greek text upon which he based his commentary.[47] The story of Tischendorf's discovery of the manuscript is briefly recounted. Interestingly, it is implied that perhaps Mk 16.9-20 was included in the portions of the manuscript Tischendorf thought he saw being thrown into the fire. (2) An

---

[44] P.D. Dugas, ed. *The Life and Writings of Elder G.T. Haywood* (Portland, OR: Apostolic Book Publishers, 1984), p. 22.

[45] Haywood, 'These Signs Shall Follow Them' in M. Crawford, ed., *The Pentecostal Flame The Crawford Revival Special* (Los Angeles, CA: Mattie Crawford, n.d.), p. 88.

[46] *Apostolic Faith* 1.2 (October, 1906), p. 3.

[47] W.B. Godbey, a holiness scholar who, despite his sharp polemics against tongues was highly regarded in the burgeoning Pentecostal movement, authored a seven volume *Commentary on the New Testament* (Cincinnati: God's Revivalist Office, 1900). In his comments on the Gospels (vol. 7, pp. 406-97) Godbey notes that the last twelve verses in Mark are not found in the 'Sinaitic' manuscript, which he has used as the basis of his commentary. Surprisingly, one aspect of Godbey's comments not mined by Pentecostals at this point is the following: 'This fact of these last twelve verses not appearing in the old authoritative manuscripts, does not necessarily invalidate their claims to inspiration, as the author might have been inspired for aught we know, though we have no idea as to his name'. Godbey believes that someone took it upon themselves to finish out the Gospel 'somewhat after the order of Matthew's which had been written A.D. 48.'

existential reason for the inclusion of Mk 16.9-20 follows by appeal to the reality of the events described in the longer ending as manifested in the Azusa Street revival.

A.J. Tomlinson acknowledges that a portion of the ending of Mark is disputed but responds that 'no one has ever yet been successful in convincing us that any part of these sacred verses should be left out'.[48] In a more extensive defense of the longer ending of Mark,[49] Tomlinson appeals primarily to the fact that despite the textual problems often raised by many Bible scholars, no bible houses anywhere are publishing the Gospel of Mark without 16.9-20. He goes so far as to say that if anyone bought a Bible which did not include these verses, it would immediately be returned by the purchaser. In very popular language, Tomlinson raises the question of canonicity: Mk 16.9-20 is widely regarded as part of the canonical text.

In answer to the question 'Is Mark 16.9-20 in the original manuscripts?' E.N. Bell responds that two of the five most ancient manuscripts omit the verses. He then cites the discovery and copying of Codex Washingtonius which Dr Frodsham is said to have examined. Given the inclusion of these verses in Washingtonius, Bell concludes that '... IT IS NOW OUT OF DATE AND GROSS IGNORANCE FOR ANYONE TO CLAIM JESUS NEVER SPOKE THESE VERSES'. For emphasis Bell placed the final statement all in caps![50]

In response to the question 'Is Mark 16:17-20 in the original Greek?' a short article by G.F. Taylor[51] makes the following points: the original manuscripts are not extant; a number of existing manuscripts do contain Mark 16.9-20; the Greek text compiled by Westcott and Hort include these verses by putting them in brackets, implying doubt about their authenticity; but good reason exists to include them. The reader is then directed to a tract on the topic published in the UK.

Arthur Frodsham offers what is perhaps the most extensive and comprehensive assessment of the state of Mk 16.9-20.[52] He bases much of his response on the impact made upon this discussion by the discovery of Codex Washingtonius. Beginning with a brief account of the purchase of Codex Washingtonius by Mr C.L. Freer, Frodsham reveals that he has personally reviewed photographic copies of the

---

[48] *Church of God Evangel* 8.14 (April 14, 1917), p. 1.
[49] *Church of God Evangel* 11.15 (April 10, 1920), p. 1.
[50] *Weekly Evangel* (March 9, 1918), p. 9.
[51] *Pentecostal Holiness Advocate* 2.8 (20 June 1918), p. 10.
[52] *Pentecostal Evangel* (April 28, 1923), p. 9.

manuscript in the British Museum. Having been assured that Washingtonius was as old as or older than the three oldest known manuscripts (Vaticanus, Sinaiticus, and Alexandrinus), he sets out to offer justification for the longer ending. His primary point is that only ℵ and B omit the reading outright and that A (which he wrongly identifies as the basis of the KJV) and W include it. He views this discovery as silencing the critics on this point. Having argued for the validity of the longer reading, Frodsham reveals his knowledge of a unique variant found only in W. Frodsham concludes that to question the authority of these last verses in Mark is now out of date. In addition, Frodsham sees the text as being 'vindicated' by God in that the discovery by Freer coincided with the outpouring of the Spirit in 1906: 'It was discovered at the very time it was needed. God had kept it hidden away all these centuries.'[53]

A later assessment of the longer ending of Mark is offered by J. Narver Gortner.[54] As in *The Apostolic Faith*, Dr Godbey's commentary is cited as an example of a scholar who questions the inclusion of these verses in Mark. Gortner has no question about the text's authenticity. However, instead of repeating earlier reasons for the verses' inclusion he offers evidence from early church history.

> There are no Greek manuscripts that we know anything about prior to the fourth century, but prior to that time a number of church fathers lived, preached and wrote, and several of them, among them Papias, Justin Martyr and Irenaeus, quote portions of the disputed passage as inspired Scripture. Ambrose, Chrysostom, Jerome and Augustine all quote the passage in part or whole; and Augustine discusses the entire passage and tells us that it is written by the evangelist Mark, and that the verses were publicly read in the churches.
>
> Some of the church fathers who have set their stamp of approval on the genuineness of the disputed passage must have known persons who had seen and conversed with the apostles, and it may be that some of these church fathers knew in their boyhood days some of the people who had seen and conversed with our Lord in the flesh. Certainly these men were in a better position to pass judgment on the genuineness of the passage in question than is any person who is living to-day or has lived during the past few centuries.

---

[53] *Pentecostal Evangel* (April 28, 1923), p. 9.
[54] *Pentecostal Evangel* (Jan 28, 1928), p. 3.

Other Responses to the Text Critical Problem

A comparison of these responses with others from roughly this same time period reveals that the controversy with regard to Mk 16.9-20 was far from settled. The testimony of ℵ and B notwithstanding, a number of writers were not prepared to remove these verses from the Gospel according to Mark. Various reasons were offered for this interpretive position. For example, the antiquity of the tradition found in these verses was thought to be so early that the author was able 'to add genuine apostolic traditions to those already recorded'.[55] The content of the passage also was thought to testify to the verses' authenticity. On the one hand, it was sometimes argued that the content was in keeping with the rest of the Gospel,[56] or that the departure from Markan style could be explained on other grounds.[57] On the other hand, the controversial nature of the content (i.e. 'the drinking of deadly poison') was thought to argue in favor of its authenticity owing to the embarrassment caused to believers by the challenge of non-believers to demonstrate the protection promised in these verses.[58] The problematic nature of a book ending with the word 'for' (γάρ), the last word in the Greek text of Mk 16.8, is also offered as a reason for retaining these twelve verses.[59] In addition to these reasons, appeal was often made to the sheer weight of the bulk of the manuscript tradition that includes these verses as part of the original text.[60] Such testimony was thought almost impossible to disregard. This argument is not unrelated

---

[55] G. Salmon, *A Historical Introduction to the Study of the Books of the New Testament* (London: John Murray, 1894), p. 150. Cf. also the hypothesis that Aristion is the author of this longer ending, F.C. Conybeare, 'Aristion, the Author of the Last Twelve Verses of Mark', *The Expositor* Fourth Series 8 (1893), pp. 241-54.

[56] H. Olshausen, *Biblical Commentary on the Gospels*, IV (trans. J. Gill and R. Garvey; Edinburgh: T. & T. Clark, 1850), pp. 300; and J.A. Broadus, 'Style of Mark xvi.9-20, As Bearing Upon the Question of Genuineness', *The Baptist Quarterly* III (1869), p. 362.

[57] J.H.A. Ebrard, *The Gospel History: A Compendium of Critical Investigations in Support of the Historical Character of the Four Gospels* (trans. J. Martin; ed. A.B. Bruce: Edinburgh: T. and T. Clark, 1863), pp. 548-59.

[58] Salmon, *A Historical Introduction to the Study of the Books of the New Testament*, pp. 150-51.

[59] H. Olshausen, *Biblical Commentary on the Gospels*, p. 301; S.W. Whitney, *The Reviser's Greek Text: A Critical Examination of Certain Readings, Textual and Marginal, in the Original Greek of the New Testament Adopted by the late Anglo-American Revisers*, I (Boston: Silver, Burdett & Company, 1892), pp. 258-59.

[60] F.H.A. Scrivener, *A Plain Introduction to the Criticism of the New Testament* (ed. E. Miller; London: George Bell & Sons, 1894), p. 344.

to those set forth that affirm the passage's canonicity, owing to the inspiration of Scripture by the Holy Spirit, regardless of the author's identity.[61] The purpose of these brief observations is not to argue for or against their validity but rather to demonstrate that the nature and shape of the early Pentecostal responses to the textual questions surrounding Mk 16.9-20 were similar to and not out of keeping with that of a number of other responses from roughly the same time period.

Mark 16.9-20 in the Textual Tradition

A Review of the Manuscript Tradition

Most students of the New Testament are aware of the various problems posed by the ending of Mark.[62] The manuscript tradition offers at least six different endings.[63]

1. The following MSS of Mark end at 16.8: ℵ B 304 (2386 and 1420 have a page missing at this point); syr^s arm^{8mss} eth^{3mss} geo^{1,A}; Clement, Origen, Eusebius mss$^{according\ to\ Eusebius}$, Jerome mss$^{according\ to\ Jerome}$.

2. The longer ending (Mk 16.9-20) is included in the following MSS: A C D E H K M S U X Y Γ Δ Θ Π Σ Φ Ω 047 055 0211 f^{13} 28 33 274 (text) 565 700 892 1009 1010 1071 1195 1230 1242 1253 1344 1365 1546 1646 2148 2174, etc.; lectionaries 60 69 70 185 547 833; Latin^{vt} aur c d^{supp}ff^2 l n o q vg syr^c p h pal cop^{sah} boh fay goth arm^{mss} geo^8; Diat$^{arabic,\ Italian,\ Old\ Dutch}$; Justin (?), Irenaeus, Tertullian, Aphraates, Apostolic Constitutions, Didymus, Hippolytus, Marinus (as quoted by Eusebius), Epiphanius.

3. Codex W (also known as the Freer Logion) expands the longer ending at v. 14, 'and they excused themselves, saying, "This age of lawlessness and unbelief is under Satan, who does not allow the truth and power of God to prevail over the unclean things of the

---

[61] S.P. Tregelles, *An Account of the Printed Text of the Greek New Testament* (London: Samuel Bagster & Sons, 1854), pp. 260-61; C.H. Hammond, *Outlines of Textual Criticism Applied to the New Testament* (Oxford: Clarendon Press, 1890), pp. 127-28; A. Brassac, *The Student's Handbook to the New Testament* (trans. J.L. Weidenhan; London: Herder, 1915), pp. 65-67; and W.C. Shearer, 'The Last Twelve Verses of St. Mark's Gospel', *ExpTim* 5 (1893-94), pp. 227-28.

[62] For the sake of continuity of argument there is some overlap at this point with a brief portion of the previous chapter.

[63] The following information is from the Institut für neutestamentliche Textforschung in Munster as given in J.K. Elliot, 'The Text and Language of the Endings to Mark's Gospel', *TZ* 27 (1971), pp. 255-62.

spirits. Therefore reveal thy righteousness now" – thus they spoke to Christ. And Christ replied to them, "The term of years for Satan's power has been fulfilled, but other terrible things draw near. And for those who have sinned I was delivered over to death, that they may return to the truth and sin no more; that they may inherit the spiritual and incorruptible glory of righteousness which is in heaven."'[64]

4. The longer ending is included in the following MSS marked with asterisks, or obeli, or with a critical note added: f¹ 137 138 1110 1210 1215 1216 1217 1221 1241^vid 1582.
5. Latin (vt. k) reads, 'But they reported briefly to Peter and those with him all that they had been told. And after this Jesus himself sent out by means of them, from east to west, the sacred and imperishable proclamation of eternal salvation.'[65]
6. The following MSS add the shorter ending (number 5 above) before the longer ending: L Ψ 099 (incomplete up to συντόμως) 0112 (omits πάν ... μετὰ δέ) 579 274^mg; lectionary 1602; syr^hmg cop^tsah mss boh^mss eth^mss.

Of these options, reading 3 can be dismissed as an expanded form of the longer ending. Metzger notes, 'The obvious and pervasive apocryphal flavour of the expansion, as well as the extremely limited basis of evidence supporting it, condemns it as a totally secondary accretion.'[66] Reading 5 can be disregarded as the original due to its scanty MS support.[67] Reading 4 obviously reflects a view of the longer ending as somewhat questionable. Reading 6 appears to be an intentional conflation of the shorter reading with the longer one and as such offers some support for both readings.

---

[64] Metzger, *A Textual Commentary on the Greek New Testament* (United Bible Societies, 1971), p. 124.

[65] B.M. Metzger, *A Textual Commentary on the Greek New Testament*, pp. 123-24.

[66] B.M. Metzger, *The Text of the New Testament* (New York and Oxford: Oxford University Press, 1968), p. 227.

[67] H.B. Swete observes, 'As to the origin of this ending there can be little doubt. It has been written by someone whose copy of the Gospel ended at ἐφοβοῦντο γάρ, and who desired to soften the harshness of so abrupt a conclusion, and at the same time to remove the impression which it leaves of a failure on the part of Mary of Magdala and her friends to deliver the message with which they had been charged. Terrified as they were, he adds, they recovered themselves sufficiently to report to Peter the substance of the Angel's words. After this the Lord Himself appeared to the Apostles and gave them orders to carry the Gospel from East to West; and these orders, with his assistance, were loyally fulfilled.' *The Gospel According to St. Mark* (London: Macmillan, 1898), p. ci.

Internal Evidence

A survey of the internal evidence reveals that a large number of words appear in 16.9-20 that occur nowhere else in Mark, in some cases the whole of the New Testament.[68] These verses also contain several strange syntactical constructions when compared to Mark, and as often noted there is an abrupt transition between vv. 8 and 9. It is, of course, possible to argue that Mk 16.9-20 was an ancient collection of resurrection appearances reworked by Mark. However, given the remarkable differences between 16.9-20 and the rest of the Gospel, it is more probable to assume that any Markan peculiarities found in 16.9-20 are either the result of the compiler's attempt to imitate Markan style or, as is more likely, coincidental.

Owing to the testimony of the manuscript tradition and the nature of the internal evidence it appears safe to assume that the most ancient extant version of the Gospel of Mark is one that ends at 16.8. However, does non-Markan, mean non-canonical? To come to terms with this question, some attention must be devoted to the origins of Mk 16.9-20 and then to the authority of this 'longer ending'.

The Origins of Mark 16.9-20

If these verses do not originate with the author of the Gospel according to Mark, what might be known of their origin? One way to gain some leverage on this topic is to determine, as nearly as possible, the date of composition of the 'longer ending'. The first unambiguous citation of the 'longer ending' occurs ca. 180 CE in the writing of Irenaeus, where the Gospel is called by name before a quotation of 16.19.[69] There is also evidence that Tatian's Diatessaron, a reworking of the Four Gospels into one narrative around ca. 172, makes use of the tradition found in Mk 16.9-20.[70] Earlier still are allusions to portions of these verses in the writing of Justin Martyr. In describing the apostles' post ascension deeds, Justin uses language very much like, and at one point identical to, that of Mk 16.20. He says, 'the powerful word of the apostles, going out from Jerusalem, preached everywhere'

---

[68] This statement is based on the more detailed analysis in the previous chapter.

[69] Irenaeus, *Against Heresies*, 3.10.5.

[70] J.A. Kelhoffer, *Miracle and Mission: The Authentication of Missionaries and Their Message in the Longer Ending of Mark* (WUNT 112; Tubingen: Mohr Siebeck, 2000), p. 170. Kelhoffer's excellent study offers the most extensive examination of Mark 16.9-20 to date.

(*Apology*, I.45.5). Arguments in favor of Justin's familiarity with Mk 16.20 are the post ascension context of both texts, an emphasis upon the word of the Lord in both, and the words 'going out they preached everywhere' (ἐξελθόντες πανταχοῦ ἐκήρυξαν in Justin, ἐξελθόντες ἐκήρυξαν πανταχοῦ in Mk 16.20).[71]

It would appear plausible that if the 'longer ending' was not only known to Justin, but also had the authority of Scripture for him in argumentation, its date of origin must be earlier still. Given the reflection of, if not dependence upon, the content of the canonical Gospels and Acts in Mk 16.9-20, a topic touched upon briefly in the next section, the 'longer ending' likely appeared after the Four Gospels began to appear together, a date probably not before 110 CE.[72] It would appear consistent with the evidence to assign a date between 115-130 CE for the composition of Mk 16.9-20. Thus, the ending is indeed an ancient one.

Sources (Written and Oral)

An examination of the content of Mk 16.9-20 reveals a number of affinities with other documents. While extensive source critical analyses have been conducted,[73] at this point this study simply identifies places where the 'longer ending' overlaps with other documents, rather than offer an explanation of how the sources were utilized. This approach is taken for two primary reasons. First, source critical reconstructions are notoriously hypothetical with consensus of thought rarely achieved. In the case of Mk 16.9-20 it is especially challenging to determine whether the text reflects a particular Gospel or the tradition(s) underlying a particular Gospel. Second, often such historical critical work can be greatly informed by the results of a prior literary analysis of the text. This said, the following portions of the 'longer ending' show signs of affinity with other documents.

The mention of Mary Magdalene in the context of resurrection appearances is not surprising as she is mentioned in all four of the canonical Gospels in such a context. However, her description as the

---

[71] For other allusions to Mk 16.9-20 in Justin cf. C. Taylor, 'Some Early Evidence for the Twelve Verses St. Mark 16, 9-20', *The Expositor* Fourth Series 8 (1893), pp. 71-80 and Kelhoffer, *Miracle and Mission*, pp. 170-75.

[72] This date is consistent with the likely emergence of the Fourth Gospel from the Johannine community into the broader early Christian communities.

[73] On this cf. J. Hug, *La Finale de L'Evangile de Marc* (Paris: J. Gabalda, 1978), pp. 163-76 and Kelhoffer, *Miracle and Mission*, pp. 123-56.

one from whom Jesus cast out the seven demons is paralleled only in Lk. 8.2.

The nearest parallel to the reference to Jesus' resurrection appearance in vv. 12-13 is found in the story of the two disciples on the Road to Emmaus in Lk. 24.13-32, though the version in the 'longer ending' is quite abbreviated.

As for the rest of the 'longer ending', there are a number of places at which one can show a given word or practice as being paralleled in John, Luke, Matthew, or Acts. However, the general impression gained from a comparison of the 'longer ending' with these other texts is that if Mk 16.9-20 is literarily dependent upon these other documents, it represents such a remarkable integration of these Gospel traditions that it is next to impossible to demonstrate the nature of the literary dependency with any degree of certainty. As with the other Gospel compositions, it is also possible, some would say likely, that the 'longer ending' also utilized traditional material from oral sources[74] making the source critical challenge all the more difficult. Suffice it to say that the composition process of the 'longer ending' may not be markedly different from the way in which a variety of sources were utilized in the composition of Matthew, Mark, Luke, and John, with the exception that more sources were available owing to the passage of time.

What can be gauged with much more certainty is the authority of Mk 16.9-20 within the church. It is this issue that is now taken up.

The Authority of Mark 16.9-20

Is it possible, owing to the antiquity of the 'longer ending' and the way a variety of Gospel traditions have been integrated into it, that Mk 16.9-20, while non-Markan, should be regarded as canonical nonetheless? A brief survey of the evidence suggests that with few exceptions, the 'longer ending' was regarded to be and functioned as part of the canon of Scripture confessed by the church. Part of the evidence for this assertion comes in the form of the manuscript tradition. Owing to the limitations of space it should simply be noted that the great preponderance of manuscripts include these verses as part of the Gospel according to Mark.[75] In addition to the manuscript tradition, evidence

---

[74] As does Hug, *La Finale de L'Evangile de Marc*.

[75] On this cf. Metzger, *A Textual Commentary on the Greek New Testament*, p. 124. Even the evidence of Codex Vaticanus, which omits these verses, may be somewhat ambiguous owing to the fact that a blank space (one and one-fourth columns) appears

for the authority of Mk 16.9-20 comes in the form of its frequent use in the works of a variety of early Christian writers.[76] Its acceptance at large, prompts Kelhoffer to observe, 'It thus comes as no surprise that Mark's Longer Ending was met with almost universal acceptance before the nineteenth century'.[77]

One way to assess the canonical authority of the 'longer ending' is by means of a comparison with other New Testament texts about which there are textual questions and with other early Christian documents contained in the early manuscript tradition. One somewhat analogous text is the so-called 'Adulterous Woman' pericope. This passage is absent from a rather large number of the earliest manuscripts, and is located at various places in the text of John (after 7.52; 7.36; 7.44; or 21.44) and even Luke (after 21.28) in the manuscripts that do contain it. It departs significantly from Johannine style and interrupts the flow of thought wherever it is located. Thus, it is clearly non-Johannine.[78] However, despite the fact that the passage clearly does not belong at a specific place in the Fourth Gospel (or Luke for that matter!), it does show signs of being an authentic piece of the Jesus tradition as it passes one or more of the criteria of authenticity.[79] In addition to its signs of authenticity may be added the fact that the passage is accepted by one or more later church councils as part of the canon.[80] By comparison, the evidence for the canonical standing of Mk 16.9-20 is much stronger indeed.[81]

---

after Mk 16.8. Owing to the fact that Mk 16.9-20 could possibly be fitted into this space, it has been argued that the blank space is evidence that the scribe knew of the 'longer ending' and left sufficient space for the future owner of the manuscript to add 16.9-20 if desired. For this suggestion cf. W. Farmer, *The Last Twelve Verses of Mark* (London: Cambridge University Press, 1974), p. 57.

[76] This statement can be readily documented with regard to the place of Mk 16.9-20 amongst early Christian writers by consulting allusions to and quotations of this passage in *Biblia patristica: index des citations et allusions bibliques dans la littérature patristique* (Paris: Editions du Centre de la recherche scientifique, 1975-87), vols. 1-4.

[77] Kelhoffer, *Miracle and Mission*, p. 6. Cf. also p. 6 n. 20 which contains examples of the kinds of appeals made to the text of Mark 16.9-20 in the writings of the church.

[78] Cf. Metzger, *A Textual Commentary on the Greek New Testament*, pp. 219-22.

[79] On this whole issue cf. G.M. Burge, 'A Specific Problem in the New Testament Text and Canon: The Woman Caught in Adultery', *JETS* 27 (1984), pp. 141-48.

[80] Cf. Burge, 'A Specific Problem in the New Testament Text and Canon: The Woman Caught in Adultery', p. 148.

[81] Comparison could also be made to the theological summary found in the Johannine comma of 1 Jn 5.7, where the Greek manuscript support is almost non-existent, but the verse has had a significant place in the life of the church. In this case, it appears that there are very few claims to canonical standing.

Another kind of comparison might also help to gauge the canonical standing of the 'longer ending'. There are several documents, coming from the same general time period as Mk 16.9-20, for which 'canonical authority' might be claimed, owing to the manuscript tradition and usage in the church. For example, 1 Clement, the Shepherd of Hermas, and the Epistle of Barnabas are all found in Codex ℵ, which omits the 'longer ending'. Each of these documents had some following in the early church but eventually were not regarded as canonical. Again, the claims for the canonical standing of the 'longer ending' are much stronger than these near contemporaries.

Toward the Re-appropriation of Mark 16.9-20

This chapter began with an examination of Mk 16.9-20 by means of *Wirkungsgeschichte*, specifically, it described the effect of this text upon early Pentecostalism. A knowledge of the extraordinary impact of this text upon Pentecostalism led to a text critical study of the end of the Gospel according to Mark. The text critical discussion, in turn, led to a discussion of the canonical authority of Mk 16.9-20. Given the impact of this text in the Pentecostal tradition, its antiquity, its integration of a variety of Gospel traditions, and its near universal acceptance as part of the church's canon of Scripture, it would seem appropriate to close this presentation with some comments on the text of Mk 16.9-20 and the identification of the theological implications of this text for Pentecostal theology and practice.

Structural, Literary, and Canonical Observations

Mark 16.9-20 is structured around three resurrection appearances of Jesus to various followers (vv. 9-14), an extended discourse in which the disciples are commissioned to take the Gospel to all creation (vv. 15-18), and a concluding section that describes Jesus' actions of ascension to heaven and being seated at the right hand of God, as well as his actions of accompanying those who went out to preach everywhere (vv. 19-20).

The first two resurrection appearances result in the proclamation of the resurrection to those who had been with Jesus (v. 10), who were mourning and weeping, and to the rest (v. 13). On both occasions these proclamations were met with unbelief (vv. 11 and 13). Even the third resurrection appearance to the Eleven appears to meet with unbelief, for Jesus himself denounces the disciples for their unbelief and their hardness of heart, which kept them from believing the reports of those who had seen him (v. 14). Each of the resurrection appearances end with a form of the same word translated 'they did not believe' (ἠπίστησαν in v. 11 and ἐπίστευσαν in vv. 13 and 14).

The third resurrection appearance provides the context for the commission of the disciples by the resurrected Jesus to go into all the world and preach the Gospel to every creature. The commission to go and preach is followed by a promise and warning: each one who believes and is baptized will be saved while the one who does not believe will be condemned. On the heels of this promise and warning is the promise of signs following believers. The words which follow have an almost formulaic or credal feel to them. In the Greek text, in each instance the noun is followed by the verb, reading somewhat literally: 'demons they will cast out' (δαιμόνια ἐκβαλοῦσιν), '(with) tongues they will speak' (γλώσσαις λαλήσουσιν), 'serpents they will take up' (ὄφεις ἀροῦσιν), 'deadly poison...will not hurt them' (θανάσιμόν ... βλάψῃ), 'upon the sick hands will be laid' (ἐπὶ ἀρρώστους χεῖρας ἐπιθήσουσιν). It is clear from the context that these signs are expected to accompany the disciples as they preach the Gospel, an expectation fulfilled in the 'longer ending' itself (v. 20).

The final section (vv. 19-20) is structured around a (μὲν ... δέ) grammatical construction, best translated 'on the one hand' and 'on the other hand', indicating that these verses stand together around the actions of Jesus. These actions include his 'heavenly' actions (ascension to heaven and being seated at the right hand of God), on the one hand, and his earthly ones (working with them and confirming his word by the signs which accompanied them), on the other hand. Two aspects of v. 20 should be mentioned at this point. First, the commission to go and preach (v. 15) and the promise of signs following the believers (vv. 17-18) are treated as being fulfilled in this verse. Second, it is very clear that despite his physical absence Jesus continues to be present with his disciples, working with them in their mission.

Some of the other significant aspects of Mk 16.9-20 are set forth in the following observations. One of the dominant themes found in the 'longer ending' is the issue of unbelief and belief. On seven occasions in these twelve verses the verb 'to believe' (πιστεύω) or its counterpart 'not to believe' (ἀπιστεύω) appear. The latter term appears in vv. 11, 13, 14a, b, while the former appears in vv. 16 and 17. The liabilities of unbelief are clearly warned against, just as belief is encouraged. Proclamation is another clear emphasis of this passage. Twice (vv. 10 and 13) the resurrection of Jesus is proclaimed (ἀπαγγέλλω) by those who have seen him. Twice the word 'preach' (κηρύσσω) is used to describe the activity of the disciples: once as part of their commission (v. 15), and again to describe their resulting activity (v. 20). Exorcism is underscored twice; once in the description of Mary Magdalene, 'from whom he cast out seven demons' and once in the list of signs which are to follow the believers, 'in my name they shall cast out demons'. Given the nature of the signs and the content of the other Gospel accounts of the post-resurrection Jesus, it is almost unbelievable that there is no mention whatsoever of the Spirit in Mk 16.9-20. Perhaps this absence is to be explained by the emphasis placed upon the person of Jesus in the 'longer ending', making it one of the most Jesucentric texts in the New Testament.

If Mk 16.9-20 is to be treated as part of the canon, how do these verses function canonically? Perhaps the following observations will suggest something of the promise of further reflection on this topic. First, the mention of Mary Magdalene in v. 9 reveals something of the depth of her role in the resurrection story, as she is mentioned in all fours Gospels as well as the 'longer ending', and anticipates her mention in Luke (8.2) as one from whom seven demons were cast out. Second, the description of the two disciples in vv. 12-13 clearly anticipates the more extensive story of the disciples on the Road to Emmaus found in Luke (24.13-35). Third, the theme of unbelief, which appears rather consistently in 16.9-20, develops the theme of unbelief on the part of some to whom Jesus appeared after the resurrection in Mt. 28.17. It also continues the theme of unbelief on the part of the disciples in the Gospel according to Mark. Fourth, the commission of 16.15 develops further that found in Mt. 28.18-20, especially with regard to the extent of their mission and a more precise understanding of how Jesus will be with them until the end of the age. Fifth, it is also noteworthy that canonically, the mention of baptism in 16.16, unlike those found in Mt. 28.19 and Acts 2.38, does not include a baptismal formula. Sixth, the mention of signs following believers connects with the unfulfilled promise of Mt. 10.7-8 as well as the previous activity of the disciples in Mk 6.12. It also points forward to their activity in Luke as well as Acts. Specifically, the casting out of demons in Jesus' name anticipates the apparent practice of Paul alluded to in Acts 19.11-20, as speaking in new tongues does the phenomenon of glossolalia described in Acts 2, 10, 11, 19 and 1 Corinthians 12 and 14. Neither is the problematic 'taking up serpents' without its canonical function. Owing to the broad meaning of the term rendered 'take up' (αἴρω),[82] its appearance here both points forward to Jesus' words to his disciples about treading upon serpents in Lk. 10.19, as well as Paul's experience on Malta in Acts 28.1-6. It should also be noted that the positive mention of signs in the 'longer ending' serves as the canonical transition where the somewhat negative view of signs found in Matthew (16.1-4) and Mark (8.11-12) gives way to their more positive role in Luke, John, and Acts.[83] Seventh, reference to the ascension points forward to its double mention in Luke-Acts (Lk. 24.50-53; Acts 1.6-11), while the mention of Jesus' being seated at the right hand of the Father points ahead to the words of Stephen, who sees the Son of Man at the right hand of God (Acts 7.54), and those of the author of Heb. in 12.2. Finally, the presence of Jesus during the disciples' mission activity clearly anticipates much which follows in Acts, beginning with the words to Theophilus (1.1), including Jesus' activity as Spirit Baptizer, his appearance at God's right hand (7.54), and his appearance to Saul and Ananias (9.1-19).

Implications for Pentecostal Theology and Ministry

Though often observed that the Acts narrative is the defining paradigm for Pentecostal doctrine and practice, in point of fact Mk 16.9-20 functions as the 'litmus test' of the early Pentecostal Movement's fulfilling of the apostolic mandates given by Jesus and carried out by the church. Owing to this text's unrivaled significance in early Pentecostalism, perhaps biblical scholars working in the tradition have been too quick to dismiss the role of this text in the canon, owing to its non-Markan origins. Perhaps historical theologians working in the tradition should rethink the defining paradigm of Pentecostal identity as one which integrates Acts and the 'longer ending'. Perhaps theologians working within the tradition should be more intentional about its importance in the articulation of contemporary Pentecostal theology.

---

[82] The term can mean 'take up', 'carry', 'remove', or 'destroy'. Cf. W. Radl, 'αἴρω', *EDNT*, I (ed. H. Balz and G. Schneider; Grand Rapids: Eerdmans, 1990), p. 41.

[83] This point is based on an observation by B.B. Charette made in his helpful though critical response to our presentation at the Society for Pentecostal Studies at Southeastern College Lakeland, FL on 15 March, 2002.

7

The Composition of the Fourth Gospel

The history of the composition of the Fourth Gospel has long presented a special challenge to interpreters. This chapter seeks to contribute to this discussion by offering an overview of the major categories of aporias found within the Gospel, identify the prominent theories of composition history, and offer a modest proposal as to how to best approach this issue.

Aporias

A number of aporias appear in the text of the Fourth Gospel. These problems may be classified into the following categories for easier examination: additions to the original text, tensions within the text, and breaks in sequence.

1. Additions to the Original Text

Several passages in the Fourth Gospel have features that suggest they were not originally part of the text. The most obvious example of this is the adulterous woman pericope, Jn 7.53-8:11. This passage, which is quite distinct from the Fourth Gospel in style and vocabulary, has little textual support for inclusion in the Fourth Gospel.[1] Apparently, this story came to have a place in the text long after the composition of the Fourth Gospel.

A less conspicuous pericope is the epilogue, ch. 21. In this case there is absolutely no textual evidence that the Fourth Gospel ever circulated without this chapter. However, several internal considerations seem to indicate that ch. 21 was added after the Gospel was completed. The primary evidence of the pericope's later addition is the

---

[1] The manuscript support is scant with some witnesses placing the pericope at different locations in John's Gospel (21.24 and 7.36) while others even locate the passage in Luke (21.38).

nature of Jn 20.30, 31, which appear to function as the conclusion of the Gospel. Verse 30 states the rationale for the selection and inclusion of the signs, while v. 31 sets out the book's purpose. That the Gospel then continues with ch. 21 and an abrupt geographic shift from Jerusalem to Galilee is awkward both in style and narrative flow. There are also some differences between the vocabulary of John 21 and the rest of the Fourth Gospel.[2] However, despite such evidence, the context and most of the vocabulary of ch. 21 cohere quite well with the Fourth Gospel,[3] enabling a few scholars to argue that the author of the Fourth Gospel added this material personally.[4] Others conclude that while the traditions of ch. 21 may very well derive from the evangelist, a disciple or associate is responsible for its composition and addition to the Gospel.[5] Still others are unconvinced that there is any connection between the author and the one who adds the chapter.[6]

Some scholars have argued that the Prologue, Jn 1.1-18, also may not have originally been part of the Fourth Gospel. One of the most compelling arguments for this view is that the Prologue is able to stand on its own, apart from the rest of the Fourth Gospel. Thus, it is at least possible that the Prologue was at one time an early Christian hymn

---

[2] Such stylistic evidence is evaluated differently by various scholars.

[3] Cf. R.E. Brown, *The Gospel according to John*, II (Garden City, NY: Doubleday, 1970), p. 1079; B. Lindars, *The Gospel of John* (London: Oliphants, 1972), pp. 621-22; C.K. Barrett, *The Gospel according to St. John* (Philadelphia: Westminster, 1978), p. 577; S.S. Smalley, *John: Evangelist and Interpreter* (Nashville: Nelson, 1984), p. 96.

[4] B.F. Westcott, *The Gospel According to St. John* (Grand Rapids: Eerdmans, 1975), pp. 191-92; A. Plummer, *The Gospel according to St. John* (Cambridge: Cambridge University Press, 1902), p. 367; H. Bernard, *A Critical and Exegetical Commentary on the Gospel according to John*, II, (Edinburgh: T. & T. Clark, 1928), pp. 687-92; A. Schlatter, *Der Evangelist Johannes* (Stuttgart: Calwer, 1930), p. 363; W. Bauer, *Das Johannesevangelium* (Tübingen: Mohr-Siebeck, 1933), p. 235; E.C. Hoskyns & F.M. Davey, *The Fourth Gospel* (London: Faber & Faber, 1956), p. 550; H. Thyen, 'Entwicklungen innerhalb der johanneischen Theologie und Kirche im Spiegel von Joh 21 und der Lieblingsjüngertext des Evangeliums', in *L' Evangile de Jean: Sources, rédaction, théologie* (BETL 44; ed. M. de Jonge; Gembloux: Leuven University Press, 1977), pp. 259-99; E. Ruckstuhl, *Die literarische Einheit des Johannesevangeliums* (Freiburg: Paulus, 1951), pp. 141-49; L. Morris, *The Gospel according to John* (Grand Rapids: Eerdmans, 1971), p. 859.

[5] Brown, *The Gospel according to John*, II, p. 1080; Lindars, *The Gospel of John*, p. 622; Barrett, *The Gospel according to St. John*, p. 577; Smalley, *John: Evangelist and Interpreter*, p. 120; G.R. Beasley-Murray, *John* (Waco, TX: Word, 1987), p. 396; R. Schnackenburg, *The Gospel according to St. John*, III (trans. D. Smith & G.A. Kon; New York: Crossroads, 1987), pp. 341-51.

[6] R. Bultmann, *The Gospel of John* (trans. G.R. Beasley-Murray; Philadelphia: Westminster, 1971), pp. 700-706; Haenchen, II 229-34.

with an existence of its own independent of the Gospel. In addition, the Prologue betrays a rather poetic structure and rhythm that is not characteristic of the style of the narrative in general. Thematic and vocabulary emphases also distinguish the Prologue form the remainder of the Fourth Gospel. Certain key terms in the Prologue, such as λόγος, χάρις, and πλήρωμα, are absent from the Gospel itself. However, despite such obvious distinct characteristics there is a good deal of continuity between the Prologue and the rest of the Fourth Gospel. Verses 11 and 12 sum up the contents of the two main divisions of the Fourth Gospel, the Book of Signs and the Book of Glory respectively.[7] Several of the ideas of the Prologue appear in the main body of the Gospel: ζωή, φῶς (v. 4), μαρτυρία (v. 7), ἀληθινός (v. 9), κόσμος (v. 10), δόξα, ἀλήθεια (v. 14),[8] as well as various themes: pre-existence, the only Son, no one has seen the Father except the Son, and the role of John (the Baptist).[9]

A variety of proposals have been set forth to explain the Prologue's origin, history, and purpose. Several scholars argue that the Prologue was constructed after the completion of the Gospel to introduce it to the readers.[10] A few writers have suggested that the Prologue serves as an outline to the Fourth Gospel.[11] Currently, the majority of authors conclude that behind the Prologue is a hymn, which has been modified to meet the specific needs of the Fourth Gospel.[12] The original

---

[7] Brown, *The Gospel According to John*, I, p. 19.
[8] Barrett, *The Gospel according to St. John*, p. 151.
[9] Brown, *The Gospel According to John*, I, p. 19; J.A.T. Robinson, 'The Relation of the Prologue to the Gospel of St. John', *NTS* 9 (1962-63), p. 122.
[10] Cf. A. von Harnack, 'Über das Verhältnis des Prologs des vierten Evangeliums zum ganzen Werk', *ZTK* 2 (1892), pp. 189-231; Bultmann, *The Gospel of John*, pp. 13-4; C.H. Dodd, *The Interpretation of the Fourth Gospel* (Cambridge: Cambridge University Press, 1970), pp. 92-296; Lindars (*The Gospel of John*, pp. 76-82) views this introduction as added to the second edition of the Gospel, while E. Haenchen (*John*, I [trans. R.W. Funk; ed. R.W. Funk & U. Busse; Philadelphia: Fortress, 1984], p. 101) understands the Prologue as a preface. Schnackenburg (*The Gospel according to John*, I, p. 224) argues that the Evangelist composes the Prologue as a 'pre-history' or 'opening narrative'.
[11] Cf. F.L. Godet, *Commentary on the Gospel of John*, I (trans. T. Dwight; Grand Rapids: Zondervan, 1969), p. 291; Hoskyns & Davey, *The Fourth Gospel*, p. 137; R.H. Lightfoot, *St John's Gospel* (Oxford: Oxford University Press, 1960), p. 78; Morris, *The Gospel According to John*, pp. 71-72.
[12] These views range from the idea that the Prologue comes from a pre-Christian hymn that has been rehabilitated (Bultmann, *The Gospel of John*, pp. 16-18) to the proposal that the hymn originated within the Johannine circle (Brown, *The Gospel According to John*, I, p. 20).

extent of the Prologue material notwithstanding, the inherent connections between the Prologue and the rest of the Gospel reveal an intrinsic unity and suggest that the Prologue serves as an introduction to the rest of the Gospel.[13]

2. Tensions in the Text

In addition to the fact that certain portions of the Fourth Gospel seem to have been added to the text of the Gospel after it had taken a definite shape, tension between certain passages raise the question of the basic unity of the document. Three problems are commonly acknowledged.

John 3.22-30 recounts that through his own work Jesus was beginning to attract greater crowds than John the Baptist. Verse 22 even describes Jesus himself as baptizing those who came to him, which is confirmed in 4.1. However, a parenthetical statement in 4.2 makes it very clear that it was Jesus' disciples (with Jesus' approval) not Jesus himself who did the baptizing. Such sharp tension prompts Brown to conclude that 4.2 'serves as almost indisputable evidence of the presence of several hands in the composition of John.'[14] While not quite as vehement as Brown, most scholars suspect that a redactor is responsible for v. 2.[15] However, certain aspects of v. 2 cause other commentators to be less emphatic[16] and even to question the logic of such an affirmation,[17] with a few scholars concluding that the evangelist is responsible for the verse, in order to clarify his earlier statements concerning baptism.[18]

A similar problem occurs in John 7. In v. 3 Jesus' unbelieving brothers urge Him to go up to Jerusalem for the Feast of Tabernacles so that He might manifest His works there. Jesus flatly refuses such advice (v. 8)[19] and the impression is left that he will not go to this feast.

---

[13] Smalley, *John: Evangelist and Interpreter*, p. 95.

[14] Brown, *The Gospel according to John*, I, p. 164.

[15] Schnackenburg (*The Gospel according to St. John*, I, p. 422 n. 6) notes, 'Signs of redactional composition in vs. 2 are: καίτοιγε is singular, ʼΙησοῦς without the article is at least remarkable, if not a criterion of the style of the redaction.' Also cf. Bultmann, *The Gospel of John*, p. 168 and Lindars, *The Gospel of John*, p. 177.

[16] Barrett, *The Gospel according to St. John*, p. 230 and Beasley-Murray, *John*, p. 58.

[17] Haenchen, *John*, I, p. 218.

[18] Morris, *The Gospel According to John*, p. 252 and J.R. Michaels, *John* (New York: Harper & Row, 1984), p. 53.

[19] It appears that οὔπω was substituted for οὐκ very early on ($\mathfrak{p}^{66, 75}$) to alleviate the apparent discrepancy between Jesus' refusal to go to the feast and his later action (v.

However, two verses later (v. 10) Jesus does go up to the feast, albeit without fanfare,[20] raising the question of the narrative's literary unity. Interestingly enough, the vast majority of scholars attribute both these verses to the Evangelist.[21] This conclusion is defended by labeling the contradiction as superficial,[22] by offering a double meaning for ἀναβαίνω,[23] or by simply asserting that, despite the inability to explain the contradiction, the Evangelist is responsible for the pericope.[24] Similarly, despite certain tensions between those passages where Jesus claims or is imputed to have the authority to judge (3.18-19; 8.16; 12.48) and those passages where he insists that he did not come to judge (3.17; 8.15; 12.47), most scholars still say the Evangelist wrote both sets of texts.

A final example concerns the eschatological views represented in the Gospel. It is well known that the Fourth Gospel reflects a distinctively realized eschatology. The basic assumption is that the salvific effects of Jesus' life, death, and resurrection are already present. For example, the one who does not believe is already judged (3.18-19), the 'coming hour' is already here (4.23), and the one who hears and believes has eternal life here and now (5.24, 25). These passages illustrate John's emphasis upon the present situation of the believer. Yet, there are several places where a future eschatology is not only presupposed but is also explicitly stated. The most prominent of these passages are: 5.28-29, where individuals will participate in the resurrection of life or of judgment; 6.39-40, 44 and 54, where Jesus promises to raise those who believe 'in the last day'; and 12.48, where the word spoken by Jesus will judge 'in the last day'. The dilemma is: how do these divergent eschatological views come together in the Fourth Gospel? One way to explain this situation is to attribute the apocalyptic statements to the hand of a redactor, who sought to make the eschatological dimension of the Fourth Gospel more orthodox. On this view, the original document contained only a realized eschatology and for this

---

10). Cf. B.M. Metzger, *Textual Commentary on the Greek New Testament* (London: United Bible Societies, 1971), p. 216.

[20] A similar situation exists in 2.1-11 where Mary makes a request of Jesus. At first he appears to refuse her, but he then acts in accord with the petition.

[21] Haenchen (*John*, II, p. 7) is one of the few exceptions and he is less than dogmatic.

[22] Barrett, *The Gospel according to St. John*, p. 372 and Beasley-Murray, *John*, p. 107.

[23] Brown, *The Gospel according to John*, I, p. 308.

[24] Lindars, *The Gospel of John*, p. 285.

reason was rehabilitated by apocalyptic additions.[25] Another approach argues that while many of the futuristic statements may have been added by a later editor, such additions are in keeping with and are an extension of the Evangelist's thought.[26] Other scholars hold that while the main emphasis of John's work is devoted to a realized eschatology, the apocalyptic verses are a genuine part of the Evangelist's perspective.[27]

Regardless of one's compositional approach to these several problems, the question concerning the literary unity of the Fourth Gospel must be acknowledged.

3. Breaks in Sequence

In addition to the problems already noted, the Fourth Gospel contains several apparent breaks in sequence, which have caused scholars to question the basic literary unity of the Gospel. Two of the most notorious examples are surveyed here.

It has often been observed that chs. 5 and 6 exhibit so many tensions in their present order that they should be transposed. The primary reason offered for such a transposition is the irregularity of the geographical progression of chs. 4-7. In 4.54 Jesus is described as going from Judea to Galilee. However, 5.1 notes that he now goes up to Jerusalem for a feast of the Jews. When the narrative is resumed in 6.1 Jesus is crossing the Sea of Galilee, as the Passover approaches (6.4). Another difficult transition follows in 7.1, where 'after these things Jesus walks in Galilee'. It has been suggested that a transposition of chs. 5 and 6 corrects these numerous tensions. Simply put, Jesus goes to Galilee in 4.54, crosses Lake Tiberias in 6.1 (with the Passover near), then goes up to Jerusalem (5.1) for the feast of the Jews, and finally retreats to Galilee (7.1) because of Judean opposition. Not only are the breaks in sequence adjusted, but this new order demonstrates remark-

---

[25] Bultmann is the major advocate of this proposal, which has wielded a great deal of influence. Also cf. Haenchen, *John*, I, pp. 254-55.

[26] Schnackenburg, *The Gospel according to St. John*, II, pp. 114-17, 426-37; Brown, *The Gospel according to John*, II, pp. cxv-cxxi, 220; R. Kysar, 'The Eschatology of the Fourth Gospel: A Correction of Bultmann's Redactional Hypothesis', *Perspective* 13 (1972), pp. 26-31.

[27] Barrett, *The Gospel according to St. John*, pp. 263, 294; M.-E. Boismard, 'L'évolution du thème eschatologique dans les traditions johanniques', *RB* 68 (1961), p. 524; A. Corell, *Consummatum est: Eschatology and Church in the Gospel of St. John* (London: SPCK, 1958), pp. 101-12; Lindars, *The Gospel of John*, p. 226; Morris, *The Gospel according to John*, p. 321; Smalley, *John: Evangelist and Interpreter*, pp. 235-41; Beasley-Murray, *John*, p. 92.

able similarities to the extended Galilean ministry attested in the Synoptics.[28] Despite such benefits most scholars are not prepared to transpose these two chapters.[29] The rationale varies but primarily includes: the lack of an adequate proposal explaining the dislocation in the first place,[30] the fact that despite these breaks in sequence the text still makes sense, the question concerning the legitimacy of imposing modern literary standards upon an ancient text, and the problems of the new contexts created by the transposition.[31]

One of the other major breaks in sequence occurs in 14.31. The most natural place to pick up the narrative again is in 18.1, where 'having said these things' Jesus and his disciples go out and cross the Kidron. The problem is that chs. 15-17 appear between these points, as if 14.31 did not exist. Obviously, there is a break in sequence, but what best accounts for such an interruption? Bultmann suggests that accidental dislocation accounts for this confusion. However, few scholars follow him at this point. Brown argues that chs. 15-17, which he deems to be authentic Johannine tradition, have been added by an editor who felt unworthy to tamper with the statement in 14:31.[32] Lindars argues that the evangelist possibly added 15-17 in a second edition of the Fourth Gospel.[33] Even though he believes an editor added chs. 15-17, Haenchen maintains that John intends the material to be understood as topics of discussion between Jesus and the disciples along the way, despite the disjunctive nature of the insertion.[34] As for the statement in 14.31, Haenchen argues that the stature of the Synoptic tradition necessitates its inclusion at this point.[35] Barrett and Beasley-Murray conclude that 15-17 is an alternate version of the farewell discourse as recorded in chs. 13 and 14.[36]

---

[28] Schnackenburg, *The Gospel according to St. John*, II, p. 6.

[29] Outside of Bultmann and Bernard, who seem to transpose at will, Schnackenburg is the most prominent Johannine scholar to adopt such a course of action with regard to chs. 5 and 6.

[30] Schnackenburg (*The Gospel according to St. John*, II, pp. 5-9) offers the best justification for reversing the order of chs. 5 and 6.

[31] Cf. the excellent discussion in Barrett, *The Gospel according to St. John*, pp. 21-6; Brown, *The Gospel according to John*, I, pp. xxvi-xxviii; Haenchen, *John*, I, pp. 45-51.

[32] Brown, *The Gospel according to John*, I, p. xxxvii and II, p. 656.

[33] Lindars, *The Gospel of John*, pp. 50-51.

[34] Haenchen, *John*, II, pp. 128, 164.

[35] Haenchen, *John*, II, p. 164.

[36] Barrett, *The Gospel according to St. John*, pp. 454-55; Beasley-Murray, *John*, pp. 223-24.

7. The Composition of the Fourth Gospel 123

A number of other problems in the text could be cited, but these should be sufficient to demonstrate the difficulties the student of the Fourth Gospel encounters. Such aporias have resulted in a number of theories of composition which propose to provide the answer to the literary peculiarities of the Fourth Gospel.

Prominent Theories of Composition

A variety of theories have been proposed as solutions to the literary enigma of the Fourth Gospel. While numerous views have been set forth only the most prominent suggestions are examined here.

1. Sources

One of the ways by which the challenge of the composition of the Fourth Gospel has been addressed is by appeal to the use of sources by the writer(s). Any discussion of source criticism and the Fourth Gospel must begin with the contribution of Rudolf Bultmann. Although dated, his proposal has had enormous influence. Bultmann works with the conviction that John drew from several sources. A very brief section of the introduction to his commentary (pp. 4-5) is devoted to a statement about this topic. Bultmann identifies three different sources. First, he assumes the use of a Passion source. While similar to the Passion narrative found in the Synoptics, there are also a sufficient number of differences from both the Synoptics and the tendencies of the Evangelist to warrant the conclusion that John employs a written Passion source.[37]

A second proposed source is a miracle/signs source. This conclusion is based on the following evidence: (1) some of these miracles have no parallel in the Synoptic materials; (2) the miracle stories which have a parallel in the Synoptics are so fundamentally distinct that the differences could not have been introduced by the Evangelist; (3) two of the stories are numbered (2.11; 4.54); and (4) the concluding expression found in 20.30 appears to be taken from the source itself.[38] Bultmann maintains that John's use of the signs 'is more complex than that of the naive miracle story'.[39] The Evangelist uses the miraculous as a symbol not of a wonder-worker but of Jesus the Revealer.[40]

---

[37] Bultmann, *The Gospel of John*, p. 6.
[38] Bultmann, *The Gospel of John*, pp. 6-7.
[39] Bultmann, *The Gospel of John*, p. 114.
[40] Bultmann, *The Gospel of John*, p. 119. The following materials are assigned to Bultmann's semeia source by D.M. Smith (*The Composition and Order of the Fourth*

The most important source, according to Bultmann, is that from which John drew the 'revelation discourses', as Bultmann calls the speeches in John. These discourses have three distinct movements: 'First the Revealer presents himself and His significance; then follows the invitation to come to him; lastly the consequence of the acceptance or rejection of the Revealer is made known in promise and threat'.[41] Bultmann suggests that the close affinity of these discourses with Gnostic revelatory writings is due to the fact that the source is a non-Christian Gnostic document which has been used by the Evangelist who is a Christian and shares a 'common cultural and religious milieu'.[42]

While a number of other source critical theories have been proposed for the Fourth Gospel,[43] the reconstruction set forth by Robert T. Fortna appears to be the most highly regarded by scholars.[44] In order to uncover the source(s) of John, Fortna examines the aporias of the Fourth Gospel for, 'they themselves contain the means to their own solution'.[45] The signs source is the beginning point for Fortna, and is the most important source. Although John has recorded eight miracle stories, there are actually seven, for the two found in John 6 should be taken together. He agrees with Bultmann that the first two signs are numbered, 2.11 and 4.54, but counts the miraculous catch of fish in John 21 as a transposed third sign.[46]

In addition to the signs source Fortna identifies source material underlying the passion and resurrection narrative. He also goes to great

---

Gospel [New Haven: Yale University Press, 1965], pp. 34-35): the calling of the disciples, 1.35-51 (probable); the miracle at Cana, 2.1-12; the story of the Samaritan woman, 4.1-42 (probable); the healing of the ruler's son, 4.43-54; the feeding of the multitude, 6.1-14; Jesus' walking on the water, 6.16-26; Jesus' conversation with his brothers, 7.1-13; the healing of the impotent man, 5.1-16; the healing of the man blind from birth, 6.1-30; the transition in 10.10-22 (probable); the raising of Lazarus, 11.1-44; the conclusion of the whole Gospel, 20.30-31.

[41] Bultmann, *The Gospel of John*, p. 7.

[42] Cf. Bultmann, *The Gospel of John*, pp. 7-9; Smith, *The Composition and Order of the Fourth Gospel*, p. 16.

[43] Cf. especially the following works: W. Nicol, *The semeia in the Fourth Gospel* (Leiden: E.J. Brill, 1972); H.M. Teeple, *The Literary Origin of the Gospel of John* (Evanston: Religion and Ethics Institute, Inc., 1974); S. Temple, *The Core of the Fourth Gospel* (London: Mowbrays, 1975); U. von Wahlde, *The Earliest Version of John's Gospel: Recovering the Gospel of Signs* (Wilmington, DE: Michael Glazier, 1989).

[44] R.T. Fortna, *The Gospel of Signs* (Cambridge: Cambridge University Press, 1970).

[45] Fortna, *The Gospel of Signs*, p. 20.

[46] Fortna, *The Gospel of Signs*, pp. 29, 109.

lengths to demonstrate the existence of other pre-Johannine material.[47] Fortna concludes that the source material which he has identified is in actuality a gospel in its own right.[48] He gives the following overall description of this gospel:

> At the center is the stylized series of seven miracles. These divide into two groups, four in Galilee and three in Judea. Introducing each group is a narrative (set in Samaria?) in which an unlikely person (skeptical Nathanael, the Samaritan woman) encounters Jesus and, the course of a conversation with him, believes. what precedes the ministry of signs is patterned also: the three denials by the Baptist, the chain reaction of witness ... the narrative ... begins, as does the series of signs, with a double confession of Jesus, and it may not be accidental that the Jerusalem period (i.e. the last three signs together with the passion) begins and ends with accounts of resurrection (of Lazarus and Jesus, respectively), accounts which appear to be in contrast to each other.[49]

According to Fortna this gospel springs from a Jewish-Christian milieu, probably from Palestine around the time of the Jewish War. The source's intent is explicit.

> The gospel is a missionary tract with a single end, to show (presumably to the potential Jewish convert) that Jesus is the Messiah. It is ... this unifying purpose that differentiates the source from a mere collection of stories.[50]

Fortna is so confident of his conclusions that he includes the entire source at the end of his monograph.

Despite its acceptance in certain circles, source criticism of the Fourth Gospel has come under severe criticism.[51] Consequently, while many scholars utilize particular aspects of source criticism (i.e. the idea of a Signs Source and/or a passion narrative) few are willing to identify sources as have Bultmann, Fortna, and others. Therefore, source criticism alone is not viewed as holding the key to unlock the literary mysteries of the Fourth Gospel.

---

[47] Fortna, *The Gospel of Signs*, pp. 114-200.
[48] Fortna, *The Gospel of Signs*, p. 221.
[49] Fortna, *The Gospel of Signs*, p. 222.
[50] Fortna, *The Gospel of Signs*, p. 225.
[51] Cf. the discussions in Brown, *The Gospel according to John*, II, pp. xxviii-xxxii; B. Lindars, *Behind the Fourth Gospel* (London: SPCK, 1971), pp. 27-42; D.A. Carson, 'Current Source Criticism of the Fourth Gospel: Some Methodological Questions', *JBL* 97 (1978), pp. 411-29.

2. Editors

A common way of explaining the literary complexities of the Fourth Gospel is the proposal that more than one hand is responsible for the final form of the Gospel. Such hypotheses differ with regard to the way in which the editor/redactor is perceived as agreeing or disagreeing with the earlier work of the Evangelist.

Again the discussion must begin with the seminal work of Rudolf Bultmann. For Bultmann, the present order (or lack of order) of the Fourth Gospel cannot be derived from the author.[52] In fact the text has a complicated history. Somehow, the text, as originally arranged by the author, fell into disarray. Just how this accident took place cannot now be determined. Next, the ecclesiastical redactor not only rearranged the text but made a number of specific editorial additions. Because the original gospel was non-sacramental and exhibited a realized eschatological perspective, the more orthodox ecclesiastical redactor made appropriate additions to include information relating to the Eucharist and baptism (3.5; 6.51b-58; 19.34b-35) and to include passages which include an apocalyptic expectation of the future (5.28-29 and 6.39-40, 44). In addition, several glosses are regarded as editorial (3.24; 4.2; 18.9, 32). Therefore, Bultmann sees at least two different hands responsible for the Fourth Gospel. To be more exact, the ecclesiastical redactor worked to make the original gospel acceptable to a more orthodox audience.[53]

Currently, the most popular editorial theory is that set forth by Raymond Brown. Aware of the peculiar problems of the Fourth Gospel, Brown proposes a theory that seeks to explain the various perplexities and at the same time gives primary attention to the text as it now stands. He suggests that the history of composition may be divided into at least five stages.[54] Stage One finds the existence of a body of material similar to but independent of the Synoptics. The source of this material is identified as the Beloved Disciple.[55] In Stage Two this material was molded and formed into distinctive Johannine patterns where the various techniques of Johannine storytelling are introduced. Although one dominant source may be responsible for what has gone into the Gospel, a close-knit school is ultimately the source. Toward the end of this period some written forms took shape. Stage Three is the point at which the first edition of the Fourth Gospel

---

[52] Bultmann, *The Gospel of John*, p. 10.
[53] Bultmann, *The Gospel of John*, pp. 10-11.
[54] Brown, *The Gospel According to John*, I, pp. xxxiv-xxxix.
[55] Brown, *The Gospel According to John*, I, pp. xcvii-civ.

is produced. The dominant teacher/preacher and theologian is, no doubt, at the very center of such an enterprise, which accounts for the basic cohesiveness of John. Brown thinks that a number of Johannine traditions were left out of the first version. In Stage Four the Evangelist addresses new situations and adds new material as a result. This work amounts to a second edition of the Fourth Gospel. Stage Five sees a final redactor, most likely a close friend or student of the Evangelist, incorporating other Johannine materials which had not been included by the Evangelist (e.g. Jn 21; 3.31-36; 15.1-16.33; 13.12-20). Such a redactor would account for certain duplications in the text and various difficulties in transition, on the theory that the redactor merely contributed additional material without modifying the work of the Evangelist. Brown proposes that this theory preserves 'the substantial unity of the Gospel' while explaining 'the various factors that militate against unity'.[56] A number of other scholars work with views similar in many respects to Brown's hypothesis, while emphasizing the centrality of the Evangelist.[57]

3. Literary Unity

Despite the many difficulties present in the Fourth Gospel there are several scholars who maintain the Gospel is a literary unit. In the face of theories that questioned the literary unity of John, Eduard Schweizer argued that while the evangelist may have utilized source material, the Fourth Gospel exhibits such a uniformity of style that it is impossible to separate the sources.[58] Schweizer sets a list of 33 stylistic characteristics found in Johannine literature. In particular, he lists the number of times a given stylistic characteristic occurs in John, 1-3 John, the rest of the New Testament, and the Synoptics.[59] By employing this stylistic evidence he concludes that none of the partition theories is established and that the Fourth Gospel is a stylistic unity.[60]

Eugen Ruckstuhl builds upon the work of Schweizer, expanding the list of stylistic criteria to fifty.[61] The selection of the characteristics is determined by (1) the infrequency of the feature in the New Testa-

---

[56] Brown, *The Gospel According to John*, I, p. xxxix.
[57] Cf. W. Wilkens, *Die Entstehungsgeschichte des vierten Evangeliums* (Zollikon: Evangelischer Verlag, 1958); Schnackenburg, *The Gospel according to St. John*, I, pp. 72-74; Lindars, *The Gospel of John*, pp. 46-54.
[58] Eduard Schweizer, *Ego Eimi* (Göttingen: Vandenhoeck & Ruprecht, 1939).
[59] Schweizer, *Ego Eimi*, pp. 82-112.
[60] Schweizer, *Ego Eimi*, p. 105.
[61] E. Ruckstuhl, *Die literarische Einheit des Johannesevangeliums, der gegenwärtige Stand der einschlägigen Erforschung* (Freiburg: Paulus, 1951), pp. 203-19.

ment, (2) the frequency of the feature in John and (3) the improbability that the feature would be imitated. Ruckstuhl then divides these characteristics into three categories: (1) 19 characteristics which are the most important, (2) 12 characteristics which are next in significance, and (3) 19 characteristics which are least in importance. One of the primary objectives is to test the source hypothesis set forth by Bultmann. Ruckstuhl concludes that the Fourth Gospel was a stylistic unity that rules out the possibility of written sources.[62]

The conviction that the Fourth Gospel is a stylistic unity has prompted several scholars to conclude that John is essentially the work of one author.[63]

4. A Modest Proposal

In light of such diversity of opinion and the debated pieces of evidence, the following assumptions might be set forth concerning the compositional history of the Fourth Gospel.

First, at the center of the issue is the Beloved Disciple. The position of this enigmatic figure is unrivaled in the Fourth Gospel. Not only does he function as a very close associate of Jesus, but he always appears in a manner which is complimentary. Another very important piece of information is that the Beloved Disciple is identified as the source of the Fourth Gospel's traditions. This evidence is stated clearly in 19.35 and 21.24. It would seem safe to assume that at the first level of the Fourth Gospel's composition stands the testimony and witness of the Beloved Disciple. Such a conclusion is in harmony with Brown's first stage[64] and appears to be in basic agreement with Schnackenburg,[65] A.M. Hunter,[66] Smalley,[67] and Beasley-Murray.[68] As for the nature of the testimony, while parts of the tradition may have

---

[62] Ruckstuhl, *Die literarische Einheit des Johannesevangeliums*, pp. 218-19. Ruckstuhl has been criticized for such an extreme conclusion. Cf. Smith, *The Composition and Order of the Fourth Gospel*, pp. 70ff.; Fortna, *The Gospel of Signs*, pp. 204-205; Teeple, *The Core of the Fourth Gospel*, pp. 20-21.

[63] Cf. M.-J. Lagrange, *Evangile selon Saint Jean* (Paris: Gabalda, 1925); Barrett, *The Gospel according to St. John*, pp. 20-21; R.H. Strachan, *The Fourth Gospel* (London: SCM Press, 1960), pp. 79-82; Morris, *The Gospel according to John*, pp. 8-30. The conclusions of Lindars, Schnackenburg, Smalley, and Beasley-Murray emphasize the role of one dominant writer.

[64] Brown, *The Gospel according to John*, I, pp. xcii-xciv.

[65] Schnackenburg, *The Gospel according to St. John*, II, pp. 85-91.

[66] A.M. Hunter, *The Gospel according to John* (Cambridge: Cambridge University Press, 1965), pp. 12-13.

[67] Smalley, *John: Evangelist and Interpreter*, pp. 119-20.

[68] Beasley-Murray, *John*, p. lxxiii.

been in a written form, as for instance the so-called signs source, it is very difficult to identify with precision the source materials themselves.

Second, while someone else may have been the Evangelist, there are no compelling reasons to regard the Beloved Disciple as far removed from the actual composition of the Fourth Gospel. Several reasons may be offered for such a rationale. (1) The Gospel does identify the Beloved Disciple as the author (21.24). (2) It would appear from the last pericope of the epilogue (21.20-23) that the Beloved Disciple lived to an old age. If there is any kernel of historicity in this statement then surely he must have had more than a foundational influence on the Gospel. (3) Most of the more plausible composition theories argue for a rather long period of development when the Evangelist shaped and gave form to the traditions.[69] The Beloved Disciple qualifies for such homiletic activity as easily as does an anonymous Evangelist. This suggestion does not rule out the possibility that the Beloved Disciple relied upon others in the composition process.

Third, the Fourth Gospel was not written in a short period of time but grew rather slowly through periods of teaching/preaching and discussion. Martin Hengel, who attributes the bulk of the Fourth Gospel to the Beloved Disciple, suggests that the discussions themselves lead to many of the breaks in sequence and that a number of the tensions are natural for a 'towering creative teacher' who ventured to take up new positions and correct himself occasionally.[70] The placement of chs. 15-17 most likely reflects such a process. This sort of addition fits well with a multiple-edition theory.

Fourth, it also appears that the Fourth Gospel was essentially complete when the Beloved Disciple died. The basic stylistic unity of the work lends support to the conclusion that one writer is primarily responsible for the work. However, before the Gospel's publication various additions were made by a disciple/redactor. The redactor's additions for publication of the Fourth Gospel include at least ch. 21, 19.35, references to the Beloved Disciple, as well as the title.[71] While other materials may have been added at this time, these seem to be the most plausible additions.

---

[69] For example, both Brown and Lindars propose two editions of the Fourth Gospel from the same author composed over a rather long period of time. In addition, Brown concedes (*The Gospel according to John*, I, p. cii) that John 21 implies the Beloved Disciple not only remained alive but continued to be influential during the period in which the Fourth Gospel was being written.

[70] M. Hengel, *The Johannine Question* (trans. J. Bowden; London: SCM Press, 1989).

[71] On this whole question cf. Hengel, *The Johannine Question*.

8

The Fourth Gospel and Rabbinic Judaism

Over the years New Testament scholars have been fascinated by the relationship between the Fourth Gospel and Judaism, especially rabbinic Judaism. Yet, despite a number of affinities between the respective materials, historical conclusions drawn have been tenuous at best. For, as Stephen S. Smalley has recognized:

> Here we are on difficult and sometimes speculative ground, because the rabbinic documents are not easy to date. They belong to the Christian period, and often preserve early (even pre-Christian) material. But we can never be certain that rabbinic parallels in the Gospel of John echo first century Jewish thought.[1]

John A.T. Robinson concurs:

> ... the process of setting John in this [rabbinic] context is always one of reading back from much later evidence in the Mishnah and the Talmud and the Midrashim. All one can be sure of is that John stands within a continuing Jewish tradition and is often our earliest witness to it. There is little if anything that antedates John – or anything here that affords a background for his distinctive categories.[2]

Such cautious remarks serve as ominous warnings about the inherent dangers of utilizing rabbinic materials in the study of the New Testament. Unfortunately, such admonitions are sorely needed.

Often, New Testament scholars have utilized rabbinic traditions in an uncritical manner. Documents spanning several centuries are cited in argumentation without due concern for the dating of the various traditions which are taken at face value. This approach produces the assumption that all the materials are of equal value for New Testament concerns, whether mishnaic or talmudic. As Philip S. Alexander notes, 'Many New Testament scholars are still guilty of massive and sustained

---

[1] S.S. Smalley, *John: Evangelist and Interpreter* (Nashville: Thomas Nelson, 1984), p. 64.
[2] J.A.T. Robinson, *The Priority of John* (Oak Park, IL: Meyer-Stone, 1987), pp. 42-43.

anachronism in their use of Rabbinic sources. Time and again we find them quoting *texts from the 3rd, 4th or 5th centuries AD, or even later, to illustrate Jewish teaching in the first century.*³ Consequently, the conclusion is drawn that the Talmud is full of information that goes back to the time of the Pharisees. Older works that exhibit such a weakness, despite other very helpful contributions, include those by George Foote Moore,⁴ Herman L. Strack, and Paul Billerbeck.⁵

Much of the very best New Testament scholarship rests upon the work of these men for their analysis of the rabbinic literature. For example, it is not uncommon to see references made in standard New Testament works to Strack–Billerbeck instead of the rabbinic materials themselves. Consequently, there is little or no first-hand examination of the rabbinic texts. Sadly, much of New Testament scholarship continues to utilize this approach.

Recently, Philip S. Alexander has sought to address this issue by chiding New Testament scholars for their lack of critical instincts when examining rabbinic texts, identifying a number of errors common to New Testament analyses.⁶ At the same time, Alexander encourages New Testament scholars to continue in their study of the rabbinic texts. He advocates utilizing the critical approach offered by Jacob Neusner because:

> Neusner has written extensively and incisively on the problems of method in the study of early Judaism. His writings are readily accessible, and congenial to the New Testament critic.⁷

Neusner challenges traditional rabbinic studies and rejects the direct tie between Pharisaism and rabbinic Judaism.⁸ Neusner and his students attempt to distinguish between the more recent layers of tradition and the older strata of rabbinic materials, which allows for the observation of the developments within a given tradition. In this regard, he begins with the Mishnah, generally considered to be the

---

³ P.S. Alexander, 'Rabbinic Judaism and the New Testament', *ZNW* 74 (1983), p. 244.

⁴ G.F. Moore, *Judaism in the First Three Centuries of the Christian Era: The Age of the Tannaim* (3 vols.; Cambridge: Harvard University Press, 1927-30).

⁵ H.L. Strack & P. Billerbeck, *Kommentar zum Neuen Testament aus Talmud und Midrasch* (7 vols.; München: C.H. Beck, 1926).

⁶ Alexander, 'Rabbinic Judaism and the New Testament', pp. 237-46.

⁷ Alexander, 'Rabbinic Judaism and the New Testament', p. 237.

⁸ In particular he rejects the notion that the traditions of the Pharisees are to be identified as the Oral Torah. Of course, this conclusion has implications for the way rabbinic texts are used in New Testament studies. Cf. *Method and Meaning in Ancient Judaism* (Missoula, MT: Scholars Press, 1979), pp. 59-75.

earliest of the rabbinic documents, and works his way back in a fashion similar to many New Testament form critics.[9] Neusner maintains that the evidence must be examined carefully before any mishnaic text is taken to represent an attitude present in the first century. Such an approach demands that the texts be treated with a critical appreciation for the traditions on their own terms.

In keeping with Alexander's recommendations, the following survey seeks to assemble those rabbinic texts that may legitimately be drawn upon as background against which the Fourth Gospel may be read. Specifically, this study attempts to identify those pieces of rabbinic tradition which are of relevance to the Gospel according to John and which most likely pre-date or are contemporaneous with the Fourth Gospel.[10] Owing to the fact that most Johannine scholars be-

---

[9] Although Neusner would personally distance himself from New Testament form critics due to the nature of the materials. Cf. *Method and Meaning in Ancient Judaism* Third Series (Chico, CA: Scholars Press, 1981), pp. 71-72 and 117-18.

[10] This study does not seek to define the differences between Pharisaism and emerging rabbinic Judaism nor propose a history for either group. Despite the differences between the groups and the distinctive dynamics which produced the movements it is appropriate to treat them together here. There are two basic reasons for this approach. First, the purpose of the inquiry is to document John's knowledge of Jewish practices of a particular kind in the latter part of the first century. In that regard it matters little whether a certain practice is Pharisaic or rabbinic proper. The real issue is whether the topic under consideration is pre-90 and comes from one of those circles. A second reason for such an approach is tied to the definition assigned by Neusner to the Pharisees and the group responsible for the pre-70 mishnaic materials. In describing the Pharisees Neusner observes: 'One primary mark of Pharisaic commitment was the observance of the laws of ritual purity outside of the Temple, where everyone kept them. Eating one's secular, that is, unconsecrated, food in a state of ritual purity, as if one were a Temple priest in the cult, was one of the two significations of party membership. The manifold circumstances of every day life required the multiplication of concrete rules. Representative of the former category may be the laws of tithing and other agricultural taboos. Pharisees clearly regarded keeping the agricultural rules as a primary religious duty. And the agricultural laws, just like the purity rules, in the end affected table-fellowship, namely, what one might eat' (*Judaism in the Beginning of Christianity* [Philadelphia: Fortress Press, 1984], p. 57). Compare this statement about the Pharisees with the following which describes the group responsible for the pre-70 mishnaic materials: 'It seems to me no accident at all that those strata of Mishnaic law which appear to go back to the period before the wars deal specifically with the special laws of marriage (in Yebamot), distinctive rules on when sexual relations may and may not take place (in Niddah), and the laws covering the definition of sources of uncleanness and the attainment of cleanness, with specific reference to domestic meals (in certain parts of Chalot, Zabim, Kelim, and Miqvaot).... The Mishnah before the wars begins its life among a group of people who are joined together by a common conviction about the eating of food under ordinary circumstances in accord with cultic rules

lieve that the final composition of the Fourth Gospel occurred between 85 and 95 CE, this inquiry will seek to isolate rabbinic attitudes and pieces of tradition contained in the Mishnah that represent a pre-90 *Sitz im Leben*. A brief comparison will then be made between these materials and the text of the Fourth Gospel. The results of Neusner's work are used to guide the investigation, with an occasional divergence where such seems warranted for methodological reasons. Such a methodology should both protect against some of the mistakes of which Alexander warns and should provide an appropriate context for an examination of specific points in John, while treating the rabbinic texts with integrity.

John 2.1-11

John 2.1-11 describes the miracle of Jesus turning water into wine at a marriage in Cana. Of particular interest is v. 6, ἦσαν δὲ ἐκεῖ λίθιναι ὑδρίαι ἓξ κατὰ τὸν καθαρισμὸν τῶν Ἰουδαίων κείμεναι. Here the most interesting point is not John's knowledge of Jewish purification, which almost anyone familiar with first-century Palestinian Judaism would have. The important thing is that John is aware of the particular utensils used in purification activities. Stone jars are used because they are not susceptible to uncleanness as are clay or earthenware vessels. This notion in part goes back to Lev. 11.29-38.

> [29]Of the animals that move about on the ground, these are unclean for you: the weasel, the rat, any kind of great lizard, [30]the gecko, the monitor lizard, the wall lizard, the skin and the chameleon. [31]Of all those that move along the ground, these are unclean for you. Whoever touches them when they are dead will be unclean till evening. [32]When one of them dies and falls on something, that article, whatever its use, will be unclean, whether it is made of wood, cloth, hide or sackcloth. Put it in water; it will be unclean till evening, and then it will be clean. [33]If one of them falls into a clay pot, everything in it will be unclean, and you must break the pot. [34]Any food that could be eaten but has water on it from such a pot is unclean, and any liquid that could be drunk from it is unclean. [35]Anything that one of their carcasses falls on becomes unclean; an oven or cooking pot must be broken up. They are unclean, and you are

to begin with applicable, in the mind of the priestly lawyers of Leviticus and Numbers, to the Temple alone. This group, moreover, had other rules which affected who might join and who might not. As I said, these laws formed a protective boundary, keeping in those who were in, keeping out those who were out' (*Judaism: The Evidence of the Mishnah* [Chicago: University of Chicago Press, 1981], pp. 69-70).

to regard them as unclean. ³⁶A spring, however, or a cistern for collecting water remains clean, but anyone who touches one of these carcasses is unclean. ³⁷ If a carcass falls on any seeds that are to be planted, they remain clean. ³⁸But if water has been put on the seed and the carcass falls on it, it is unclean for you.

Here is an explicit statement that if an unclean substance falls into a clay pot, the contents of the vessel become unclean and the pot itself must be destroyed. However, there is no mention of stone vessels. It appears that the move to use stone vessels is a later development.[11] By the time of the Mishnah, it is assumed that stone utensils are best suited for purposes of purification. As Neusner notes, it is important to discern 'what the framers of Mishnah take for granted and treat as settled facts of law and life.'[12] It appears that such is the case with stone vessels and purification. Several discussions in Mishnah confirm such a situation, three of which are examined here. In *Kelim*,[13] a tractate devoted to a discussion of the contamination and purification of vessels, stone utensils appear to occupy a peculiar position. When discussing baking ovens and stoves and their susceptibility to uncleanness *Kelim* 5.11 states:

> A. An oven made of stone or metal is clean [so far as the laws governing clay utensils are concerned]. And it [the metal one] is unclean on account of a vessel made of metal. (Danby: 'Yet this last is susceptible by virtue of being a vessel of metal.' Note: 'It is not susceptible through its airspace like an earthenware vessel; and it can be made clean by immersion.')
> B. [If] it was perforated, damaged, or cracked, [and] one made for it a plaster [lining] or a patch [rim] of clay [to fill up the holes or cracks], it is unclean [as a clay utensil, for it now relies on the clay patch for its functioning].
> C. How much must the perforation be? Sufficient for flame to exude through it.
> D. And so with respect to a stove:
> E. A stove made of stone or of metal is clean.
> F. And it is susceptible to uncleanness on account of being a vessel of metal.

---

[11] Cf. R.E. Brown, *The Gospel According to John*, I (Garden City: Doubleday, 1966), p. 170.

[12] Neusner, *Method and Meaning in Ancient Judaism*, Third Series, p. 75.

[13] That *Kelim* is an appropriate starting place is supported by the suggestions made by Neusner, 'the specific subject matter (Kelim) is especially interesting, because it certainly derives from the interests of pre- and early post-70 Pharisaism, and, because of its substance, is to be regarded as distinctive of the Pharisaic sect. If any anonymous saying may ever be assigned to a pre-70 setting, some of these should stand among them (Neusner, *Method and Meaning in Ancient Judaism*, Third Series, pp. 119-20).

G. [If] it is perforated, damaged, or cracked, [and] one made for it clay props, it is unclean [as a clay utensil].
H. [If] he plastered it with clay, whether on the inside or on the outside, it remains clean.
I. R. Judah says, '[If the plastering is] on the inside, it is unclean, and [if it is] on the outside, it is clean.'[14]

The primary thrust of the discussion concerns that which renders such an oven or stove susceptible to uncleanness. In the midst of this discussion it is twice observed that an oven or stove of stone is not susceptible to uncleanness. This basic premise is not challenged, even though a qualification is made concerning a metal oven or stove which is classified with its stone counterpart. Such a concern is exactly what one would expect to find in pre-70 thought.[15] In addition, the opinion of R. Judah reflects an idea present in the Yavnean period.[16]

A second example of the underlying assumption concerning the suitability of stone jars in purification rites is found in *Besah* 2.3. This tractate is devoted to a discussion of the suitability of various actions on a festival day. In particular, there is a discussion devoted to rendering unclean water as clean. The issue in 2.3 grows out of 2.2 where it is stated that, in general, vessels should be immersed the day before the Sabbath, when the Festival-day follows it:

2.2
A. [If the festival-day] coincided with the day after the Sabbath [Sunday],
B. the House of Shammai say, 'They immerse everything before the Sabbath.'
C. And the House of Hillel say, 'Utensils [are to be immersed] before the Sabbath.
D. But man [may immerse] on the Sabbath [itself].'

2.3
A. And they concur that they effect surface contact between water [which is unclean], contained in a stone utensil [which is insusceptible to

---

[14] Unless otherwise noted, all quotations of the Mishnah are taken from J. Neusner, *The Mishnah: A New Translation* (New Haven: Yale University Press, 1988). However, some explanatory glosses have been retained from his earlier translations for the sake of clarity. When these glosses are retained the original work will be cited. Cf. the translation of J. Neusner, *A History of the Mishnaic Law of Purities: Part One: Kelim* (Leiden: E.J. Brill, 1974), pp. 150-51.

[15] J. Neusner, *Judaism: The Evidence of the Mishnah* (Chicago: University of Chicago Press, 1981), p. 67.

[16] Cf. *Kelim* 25.7-8, which reflects this pre-70 idea. For Neusner's treatment cf. his *Method and Meaning in Ancient Judaism*, Third Series, pp. 155-64.

uncleanness, with the water of an immersion pool] in order to render [the unclean water] clean.
B. But they do not immerse [unclean water in an unclean utensil which contains it].
C. And they immerse [utensils] [if they are to be changed] from one use to another use,
D. or [at Passover] from one association [joined to make use of a single Passover lamb] to another [such] association.[17]

The introduction of the stone vessel is neither contested nor, it seems, unexpected. It does not appear to be a late concern but the assumed way of rendering unclean water clean. It seems to be taken for granted that stone vessels are best suited for these practices. Neusner indicates that the idea of this section of the tractate is pre-70.[18] It is precisely this kind of concern which characterizes the Pharisees.

Another reference to stone utensils is found in *Parah*, a tractate devoted to a discussion of the burning of the Red Heifer. Chapter 3 describes the process of the sacrifice itself and the gathering of the ashes. Of particular interest is 3.2:

A. There were courtyards in Jerusalem, built on rock, and under them was a hollow, [which served as protection] against a grave in the depths.
B. And they bring pregnant women, who give birth there, and who raise the sons there.
C. And they bring oxen, and on them are doors, and the youngsters sit on top of them, with cups of stone in their hands.
D. [When] they reached the Siloam, they descended and filled them, mounted and sat on top of them.
E. R. Yose says, 'From this place did he let down and fill [the cup, without descending].'[19]

Here the emphasis is upon 'provision for the nurture of young priests who have never been made unclean'.[20] A number of precautions are taken to ensure the young priests' clean condition. In this regard, the young priests used cups made of stone 'which are not susceptible to

---

[17] J. Neusner, *A History of the Mishnaic Law of Appointed Times: Part Four* (Leiden: E.J. Brill, 1983), p. 216.

[18] J. Neusner, *A History of the Mishnaic Law of Appointed Times: Part Five: The Mishnaic System of Appointed Times* (Leiden: E.J. Brill, 1983), pp. 152-53.

[19] J. Neusner, *A History of the Mishnaic Laws of Purities: Part Nine: Parah, Translation and Explanation* (Leiden: E.J. Brill, 1976), p. 49.

[20] Neusner, *A History of the Mishnaic Laws of Purities: Part Nine: Parah, Translation and Explanation*, p. 50.

uncleanness'.[21] Although ch. 3, as a whole, seems to reflect an Ushan date,[22] the detail about the cups of stone is assumed, not debated. This fact seems to imply that there was no question as to the use of such utensils in ceremonies demanding the utmost in purity. Such a concern is certainly pre-Ushan.

On the basis of the three Mishnah texts examined here, there should be little doubt that stone jars figured prominently in first-century Jewish purity concerns. Wherever stone utensils appear, their introduction is never controversial, nor is their status questioned. Their insusceptibility to uncleanness is presumed. John reflects an understanding of such subtleties, which suggests his familiarity with Pharisaic and/or emerging rabbinic practices.

John 4.9

Another indication of familiarity with first-century Jewish customs is found in ch. 4, where John narrates a passage of Jesus through Samaria and a conversation with a Samaritan woman. Jesus surprises the woman by requesting her to give him a drink of water. The reasons for her surprise are detailed in an editorial aside found in v. 9: οὐ γὰρ συγχρῶνται Ἰουδαῖοι Σαμαρίταις. This phrase is disputed textually, being omitted by ℵ* D it^{a,b,e,j} cop^{fay}. While some scholars reject the words as a later gloss,[23] representing attitudes of the second century CE, there is good reason to accept the phrase as original.

The external evidence for inclusion is early, well-distributed, and strong. This testimony is even more impressive since it appears that ℵ was corrected before the manuscript left the scriptorium.[24] The corrector includes the editorial aside. In addition, such remarks from the editor occur in a variety of places in the Fourth Gospel (1.38, 41; 3.24; 4.8, 9, 25, 44; 6.1, 71; 7.22; 9.7; 14.22; 18.10; 19.13, 17; 20.9, 16, 14; 21.2, 7, 20). Consequently, inclusion is consistent with the style of the author. As for the reason the phrase is omitted by certain witnesses, it

---

[21] Neusner, *A History of the Mishnaic Laws of Purities: Part Nine: Parah, Translation and Explanation*, p. 50.

[22] Neusner, *A History of the Mishnaic Laws of Purities: Part Nine: Parah, Translation and Explanation*, pp. 44-47.

[23] R. Schnackenburg, *The Gospel according to St. John I* (trans. K. Smyth; New York: Crossroad, 1987), p. 425 n. 19; F. Blass & A. DeBrunner, *A Greek Grammar of the New Testament* (ed. R.W. Funk; Chicago: University of Chicago Press, 1961), p. 104.

[24] B.M. Metzger, *The Text of the New Testament* (Oxford: Oxford University Press, 1968), p. 46.

is probable that the omission is a result of a 'scribal opinion that the statement is not literally exact and therefore should be deleted'.[25] Of course, it is possible that the omission is merely an accident in the copying process.

Animosity between the Samaritans and Jews has a long history. The earliest evidence of Jewish suspicions concerning Samaritan purity is found in 2 Kings 17. In this account of Israel's fall to Assyria, people from Babylon, Cuhah, Avva, Hamath, and Sepharaim are settled in the towns of Samaria. This move results in syncretistic worship. The passage implies that the Samaritans lose their ethnic and cultic purity.[26] Traces of the polemic are found in Ezra, Nehemiah, and Sir. 50.25, 26. 1 Maccabees 6.1, 2 charges the Samaritans with changing the name of their temple to 'The Temple of Zeus, the Friend of Strangers'. Eventually, such tensions led to the destruction of the Samaritan Temple on Mt Gerizim by John Hyrcanus (ca. 128-126 BCE). Nearer the time of the Fourth Gospel, Josephus (Ant. IX 291) alleges that the Samaritans associate with the Jews only when the Jews are prospering. The final break between Samaritans and Jews perhaps occurred as the result of the Bar Kochba War when the Samaritans aligned themselves with the Romans instead of the Jews.[27]

Taken literally, the editorial comment οὐ γὰρ συγχρῶνται Ἰουδαῖοι Σαμαρίταις means that the Jews and Samaritans have no dealings together. It is apparent that such a meaning is unintended, for both 4.8 and 4.27 imply that certain associations take place between the groups. After a thorough examination of συγχράομαι in both Christian and non-Christian texts, David Daube observes:

> The conclusion is obvious. Unless John applies the verb in a way recurring nowhere else – and it may be repeated that this is just possible – it must signify either 'to use something together with another person', or 'to use two things together' ... or simply 'to use something'. The mean-

---

[25] B.M. Metzger, *A Textual Commentary on the Greek New Testament* (United Bible Societies, 1971), p. 206.

[26] Whether 2 Kings 17 is legendary, cf. H.H. Rowley, 'The Samaritan Schism in Legend and History' in *Israel's Prophetic Heritage* (ed. B.W. Anderson & W. Harrelson; London: Preacher's Library, 1962), or represents the actual religious situation of the times, cf. J.D. Purvis, *The Samaritan Pentateuch and the Origin of the Samaritan Sect* (Cambridge, MA: Harvard University Press, 1968), it is clear that 2 Kings 17 is a polemic directed toward the Samaritans which voices Jewish suspicions about Samaritans.

[27] This suggestion is made by L.H. Schiffman, 'The Samaritans in Tannaitic Halakah', a paper presented to the Brown University Conference, 'To See Ourselves As Others See Us' (August, 1984).

ing 'to use two things together', rare in any case, does not fit. Neither does the simple 'to use something'. A statement to the effect that Jews do not make use of Samaritans would be neither true nor – and this is decisive – to the purpose in this particular context: the woman must be referring to some plain unkindness on the part of the Jews. It should be observed, incidentally, that even if this argument is not accepted, we arrive only at 'to use' and at 'to associate on friendly terms'. The result is that, in all probability, the prefix is stressed together with another person: Jews do not use vessels together with Samaritans, most definitely not with Samaritan women.[28]

The parable of the Good Samaritan (Lk. 10.25-37) confirms Jewish prejudices concerning the Samaritans.

However, it is difficult to acquire an accurate picture of first-century Samaritanism from the mishnaic documents. In part, this is due to the fact that many references to the Cuttim, the mishnaic term for the Samaritans, show signs of being Ushan in date.[29] It appears that many of these strong statements enter the rabbinic discussions as a result of the Bar Kochba War. As hostilities increased, the rhetoric, no doubt, escalated. Such a situation is further suggested by the fact that in a number of places the references to Samaritans appear to be unrelated to the immediate discussions.

Despite these hindrances, the Mishnah still yields some information about first-century Jewish attitudes toward the Samaritans. Three passages merit consideration. Neusner suggests:

> The bulk of materials in Berakhot for the period before 70 ... deals with conduct of a meal. At issue are the particular blessings to be said over various kinds of food and in diverse circumstances, and the order of these blessings and of other rituals in connection with a common meal.[30]

He goes on to infer that *Berakoth* 8.8 may very well be pre-70.[31]

> A. [If] wine came to them after the meal,
> B. and there is only that [one] cup –
> C. the House of Shammai say, 'One recites the blessing for the wine, and then one recites the grace after the meal.'
> D. But the House of Hillel say, 'One recites the grace after the meal, and then one recites the blessing for wine.'

---

[28] D. Daube, *The New Testament and Rabbinic Judaism* (New York: Arno Press, 1973), p. 379.
[29] For example, Neusner assigns almost all of the references to the Ushan period.
[30] Neusner, *Judaism: The Evidence of the Mishnah*, p. 53.
[31] Neusner, *Judaism: The Evidence of the Mishnah*, pp. 53-54.

> E. They respond 'Amen' after an Israelite who recites a blessing, but they do not respond 'Amen' after a Samaritan who recites a blessing,
> F. until one hears the entire blessing.

In this reference, the Samaritan, while not above suspicion as the 'amen' must wait until the end of the prayer, is deemed acceptable to be included in a minimum number needed for saying the Common Grace.[32]

An extremely late passage, *Niddah* 4.1, is also helpful in this discussion:

> A. Samaritan women are deemed menstruants from their cradle.
> B. And the Samaritans convey uncleanness to a couch beneath as to a cover above, (Danby: 'uncleanness to what lies beneath them in like degree as [he that has a flux conveys uncleanness] to what lies above him')
> C. because they have intercourse with menstruating women,
> D. And [Because] they [Samaritan women] continue [for seven days] unclean for any sort of blood.
> E. But those [who have contact] with them are not liable for entering the sanctuary, and they do not burn heave offering on their account,
> F. because their uncleanness is in doubt.[33]

This law, which Neusner assigns to an Ushan date, is important because, even though Samaritan women are deemed to be menstruants from the cradle, they are, nonetheless, regarded as Israelites '... therefore their blood is unclean. If they were regarded as wholly outside the community of Israel, their menstrual blood would be deemed clean.'[34]

---

[32] To this might be added *Berakoth* 7.1, which agrees with this basic attitude.

A. Three who ate together are obliged to [appoint one of their number] to invite [the others to recite the grace after the meal].

B. One who ate (1) produce about which there is doubt whether or not it was tithed, or (2) first tithe from which heave offering [of the tithe] was taken, or [who ate] (3) second tithe or [produce which had been] dedicated [to the Temple] and [then] redeemed, or (4) a servant who ate an olive's bulk [of food], or (5) a Samaritan – they may invite others [to say the grace after the meal] on their account [these individuals are included in the required three, A].

C. But one who ate (1) produce which is subject to the separation of tithes, or (2) first tithe from which heave offering [of the tithe] was not separated or [who ate] (3) second tithe or [produce which had been] dedicated [to the Temple] but which was not redeemed, or (4) the servant who ate less than an olive's bulk, or (5) the gentile – they may not invite others [to say the grace after the meal] on their account.

[33] Cf. the translation of J. Neusner, *A History of the Mishnaic Law of Purities: Part Fifteen: Niddah* (Leiden: E.J. Brill, 1976), p. 63.

[34] J. Neusner, *A History of the Mishnaic Law of Purities: Part Twenty-two: The Mishnaic System of Uncleanness* (Leiden: E.J. Brill, 1977), p. 210.

That the Samaritans are regarded as not 'wholly outside the community of Israel' is remarkable in that such a position is clearly in a post-Bar-Kochba situation. If that kind of attitude exists after the wars, in all probability the Samaritans hold a more acceptable position before 70.

Without doubt the most important piece of evidence from Mishnah dealing with the Samaritans is found in a much debated passage, *Shebiith* 8.10:

> A. And they further said before him [R. Aqiba], 'R. Eliezer used to say, "One who eats the bread [baked] by Samaritans is like to one that eats pork."
> B. He said to them, "Shut up [dummies]! I will not tell you what R. Eliezer meant by this".'

From this verse Neusner concludes that by the time of Eliezer 'Pharisaism almost certainly forbade Samaritans' cooking, thus intercourse with them'.[35] Such a state of affairs is exactly as John portrays them. Although the Samaritans are under the broader umbrella of Judaism, they are not fit to engage in ritual relations. Consequently, the Johannine 'Jews' do not use dishes together with them. The Fourth Gospel seems to reflect an accurate knowledge of Pharisaic and/or emerging rabbinic attitudes on this point.

The Sabbath

One of the characteristic practices of Judaism is Sabbath observance. The earliest instructions concerning the Sabbath regulations appear in Exod. 20.8-11:

> [8]Remember the Sabbath day by keeping it holy. [9]Six days you shall labor and do all your work, [10]but the seventh day is a Sabbath to the Lord your God. On it you shall not do any work, neither you, nor your son or daughter, nor your manservant or maidservant, nor your animals, nor the alien within your gates. [11]For in six days the Lord made the heavens and the earth, the sea, and all that is in them, but he rested on the seventh day. Therefore, the Lord blessed the Sabbath day and made it holy.

The primary emphasis of these verses is devoted to the cessation of labor. By the time of Jeremiah (17.21-22) specific stipulations are given to clarify the Torah's intent:

---

[35]J. Neusner, *Eliezer ben Hyrcanus: The Tradition and the Man, Part Two: Analysis of the Tradition, the Man* (Leiden: E.J. Brill, 1973), p. 300.

> [21] This is what the Lord says: Be careful not to carry a load on the Sabbath day or bring it through the gates of Jerusalem. [22] Do not bring a load out of your houses or do any work on the Sabbath, but keep the Sabbath day holy, as I commanded your forefathers.

Again, abstaining from work is stressed, but here a heavy emphasis is placed upon the carrying of burdens and the transferring of them from one place to another. Nehemiah (13.19) builds upon such stipulations and takes precautions to ensure that Sabbath violations would not take place:

> When evening shadows fell on the gates of Jerusalem before the Sabbath, I ordered the doors to be shut and not opened until the Sabbath was over. I stationed some of my own men at the gates so that no load could be brought in on the Sabbath day.

By the first century, there is a proliferation of Sabbath regulations. Perhaps the most extreme understanding is that of the Qumran community. Geza Vermes offers this summary of the Essenes' view:

> The secretary was not only to abstain from labour 'on the sixth day from the moment when the sun's orbe is distant by its own fullness from the gate (wherein it sinks)' (CD 10:15-16 - *DSSE* 112), he was not even to speak about work. Nothing associated with money or gain was to interrupt his Sabbath of rest (CD 10:18-19 - *DSSE* 112). No member of the Covenant of God was to go out of his house on business on the Sabbath. In fact, he was not to go out, for any reason, further than one thousand cubits (about 500 yards), though he could pasture his beast at a distance of two thousand cubits from his town (CD 10:21; 11:5-6 - *DSSE* 112). He could not cook. He could not pick and eat fruit and other edible things 'lying in the fields'. He could not draw water and carry it away, but must drink where he found it (CD 10:22-23 - *DSSE* 112). He could not strike his beast or reprimand his servant (CD 11:6, 12 - *DSSE* 112-13). He could not carry a child, wear perfume or sweep up the dust in his house (CD 11:10-11 - *DSSE* 112-13). He could not assist his animals to give birth or help them if they fell into a pit; he could however, pull a man out of water or fire with the help of a ladder or rope (CD 11:13-14, 16-17 - *DSSE* 113). Interpreting the Bible restrictively (Lev. 23:38), the sect's lawmaker (or makers) commanded him to offer nothing on the Sabbath save the Sabbath burnt offering, and never to send a gift to the Temple by the hand of one 'smitten with any uncleanness permitting him to defile the altar' (CD 11:19-20 - *DSSE* 113). And as has been said earlier (p. 97), he was also never to have intercourse while in the 'city of the Sanctuary' (CD 12:1-2 - *DSSE* 113).

The punishment imposed for profaning the Sabbath and the feasts in any of these ways was not death as in the Bible (Num. 15:35), and not even expulsion as in the Community Rule. It was seven years of imprisonment. 'It shall fall to men to keep him in custody. And if he is healed of his error, they shall keep him in custody for seven years and he shall afterwards approach the assembly (CD 12:4-6 - *DSSE* 114).'[36]

As near as can be determined, the Samaritans were also quite rigid in Sabbath observance,[37] although it is extremely difficult to be certain on this point.

John 5.1-18

On two occasions the Fourth Gospel narrates Sabbath infractions in which Jesus is directly or indirectly involved. The first incident, which occurs in 5.1-18, depicts the healing of a lame man at the pool of Bethesda. Verse 9b adds, as almost an afterthought, ῏Ην δὲ σάββατον ἐν ἐκείνῃ τῇ ἡμέρᾳ. The charge of 'the Jews' is not that it is unlawful to heal on the Sabbath, as might be expected from the Synoptics (cf. Mk 3.1-6), but that οὐκ ἔξεστίν σοι ἆραι τὸν κράβαττόν σου. No doubt this accusation comes on the basis of the biblical prohibition of carrying burdens on the Sabbath. However, it is possible that John reflects knowledge of an emerging concern about public servile labor on the Sabbath. Neusner suggests that certain themes related to the Sabbath begin in a pre-Ushan setting:

> One line of thought concerns the definition of Sabbath boundaries and limits, and it seems likely that the notion of public and private domain – which Scripture requires in referring to a person's not leaving his own home, so implying that here is a domain which is private, and by contrast, one which is public – is extended and refined.[38]

In this regard *Shabbat* 11.1-2 is particularly relevant.

11.1
A. He who throws [an object] from private domain to public domain, [or] from public domain to private domain, is liable.

---

[36] G. Vermes, *The Dead Sea Scrolls: Qumran in Perspective* (Cleveland: Collins & World Publishing Co., 1978), pp. 101-102.

[37] R.J. Coggins, *Samaritans and Jews: The Origins of Samaritanism Reconsidered* (Atlanta: John Knox, 1975), pp. 133-34.

[38] J. Neusner, *A History of the Mishnaic Law of Appointed Times: Part Five: The Mishnaic System of Appointed Times* (Leiden: E.J. Brill, 1983), p. 71.

B. [He who throws an object] from private domain to private domain, and public domain intervenes –
C. R. Aqiba declares [him] liable [to a sin offering].
D. And sages exempt [him].

11.2
A. How so?
B. Two balconies opposite one another [extending] into the public domain –
C. he who stretches out or throws [an object] from this one to that one is exempt.
D. [If] both of them were [different private domains on the same side of the street and] at the same story,
E. he who stretches [an object over] is liable, and he who throws from one to the other is exempt.
F. For thus was the mode of labor of the Levites:
G. Two wagons, one after the other, in the public domain –
H. they stretch beams from this one to that one, but they do not throw [them from one to the other].
I. The bank of a cistern and the rock ten handbreadths high and four broad –
J. he who takes [something] from that area or who puts something onto that area is liable.
K. [If they were] less than the stated measurements he is exempt.[39]

In assessing the date of themes in these verses Neusner observes:

> This pericope assigns to Yavneans as exercised in the second level analysis of the matter of not transporting an object from one domain to another. Certainly Ushans know full well that doing so is prohibited; their problems take that fact for granted. It is not at all farfetched therefore to maintain that at the outset, long before the time of Yavneh, comes the distinction between public and private domain. Yavneans take up the subsidiary question before us. Ushans introduce the notion of a neutral domain. There is no reason to doubt that the present entry belongs in Yavneh.[40]

It appears that the former lame man is guilty of just such a violation, i.e. transporting an object from one domain to another. In the former lame man's case, the pool, with its five covered colonnades would be considered his private domain, since he is said to have been confined

---

[39] J. Neusner, *A History of the Mishnaic Law of Appointed Times: Part One: Sabbath* (Leiden: E.J. Brill, 1981), p. 109.

[40] Neusner, *A History of the Mishnaic Law of Appointed Times: Part One: Sabbath*, pp. 65-66.

there for 38 years. In walking from the pool to the Temple, he moves from a private domain to a public one.[41] If the issue of public and private domain begins when Neusner suggests, John's knowledge of such views is not unlikely.

John 9

The other Sabbath incident is recorded in ch. 9, where a man born blind receives his sight. In this pericope it is Jesus who is charged with breaking the Sabbath. Again, the specific accusation of healing on the Sabbath is missing.[42] Instead, the Evangelist focuses attention upon the actions of Jesus in the healing. Namely, Jesus makes mud from spittle and dirt, places it upon the blind man's eyes and instructs him to go wash in the pool of Siloam. On three occasions John mentions Jesus' actions (vv. 6-7, 11, 15). It appears, then, that the Fourth Gospel wishes to draw attention to the actions of Jesus in the course of the healing as well as to the miracle itself. More than likely the alleged Sabbath violations concern three acts of labor: kneading (making mud), healing (placing the mud upon the eyes), and anointing (with the intent of facilitating the healing). Each such action is documented in the Mishnah. Unfortunately, in each case the passages are assigned Ushan dates by Neusner.[43] There is no quarrel here, with the attribution of these tractates to a late date. However, two pieces of evidence must be borne in mind. First, the prohibition against kneading, *Shabbat* 7.2, and some of the prohibitions against healing on the Sabbath come from anonymous traditions in the Mishnah, *Shabbat* 22.5, 6. While these traditions seem to cohere with the later materials, it is notoriously difficult to demonstrate conclusively the date of such materials. Second, as Neusner notes, 'I need hardly repeat that innumerable facts of the tractate go back long before 70.'[44] It does not exceed the bounds of plausibility to suggest that the issues under consideration in John 9 belong to that set of innumerable facts. When the independent evidence of the Synoptics is added to John 5 and 9, there is little doubt that Sabbath regulations, particularly in regards to healing, were in the

---

[41] Carrying a mat is specifically condemned in later mishnaic formulations (*Shabbath* 10.5).

[42] However, such an attitude can be detected here, which coheres with the Synoptic materials.

[43] Neusner, *The Mishnaic System of Appointed Times: Part Five*, pp. 69-70, 79.

[44] Neusner, *The Mishnaic System of Appointed Times: Part Five*, p. 80.

process of development during the first century CE. John demonstrates a knowledge of such tendencies.

The Fourth Gospel demonstrates still another point of acquaintance with Sabbath regulations. While teaching at the Feast of Tabernacles (7.14-24), Jesus responds to charges of Sabbath violations by pointing to the practice of his opponents, who allow circumcision to take precedence over the Sabbath. By this time, such an attitude appears to be an accepted procedure. Torah (Lev. 12.3) simply states:

> On the eighth day the boy is to be circumcised.

There is no mention of the Sabbath nor the relationship between the rite of circumcision and Sabbath observance. However, there is plenty of evidence that at the time of the final compilation of the Fourth Gospel the question of circumcision and the Sabbath is a living issue. *Shabbat* 19.1 is particularly helpful:

> A. R. Eliezer says, 'If one did not bring a utensil [used for circumcision] on the eve of the Sabbath, he brings it openly on the Sabbath.'
> B. And in the time of the danger, one covers it up in the presence of witness.
> C. And further did R. Eliezer state, 'They cut wood to make coals to prepare an iron utensil [for circumcision].'
> D. An operative principle did R. Aqiba state, 'Any sort of labor [in connection with circumcision] which it is possible to do on the eve of the Sabbath does not override [the restrictions of] the Sabbath, and that which is not possible to do on the eve of the Sabbath does override [the prohibitions of] the Sabbath.'[45]

Eliezer ben Hyrcanus grants much flexibility to the one who performs circumcision on the Sabbath. It is taken for granted in the passage that circumcision overrides the Sabbath. Eliezer goes beyond this premise to permit the circumcision knife to be made on the Sabbath. This attitude is consistent with Eliezer's view of the Sabbath and Passover (cf. *Pesahim* 6.2). Neusner affirms the reliability of this tradition by observing, 'We may therefore assign to Eliezer both the principle that the Passover and circumcision override the Sabbath, and the view that that principle is interpreted in a most lenient way.'[46]

Corroborating evidence is found in *Shabbat* 19.3.

---

[45] J. Neusner, *The Mishnaic System of Appointed Times: Part One*, p. 170.
[46] Neusner, *Eliezer ben Hyrcanus*, p. 179. Also cf. Neusner, *The Mishnaic System of Appointed Times*, p. 114. It should be noted that Eliezer declares guilty one who mistakenly circumcises an infant on the Sabbath (*Shabbat* 19.4).

A. They wash off the infant.
B. both before the circumcision and after the circumcision,
C. and they sprinkle him,
D. by hand but not with a utensil.
E. R. Eleazar b. Azariah says, 'They wash the infant on the third day after circumcision [even if it] coincides with the Sabbath,
F. "since it says, And it came to pass on the third day when they were sore (Gen. 34:25)."'
G. [If the sexual traits of the infant are a matter of] doubt, or [if the infant] bears the sexual traits of both sexes, they do not violate the Sabbath on his account.
H. And R. Judah permits in the case of an infant bearing the traits of both sexes.[47]

Eleazar ben Azariah not only allows for circumcision on the Sabbath, which is implied but not stated, he also allows for therapeutic washings on the Sabbath. These ideas, which come from the same general time as the Fourth Gospel, cohere well with Jn 7.21-23.[48]

John 5.31-47 and 8.13

On two occasions John portrays discussions about the validity of self-witness. In 5.31-47, Jesus brings up the issue by acknowledging, 'If I testify about myself, my testimony is not valid.' He then proceeds to demonstrate that his words are due to his witnesses, the Father (vv. 36-44), John the Baptist (vv. 33-35), Moses (v. 45), and the Scriptures (vv. 46-47). The Pharisees initiate the discussion in 8.13 by accusing, 'You are testifying on your own behalf, your testimony is not valid'. On this occasion, Jesus argues that his words are valid on the basis of his Father's testimony.

The Torah is consistent in requiring more than one witness in capital crimes:

> Anyone who kills a person is to be put to death as a murderer only on the testimony of witnesses. But no one is to be put to death on the testimony of only one witness (Num. 35.30).
> On the testimony of two or three witnesses a man shall be put to death, but no one shall be put to death on the testimony of only one witness (Deut. 19.15).

---

[47] Neusner, *The Mishnaic System of Appointed Times: Part One*, p. 171.
[48] Cf. T. Zahavy, *The Traditions of Eleazar ben Azariah* (Missoula, MT: Scholars Press, 1977), pp. 40, 288.

> One witness is not enough to convict a man accused of any crime or offense he may have committed. A matter must be established by the testimony of two or three witnesses (Deut. 19.15).

It is clear that in these cases the law requires more than one witness, but it says nothing about non-capital cases or the validity of self-witness. Torah, by itself, does not explain the issues of John 5 and 8. Jesus is not on trial for a capital crime but is arguing that he is who he claims to be. Two tractates from the Mishnah shed light upon these verses. A passage which contains ideas attributed to the pre-Yavnean period is found in *Yebamot* 15.1-2:[49]

> 15.1
> A. The woman who went, she and her husband, overseas –
> B. there was peace between her and him, and the world was at peace –
> C. and she came and said, 'My husband died' –
> D. she may remarry.
> E. 'My husband died' –
> F. she may enter into levirate marriage.
> G. [If] there was peace between her and him but war in the world –
> H. strife between him and her, but the world was at peace –
> I. and she came and said, 'My husband died' –
> J. she is not believed.
> K. R. Judah says, 'Under no circumstances is she believed unless she came in tears, with the garments torn [as a sign of mourning].'
> L. They said to him, 'All the same [are one who cries wearing torn garments] – she may remarry [under the stated circumstances].'
>
> 15.2
> A. The House of Hillel say, 'We have heard [that the woman's testimony concerning the death of her husband is accepted] only in a case in which she comes back from the grain harvest and is in the same territory.' 'And [these facts are accord with] a case which actually took place.'
> B. Said to them the House of Shammai, 'All the same are one who comes home from the grain harvest, and one who comes home from harvesting olives, and one who comes from cutting grapes, and one who comes home from one province to another.'
> C. 'Sages spoke about the grain harvest only because that is commonplace.'
> D. The House of Hillel reverted and taught the law in accord with the opinion of the House of Shammai.[50]

---

[49] J. Neusner, *A History of the Mishnaic Law of Women: Part Five: The Mishnaic System of Women* (Leiden: E.J. Brill, 1980), p. 71.

[50] J. Neusner, *A History of the Mishnaic Law of Women: Part One: Yebamot* (Leiden: E.J. Brill, 1980), pp. 192-93.

The debate between the Houses revolves around the issue of the widow's self-witness. The Shammaites argue for a lenient understanding of the self-witness and eventually convince the House of Hillel of their position. This testimony does not involve a capital crime but demonstrates that one could in certain circumstances testify concerning his or her own situation and that such testimony is valid.

A passage containing Yavnean ideas[51] focuses on still another aspect of self-witness in *Ketubot* 1.6-9:

1.6
A. He who marries a woman and did not find tokens of virginity
B. she says, 'After you betrothed me, I was raped, and your field has been flooded,'
C. and he says, 'Not so, but it was before I betrothed you, and my purchase was a bargain made in error' –
D. Rabban Gamaliel and R. Eliezer say, 'She is believed.'
E. R. Joshua says, 'We do not depend on her testimony. But lo, she remains in the assumption of having sexual relations before she was betrothed and of having deceived him,
F. until she brings evidence to back up her [contrary] claim.'

1.7
A. She says, 'I was injured by a piece of wood,'
B. and he says, 'Not so, but you have been laid by a man' –
C. Rabban Gamaliel and R. Eliezer says, 'She is believed.'
D. And R. Joshua says, 'We do not depend on her testimony. But lo, she remains in the assumption of having been laid by a man,
E. until she brings evidence to back up her [contrary] claim.'

1.8
A. [If] they saw her [sexually] conversing with a man in the market,
B. [and] they said to her, 'What is the character of this one?'
C. [and she said,] 'It is Mr. So-and-so, and he is a priest' –
D. Rabban Gamaliel and R. Eliezer say, 'She is believed.'
E. And R. Joshua says, 'We do not depend on her testimony. But lo, she remains in the assumption of having had sexual relations with a Netin or a mamzer,
F. until she brings evidence to back up her claim.'

1.9
A. [If] she was pregnant, and they say to her, 'what is the character of this foetus?'
B. [and she said,] 'It is by Mr. So-and-so, and he is a priest' –

---

[51] J. Neusner, *A History of the Mishnaic Law of Women: Part Five*, pp. 87-88.

C. Rabban Gamaliel and R. Eliezer say, 'She is believed.'

D. And R. Joshua says, 'We do not depend on her testimony. But lo, she remains in the assumption of having been made pregnant by a Netin or mamzer,

E. until she brings evidence to back up her claim.'[52]

The groups of authorities are consistent in the disagreements concerning the claim of a woman who had been raped. Eliezer and Gamaliel consistently accept her claim, without corroborating evidence, while Joshua wants her to prove her claim.

The basic agreement with the perspective of the Fourth Gospel is clear. The issue of the validity of self-witness, in non-capital situations, characterizes discussions before the Wars and at Yavneh.

John 13.8-9

Another aspect of John's familiarity with Pharisaic and/or emerging rabbinic practices may be contained in Jn 13.8-9. When Jesus attempts to wash Peter's feet, Peter misunderstands his Master's action as merely an hospitable gesture and refuses the washing in the strongest possible language (Οὐ μὴ νίψῃς μου τοὺς πόδας εἰς τὸν αἰῶνα).[53] When Jesus responds that Peter will have no μέρος with him if he does not submit to the footwashing, the disciple again misunderstands. It appears that he now believes Jesus is talking about ritual purity. Therefore, Peter suggests particular kinds of washing which, in his way of thinking, are much more needed than washing the feet. He is willing to submit to the footwashing as an attempt to request more extensive washings (13.9).

It is significant that Peter does not request a bath, but offers particular parts of his body for washing. One of the points most obvious concerning the Gospels' Pharisees is that they are scrupulous about washing their hands before eating. Mk 7.3 confirms this fact.

---

[52] Neusner, *A History of the Mishnaic Law of Women: Part Two: Ketubot* (Leiden: E.J. Brill, 1980), pp. 18-19.

[53] Blass, Debrunner, Funk (*A Greek Grammar of the New Testament and Other Early Christian Literature* [Cambridge: Cambridge University Press, 1961], p. 184) note, 'Οὐ μή with the aorist subjunctive or future indicative, both of which are classical, is the most definite form of negation regarding the future.' H.E. Dana and Julius R. Mantey concur, 'we can now say unreservedly that the negatives were doubled for the purpose of stating denials or prohibitions for the purpose of stating denials or prohibitions emphatically' (*A Manual Grammar of the Greek New Testament* [Toronto: Macmillan, 1957], p. 266).

> The Pharisees and all the Jews do not eat unless they give their hands a ceremonial washing, holding to the tradition of the elders.

Not only do the disciples come under the scrutiny of the Pharisees on this issue (cf. Mk 7.1-23; Mt. 15.1-20), but Jesus himself is challenged on this point (cf. Lk. 11.37-54). As Neusner observes, 'There can be no doubt whatsoever that Pharisees washed hands before eating.'[54] According to Josephus (*Wars* II 133) the Essenes also practiced some sort of washing before meals (ζωσάμενοί τε σκεπάσμασιν λινοῖς οὕτως ἀπολούονται τὸ σῶμα ψυχροῖς ὕδασιν).

The reason for washing the hands becomes explicit during the Yavnean period. *Yadayim* 3.1-2 states:

> 3.1
> A. He who pokes his hands into a house afflicted with [a Father of uncleanness] –
> B. 'his hands are in the first remove of uncleanness,' the words of R. Aqiba.
> C. And sages say, 'His hands are in the second remove of uncleanness.'
> D. Whoever imparts uncleanness to clothing, when in contact [with them], imparts uncleanness to the hands –
> E. 'So that they are in the first remove of uncleanness,' the words of R. Aqiba.
> F. And sages say, 'So that they are in second remove of uncleanness.'
> G. Said they to R. Aqiba, 'When do we find that the hands are in the first remove of uncleanness under any circumstances whatsoever?'
> H. He said to them, 'And how is it possible for them to be in the first remove of uncleanness without his [whole] body's [being] made unclean, outside of the present case [which is exceptional]?'
> I. 'Food and utensils which have been made unclean by liquids [which food and utensils are in the second remove] impart uncleanness to the hands so that they are in the second remove of uncleanness,' the words of R. Joshua.
> J. And sages say, 'That which is made unclean by a Father of Uncleanness [and so in the first remove] imparts uncleanness to the hands [up to the wrist]. [That which has been made unclean] by an Offspring of Uncleanness [made unclean by something in the first remove and so itself is in the second remove] does not impart uncleanness to the hands.'
> K. Said Rabban (Simeon b.) Gamaliel, 'M 'SH B: A certain woman came before her father.
> L. 'She said to him, "My hands entered the [unclean] contained airspace of a clay utensil."'

---

[54] J. Neusner, *A History of the Mishnaic Law of Purities: Part Twenty-two: The Mishnaic System of Uncleanness* (Leiden: E.J. Brill, 1977), p. 89.

M. 'He said to her, "My daughter, By what had it been made unclean [a Father or an Offspring]."
N. "But I did not hear what she said to him."
O. Said sages, 'The matter is clear. That which has been made unclean by a Father of Uncleanness imparts uncleanness to the hands. [That which has been made unclean] by an Offspring of Uncleanness does not impart uncleanness to the hands.'

3.2
A. 'Whatever imparts unfitness to heave offering imparts uncleanness to hands, putting them into the second remove of uncleanness."
B. One hand [which is made unclean] imparts uncleanness to the second,' the words of R. Joshua.
C. And sages say, 'That which is unclean in the second remove does not put [something else into a state of uncleanness at] the second remove.'
D. He said to them, 'And do not sacred scriptures, unclean in the second remove, impart uncleanness to hands?'
E. They said to him, 'They do not draw inferences about rulings of the Torah from rulings of scribes, nor about rulings of scribes from rulings of Torah, nor about rulings of scribes from rulings of scribes.'[55]

Akiba and Joshua debate the degree to which the hands may be unclean. It is in the Yavnean period that the whole question of the removes of uncleanness becomes prominent. For example, solid food which comes into contact with a Father of Uncleanness (e.g. corpse, menstruant woman, man with an issue) is rendered unclean in the first remove. That which touches food unclean in the first remove is rendered unclean in the second remove. That which touches food unclean in the second remove is rendered unclean in the third remove, and so on.[56] In *Yadayim* 3.1, Akiba argues that the hands may become unclean in the first remove, while Joshua maintains that the hands may become unclean in the second remove. Eventually, the hands are regarded as always being unclean in the second remove, unless they had just been washed. The ultimate implication of all this is that the hands can render the entire person unclean (cf. *Hagigah* 2.5; *Eduyoth* 3.2).

When Peter requests that his hands be washed, he is suggesting that if any part of the body is in constant need of ritual washing, it is the

---

[55] Cf. the translation of J. Neusner, *A History of the Mishnaic Law of Purities: Part Nineteen: Tebul Yom and Yadayim* (Leiden: E.J. Brill, 1977), pp. 137-40.

[56] Neusner, *A History of the Mishnaic Law of Purities: Part Nineteen: Tebul Yom and Yadayim*, p. 160.

hands. From their experience with the Pharisees, the disciples would, no doubt, be quite sensitive to this practice.[57]

John 18.28

A final passage relevant for this inquiry is located in Jn 18.28, where the Jews are taking Jesus from Caiaphas to Pilate:

> Then they led Jesus from Caiaphas to the praetorium of the Roman governor. By now it was early morning, and to avoid ceremonial uncleanness the Jews did not enter the palace; they wanted to be able to eat the Passover.

The major issue here concerns the uncleanness that would be contracted by entrance into the praetorium. According to the Torah, uncleanness which disqualifies one from observing the Passover, or postponing its observance for a month, is that which results from contact with a corpse. Numbers 9.10-12 states:

> [10]"Tell the Israelites: "When any of you or your descendants are unclean because of a dead body or are away on a journey, they may still celebrate the Lord's Passover. [11]They are to celebrate it on the fourteenth day of the second month at twilight. They are to eat the lamb, together with unleavened bread and bitter herbs. [12]They must not leave any of it till morning or break any of its bones. When they celebrate the Passover, they must follow all the regulations."'

---

[57] Peter's suggestion that the head be washed is also significant. In ancient Greek κεφαλή came to represent the whole person, life itself. For this reason curses are called down upon the head. The same basic idea develops in the LXX where, 'The head can be used as the equivalent of the person and his(/her) whole existence.' Therefore, κεφαλή is used to express the whole person and the part (standing for the whole) where blessings (Gen. 48.14, 18; 49.26), curses (2 Sam. 1.10; 3.29; Ezek. 33.4; Joel 3.4, 7; Obad. 15), dust/ashes (Josh. 7.6; Neh. 9.1; Lam. 2.10), and anointings (Exod. 29.8; Lev. 8.12; 1 Sam. 10.1) are placed. In the New Testament two uses are significant: anointing (Mt. 6.17; 26.17; Mk 14.3; Lk. 7.46) and judgment (Acts 18.6). Peter's request that his head be washed expresses the view that the head represents the person. Since this is the case, it makes sense to Peter that an efficacious washing be devoted to the head. According to Peter's viewpoint, both the hands and the head are appropriate for such significant washings.

Clearly, this passage places emphasis upon the way in which contact with a corpse disqualifies one from observing Passover at the appointed time. It is also obvious that there is no mention of Gentile dwellings.

However, by the time of Mishnah this issue has emerged. *Oholot* 18.7-9 gives evidence of such a concern:

> 18.7
> A. He who buys a field in Syria, near the land of Israel, if he can enter it in a state of cleanness, it is clean, and it is subject to the laws of tithes and the seventh year. If he cannot enter it in a state of cleanness, it is unclean, but it [still] is liable to the laws of tithes and the seventh year.
> B. Dwelling places of gentiles [in the Land of Israel] are unclean.
> C. How long must [the gentiles] remain in them for them to require examination [to determine their status]? Forty days, even though there is no woman with him.
> D. And if a slave or an [Israelite] woman was watching over it, it does not require an examination.
>
> 18.8
> A. What do they examine? The deep drains and the foul waters.
> B. The House of Shammai say, 'Also the rubbish heaps and loose dirt.'
> C. And the House of Hillel say, 'Any place which the pig or the weasel can reach does not require examination.'
>
> 18.9
> A. Colonnades are not subject to the law applying to the dwellings of gentiles.
> B. Rabban Simeon b. Gamaliel says, 'A city of gentiles which was laid waste is not subject to the law applying to the dwellings of gentiles.'
> C. East of Qisrin and west of Qisarion [Caesarea Philippi] are graveyards. [The area] east of Akko was in doubt, and sages declared it clean.
> D. Rabbi and his court voted concerning Qeni and declared it clean.

Although the dwellings of gentiles is not an important aspect of this tractate,[58] the idea that a gentile's dwelling is unclean is quite ancient, perhaps finding its origin before the first century CE.[59] The declaration that gentile dwellings are unclean is made upon the assumption that gentiles dispose of abortions there. Mention of a concern about the contracting of ritual uncleanness in Jn 18.28 demonstrates that the

---

[58] J. Neusner, *The Mishnah before 70* (Atlanta: Scholars Press, 1987), p. 89.

[59] Neusner, *The Mishnah before 70*, p. 89. Cf. also J. Neusner, *A History of the Mishnaic Law of Purities: Part Twenty-two: The Mishnaic System of Uncleanness* (Leiden: E.J. Brill, 1977), pp. 55 and 116.

Fourth Gospel exhibits an intimate acquaintance with this purity idea which was important to Pharisaic Judaism.

Conclusions and Implications

Two major conclusions may be drawn from this survey. First, this investigation has shown that the Fourth Gospel exhibits an acquaintance with many of the issues that were of concern for pre-90 Pharisaism and/or emerging rabbinic Judaism. Second, in each instance, the emphasis of the Fourth Gospel coincides with mishnaic ideas to which Neusner assigns a pre-90 date. Although simple, such conclusions are not unimportant but have significant implications for several areas of research.

1. The close parallel between the Fourth Gospel's acquaintance with Pharisaic and/or emerging rabbinic thought and the mishnaic materials to which Neusner assigns a pre-90 date indicates that Alexander's recommendations concerning the use of rabbinic texts by New Testament scholars is on the right track and worth pursuing. Consequently, one methodological implication of this investigation is that Neusner's work can be used to guide and inform New Testament exegesis as it seeks to utilize rabbinic texts.

2. The accuracy of the Fourth Gospel's knowledge of some of the practices and thought of Pharisaism and/or emerging rabbinic Judaism and the inert quality of the facts[60] may serve to confirm the observations of several Johannine scholars that either the author or the source(s) of the Fourth Gospel originated in Palestine.[61]

3. Identification of the Fourth Gospel's acquaintance with several aspects of Pharisaic and/or emerging rabbinic thought may also have implications for those who wish to gauge the extent to which the Fourth Gospel seeks to engage the Judaism which emerged after 70.[62]

---

[60] On the distinction between inert facts which may be important but not central to a religious system and facts which form the centerpieces of religious systems cf. J. Neusner, 'The Absoluteness of Christianity and the Uniqueness of Judaism: Why Salvation is not of the Jews', *Int* 43 (1989), pp. 18-31.

[61] Cf. most recently, M. Hengel, *The Johannine Question* (London: SCM Press, 1989), pp. 109-14. Cf. also Robinson, *The Priority of John*, pp. 36-122; R. Kysar, *The Fourth Evangelist and His Gospel* (Minneapolis: Augsburg, 1975), pp. 144-46; Smalley, *John: Evangelist and Interpreter*, pp. 68-74.

[62] For recent attempts cf. W.A. Meeks, 'The Man from Heaven in Johannine Sectarianism', *JBL* 91 (1972), pp. 44-72; J.L. Martyn, *The Gospel of John in Christian History* (New York: Paulist, 1978); D. Rensberger, *Johannine Faith and Liberating Community* (Philadelphia: Westminster, 1988).

4. If, as many Johannine scholars believe, the Fourth Gospel was written in Asia Minor between 85-95 CE then some of these rabbinic ideas may be a bit older than even Neusner has suggested. Enough time must have transpired either for the author and/or sources to have traveled from Palestine to Asia Minor or for the ideas to have been transmitted to Asia Minor via the Jewish community. In either case, the rabbinic ideas contained in the Fourth Gospel not only pre-date the Fourth Gospel's composition, but may be as old as or older than the Johannine traditions themselves. Consequently, a responsible utilization of rabbinic texts by New Testament scholars may even assist rabbinic scholars in assigning more precise dates to some of the Pharisaic and/or emerging rabbinic ideas.

9

The Spirit in the Fourth Gospel: Narrative Explorations

The pneumatology of the Fourth Gospel has been of more than passing interest to a variety of New Testament scholars over the years, with a great deal of attention devoted to John's use of the somewhat enigmatic term παράκλητος.[1] Several things have encouraged my own interest in this topic. First, for over two decades now, it has been my happy privilege to teach a course on the Fourth Gospel at least once a year. One of the results of this extensive and regular engagement with the text has been a general dissatisfaction with a number of approaches to this topic from a purely historical critical perspective. My own thoughts about the Spirit in the Fourth Gospel have taken shape in part as a result of these times of dialogue with a variety of graduate students from all around the world. Second, the kind invitation from Southeastern College in Lakeland, Florida to deliver the Staley Lectures in 1997 afforded me an opportunity to formalize some of my ideas about the Holy Spirit/Paraclete in the Farewell Materials of the Fourth Gospel.[2]

---

[1] Cf. for example the work of H. Windisch, *The Spirit-Paraclete in the Fourth Gospel* (trans. J.W. Cox; Philadelphia: Fortress, 1968); F. Mussner, 'Die johanneische Parakletsprüche und die apostolische Tradition', *BZ* 5 (1961), pp. 56-70; O. Betz, *Der Paraklet: Fürsprecher im häretischen Spätjudentum, im Johannes-Evangelium und in neu gefundenen gnostischen Schriften* (AGSU 2; Leiden: Brill, 1963); R.E. Brown, 'The Paraclete in the Fourth Gospel', *NTS* 13 (1966-67), pp. 113-32; G.W. Locher, 'Der Geist als Paraklet: Eine exegetisch-dogmatische Besinnung', *EvT* 26 (1966), pp. 565-79; G. Johnston, *The Spirit-Paraclete in the Gospel of John* (Cambridge: Cambridge University Press, 1970); U.B. Müller, 'Die Parakleten-vostellung im Johannesevangelium', *ZTK* 71 (1974), pp. 31-77; F. Porsch, *Pneuma und Wort: Ein exegetischer Beitrag zur Pneumatologie des Johannesevangeliums* (Frankfurt: J. Knecht, 1974); R. Schnackenburg, *The Gospel according to St John*, III (trans. D. Smith & G.A. Kon; New York: Crossroad, 1982), pp. 138-54; E. Frank, *Revelation Taught: The Paraclete in the Gospel of John* (ConBNT 14; Lund: Gleerup, 1985); G.M. Burge, *The Anointed Community: The Holy Spirit in the Johannine Tradition* (Grand Rapids: Eerdmans, 1987); J. Breck, *Spirit of Truth: The Origins of Johannine Pneumatology* (Crestwood, NY: St Vladimir's Seminary Press, 1991).

[2] Cf. now J.C. Thomas, *He Loved Them until the End: The Farewell Materials in the Gospel according to John* (Pune, India: Fountain Press, 2003).

Third, a recent dialogue with Max Turner and his new book on the Spirit[3] has served to prod me further along in my reflection about the pneumatology of the Fourth Gospel. Fourth, as a Pentecostal I am continually amazed at how differently any number of biblical and theological topics appear when approached afresh from more distinctively Pentecostal approaches.[4] My own conviction is that there is much to learn about the Spirit's role in the Fourth Gospel from a Pentecostal perspective.[5]

For the most part, previous investigations devoted to the pneumatology of the Fourth Gospel have focused upon the topic from the methodological perspective of historical criticism. While such attempts have contributed a great deal to an understanding of the Spirit's role in the Fourth Gospel, these enquiries have usually not paid sufficient attention to the story of the Holy Spirit as it unfolds within the narrative of the Fourth Gospel itself. Unfortunately, this lack of attention to the narrative has resulted in a number of false turns in seeking clarity on the role of the Holy Spirit in the Fourth Gospel. What has been missing is a reading of the Fourth Gospel which informs the reader of the Spirit's role as the narrative unfolds.[6] In what follows, I seek to offer some reflections on the shape of the pneumatology of the Fourth Gospel from the perspective of narrative analysis. Rather than being a summary of extensive published research, this essay is offered as an initial exploration of this pneumatological territory. Limitations of space necessitate that what follows be no more than a survey of the relevant texts.

John 1.32-33

The first mention of the Spirit's activity in the Fourth Gospel comes in the testimony of John (the Baptist) with regard to Jesus' identity. Here

---

[3] Cf. J.C. Thomas, 'Max Turner's *The Holy Spirit and Spiritual Gifts: Then and Now* (Carlisle: Paternoster Press, 1996): An Appreciation and Critique', *JPT* 12 (1998), pp. 3-22; Max Turner, 'Readings and Paradigms: A Response to John Christopher Thomas', *JPT* 12 (1998), pp. 23-38.

[4] Cf. J.C. Thomas, 'Pentecostal Theology in the Twenty-First Century', *Pneuma* 20 (1998), pp. 3-19 esp. pp. 13-19.

[5] For an overview of an earlier dialogue on the pneumatology of the Fourth Gospel from a Pentecostal perspective cf. W.G. MacDonald, 'Exegetical Circles: An Innovation at the Charlotte Meeting', *Pneuma* 4 (1982), pp. 19-31.

[6] Cf. the helpful studies of R.A. Culpepper, *The Anatomy of the Fourth Gospel* (Philadelphia: Fortress, 1983); J.L. Staley *The Print's First Kiss: A Rhetorical Investigation of the Implied Reader in the Fourth Gospel* (SBLDS 82; Atlanta: Scholars Press, 1988); esp. J. Becker, 'Das Geist- und Gemeindeverständnis des vierten Evangelisten', *ZNW* 89 (1998), pp. 217-34. For the application of this approach to two specific pneumatological texts in the Fourth Gospel cf. P. Letourneau, 'Le double don de l'Esprit et la Christologie du quatrième évangile', *Science et Esprit* 44 (1992), pp. 281-306.

John testifies that he saw the Spirit come down as a dove and remain upon Jesus, who has previously been identified as the Lamb of God in 1.29. Not only is this descent of the Spirit God's way of revealing Jesus' identity to John, who in turn reveals it to others, but it is also the means by which it is revealed that the one upon whom the Spirit remains is the one who will baptize with the Holy Spirit. At least two things are important about this text for the unfolding of the Fourth Gospel's pneumatological story. First, it is truly remarkable that Jesus, who earlier in the narrative is clearly identified as the pre-existent Logos, should be described as being anointed by the Spirit. Given the Logos' identification with and as God (1.1, 18), his role in the creation of all things (1.2), and his description as the unique Son of God (1.14, 18), the reader is tempted to wonder why such a one would need an anointing by the Spirit. In point of fact, many readers of the Fourth Gospel appear to be so overwhelmed by the Logos Christology of the Fourth Gospel that they scarcely even notice the Christological implications of 1.32-33.[7] Yet, standing alongside the rather obvious Logos Christology is an equally obvious Spirit Christology. Such a narrative placement indicates that for John, these Christological understandings are complementary rather than contradictory.[8] Second, it is only natural that the one upon whom the Spirit remains is the one who will baptize with the Holy Spirit. In the Fourth Gospel, it is only after the descent of the Spirit upon Jesus is described that John (the Baptist) identifies Jesus as the Holy Spirit Baptizer. Whether or not Jesus will baptize individuals with the Holy Spirit within the confines of the narrative of the Fourth Gospel (something which none of the Synoptics appear to describe despite the citation of this same prophecy), it is clear from this point that Jesus is connected with the Spirit in a unique way.

John 3

In the passage devoted to Jesus' dialogue with Nicodemus, Jesus discloses (3.3) that in order to see the kingdom of God it is necessary to be born "from above" (ἄνωθεν). This statement rather obviously is to be taken as clarification of the words of the Fourth Gospel's Prologue. In 1.12 the reader learns that all who received him (that is 'believed in his name') were given the authority to become children of God. John

---

[7] Cf. R. Bultmann, *The Gospel of John* (trans. G.R. Beasley-Murray, R.W.N. Hoare, & J.K. Riches; Philadelphia: Westminster, 1971), p. 92 n. 4; E. Schweizer, 'πνεῦμα', *TDNT*, VI (ed. G. Kittel & G. Friedrich; trans. G.W. Bromiley; Grand Rapids: Eerdmans, 1968), p. 438.

[8] On this cf. the very perceptive comments of C.H. Pinnock, *Flame of Love: A Theology of the Holy Spirit* (Downers Grove, IL: IVP, 1996), pp. 80-111.

goes on to make clear that this birth is not the result of physical, sexual, or human means but comes from God himself (1.13).[9] Thus, Jn 3.3 begins to reveal how one becomes a child of God.[10] This birth, appropriately enough, comes 'from above'. As Jesus continues this explanation he indicates that one must be born of water and Spirit in order to enter the Kingdom of God. The debate which surrounds the meaning of water in this verse is well known, with a variety of interpretive options offered.[11] While uncertainty with regard to the meaning of water in 3.5 exists, there appears to be little uncertainty as to the meaning of Spirit. The following verses (3.6-8) continue to emphasize, by means of appeal to the Spirit, that birth from above is a necessity (v. 7). The Spirit (πνεῦμα), like the wind (πνεῦμα), blows where it will, it comes from another world – the world of God. There can be little question that this text serves to define for the reader the way in which being born of God is accomplished. Therefore, the reader learns that all who become children of God in the Fourth Gospel, all who believe in his name, are born of the Spirit. Despite the intricate connection with Jesus' exaltation on the cross (3.14-15), such a spiritual experience is already available to those who hear Jesus. In the verses that follow it becomes apparent that this spiritual birth, which comes from God not humankind, brings eternal life (3.16-21). Jesus, who is sent by God (from the realm of God!), is the agent of such a work of the Spirit, for he has received the Spirit without measure (3.34), a clever allusion both to Jesus' place of origin (from above, which is the place of the Spirit) and to his anointing by the Spirit in 1.32-33. The fact that Jesus' role as Spirit Baptizer is not emphasized at this point may suggest that perhaps his function as Spirit agent is multi-dimensional.

John 4

The emphasis on the Spirit continues in Jesus' dialogue with the Samaritan woman in John 4. Using double meaning, a favorite Johannine literary technique, Jesus speaks of ὕδωρ ζῶν (v. 10), a phrase which can

---

[9] For a history of the interpretation of John 1.12-13 cf. M. Vellanickal, *The Divine Sonship of Christians in the Johannine Writings* (Rome: Biblical Institute Press, 1977), pp. 105-12.

[10] Vellanickal, *The Divine Sonship of Christians in the Johannine Writings*, p. 163.

[11] For some of the options cf. Z.C. Hodges, 'Water and Spirit – John 3:5', *BibSac* 35 (1978), pp. 206-20. Cf. esp. the intriguing suggestion that water has at least a secondary reference to baptism as a boundary marker by D. Rensberger, *Johannine Faith and Liberating Community* (Philadelphia: Westminster, 1988), pp. 66-70. For a history of interpretation of this passage cf. I. de la Potterie & S. Lyonnet, *The Christian Lives by the Spirit* (trans. J. Morriss; Staten Island, NY: Alba House, 1970), pp. 1-12; Vellanickal, *The Divine Sonship of Christians in the Johannine Writings*, pp. 179-86.

mean 'running water', as the running water of a stream as opposed to the still water of a cistern, as well as 'living water'. The 'living water' of which Jesus speaks is not the stream of running water at the bottom of Jacob's well, as the woman supposes. Rather this water can quench thirst forever, becoming in the one who drinks 'a well of water leaping up into eternal life' (v. 14). Just as there is a connection between 'birth from above' (by means of the Spirit) and eternal life in ch. 3, so here there is a connection between drinking of the 'living water' and eternal life (v. 14). The reader of the Fourth Gospel is not surprised by such an association, given the earlier significant occurrences of water to this point in the narrative.[12]

Sensing that Jesus is more than a weary pilgrim, the woman poses a question which according to Samaritan expectations would be answered by the prophet like Moses (the Taheb); where is the true place of worship? Jesus' surprising response both rejects Jerusalem and this mountain (Mt Gerizim) as the true place of worship (v. 21), and reveals that by cutting themselves off from important parts of redemptive history, the Samaritans find themselves in an inferior position to the Jews with regard to salvation (v. 22). At this point Jesus reveals that 'an hour comes and now is when true worshipers will worship the Father in Spirit and Truth' (v. 23). Here the reader learns that the Spirit is not only the means by which one is 'born from above', but the Spirit also makes true worship possible. One implication of this statement is that true worship of the Father is possible only for those who are children of God, those born from above by means of the Spirit. It is not surprising that true worship of the Father is also 'in Truth'. For the reader of the Fourth Gospel, mention of 'Truth' is a subtle reference to Jesus,[13] for he is the one who is full of grace and truth (1.14), out of whose fullness all have received one grace after another (1.16), the one who has given grace and truth (1.17). It naturally follows that 'the one who does the truth comes to the Light' (3.21). Such an interpretation of 'Truth' in 4.23 is not only appropriate in the light of these previous associations of truth with Jesus in the narrative, but is also in keeping with the later explicit claim of Jesus in 14.6, 'I am the Way, the Truth, and the Life'. Thus, it would not appear to be going too far to suggest that true worship in this text has a trinitarian dimension (at least in embryonic form) – an understanding not unlike that found in Rev. 1.4-5.

---

[12] J.C. Thomas, *Footwashing in John 13 and the Johannine Community* (JSNTS 61; Sheffield: JSOT Press, 1991), pp. 88-89. Cf. now the comprehensive study by L.P. Jones, *The Symbol of Water in the Gospel of John* (JSNTS 145; Sheffield: Sheffield Academic Press, 1998).

[13] I am indebted to my colleague R.H. Gause, for drawing my attention to this interpretive possibility. Cf. the discussion in Burge, *The Anointed Community*, pp. 193-95.

From the beginning of the Fourth Gospel the reader has known of the unique relationship which exists and the unique nature of the identity between God (the Father) and the Word (Jesus). Now in 4.24 the reader learns of the special identity that is shared by God and the Spirit when Jesus says, 'God is Spirit'. Such a statement reveals that not only is the Spirit essential to true worship, owing to the Spirit's role in the believer's birth from above, but the Spirit is also essential to true worship owing to the Spirit's shared identity with God.

Unlike Nicodemus, who disappears from the narrative in ch. 3 without believing, many (πολλοί) of the Samaritans believe in Jesus (4.39-42). Given the earlier clues in the narrative, the Samaritans' belief means that they become children of God, they experience eternal life by drinking of the living water, and are able now to worship the Father in Spirit and Truth.

John 6.63

The next reference to the Spirit in the Fourth Gospel is found in 6.63 just after the bread of life discourse. On this occasion a connection is made between Jesus' scandalous words and the Spirit. Earlier in the passage Jesus speaks of the necessity of eating his flesh and drinking his blood in order to have eternal life (6.53). In 6.63 the reader learns that there is a very tight interplay between eating the flesh and drinking the blood on the one hand and the work of the Spirit on the other. Just as drinking of the living water brings eternal life, so eating his flesh and drinking his blood is tied to eternal life. Jesus' statement that his words are Spirit and life are consistent with the fact that from the beginning of the Fourth Gospel Jesus (the Word) is closely identified with life (1.3-4), and in 14.6 he will make this identification explicit. Neither is it surprising that the one upon whom the Spirit descends and remains (1.32), the one who will baptize with the Holy Spirit (1.33), and the one who has been given the Spirit without measure (3.34) should speak words which bring life.[14] Such a statement reinforces the idea of the close relationship that exists between the Spirit and the Truth suggested earlier in 4.23. In contrast to the many disciples who depart and no longer walk with Jesus, Peter, as spokesman for the Twelve, reveals that he and they have paid careful attention to Jesus' teaching at this point and believed in him (6.68).

---

[14] Porsch (*Pneuma und Wort*, pp. 210-12) argues that Jesus conveys the Spirit through his words.

John 7.37-39

Another clear reference to the Holy Spirit found in the Book of Signs (John 1-12) occurs in 7.39, a text filled with interpretive challenges. The narrative context of the verse is the last great day of the feast (of Tabernacles). Jesus stands and cries out inviting all who are thirsty to come and drink. But at this point in the passage there arises a host of questions, all of which have some bearing upon the meaning of the text. The major questions concern the punctuation of the text, the location of the Scripture quotation in v. 38, the antecedent of the pronoun 'his' in the phrase 'out of *his* belly', and the nature of the Spirit's work mentioned in v. 39. While limitations of space naturally preclude a full discussion of these questions, the following observations may be offered.

With regard to the punctuation of the text, the main question is, does the phrase 'the one who believes in me', which in the Greek text is grammatically independent, stand with that which precedes it in v. 37 or with that which follows it in v. 38? If the former, the sentence would read:

> Jesus stood and cried saying, 'If anyone thirsts let that one come to me and drink, the one who believes in me. Just as the Scripture said, "Out of his belly will flow rivers of living water".'

If the latter, the sentence would read:

> Jesus stood and cried saying, 'If anyone thirsts let that one come to me and drink. The one who believes in me, just as the Scripture said, "Out of his belly will flow rivers of living water".'

Although certainty on this issue may very well be beyond the reach of the interpreter, it appears that on balance the former option is to be preferred – if only slightly – owing to the punctuation found in the earliest papyri,[15] this preference among a number of the earliest patristic writers, and certain grammatical considerations with regard to the phrase 'the one who believes'.[16]

The second question focuses on the identity of the person to whom the pronoun αὐτοῦ has reference in the phrase 'out of his belly'. From whom will the rivers of living water flow; from the one who believes in him or from Jesus? If 'the rivers of living water' are promised to

---

[15] Cf. the punctuation of these verses in $\mathfrak{p}^{66}$ and $\mathfrak{p}^{75}$ in *The Complete Text of the Earliest New Testament Manuscripts* (ed. P.W. Comfort & D.P. Barrett; Grand Rapids: Baker, 1999), pp. 405 and 578-79.

[16] On this whole question cf. the very helpful discussion in M.J.J. Menken, *Old Testament Quotations in the Fourth Gospel: Studies in Textual Form* (Kampen: Pharos, 1996), pp. 189-92. For an opposing view cf. Burge, *The Anointed Community*, pp. 88-93.

gush forth from the one who believes in Jesus, this experience seems to be somewhat different from the 'well of water leaping up into eternal life' promised to the Samaritan woman.[17] If the rivers gush forth from Jesus, this would be in accord with some of Jesus' previous promises as Spirit agent. Although it is often assumed that a decision in favor of the former punctuation option necessitates that αὐτοῦ in v. 38 must have reference to the believer,[18] this conclusion does not necessarily follow. Given the wilderness imagery of the Fourth Gospel, the fact that later in the narrative blood and water do indeed flow from Jesus' side (19.34), and the fact that the believers are to receive the Spirit after Jesus is glorified, it would appear safe to assume that the rivers of living water will flow from Jesus' belly.[19] However, given the Fourth Gospel's love of double meaning and the ambiguity of the text it should not be thought impossible that the reader would see a reference both to Jesus and the one who believes in him in this verse.

As to the location of the Scripture to which v. 38 refers, it is important to remember that John does not always make clear the exact location of a reference to Scripture (cf. 20.9). Thus the exact location may not be as important as is sometimes thought. Nor is it always the case that a single text serves as the referent of the Scripture citation. Rather, 'Scripture may be found to ground *the entire matrix of thought* found in vv. 37-38'.[20] Despite a host of other texts proposed as the Scripture to which v. 38 refers, Deut. 8.15-16 may merit serious consideration as a viable candidate, given the way its content matches so remarkably the content of the Fourth Gospel.[21]

> He led you through the vast and dreadful desert, that thirsty and waterless land, with its venomous snakes and scorpions. He brought you water out of hard rock. He gave you manna to eat in the desert, something your fathers had never known, to humble and test you so that in the end it might go well with you.

It is significant that this text makes reference to three events in Israel's history to which the Fourth Gospel also makes reference: the serpent

---

[17] Cf. the comments of H.M. Ervin, *Spirit Baptism: A Biblical Investigation* (Peabody, MA: Hendrickson, 1987), pp. 171-73. Cf. also, D.N. Bowdle, *Redemption Accomplished and Applied* (Cleveland: TN; Pathway Press, 1972), p. 83.

[18] R.E. Brown, *The Gospel according to John I-XII* (Garden City, NY: Doubleday, 1966), pp. 320-23; Porsch, *Pneuma und Wort*, p 58.

[19] Again, Menken's discussion [*Old Testament Quotations in the Fourth Gospel*, pp. 192-94] is a model of clarity. For the view that the rivers of living water come from the disciples cf. Johnston, *The Spirit-Paraclete in the Gospel of John*, pp. 7-9.

[20] As pointed out by D.A. Carson, *The Gospel according to John* (Leicester: IVP, 1991), pp. 325-26.

[21] For this suggestion cf. A.D. Palma, 'Out of *whose* innermost being?' *Advance* 12 (August 1976), p. 23.

in the wilderness (3.14), manna from heaven (6.22-59), and water from the rock (7.38). However, given the general uncertainties surrounding this text, it might be best to leave open the question of the identity of the Scripture.

But even with these tentative answers what is the meaning of the words found in v. 39?

> He said this concerning the Spirit which those who believed in him were about to receive. For the Spirit was not yet, because Jesus had not yet been glorified.

What do the words 'the Spirit was not yet' (οὔπω γὰρ ἦν πνεῦμα) mean in this verse? Clearly, they cannot be taken literally to mean that the Spirit was not yet in existence.[22] Nor does the reader understand them to mean that the Spirit can only work apart from Jesus - after his glorification - for the Fourth Gospel has gone to great lengths to indicate that the Spirit is extraordinarily active in Jesus and his ministry.[23] Nor does it appear that the reader would be inclined to take this statement to mean that the Spirit was not yet active in the lives of those who already believe in Jesus. It has been made very clear that those who believe in Jesus are given the authority to become children of God (1.12), a birth which takes place only by means of the Spirit (3.5); that those who drink of the living water which Jesus gives will have 'a well of water leaping up into eternal life' (4.14); and that those who so experience the Spirit ('an hour is coming and now is') are true worshippers who worship the Father in Spirit and Truth (4.23-24). The unequivocal belief of the Samaritans and the disciples in Jesus, as revealed within the narrative world of the Fourth Gospel, strongly suggests that the Spirit is already active to some extent in their lives, a reality that will be reaffirmed later (14.17).

A reading of 7.39 which does not take into account the text's narrative context can result in a one-dimensional understanding of the Spirit's activity in John, an interpretation which the narrative itself tends to subvert. What then does the phrase 'the Spirit was not yet' mean? It is interesting to note that if Jesus is the source of the rivers of living water, this imagery fits rather well with the imagery found in Jesus' dialogue with the Samaritan woman. There the reader learns that those who drink of the living water will have in themselves 'a well of water leaping up to eternal life'. As is revealed from the dialogue in John 4, it is clear that a well is not a source of water but rather a chan-

---

[22] However, cf. the attempt to take the phrase literally by H. Boer, *Pentecost and Missions* (Grand Rapids: Eerdmans, 1975), pp. 77-87.

[23] Despite his acknowledgement of this fact, D. Holwerda (*Holy Spirit and Eschatology in the Gospel of John* [Kampen: Kok, 1959], pp. 1-2) still regards the Holy Spirit as 'primarily a post-ascension figure in the Gospel of John'.

nel by which one gains access to a source of water. Just as Jacob's well tapped into a stream or river of subterranean running water, so the one who drinks of the living water which Jesus provides has within him/herself a well which taps into the living water which has its origin in Jesus. It comes as little surprise, then, when the reader learns in 7.38-39 that rivers of living water come from Jesus. On this reading, this passage is in continuity with that which has come before it in the narrative. At the same time, there also appears to be some degree of discontinuity with what precedes, for the reader would not expect from the imagery of 'a well of water leaping up into eternal life' to find 'rivers of living water' as the source but a river of living water. Therefore, the imagery found in 7.38-39 is pregnant with meaning. While the rivers of living water certainly include the idea of salvation (and that in Jesus there is an abundant supply – as stated in 3.34), it suggests that there is more in store for those who believe in him than they have previously understood. This dimension of the Spirit's work (which at this point in the narrative is not explained) will only be experienced after Jesus' glorification. With this, the reader detects a rather subtle shift in emphasis on the Spirit's work in the Fourth Gospel. The tension created by the statement in v. 39 that 'the Spirit was not yet' despite the Spirit's activity earlier in the narrative, prepares the reader for the extensive teaching about the future role of the Paraclete which awaits in John 14-16 and may be a way of reminding the reader that Jesus is the one who will baptize in the Holy Spirit (1.33).

John 11.33 and 13.21

The Greek term πνεῦμα occurs in both Jn 11.33 and 13.21, but in neither of these texts is there a reference to the Holy Spirit. Rather they refer to Jesus' (human) spirit, which is part of his life as a human being. With both uses one is not far from a description of the inward emotions of Jesus. The significance of this use of πνεῦμα is seen later in the Fourth Gospel.

John 14.15-31

The story of the Spirit in the Fourth Gospel continues in the Farewell Materials. In fact, the bulk of the Fourth Gospel's teaching about the Spirit is found in chs. 14-16, where Jesus' farewell discourse includes two major sections and one minor one devoted to this subject. The first Paraclete passage is found in 14.15-31.[24] Throughout this passage there is an emphasis upon Jesus' departure, the relationship between loving Jesus and keeping his words, and the work of the Paraclete during Jesus' absence. In point of fact, the work of the Paraclete in this section is linked both to Jesus' departure and the keeping of his words. Several aspects of the Spirit's nature and identity are revealed in this section.

First, the Paraclete comes from the Father as a result of Jesus' own request. Jesus, who had earlier encouraged the disciples to ask the Father for anything in his name (14.13-14), states in v. 16 that 'Even I (κἀγώ) will ask', a statement that serves to encourage the disciples to ask. It might at first glance be surprising that the one who is anointed by the Spirit, who has been given the Spirit without measure and who will baptize with the Spirit, would have to ask that the Father send the Paraclete. However, it should be remembered that in the Fourth Gospel Jesus does nothing on his own but only those things which the Father desires that he do.

Second, the Paraclete is called 'another Paraclete' in v. 16 implying that Jesus himself functions as a Paraclete, a point made explicit in 1 Jn 2.1. Not only does this statement point to the intimate relationship of Jesus and the Paraclete, but it also serves to underscore the fact that the Spirit is to function in a way analogous to Jesus in the lives of the disciples. While Jesus is soon to depart, the Paraclete will be with them forever.

Third, it comes as no surprise to the reader that the Paraclete is called the Spirit of Truth, for earlier in the Fourth Gospel Jesus is said to be 'full of truth' (1.14) and identifies himself as 'the Truth' in 14.6. This title or name underscores the intimate connection between Jesus and the Spirit, indicates the trustworthiness of the Spirit, and reminds the reader of the relationship between Spirit and Truth found in 4.23.

Fourth, like Jesus (cf. 1.10-11), the Paraclete is not received by the world for he is not seen or known by it (v. 17). In contrast, the believers know the Spirit for he remains among them and *is* in them (v. 17).[25] Picking up on the hints in 7.37-39, this statement at once affirms

---

[24] The origin of the term παράκλητος has been much debated. For an intriguing proposal with regard to the word's etymology cf. G.E. Ladd, *A Theology of the New Testament* (Grand Rapids: Eerdmans, 1974), p. 293. Cf. also the works cited in n. 1.

[25] Following the textual tradition which supports the present tense verb ἐστιν rather than the future tense ἔσται. The manuscript support for ἐστιν [𝔓⁶⁶* B D* W] is slightly better than that for ἔσται [𝔓⁶⁶ᶜ 𝔓⁷⁵ᵛⁱᵈ ℵ A Dᵇ L], given the combination of B and D* with the original reading of 𝔓⁶⁶, and in this context ἐστιν would not only be the more difficult reading, but also the reading which best explains the origin of the other reading since a scribe would be more likely to change the present to the future to conform to the future context of the promise of the coming Paraclete.

the basic continuity between the Spirit's work with the disciples to this point in the narrative, while pointing to the discontinuity of his future work. Not only has the Paraclete been present among the disciples through the ministry of the Spirit-anointed Jesus, but he is also in those (mainly the disciples, but others as well) who, believing in his name, have become children of God through birth by the Spirit, who have drunk of the living water and have *in* them 'a well of living water leaping up into eternal life'.[26]

Fifth, in the latter part of the text (v. 26) the Spirit is called the Paraclete, the Holy Spirit, and is identified as coming from the Father. In this section, which gives pride of place to the disciples' relationship to the words of Jesus, the Spirit will do two things. (1) He will teach the disciples all things. The reader of the Fourth Gospel knows that one of Jesus' primary roles is that of teacher (1.38; 3.2; 6.59; 7.14, 28, 35; 8.20; 11.28; 13.13, 14; cf. also 18.20; 20.16). Thus the Paraclete, the Spirit of Truth, the one who is sent by the Father, will do precisely what Jesus has done - teach! This function is necessitated by Jesus' departure. (2) The Paraclete will remind the disciples of the things which Jesus said to them. Although the disciples believe throughout the Fourth Gospel, they do not always fully understand what Jesus has done or said. The first time the reader learns this is after Jesus has cleansed the Temple (2.22). It also occurs in 12.16 and is implied in 13.7. In 14.26 Jesus promises that the Paraclete will play an active role in the disciples' memory and understanding. It is significant that both in 2.22 and 12.16 the disciples remember after the resurrection/glorification of Jesus. In retrospect the reader is able to understand that it is the Paraclete who is responsible for the disciples remembering the things which Jesus said and did.

John 15.26

In Jesus' words about the world's hatred of him and the disciples, the Paraclete is mentioned again. Here the reader learns that while the Paraclete comes from the Father, Jesus himself has a role in his sending. Identified again as the Spirit of Truth, emphasizing the intimacy between the Spirit and the Truth, it is now revealed that the Paraclete will be active in his witness to Jesus. Although the text does not explicitly state that the Spirit will inspire the witness of the disciples, the following verses (15.27-16.4a) strongly suggest that the disciples will

---

[26]For an interpretation which builds on the future tense ἔσται and sees the presence of the Spirit among the disciples as confined to the ministry of Jesus cf. I. de la Potterie, 'Parole et esprit dans S. Jean', *L'Évangile de Jean: Sources, Rédaction, Théologie* (ed. M. de Jonge *et al.*: Leuven: Leuven University Press, 1987), pp. 192-93.

not experience the persecution of a hating world passively, but will offer witness to Jesus which is anointed by the Spirit.[27]

John 16.4b-15

The second major passage devoted to the role of the Paraclete in the Farewell Discourse (16.4b-15) follows those words about the witness of the Paraclete and the disciples. This passage, also set in the context of Jesus' departure - an event which brings grief to the disciples (vv. 5-6), for the first time reveals that Jesus must depart in order for the Paraclete to come (v. 7). Although unexpected, this revelation coincides with the fact that the Paraclete will in many ways be to the disciples what Jesus has been. While the promise of the Paraclete in the first passage focused primarily upon his work within the circle of believers, this passage focuses primarily upon his role in relation to the world, a theme introduced in 15.26.

The Fourth Gospel consistently presents the story of Jesus as a trial, with terms like testimony, interrogation, belief, and judgment appearing frequently. Continuing this motif v. 8 reveals that the Paraclete will serve as a legal representative. However, instead of being an advocate, as the term Paraclete is sometimes translated, he will serve as a prosecuting attorney, convicting the world on three counts: sin, righteousness, and judgment. On more than one occasion in the Fourth Gospel, Jesus' Jewish opponents confront him about the matter of sin, even accusing him of being a sinner (cf. esp. 9.24). The Paraclete will convict the world of sin because they did not believe in Jesus. Not only will the world be proven wrong about its accusations, it will also discover that its refusal to believe Jesus is itself sin (16.9)!

Righteousness ($\delta\iota\kappa\alpha\iota\sigma\sigma\nu\nu\eta$) is not used here as in Paul, where the term conveys the idea of being judged as righteous. The emphasis in 16.10 is clearly connected to the validity of Jesus' claims that he is going to the Father: 'And concerning righteousness because I am going to the Father and you will see me no longer'. The reader has been prepared for this idea as early as 5.30, where Jesus in speaking of his authority says, 'I am not able to do anything of myself; just as I hear I judge, and my judgment is righteous ($\delta\iota\kappa\alpha\iota\alpha$), because I do not seek my will but the will of the one who sent me'. This language, no doubt, includes the vindication of Jesus' frequent claims that he is going to the one who sent him and the Jews will be able to see him no longer (7.33; 8.14, 21; 13.3, 33; 14.4, 28; 16.5). As such, the language of 16.10 includes the vindication of his claims with regard to origin as well.

---

[27] For this idea cf. Holwerda, *Holy Spirit and Eschatology in the Gospel of John*, pp. 51-52.

The world will also be convicted of judgment because the ruler of this world stands judged already. Such a statement about judgment has already been signaled in 12.31, where in connection with the lifting up of the Son of Man the time has come for the world's judgment and its leader to be driven out. Clearly, the ultimate vindication of Jesus' person and work is envisaged here.

In addition to his work as prosecuting attorney, this section returns to the idea of the Paraclete's work among the disciples. Owing to the sorrow in the disciples' hearts, Jesus is unable to tell them all that he desires. Thus, much of the additional teaching they need must be conveyed by the Paraclete who may be trusted, for he is again identified as the Spirit of Truth (v. 13). Specifically, the Paraclete will guide into all truth. While such teaching will not be at variance with what Jesus has earlier taught, owing to the fact that the Paraclete's teaching will come from Jesus, it does not appear that Jesus anticipates this additional teaching by the Paraclete be identical to what precedes it. Not only is Jesus the origin of the teaching, but the Paraclete's teaching will also glorify Jesus. Verse 15 underscores the essential unity of the Father, Son, and Spirit.

John 19.30

Another reference to πνεῦμα occurs in a text devoted to the death of Jesus. Immediately following Jesus' final words on the cross ('It is completed!'), bowing his head παρέδωκεν τὸ πνεῦμα ('he gave [up] the Spirit'). It is quite certain that, at one level, the reader would take these words as describing Jesus' expiration, his giving up his life, an idea which goes back to 10.17-18 where Jesus speaks of laying down his life voluntarily. This use of πνεῦμα is also in accord with its use in 11.33 and 13.21. However, it is just possible that this phrase would convey a bit more to the reader as the phrase παρέδωκεν τὸ πνεῦμα apparently is never used in antiquity in a strict sense for 'to die'.[28] What more than Jesus' death might be present in this phrase? Owing to the fact that παραδίδωμι rather properly means 'to hand over, give, or deliver',[29] it is possible to take the phrase as having reference to the bestowal of the Spirit by Jesus at the moment of his exaltation/glorification on the cross. Attempts to see here, in the light of 19.26-27, a bestowal of the Spirit which constitutes the foundation of the community of believers

---

[28] Letourneau, 'Le double don de l'Esprit et la Christologie du quatrième évangile', p. 283. Cf also Porsch, *Pneuma und Wort*, p. 328.

[29] W. Bauer, W. Arndt, F.W. Gingrich & F.W. Danker, *A Greek-English Lexicon of the New Testament and Other Early Christian Literature* (Chicago: University of Chicago Press, 2nd edn, 1958), p. 619.

appear to go beyond the evidence of the text.[30] Based on the distinctive formula used to describe Jesus' death, the connections between water and Spirit in 7.37-39 and (apparently) in 19.34, as well as the numerous promises of the coming of the Paraclete, it may very well be that this phrase points to the future bestowal of the Spirit in a symbolic or proleptic way.[31]

John 20.22

The Fourth Gospel's pneumatological story concludes in 20.22, the meaning of which has been widely debated. The location of this final pneumatological text occurs very near the narrative's conclusion. The broader context (20.19-23) describes an encounter between the risen Jesus and his disciples who are behind locked doors on account of the 'fear of the Jews'. Given its previous connotations in the narrative, mention of the 'fear of the Jews' suggests to the reader that the disciples are in danger of not remaining in Jesus and his word (cf. 8.31). After speaking peace to the disciples, he shows them his side and hands, thereby prompting great rejoicing, and again he speaks peace to them. Jesus then commissions the disciples to be sent just as the Father had sent him. At this point 'he breathed (on them?) and says to them, λάβετε πνεῦμα ἅγιον ('Receive the Holy Spirit') and authorizes them to forgive and retain sins.

The primary question facing the interpreter at this point is how would the reader understand the phrase 'Receive the Holy Spirit'? If the aorist imperative λάβετε is taken to signify an 'immediate and forthright reception of the Holy Spirit',[32] the phrase 'Receive the Holy Spirit' might be interpreted in one of several ways. On this interpretation of λάβετε the phrase could be taken as having reference to (1) the disciples' regeneration or birth by the Spirit,[33] (2) an equipping of the

---

[30] For this position cf. esp. M.-A. Chevallier, *Souffle de Dieu: Le Saint-Esprit dans le Nouveau Testament*, II (Paris: Beauchesne, 1990), pp. 409-564; J.P. Heil, *Blood and Water: The Death and Resurrection of Jesus in John 18-21* (CBQMS 27; Washington, DC: Catholic Biblical Association, 1995), pp. 102-109; Letourneau, 'Le double don de l'Esprit et la Christologie du quatrième évangile', pp. 281-306.

[31] For this general idea cf. Brown, *The Gospel according to John XIII-XXI*, pp. 951; Burge, *The Anointed Community*, pp. 134-35. *Contra* Porsch (*Pneuma und Wort*, pp. 332-39).

[32] So F.L. Arrington, 'The Indwelling, Baptism, and Infilling with the Holy Spirit: A Differentiation of Terms', *Pneuma* 3 (1981), p. 5.

[33] H.M. Ervin, *Spirit Baptism: A Biblical Investigation* (Peabody, MA: Hendrickson, 1987), pp. 14-21 and B. Aker, '"Breathed": A Study on the Biblical Distinction Between Regeneration and Spirit-Baptism', *Paraclete* 17 (Summer, 1983), pp. 13-16. This suggestion is also made by J.D.G. Dunn, *Baptism in the Holy Spirit* (Philadelphia: Westminster, 1970), p. 180 and appears to be followed by H.D. Hunter, *Spirit-Baptism:*

disciples for ministry, especially with regard to the forgiving of sins,[34] (3) a special measure of the Spirit given to the disciples before Pentecost owing to their unique situation in salvation history,[35] (4) a gift of the Spirit which enables them to have Easter faith,[36] (5) a gift of the Spirit which later assumes the functions of the Paraclete,[37] or (6) the Johannine Pentecost.[38]

However, most of these views fail to convince owing, to textual indicators in the narrative of the Fourth Gospel which are at odds with taking λάβετε to demand an immediate and forthright reception of the Spirit. One of the more significant textual indicators is the fact that earlier in the narrative Jesus reveals the Paraclete cannot come unless he departs. It is only after Jesus' departure that he will send the Paraclete (16.7), which may suggest that Jesus' glorification of which the Fourth Gospel speaks in 7.37-39 includes more than his exaltation on the cross. In point of fact, Jn 17.5 seems to state just this point.[39] Therefore, while the grammar might be taken to imply that the Spirit was received at this time (in 20.22), there are indications in the narrative that the Paraclete will not come until Jesus' departure.

Another aspect of the narrative can be seen to subvert such an understanding of λάβετε. Despite the fact that Jesus commands the disciples to 'Receive the Holy Spirit', their later conduct and behavior do not reveal any perceptible change. Most notably, instead of bearing Paraclete-inspired witness to Jesus, something implicitly anticipated in 15.26-16.4, the disciples are still hiding behind locked doors in the very next pericope (20.26) after they have received the command to receive the Spirit. This is a clear indication that their 'fear of the Jews' had not diminished. Thus, despite Jesus' commissioning of the disciples

---

A Pentecostal Alternative (Lanham, MD: University Press of America, 1983), p. 110. Cf. also a modified version of this view in M. Turner, *The Holy Spirit and Spiritual Gifts*, pp. 97-102.

[34] Windisch, *The Spirit-Paraclete in the Fourth Gospel*, pp. 33-34. Cf. also Chevallier, *Souffle de Dieu*, pp. 430-38; Letourneau, 'Le double don de l'Esprit et la Christologie du quatrième évangile', pp. 281-306; and apparently B. Aker, 'Gospel of John', *Dictionary of the Pentecostal and Charismatic Movements* (ed. S.M. Burgess & G.B. McGee; Grand Rapids: Zondervan, 1988), p. 510. Holwerda (*Holy Spirit and Eschatology in the Gospel of John*, p. 24) views 20.22 as describing the ordination of the apostles for their future ministry.

[35] S.M. Horton, *What the Bible Says about the Holy Spirit* (Springfield, MO: Gospel Publishing House, 1976), pp. 130-33.

[36] De la Potterie, 'Parole et esprit dans S. Jean', pp. 196-201.

[37] Porsch, *Pneuma und Wort*, pp. 375-76.

[38] Cf. among others Brown, *John XIII-XXI*, pp. 1038-39; Dunn, *Baptism in the Holy Spirit*, pp. 173-82; Burge, *The Anointed Community*, pp. 123-31; R. Schnackenburg, *The Gospel according to St John*, III (trans. D. Smith & G.A. Kon; New York: Crossroad, 1987), pp. 324-25.

[39] On this cf. Turner, *The Holy Spirit and Spiritual Gifts*, p. 95.

to be sent as he was sent by the Father and to forgive sins (20.21-23), the disciples remain inactive in this regard. This is the case despite Jesus' command to 'Receive the Holy Spirit'. Furthermore, there are no other anticipated activities of the Paraclete described after and as a result of Jesus' command in 20.22.[40]

In addition to these narrative indicators, the way in which 20.22 resembles 7.39 and 14.17 should also be noted. In contrast to the texts which speak of drinking from the living water (Spirit) or being born of the Spirit, these texts use the terminology of receiving to describe this Spirit experience. The fact that 'receiving' vocabulary is reserved for a post-resurrection experience of the Spirit suggests that the reader is to discern a difference in the work of the Spirit here described and the Spirit's work as described earlier in the narrative. Thus it appears that the Fourth Gospel makes room for distinct works of the Spirit.

If the narrative of the Fourth Gospel itself subverts an interpretation of 20.22 which calls for an immediate and forthright reception of the Spirit, what does the phrase 'Receive the Holy Spirit' mean to the reader? Given the fact that the Paraclete will come only after Jesus' departure, that there are no signs of the Paraclete's activity after the command to receive the Spirit in 20.22, and that the Fourth Gospel not only allows for but appears to expect distinct works of the Spirit, it appears that Jesus' action of breathing and utterance of the phrase 'Receive the Holy Spirit' should be taken as a symbolic, parabolic, and/or proleptic action which points beyond itself to a reception of the Spirit that is not described in the narrative.[41] Such a reading coincides with Jesus' anticipated work as Spirit Baptizer (1.33), the coming of the Paraclete after Jesus' departure (16.7), and the anticipated activities of the disciples after the Paraclete arrives (14-16; 20.21-23).[42] From the standpoint of narrative analysis, such an understanding of Jn 20.22 is less problematic than views which see an immediate and forthright reception of the Spirit in this verse.[43]

---

[40] Cf. Turner, *The Holy Spirit and Spiritual Gifts*, pp. 96-97.

[41] An interpretive position that goes back at least as far as Theodore of Mopsuestia. Cf. G.E. Ladd, *A Theology of the New Testament*, p. 297; D. Guthrie, *New Testament Theology* (Downers Grove: IVP, 1981), p. 534; Carson, *The Gospel according to John*, pp. 651-55; D. Petts, *The Holy Spirit: An Introduction* (Mattersey: Mattersey Hall, 1998), pp. 47-48; and apparently R.H. Gause, *Living in the Spirit: The Way of Salvation* (Cleveland, TN: Pathway Press, 1980), p. 66.

[42] In this the Fourth Gospel is not unlike the Synoptics which also leave the promise that Jesus will baptize with the Holy Spirit unfulfilled within their respective narratives.

[43] However, cf. Turner (*The Holy Spirit and Spiritual Gifts*, pp. 97-102), who understands the Spirit's work in Jn 20.22 as an eschatological new creation, which later will include the work attributed by Jesus to the Paraclete.

Concluding Remarks

This study has sought to contribute to a better understanding of the pneumatology of the Fourth Gospel from the perspective of narrative analysis. These reflections are offered not as the final word but as initial explorations from this perspective. No doubt, numerous interpreters will disagree at various points with the analysis here offered, but perhaps these reflections will serve to generate additional constructive reflection and dialogue on this important topic.

10

Healing in the Atonement: A Johannine Perspective

The doctrine that physical healing is provided in the atonement of Jesus is a common belief found amongst a variety of Pentecostal believers around the globe. For the most part, adherents of this teaching have been content simply to cite certain proof-texts as offering sufficient biblical support for this doctrine. Chief among these proof-texts stand Mt. 8.16-17 and 1 Pet. 2.24. However, in recent years this topic has been the subject of more intensive study, with at least two PhD theses and one article appearing. In the earliest of these studies, David Petts argues that Pentecostals have wrongly appropriated these texts and concludes that a differently nuanced theological statement with regard to healing in the atonement is needed within the tradition.[1] Conversely, in an essay Robert P. Menzies argues that Pentecostals are right in their understanding that healing is based in the atonement. He goes on to suggest that the movement would be well served to articulate a doctrine of healing in the atonement that is informed by the 'Christus Victor' model of the atonement.[2] The most recent of these studies, by Kimberly Ervin Alexander, offers a comprehensive analysis of healing discussions in periodical literature across the spectrum of early Pentecostalism.[3] Like Menzies, she concludes that Pentecostals have rightly understood healing as being based in the atonement and she goes on to call for the re-appropriation within the movement of a Wesleyan-Pentecostal understanding of healing in the atonement.

Various things have piqued my own interest in the relationship between healing and the atonement. First, as one who is part of and

---

[1] D. Petts, 'Healing and the Atonement' (PhD thesis, University of Nottingham, 1993).
[2] R.P. Menzies, 'Healing in the Aonement' in W.W. Menzies & R.P. Menzies, *Spirit and Power: Foundations of Pentecostal Experience* (Grand Rapids: Zondervan, 2000), pp. 159-70.
[3] K.E. Alexander, 'Models of Pentecostal Healing and Practice in Light of Early Twentieth Century Pentecostalism' (PhD thesis, St John's College, Nottingham/Open University, 2002).

works within the Pentecostal tradition and movement, I am quite interested in the theological heart of our tradition and the revisioning project to which many of us feel called.[4] Given the prominent place of 'Jesus is Healer' within the five-fold Gospel and the fact that divine healing may well be the most characteristic aspect of the Pentecostal identity,[5] my interest in a variety of aspects related to healing should be easy to understand. Second, my previous work on healing brought me into contact with various interpretations of Mt. 8.16-17, some of which seek to subvert a reading of this text as having reference to Jesus' atoning death.[6] In that encounter, I found myself unconvinced by numerous arguments put forward in support of such a subversive reading. On occasion I found the arguments to be apologetically driven or methodologically misguided.[7] Even some of the more even-handed attempts struck me as flawed to some extent or as not going far enough in articulating the implications of Mt. 8.16-17 for the doctrine of healing provided in the atonement.[8] My own reading of Mt. 8.16-17 convinced me that at least for this Evangelist there is a clear connection between Jesus' healing and exorcistic ministry and the atoning work of Jesus. Third, I owe a debt of thanks to my colleague, Kimberly Ervin Alexander, with whom I team-teach 'Divine Healing' on a yearly basis and whose collaboration continues to benefit me greatly on a variety of topics related to Pentecostal Theology. Through the dialogue generated in and around this team-taught course I have learned much about the issue of the atonement and its significance with regard to healing. Here, I should also note that it was a specific question Kimberly raised with me a few years ago that generated the reflection resulting in this study.

In this chapter I want to propose another avenue by which the relationship between healing and the atonement might be explored. Specifically, I want to explore the ways in which the Fourth Gospel

---

[4] With regard to the call to revision Pentecostal theology cf. the seminal work of S.J. Land, *Pentecostal Spirituality: A Passion for the Kingdom* (JPTS 1; Sheffield: Sheffield Academic Press, 1993).

[5] For this observation cf. D.W. Dayton, *The Theological Roots of Pentecostalism* (Peabody, MA: Hendrickson, 1987), p. 115.

[6] Cf. J.C. Thomas, *The Devil, Disease, and Deliverance: Origins of Illness in New Testament Thought* (JPTS 13; Sheffield: Sheffield Academic Press, 1998), pp. 170-74.

[7] This seems to me to be especially true with regard to the work of D. Petts, 'Healing and the Atonement', *ETPA* 12 (1993), pp. 23-37.

[8] I also find myself in apparent disagreement with my good friend Max Turner, *The Holy Spirit and Spiritual Gifts: Now and Then* (Carlisle: Paternoster, 1996), pp. 257, 340-41 as I note in J.C. Thomas, 'Max Turner's *The Holy Spirit and Spiritual Gifts: Then and Now* (Carlisle: Paternoster Press, 1996): An Appreciation and Critique', *JPT* 12 (1998), pp. 3-22 (p. 19). However, cf. his clarification in M. Turner, 'Readings and Paradigms: A Response to John Christopher Thomas', *JPT* 12 (1998), pp. 23-38 (p. 36).

affirms the connection between the two and suggest additional ways to reflect upon this issue, thereby making a small contribution to the revisioning of this doctrine. In order to accomplish this task this study will include the following components. First, I will offer a reading of the accounts of healing found within the Fourth Gospel in order to ascertain the level of explicit connection between healing and salvation within these stories. Second, I shall explore the significance of the narrative location of the signs of healing and their relationship to explicit textual referents to Jesus' exaltation upon the cross. Third, I shall offer a couple of observations on other portions of the Fourth Gospel that might be of some relevance to this topic. Fourth, I shall explore this topic further by listening to readings (testimonies, if you will) from early Pentecostalism which see some connection between healing in the atonement and the Fourth Gospel. Finally, I shall attempt to make explicit the modest implications of this discussion for a Pentecostal Theology of healing in the atonement.

Healing and Salvation in the Fourth Gospel

In the Gospel according to John, Jesus' miracles of healing are part of the Fourth Gospel's use of 'signs'. Briefly put, signs in the Fourth Gospel are miraculous events that point beyond themselves to faith in Jesus as the Son of God. Often the signs give way to an extended discourse where part of the sign's significance is made more explicit. Though they are part of the revelation of the Father through the Son, the signs are not to be understood in a mechanical fashion. For the same set of signs can produce genuine belief evidenced by a full commitment to Jesus (2.11; 4.42), faith in Jesus which is private owing to 'the fear of the Jews' (19.38), faith in Jesus which Jesus himself does not have faith in (2.24), lack of belief in Jesus (12.37), and an outright hostility to Jesus which remains constant throughout much of the Fourth Gospel. The purpose of the signs is succinctly stated near the conclusion of the Gospel:

> Therefore, there are many other signs which Jesus also did before the disciples, which are not written in this book; but these have been written in order that you might believe that Jesus is the Christ, the Son of God, and in order that believing you might have eternal life in his name (20.30-31).

Among the signs described in the Fourth Gospel one finds four specific signs of healing along with a general reference to Jesus' signs of healing. These include: the healing of the nobleman's son (4.46-54), the healing of the man at the pool (5.1-18), the general statement with regard to the signs Jesus did upon the sick (6.2), the healing of the man born blind (9.1-41), and the resurrection of Lazarus from the dead (11.1-57). When examined closely, each of the signs of healing reveal the holistic nature of healing and salvation within the Fourth Gospel, for each of the individual signs of healing conveys this very message.

The healing of the nobleman's son is described as the second sign that Jesus did when going out of Judea into Galilee, following the turning of water into wine, called the first or beginning of signs which Jesus did in Cana of Galilee. In that text it is clear that through this sign Jesus manifested his glory and his disciples believed in him (2.11). The first healing in the Fourth Gospel is strategically located near the end of the portion of the Gospel that describes the early mostly positive responses to Jesus. In this story it is clear that the nobleman seeks out Jesus for the healing of his son who is near death. The text says that, hearing that Jesus had come back into Cana of Galilee where he had made the water into wine, the man came to Jesus. Despite words of rebuke, the man makes his request. Jesus instructs him to return home and speaks words of healing. The man believes Jesus' word and obeys his command (in conformity to the words of Mary 'whatever he says to you, do it' – 2.5). When learning of his son's healing the nobleman and his whole house believe in Jesus. These details would be enough on their own to reveal the close relationship that exists between healing and salvation in the Fourth Gospel; however, there is more. For what the attentive reader learns is that a refrain runs throughout the passage that highlights the kind of (eternal) 'life' which Jesus brings (cf. 1.4; 3.15-16, 36; 4.14, 36). Jesus' response to the nobleman in v. 50 is, 'Go, your son lives' (πορεύου ὁ υἱός σου ζῇ). On the journey back to his home, the nobleman's servants meet him with the news (v. 51) that 'His son lives' (ὁ παῖς αὐτοῦ ζῇ). If that emphasis is not sufficient to speak to the reader, the text states (v. 53) that after the man heard the news from his servants and discovered the hour of his son's recovery, he knew it was the hour that Jesus said, 'Your son lives' (ὁ υἱός σου ζῇ). The relationship between this sign of healing, belief in Jesus, and the salvific life which Jesus brings, is quite clear in this first sign of healing in the Fourth Gospel.

The second sign of healing occurs in the very next pericope (5.1-18). In this episode, Jesus seeks out the man who for thirty-eight years has been lying at the pool. Several things in this passage are important for the purposes of this study. First, the vocabulary used to describe this man's transformation is not the ordinary terminology used for healing. In other words, Jesus does not ask the man if he wants to be healed, but 'Do you desire to be whole (ὑγιής)?' (v. 6). The significance of this term is revealed in part by the fact that it is used only six times in the Fourth Gospel, with each occurrence having reference to this particular man. In addition, just as Nicodemus had earlier misunderstood Jesus' use of the word ἄνωθεν (which can mean 'from above' or 'again'), and the Samaritan woman had misunderstood Jesus' reference to ὕδωρ ζῶν (which can mean 'running water' or 'living water'), so the man at the pool misunderstands ὑγιής (which can mean 'well' or 'whole'), indicating that there is more to this Johannine term than meets the eye. A second, related issue is the fact that apparently, the transformation that leads to the man being made whole, includes the forgiveness of sin, for he is later warned, 'See you have become whole! Stop sinning, in order that something worse does not come upon you' (v. 14).[9] A third significant aspect of this text is found in the man's response to the enquiries of the Jews as to the identity of the one who instructed him to carry his mat on the Sabbath. After discovering the identity of the one who healed him, the man proclaims to them that 'Jesus is the one who made him whole' (v. 15). Two things indicate the positive nature of the man's proclamation. On the one hand, he does not respond to their question with regard to the identity of the one who instructed him to carry his mat on the Sabbath, but rather he says that Jesus made him whole. On the other hand, the word used to describe the man's proclamation (ἀνήγγειλεν), is the same term used elsewhere in the Johannine literature to describe the activity of the Messiah (4.25), the activity of the Paraclete (16.13-15), and the authoritative proclamation of the Johannine church (1 Jn 1.5). Thus, in this passage the holistic nature of the healing is in full view.[10]

The next sign of healing, after the more general reference to Jesus' healing ministry connected to the signs (6.2), involves the man born blind. A number of aspects of this passage indicate that there is a close connection between healing and salvation in the giving of sight to the man born blind. One of the first things to alert the reader to the significance of the ensuing sign is Jesus' words that the man was born blind so that the 'works of God might be manifested in him' (9.3). Attention is also drawn to the way in which Jesus' identity, his mission, and this healing converge in v. 7. Here, Jesus (the One Sent by God) sends the blind man to wash ('Go and wash') in a pool called Siloam, the name of which, according to the following parenthetical statement, means 'Sent'. The effect of the healing upon the formerly blind man is immediate, and not confined to his physical recovery. For he immediately identifies the one who restores his sight as 'the man called Jesus' (v. 11), repeats the details of the healing (vv. 15-17), and while being

---

[9] A point also made by G.H. Twelftree, *Jesus the Miracle Worker* (Downers Grove, IL: IVP, 1999), pp. 203-204.

[10] For a more detailed discussion of this text cf. Thomas, *The Devil, Disease, and Deliverance*, pp. 92-109.

interrogated by the Pharisees calls Jesus a 'prophet' (v. 17). Eventually, he asks the Pharisees, 'Do you also wish to become his disciples?' (v. 27b), prompting the Pharisees to identify him as 'a disciple of that one' (v. 28). Later in the narrative the man's belief in Jesus is made explicit when he is given opportunity to confess, 'I believe, Lord' and to worship (προσεκύνησεν) Jesus, in keeping with the true worship of which Jesus spoke in his words to the Samaritan woman in 4.23 (οἱ ἀληθινοὶ ποσκυνηταὶ προσκυνήσουσιν τῷ πατρὶ ἐν πνεύματι καὶ ἀληθείᾳ).[11] Another related emphasis is the preoccupation in the passage with the question, who is a sinner? Despite the fact that Jesus clearly denies that culpability is at the root of the man's blind condition (v. 3), the Pharisees end up accusing the man of being a sinner (v. 34). They also accuse Jesus of being a sinner in the story (v. 24), a charge against which the formerly blind man defends Jesus (vv. 25-33). The other major relevant theme concerns the broader issue of who sees and who is blind. Clearly, the man's encounter with Jesus results in more than physical sight. Yet, the Pharisees, though physically sighted, remain in their spiritual blindness. The themes of sin and blindness converge as the passage concludes (vv. 39-41), offering additional evidence of the holistic nature of this sign.[12]

The final sign of healing in the Fourth Gospel is the well-known account of the resurrection of Lazarus. Given the obvious ways in which John 11 testifies to the relationship between healing and salvation, the following comments are minimal. However, several aspects of this text should be highlighted. Similar to the story in John 9, the event to follow is 'in order that the Son of God might be glorified through him' (v. 4). Upon learning that Lazarus is asleep, the disciples prophetically observe, 'Lord, if he has fallen asleep, he will be saved (σωθήσεται)' (v. 12).[13] The relationship between Lazarus' death and the belief of the disciples is underscored (v. 15). The dialogue with Martha not only highlights the fact that her confession is perhaps the most significant one in the Fourth Gospel, but also the fact that Jesus is the resurrection and the life – a point made clear in the resurrection of Lazarus (vv. 20-27). In the ensuing dialogue, Mary invites Jesus to the place of Lazarus' burial with the words, 'Come and See' (v. 34), a formula that has previously appeared in the narrative upon the lips of Jesus (1.39), Philip (1.46), and the Samaritan Woman (4.29). In each case, it invites deeper

---

[11] For this suggestion cf. J.-M. Sevrin, 'L'intrigue du quatrième évangile, ou la christologie mise en récit', A Paper Presented to the 2003 Meeting of the Studiorum Novi Testamenti Societas in Bonn, Germany.

[12] For a more detailed discussion of this text cf. Thomas, *The Devil, Disease, and Deliverance*, pp. 110-23.

[13] I would like to thank Patrick Jensen, a member of my John Seminar, for first drawing this textual detail to my attention.

exploration on the part of characters and readers with regard to Jesus' person and identity. The prayer of Jesus (vv. 41b-42), which focuses upon the belief of the crowds more than the resurrection of Lazarus, is answered later in the narrative when many of the Jews see the sign which he did and believe in him (v. 45). Suffice it to say that this sign contains overt references to Jesus' resurrection and life-giving powers which culminate in the belief of many who see this sign. The relationship between this healing and salvation is quite clear in this passage as well.

Signs of Healing and the Structure of the Fourth Gospel

Such explicit connections between healing and salvation in the individual signs of healing within the Fourth Gospel would be enough to merit expansion of the passages to be considered in any discussion of healing in the atonement. However, the holistic nature of healing in the Fourth Gospel may also be seen in the narrative placement of the signs of healing within the structure of the Fourth Gospel. Specifically, the signs of healing in the Gospel according to John are framed by two references to Jesus' exaltation upon the cross. In the discourse that develops from the dialogue with Nicodemus in ch. 3, Jesus says,

> And just as Moses lifted up the serpent in the wilderness, so it is necessary for the Son of Man to be lifted up, in order that each one who believes in him might have eternal life (3.14-15).

It is significant that this first unambiguous reference to Jesus' exaltation on the cross, which precedes all the signs of healing, is explicitly tied to an Old Testament sign that afforded physical healing (Num. 21.4-9). Not only this, but the mention of the cross in Jn 3.14 also points forward by means of anticipation to Jesus' exaltation on the cross in the passion narrative proper, culminating in the blood and water that issue from his side in 19.34. Thus, all the signs of healing occur between these two references to the cross. One might say that in the Fourth Gospel the healing signs are enveloped in the cross.[14]

Another aspect of Jesus' words in 3.14-15 worthy of comment is the way in which this event, well known from the Jewish Scriptures, is taken up and reinterpreted in the process. While the event recorded in Num. 21.9 focuses upon physical healing which preserves life and points toward spiritual healing/salvation for those involved, John's use of the text focuses upon the salvific dimension of the event, pointing in a subtle fashion toward the implications for physical healing (as part of that salvation). The emphasis upon eternal life in v. 15 underscores this

---

[14] A question by K.E. Alexander with regard to the meaning of Jn 3.14-15 was the catalyst that generated my first reflection on this issue.

primary meaning of the text and at the same time serves as a sign of the holistic nature of salvation (life) anticipating the signs of healing in the Fourth Gospel.

Before moving to the next section of this study a couple of additional points should be made about the nature of the Numbers text. First, it may not be without significance that in the instruction to set the bronze serpent upon a 'pole', 'standard', or 'sign', in the Hebrew text of Num. 21.9 the word used is הנס, which in the LXX is translated by σημεῖον, 'sign'.[15] While the lifting up of the serpent in the wilderness is not referred to as a 'sign' in the Fourth Gospel, perhaps such an association would not be lost upon some of its readers. In any case, it may be that this 'sign' association is yet another way by which the tie between healing and salvation is made.

Second, the choice of this passage from Numbers might at first appear a bit odd given the fact that one learns in 2 Kgs 18.4 that Hezekiah feels compelled to destroy the bronze serpent owing to the people's proclivity to offer incense to it, even naming the image Nehustan. The bronze serpent also troubles later interpreters who sought to reconcile its existence with the prohibition in the Torah against the making of any graven image (Exod. 20.4-6). One of the best examples of attempts to solve this apparent contradiction is found in Wisdom 16.5-13. This document, which appears to pre-date the Fourth Gospel by about a century, explains that it is God, not the serpent, who heals:

> (5) For when the terrible rage of wild beasts came upon your people and they were being destroyed by the bites of writhing serpents, your wrath did not continue to the end; (6) they were troubled for a little while as a warning, and received a symbol of deliverance to remind them of your law's command. (7) For he who turned toward it was saved, not by what he saw, but by you, the Savior of all. (8) And by this also you convinced our enemies that it is you who deliver from every evil. (9) For they were killed by the bites of locusts and flies, and no healing was found for them, because they deserved to be punished by such things; (10) but your children were not conquered even by the fangs of venomous serpents, for your mercy came to their help and healed them. (11) To remind them of your oracles they were bitten, and then were quickly delivered, lest they would fall into deep forgetfulness and become unresponsive to your kindness. (12) For neither herb nor poultice cured them, but it was your word, O Lord, which heals all people. (13) For you have power over life and death; you lead mortals down to the gates of Hades and back again (NRSV).

---

[15] This is also reflected in the Targum's choice of נסא to translate הנס. I am indebted to my colleagues R.D. Moore and L.R. Martin for bringing these details to my attention. For the theological understanding of הנס in the Hebrew Scriptures cf. M.R. Wilson, 'נסה', *TWOT* II, p. 583.

A later explanation of this conundrum comes from Philo (*Alleg.* 2.19-21 [76-81]), who interprets the serpent bites allegorically as the bites of pleasure and the bronze serpent as representing the principle of self-mastery.

The Mishnah also contains an explanation similar to that offered in the Wisdom of Solomon. After noting that the power for victory over the Amalekites was not in the hands of Moses, but rather that the lifting up of his hands was to teach the Israelites to be in subjection to their Father in heaven, Tractate *Rosh Ha-shanah* (3.8) goes on to say:

> But could the serpent slay or the serpent keep alive! – it is, rather, to teach thee that such time as the Israelites directed their thoughts on high and kept their hearts in subjection to their Father in heaven, they were healed; otherwise they pined away.[16]

Given the hermeneutical challenges raised by this passage in Numbers[17] it would be surprising indeed if the comparison of Jesus' exaltation on the cross with the lifting up of the serpent is not intended to convey something of the intertextual meaning brought to the Fourth Gospel by the Numbers text.[18] Such an intertextual understanding on the reader's part is confirmed by the healing signs encountered by the reader as the narrative continues to unfold.

Other Observations from the Fourth Gospel

If there are explicit associations between the signs of healing and salvation in the Fourth Gospel, and if the narrative's structure highlights the connections between Jesus' exaltation upon the cross and the signs of healing, are there any other pieces of corroborating evidence within this Gospel that might be offered in support of this reading? One such possible hint is found in Jn 10.10, where Jesus says,

> The thief does not come except to steal, and kill, and destroy; I come in order that they may have life and have it superabundantly.

---

[16] Cited according to the translation of H. Danby, *The Mishnah: Translated from the Hebrew with Introduction and Brief Explanatory Notes* (Oxford: Oxford University Press, 1974), p. 192.

[17] For some of the early Christian discussions of this passage cf. *EpBarn* 12.5-7; Justin Martyr, *Dialogue with Trypho* 41; 44; Origen, *On the Passion* 14-15; Tertullian, *On Idolatry* 5; Hippolytus, *Refutation of all Heresies* 11; Lactantius, *The Divine Institutes* 26; 51; Cyril of Jerusalem, *Lecture 13.20*. I am indebted to my graduate assistant, Richard Hicks, for tracking down several of these references.

[18] For an excellent attempt to develop a Pentecostal hermeneutic by means of intertextuality, cf. R.C. Waddell, *The Spirit in the Book of Revelation* (JPTS 29; Blandford Forum: Deo Publishing, forthcoming).

Given the connections between healing and the atonement found within the Fourth Gospel, is it possible that this verse offers an additional piece of evidence for this association?[19] The answer to this question is very closely connected to the meaning of περισσόν in this verse. By the time the reader of the Fourth Gospel comes upon this statement he/she has already encountered the verbal form of the term on two occasions in the account of the feeding of the 5,000 in Jn 6.1-15. Both times the word appears in this pericope (περισσεύσανταν in v. 12; ἐπερίσσευσαν in v. 13), it is used to describe the fragments that have been left over after all the multitude had eaten their fill. Clearly in this passage the term is used to underscore the fact that Jesus' provisions are more than enough; they are, in fact, superabundant. The associations between these superabundant fragments and the bread of life discourse that follows, which itself emphasizes the holistic nature of salvation (cf. esp. 6.41-58), would also function to underscore this connection for the reader. Given this understanding of Jesus' provisions and the holistic nature of life which he offers throughout the Fourth Gospel, when encountering the adjective περισσόν in 10.10,[20] the reader would be inclined to understand this promise in its fullest possible sense. Added to this is the fact that this life stands in contrast to the physical forms of destruction caused by the thief mentioned earlier in the verse.[21] Consequently, it would appear safe to assume that the statement found in 10.10 is both an indication that this superabundant life includes holistic salvation (i.e. healing as [part of] life) and an anticipation of Lazarus who will soon experience life περισσόν.[22] In fact, it might not be going too far to suggest that one would appear justified in expecting the continued identification of healing with salvation within the life of the Johannine community on the basis of this understanding of περισσόν.

---

[19] I am indebted to my good friend B.B. Charette for raising this interpretive possibility with me.

[20] About this adjective F. Hauck ('περισσός', *TDNT* VI, p. 62) notes, 'The Adjective occurs only 6 times in the NT. It denotes the superabundance of the blessing of salvation which Christ as distinct from false prophets will give believers ἵνα ζωὴν ἔχωσιν καὶ περισσὸν ἔχωσιν (Jn. 10:10)'.

[21] My thanks again to B.B. Charette for this observation.

[22] While this superabundant life is clearly to be seen as synonymous with eternal life (as most commentators note), apparently eternal life itself should be viewed more holistically, with its implications not limited simply to the realm of the 'spiritual' (as most commentators fail to note). A bit closer to the mark here than most other interpreters is J. Marsh (*Saint John* [New York: Penguin, 1968], p. 400), who observes, 'The thought is that Jesus brings true, eternal life to men, and a life that is superabundant in its quality. Its "duration" and its "quality" are both beyond measure'. To this might be added D. Mollat's note on 10.10 (*L'Évangile et les Épitres de Saint Jean* [with F.-M. Braun; Paris: Cerf, 1960], p. 128): 'La vie éternelle (v. 28). Jésus la donne (3.16, 36; 5.40; 6.33, 35, 48, 51) avec magnificence (cf. Ap 7.17; Mt 25.29; Lc 6.38).'

Early Pentecostal Readings of John 3.14-15

It is quite significant that while the Fourth Gospel is rarely consulted in contemporary discussions of healing in the atonement, early Pentecostals were not as reticent to utilize the Fourth Gospel in their attempt to offer a constructive theology with regard to healing. As early as publication of *The Apostolic Faith*, Jn 3.14 is being read in a holistic fashion:

> We read in Ex. 15. 26, "I am the Lord that healeth thee." Jesus said in John 3.14, "And as Moses lifted up the serpent in the wilderness, even so must the Son of Man be lifted up; that whosoever believeth in Him should not perish but have eternal life."
>
> Dear beloved, we see in receiving the words of Jesus, it brings not only life to our souls and spirits but to these physical bodies. For His words are medicine to our bodies through faith. "Praise God!" We find that all the apostles believed in healing of the body and practiced it, for that was a part of their commission, "Teaching them to observe all things whatsoever I have commanded you." We read in Matt. 10, 1, "And when He had called unto Him His disciples, He gave them power against unclean spirits to cast them out and to heal all manner of sickness and all manner of disease," in the name of Jesus of Nazareth these things should be done. We read in the 6th verse of the same chapter, "And as ye go preach, saying The Kingdom of heaven is at hand; heal the sick; cleanse the lepers; raise the dead, cast out devils; freely ye have received, freely give."[23]

Not only does this article make explicit the connection between Jn 3.14-15 and healing, but this passage and its contents are seen as part of a more comprehensive understanding of healing as a prominent part of Gospel proclamation, as the article goes on to argue. In some ways Jn 3.14 functions foundationally in this *Apostolic Faith* argument.

One of the more extensive expositions of Jn 3.14 in early Pentecostal literature is an article by Mrs. C. Nuzum that appeared in *Triumphs of Faith*, a periodical published by Carrie Judd Montgomery. The study offers a careful comparison of the brazen serpent incident found in Numbers 21 and Jesus' use of this text in Jn 3.14. Seeing the latter as a type of the former, Nuzum argues that Jesus' work on the cross is God's 'remedy for Satan's bite' that will 'destroy all that he has done in man'.[24] The work of Satan is identified as a good number of things including 'our sick body'. She goes on to say:

> So, beloved, as we find anything, great or small, in spirit, soul, mind, heart or body, that is not right, not good and perfect as God created man,

---

[23] *The Apostolic Faith* 1.6 (February-March, 1907), p. 6.
[24] Mrs. C. Nuzum, 'Even So: John ii.14 [sic]; and 1 John iii.8', *Triumphs of Faith* 36.4 (April 1916), pp. 93-94.

– not like Jesus, let us look at Jesus on the Cross, and say, 'God, this is in thy remedy for this thing. As I look at Jesus on the Cross, this thing must depart from me.[25]

As if to underscore the connection between healing and Jesus' work on the cross, Nuzum concludes the article with a testimony of her own healing:

I have just been healed of a very severe case of appendicitis by doing as I have written. All glory to Jesus, who bore all our sins and sicknesses upon the cross, and made us free.[26]

Thus, for this writer, the connection between healing and the atonement in Jn 3.14 could hardly be clearer.

In *The Weekly Evangel*, an early Assemblies of God periodical, Pastor D.H. McDowell writes an article entitled 'Redemption That is in Christ Jesus: Rom. 3:24'.[27] In this study appeal is made to Numbers 21, where looking upon the brazen serpent and living means being 'delivered from all the effects of the poison of sin and its attendant penalty – death.'[28] John 3.14 is then cited as evidence of the fact that one must look upon Christ on the cross, believing in order to receive the benefit of his being 'a curse for us'.[29] While healing of the body is not explicitly mentioned in this connection, given the article's preoccupation with Christ's removal of the sin's penalty, death, by means of his death on the cross, it may not be going too far to see here a connection between healing and the atonement.

The connection between healing and the atonement in Jn 3.14 is made explicit in an article entitled 'Power in Jesus (sic) Blood to Heal the Sick', appearing in *The Pentecostal Holiness Advocate* in 1919. The author writes:

When the fiery serpents were sent among the children of Israel for their sin, the Lord told Moses to make a brazen serpent and put it on a pole that all who were bitten might look and be healed. That represented the cross. Now Jesus has purchased healing for us, and all we have to do is to look to him with all our heart and be healed. When the deadly serpent had bitten any man, and he beheld the serpent of Brass he lived. Num. 21.9. Jesus had been made a curse for us. We read in John 3.14, 15, 'And as Moses lifted up the Serpent in the wilderness even so must the Son of Man be lifted up that whosoever believeth in Him should not perish but have everlasting life.' Now we see clearly that the serpent was a type of

---

[25] *Triumphs of Faith* 36.4 (April 1916), p. 94.
[26] *Triumphs of Faith* 36.4 (April 1916), p. 94.
[27] D.H. McDowell, 'Redemption That is in Christ Jesus: Rom. 3:24', *The Weekly Evangel* (June 16, 1917), pp. 3-4, 8.
[28] *The Weekly Evangel* (June 16, 1917), p. 3.
[29] *The Weekly Evangel* (June 16, 1917), p. 3.

Jesus; and if a look at the type healed the sick and dying, how much more will Jesus Himself heal our diseases. He is the same today as he was to the Israelites, so when we look at the Son of God, our broken bodies are healed.[30]

As in some of the other readings offered in this section, there is a very close relationship between Numbers 21 and the words of Jesus found in John 3.

A 1920 article by Tinnie Wheeler, appearing in the *Triumphs of Faith*, seeks to offer biblical evidence for 'Why We Believe in Divine Healing'. In discussing the four times in the Old Testament when disease appears in the wilderness, for which supernatural healing is provided, Wheeler notes the close connection between sin and sickness, obedience and healing. One of these four cases consists of:

> c. Fiery serpents, fruit of discontent and murmuring against their leader, healed by the type of the cross. Num. 21:4-9. (See John 3:14, 15).[31]

Her attribution of the healing described in Numbers 21 as the result of the cross, typologically, suggests that Wheeler also sees a connection between healing and the atonement in Jn 3.14-15.

The last reading of Jn 3.14-15 offered in this section is actually a reprint of an article by A.B. Simpson, founder of the Christian and Missionary Alliance, appearing in *The Pentecostal Holiness Advocate*. Simpson offers the following exposition of this text:

> Look again at the story of the brazen serpent. It was a clear case of physical healing through the sting of the serpent representing the power of Satan in our bodies as well as our souls. The healing was accomplishing (sic) by the uplifting of the brazen serpent, a direct type of Jesus in his atonement. It is idle to spiritualize this. True, Christ applies it to salvation of the soul, the receiving of eternal life, but eternal life in all its fulness, and Christ constantly uses the term 'life' in reference to the body as well as the soul.... What right has any man to take a narrative, whose primary reference is to a case of physical healing through a look of faith to that which symbolized a crucified Redeemer, apply it exclusively to the spiritual aspect of salvation, and, although it belongs to the broader dispensation of the gospel, actually narrow it down and make it mean less than in the day of Moses? Undoubtedly it includes the greater salvation of the soul, but does not exclude the salvation of the body and its deliverance from the venomous stroke of Satan through a look of the faith at the crucified Redeemer.[32]

---

[30] *Pentecostal Holiness Advocate* 2.59 (3 April 1919), p. 5.
[31] T. Wheeler, 'Why We Believe in Divine Healing', *Triumphs of Faith* 40.8 (August 1920), pp. 181-82.
[32] A.B. Simpson, 'Divine Healing in the Atonement', *Pentecostal Holiness Advocate* 5.30 (Nov. 24, 1921), pp. 2-3.

Simpson's forthright comments are added testimony to the other readings found in early Pentecostal literature which see a connection between healing and the atonement within the pages of the Fourth Gospel.

What do these early Pentecostal readings of Jn 3.14-15 contribute to this study? First, they offer some additional support for the main point of this enquiry, that evidence for the connection between healing and the atonement is found in passages other than Mt. 8.16-17 and 1 Pet. 2.24. Second, these readings may also suggest that if there is indeed a Pentecostal hermeneutic at work among Pentecostal interpreters of Scripture, then perhaps the voices of those who have gone before us might profitably be revisited and heard as we seek to make our own way.

Conclusions and Implications

There appear to be at least four implications of this enquiry for the study of the doctrine of healing provided for all in the atonement that I would like to highlight for future reflection.

First, it seems clear that one finds evidence in the Fourth Gospel for the idea that physical healing is grounded in the atoning life of Jesus and that physical healing is part of the eternal life which Jesus brings. In fact, there is so much evidence of such a connection that John's voice within the canonical choir might well be one of the dominant voices, if not the dominant voice.

Second, given the nature of the evidence found within the Fourth Gospel, and this Gospel's understanding of the atoning life of Jesus, basic questions about the nature of the atonement might need to be raised again by those working within the tradition. Specifically, a broader understanding of the atonement, which is informed by more than the concept of forensic righteousness, is needed to reflect more accurately the nature of the biblical witness and the experience of the Pentecostal community. For example, dialogue with the seminal work of Gustaf Aulén[33] is already generating positive results among those working on this issue within the tradition.[34]

Third, this study has shown that early Pentecostal readings of Jn 3.14-15 can be profitably consulted in the attempt to arrive at an informed understanding of this entire issue. What is perhaps surprising to some is that a number of these readings are more appreciative of the

---

[33] Gustaf Aulén, *Christus Victor: An Historical Study of the Three Main Types of the Idea of the Atonement* (New York: Macmillan, 1969).

[34] Cf. esp. the work of Menzies and Alexander mentioned earlier.

holistic nature of the life which Jesus brings than many contemporary readers. Methodologically, such a result suggests not only that *Wirkungsgeschichte* has a contribution to make in the hermeneutical challenge that lies before us, but also that hearing the voices from those who have gone before us in the tradition might be an especially edifying activity.

Fourth, if, as this study argues, there is more biblical support for the belief that healing is provided for in the atonement based upon the evidence of the Fourth Gospel, perhaps there are other biblical voices that can speak to this issue, which have previously gone unheard. Who knows what additional exploration of the biblical text would produce? At the very least, it would seem that biblical scholars working within the tradition have a role to play in ensuring that various dimensions of this topic yet unexplored receive the attention they merit.

Fifth, this examination of the Fourth Gospel reveals that a very close connection exists between healing and Jesus' atoning life. Such a finding, while in need of additional reflection and examination, suggests that Pentecostal theologians would be ill-advised to jettison this understanding, but rather would be well-advised to engage in greater exploration of this doctrine from a variety of biblical, theological, and ministerial perspectives.

11

A Note on the Text of John 13.10

Fundamental for the understanding of any literary text is the establishment of that text as it originally stood. On occasion, the interpretation of a given New Testament passage is dictated by decisions reached on the text critical level. John 13.10 is one such place, for the decision to include or omit the phrase εἰ μὴ τοὺς πόδας affects the interpretation of the entire passage. The United Bible Societies Greek New Testament identifies seven variants in this verse.

1. οὐκ ἔχει χρείαν εἰ μὴ τοὺς πόδας νίψασθαι B C* W Ψ' arm Origen Augustine.
2. οὐ χρείαν ἔχει εἰ μὴ τοὺς πόδας νίψασθαι (K ἢ μή) L Π f^{13} 892 1071 1079 1216 1230 1546 1646 l^{547} syr^{h,pal}
3. οὐκ ἔχει χρείαν (or οὐ χρείαν ἔχει) εἰ μὴ τοὺς πόδας νίψασθαι it^{a,b,e,f,ff2,l,q,p}; vg^{cl} cop^{sa,bo,ach2}
4. οὐ χρείαν ἔχει ἢ τοὺς πόδας νίψασθαι C³ E* Δ (A 1241 ἔχει χρείαν) f^1 28 700 1009 1010 1195 (1242* omit ἢ) 1242^c 1344 1365 2148 2174 Byz Lect Cyril
5. οὐ χρείαν ἔχει εἰ μὴ τοὺς πόδας μόνον νίψασθαι ($\mathfrak{p}^{66}$ οὐκ ἔχει χρείαν) Q syr^{s,p} cop$^{bo^{ms}}$ geo (Chrysostom)
6. οὐκ ἔχει χρείαν νίψασθαι ℵ it^{aur,c} vg^{ww} Tertullian Origen
7. οὐ χρείαν ἔχει τὴν κεφαλὴν νίψασθαι εἰ μὴ τοὺς πόδας μόνον (see 13.9) D it^d

One thing is immediately obvious: these seven variants can be reduced to two basic readings. Readings 1, 2, 3, 4, 5 and 7 have essentially the same sense, while reading 6 offers a truly different meaning. The basic question then is whether εἰ μὴ τοὺς πόδας should be included or omitted. It is sometimes suggested that the diversity of readings which include the phrase εἰ μὴ τοὺς πόδας is a sign that the phrase is secondary. Barnabas Lindars notes:

The variants in other MSS. betray uncertainty. The textual evidence thus suggests that they are not original, but have been added in an attempt to clarify the sense.[1]

However, such a view fails to appreciate the complexity of the evidence. On the one hand, despite their disagreements, each of the witnesses for readings 1, 2, 3, 4, 5 and 7 contains the words εἰ μὴ τοὺς πόδας. On the other hand, the kinds of variants attested in these witnesses are just the sorts of modification one might expect to appear if the phrase were original.

It is one of the basic rules of textual criticism that the shorter reading is to be preferred. In this case the shorter reading is variant 6, οὐκ ἔχει χρείαν νίψασθαι. The external evidence for this reading is relatively early and has good distribution. ℵ (fourth century) is an Alexandrian witness. Tertullian (third century), it^{aur} (seventh century), it^c (twelfth century) and vg^{ww} (fourth century) represent the Western family of witnesses. The Caesarean family is represented by Origen (third century). Even though the witnesses are early and widely distributed, as a whole the evidence is somewhat scanty.

Realizing the sparse nature of this testimony, a number of commentators have looked to internal considerations in an attempt to support the shorter reading. Several such considerations have been proposed for preferring the omission of εἰ μὴ τοὺς πόδας. Basically, they all are tied to the thesis that the footwashing prefigures the complete cleansing (v. 10) accomplished in Jesus' sacrificial death. This line of argumentation is taken by Hoskyns and Davey,[2] Bultmann,[3] Tasker,[4] Brown,[5] Marsh,[6] Dunn,[7] Lindars,[8] and Barrett.[9] This is underpinned by a number of observations.

From the conviction that John must be speaking of only one washing several deductions are made. The stern language of v. 8b (Ἐὰν μὴ

---

[1] B. Lindars, *The Gospel of John* (London: Oliphants, 1972), p. 451.
[2] E.C. Hoskyns, *The Fourth Gospel* (ed. F.M. Davey; London: Faber & Faber, 1947), p. 439.
[3] R. Bultmann, *The Gospel of John* (trans. G.R. Beasley-Murray; Philadelphia: Westminster Press, 1971), p. 470.
[4] R.V.G. Tasker, *The Gospel According to St. John* (Grand Rapids, MI: Eerdmans, 1960), pp. 157-58.
[5] R.E. Brown, *The Gospel According to John*, II (ABC 29A; New York: Doubleday, 1966), pp. 567-68.
[6] J. Marsh, *The Gospel of St. John* (London: Penguin Books, 1968), pp. 489-90.
[7] J.D.G. Dunn, 'The Washing of the Disciples' Feet in John 13:1-20', *ZNW* 61 (1970), p. 250.
[8] Lindars, *The Gospel of John*, p. 451.
[9] C.K. Barrett, *The Gospel According to St. John* (Philadelphia: Westminster Press, 1978), p. 442.

νίψω σε, οὐκ ἔχεις μέρος μετ' ἐμοῦ) indicates that the footwashing is no trivial event. Several scholars argue that if λελουμένος refers to a previous washing and not to the footwashing, then the latter becomes trivial. Hoskyns and Davey conclude:

> If the longer reading be regarded as the original, the reference might be to the need of comparatively trivial washing, represented here by the washing of the feet only, after the complete purging of baptism.... But the action of Jesus here is not even comparatively trivial.[10]

Dunn concurs: 'By referring to an earlier bathing the significance of the footwashing is lost – as though there could be an earlier, more effective cleansing than that accomplished by Christ's redemptive action on the cross.'[11] Barrett suggests that even John's employment of the two verbs λούεσθαι and νίπτεσθαι as synonyms for cleansing points toward this interpretation. Consequently, the longer reading could owe its origin to non-discerning scribes who saw a difference between the verbs.[12]

That λελουμένος refers to the footwashing is said to be supported on form critical grounds as well. Bultmann labels the saying in v. 10 as a parabolic saying which would mean, 'Just as the man who has had a bath needs no further washing, but is completely clean: so too the man who has received fellowship with me through the footwashing, needs no further cleansing.'[13] Lindars agrees with this assessment and adds that v. 10 is not a direct reply to Peter's statement (v. 9).[14] This parabolic saying would suggest that the shorter reading is original.

Another rule of textual criticism states that the reading that best explains the origin of the other readings is probably original. Lohse follows this rule and concludes:

> One would do well to render a judgment according to internal probability and to ask which type of reading will explain the origin of the other. Here, together with external reasons, everything speaks against the long text. There is absolutely no reason why εἰ μὴ τοὺς πόδας should be missing. But it is easy to understand how so many different forms of an expanded v. 10 came about. One felt the short text presented a difficulty in thought and added an interpretive expansion to solve the difficulty.[15]

---

[10] Hoskyns & Davey, *The Fourth Gospel*, p. 439.

[11] Dunn, 'The Washing of the Disciples' Feet in John 13:1-20', p. 251. Cf. also Barrett (*The Gospel According to St. John*, p. 441); Bultmann (*The Gospel of John*, p. 470).

[12] Barrett, *The Gospel According to St. John*, pp. 441-42. Cf. also Lindars, *The Gospel of John*, p. 451.

[13] Bultmann, *The Gospel of John*, p. 470.

[14] Lindars, *The Gospel of John*, p. 451.

[15] W. Lohse, 'Die Fusswaschung (Joh 13.1-20): Eine Geschichte ihrer Deutung', (Dissertation, Friedrich-Alexander-Universität zu Erlangen-Nürnberg, 1967), I, p. 8.

Most scholars who accept the shorter reading would suggest that the longer reading originated '... when the original meaning of the narrative was misunderstood.'[16] Brown offers the best summation of this view.

> The most plausible explanation is that a scribe, faced with the statement, 'The man who has bathed has no need to wash,' and not recognizing that the bath was the footwashing, thought that he had to insert an exceptive phrase to show that Jesus did not mean to exclude the footwashing when he said there was no need to wash.[17]

Therefore, in spite of its scanty external support, many scholars defend the shorter reading on the basis of internal considerations.[18]

Although such arguments in favor of the shorter reading have some force, they are not decisive. Rather than assuming that variations in the longer reading suffice to show its secondary character, it is necessary to explore these variations carefully before reaching a conclusion about the genuineness of εἰ μὴ τοὺς πόδας.

Some witnesses (those that support readings 2, 4, 5 and 7) have οὐ χρείαν ἔχει rather than οὐκ ἔχει χρείαν. However, this small difference in word order should not be overly valued. Several reasons can explain such a change. It may be that the words were transposed for the sake of euphony.[19] While this is possible it is difficult to determine whether οὐ χρείαν ἔχει would really sound better than οὐκ ἔχει χρείαν. A better suggestion is that the change was made for the sake of emphasis.[20] By placing χρείαν in a more prominent position a scribe may have wished to underscore its importance. (Then οὐκ, which is appropriate before the vowel of ἔχει, changes to οὐ when followed by the consonant of χρείαν). Or, the transposition may be simply a transcriptional error of the mind, whereby the scribe saw οὐκ ἔχει χρείαν but inadvertently wrote οὐ χρείαν ἔχει. Bruce M. Metzger notes, 'Variations in the sequence of words is a common phenomenon...'[21] Since this same kind of alteration appears in a variety of places in the New Testament, it should not seem strange that it happens here as well. Whatever the actual explanation, only the verb and noun are transposed; the negative merely conforms to its following vowel or consonant.

---

[16] Hoskyns & Davey, *The Fourth Gospel*, p. 439.

[17] Brown, *The Gospel According to John*, II, pp. 567-68.

[18] Cf. e.g. F.J. Moloney, *Glory not Dishonor: Reading John 13-21* (Minneapolis, MN: Augsburg Fortress, 1998), p. 15 n. 44.

[19] B.M. Metzger, *A Textual Commentary on the Greek New Testament* (London: United Bible Societies, 1971), p. 240.

[20] This possibility was suggested by B.M. Metzger in conversation.

[21] Metzger, *The Text of the New Testament*, p. 193.

That οὐκ is original is also supported by the fact that οὐ is found in no Greek witness until the sixth century. It appears that D is the first Greek manuscript to give this reading, joined by the third corrector of C. It is natural that the rest of the witnesses supporting οὐ are Caesarean and Byzantine, for Caesarean witnesses generally preserve a 'distinctive mixture of Western readings and Alexandrian readings',[22] and the Byzantine text is generally characterized by its lucidity and completeness.

The other variations are relatively minor. μόνον has been inserted between πόδας and νίψασθαι in a few witnesses. More than likely this specification is due to 'the influence of the preceding verse'.[23] D expands the verse by adding τὴν κεφαλήν and μόνον. Alternations of this nature are not uncharacteristic of D. The substitution of ἤ for εἰ μή might best be understood 'as though the evangelist had written something like οὐκ ἄλλου τινὸς χρείαν ἔχει'.[24] This reading is found almost exclusively in Caesarean and Byzantine texts. Since the differences among the attested longer readings are small and do not significantly change the meaning of the phrase, it is legitimate to take these together in support of εἰ μὴ τοὺς πόδας. With this in mind, the major issue may now be considered. The great preponderance of witnesses favor the inclusion of εἰ μὴ τοὺς πόδας. This reading has the support of the Proto-Alexandrian $\mathfrak{p}^{66}$ (second-third century), B (fourth century) and cop^{sa} (third century). Alexandrian witnesses include: C*,3 (fifth century), W (fifth century), and cop^{bo} (fourth century). The Western support is strong and early as well. The witnesses range from D (sixth century) to the versions syr^s (second-third century), it^a (fourth century), it^{b,c,d,e} (fifth century). The Byzantine family is represented by A (fifth century) and E* (sixth century). The Caesarean tradition includes: arm (fourth-fifth century), geo (fifth century), Origen (third century), along with some later witnesses. Thus, the support for the inclusion of εἰ μὴ τοὺς πόδας is strong, early, well-distributed and includes a number of different kinds of witnesses. If a decision were to be made on the basis of external evidence alone, a verdict would have to be rendered in favor of the longer reading.

However, several internal considerations must also be taken into account. Jean Owanga-Welo argues that when 13.10 is identified as parabolic, it supports the longer reading. Against Bultmann, he cites a

---

[22] Metzger, *The Text of the New Testament*, p. 215.
[23] Metzger, *A Textual Commentary on the Greek New Testament*, p. 240.
[24] Metzger, *A Textual Commentary on the Greek New Testament*, p. 240.

'proverbial' phrase in Seneca (*Epistulae Morales*, LXXXVI 12) which mentions complete bathing and partial washing together.

> Friend, if you were wiser, you would know that Scipio did not bathe every day. It is stated by those who have reported to us the old-time ways of Rome that the Romans washed only their arms and legs daily – because those were the members which gathered dirt in the daily toil – and bathed all over only once a week.[25]

This example, he says, demonstrates the proverbial character of v. 10 and supports the inclusion of εἰ μὴ τοὺς πόδας.[26] While the text cited by Owanga-Welo is not quite proverbial, it is apparent that Seneca is describing the Roman practices by use of 'traditional materials'. Barrett's argument that λούω and νίπτω are used as synonyms is at best a guess and goes against philological evidence.[27] Also, the view that a previous washing (λελουμένος, v. 10) makes additional washing superfluous is not compelling.[28]

If, then, there are no sound reasons to reject the longer reading, it is still necessary to explain the origin of the shorter reading. Two suggestions are quite plausible. On the one hand, the omission may be the result of 'the difficulty of reconciling εἰ μὴ τοὺς πόδας with the words ἀλλ' ἔστιν καθαρὸς ὅλος which follow'.[29] On the other hand, the omission may simply be the result of a mistake,[30] possibly homoio-

---

[25] Cited according to the translation of R.M. Gummerie, *Seneca ad Lucilium Epistulare Morales* II (London: William Heinemann, 1920), p. 317.

[26] J. Owanga-Welo, 'The Function and Meaning of Footwashing in the Johannine Passion Narrative: A Structural Approach' (PhD dissertation, Emory University, 1980), p. 241. According to Owanga-Welo, since Bultmann assumes the shorter reading he is only partially correct in identifying v. 10 as parabolic.

[27] It is now obvious that, despite John's fondness for double entendre and for synonyms, λούω and νίπτω are distinct in meaning. They appear together in a variety of contexts but never as synonyms. Owanga-Welo ('The Function and Meaning of Footwashing in the Johannine Passion Narrative', pp. 15-16) points out several citations, overlooked by most scholars, where such distinctions are apparent, cf. *Testament of Levi* 9.11, *Tobit* 7.9b, and Plutarch *Moralia* 958B. The distinction between λούω (bathe) and νίπτω (partial washing) is supported by Oepke, 'λούω,' *TDNT*, IV, p. 305 and by Hauck 'νίπτω,' *TDNT*, IV, p. 947. Cf. also the extended discussion in J.C. Thomas, *Footwashing in John 13 and the Johannine Community* (JSNTS 61; Sheffield: JSOT Press, 1991), pp. 97-107. Despite such philological evidence, some scholars persist in arguing that λελουμένος has reference to the footwashing.

[28] O. Cullmann (*Early Christian Worship* [ed. A.S. Todd, J.B. Torrance; London: SCM Press, 1953], p. 109) can argue on internal grounds for the inclusion of εἰ μὴ τοὺς πόδας, v. 10, which, in his view, refers to the continual cleansing of the Eucharist.

[29] J.H. Bernard, *Gospel According to St. John*, II (Edinburgh: T & T Clark, 1926), p. 462. Cf. also Metzger, *A Textual Commentary on the Greek New Testament*, p. 240.

[30] J.A.T. Robinson, 'The Significance of the Footwashing', *Neotestamentica et Patristica: Supplement to Novum Testamentum* (O. Cullmann FS; ed. A.N. Wilder, et al.; Lei-

teleuton. If either of these suggestions is correct then all objections to the longer reading can be answered satisfactorily.

Finally, in terms of the internal coherence of the passage the longer reading makes better sense. As Robinson notes:

> If τοὺς πόδας alone were missing, it would make sense to say that 'he who has had a bath only needs to wash,' but to say that 'he has no need to wash' cannot be squared with Jesus' insistence on the absolute necessity of the washing (v. 8).[31]

Consequently, on the basis of early and well-distributed external support and convincing internal considerations the text which includes εἰ μὴ τοὺς πόδας may be accepted as original.[32]

One of the most important implications of this text critical decision is that by retaining εἰ μὴ τοὺς πόδας the place of footwashing in the Johannine community must be reconsidered. The disciples (and in them the community) are told that since they have bathed, they have no need to wash except the feet, which implies that their bath (baptism) needs to be supplemented by footwashing. Such a view coheres better with the instructions, found in the discourse (vv. 12-17), to continue the practice. Consequently, if the longer reading is accepted, the commands of Jesus about footwashing must be given consideration in and of themselves. Such a reading opens up the possibility that not only did the Johannine community believe that Jesus washed the feet of the disciples, but that they too are to wash one another's feet.

---

den: E.J. Brill, 1962), p. 146 n. 1. Cf. also Bernard, *Gospel according to St. John*, II, p. 462 and Metzger, *A Textual Commentary on the Greek New Testament*, p. 240.

[31] Robinson, 'The Significance of the Footwashing', p. 230.

[32] This is also in accord with the conclusions of F.F. Segovia ('John 13.1-20, The Footwashing in the Johannine Tradition', *ZNW* 73 [1982], p. 44), who offers three reasons for favoring the longer reading: 'a. The external attestation is much superior; b. The reading can be satisfactorily explained in the context of the Gospel narrative; c. The shorter reading can be readily explained as an attempt to smooth out what could be construed as an irreconcilable clash with the following.' Other scholars who support the longer reading are J.N. Sanders, *A Commentary on the Gospel according to St. John* (ed. B.A. Mastin; London: A. & C. Black, 1968), p. 308; L. Morris, *The Gospel according to John* (Grand Rapids: Eerdmans, 1971), p. 618; E. Haenchen, *John*, II (trans. R.W. Funk; ed. R.W. Funk and U. Busse; Philadelphia: Fortress, 1984), p. 108; F.F. Bruce, *The Gospel of John* (Grand Rapids: Eerdmans, 1983), pp. 282-83; D.A. Carson, *The Gospel according to John* (Grand Rapids: Eerdmans, 1990), pp. 464-66; C. Niemand, *Die Fusswaschungserzählung des Johannesevangelium: Untersuchungen zu ihrer Entstehung und Überlieferung im Urchristentum* (Studia Anselmiana 114; Rome: Pontificio Ateneo S. Anselmo, 1993), pp. 252-56.

12

Footwashing in the Context of the Lord's Supper

In this chapter I attempt to answer three specific questions: (1) What is the theological justification for the practice of footwashing? (2) What does footwashing mean? and (3) What is the relationship of footwashing to the Lord's Supper and its implications for the believers' church?[1]

The Theological Justification for the Practice of Footwashing

It is, no doubt, obvious that the primary theological justification for the practice of footwashing is grounded in the explicit nature of the commands Jesus gives to his disciples to wash one another's feet in Jn 13.14-17.

> If, therefore, I your Lord and Teacher have washed your feet you are obligated to wash one another's feet. For I have given you an example in order that you should do just as I have done. Truly, truly I say to you, no servant is greater than his Lord, neither is a sent one (apostle) greater than the one who sends. If you know these things, blessed are you if you do them.

While it is true that not all readers of Jn 13.14-17 interpret these verses as calling for a literal fulfillment of the commands, those communities of faith which observe this rite are convinced of the mandatory nature of Jesus' words. Although in some communities this interpretation has resulted simply from a surface reading of the text, there is additional evidence which indicates that Jn 13.14-17 were intended to be taken to result in the actual practice of footwashing as a religious rite.

Despite the fact that a hermeneutical gap exists between twentieth century readers and their ancient counterparts it is possible to narrow that gap somewhat by examining attitudes toward and the practice of footwashing in Greco-Roman and Jewish antiquity. When this evidence is examined it becomes clear that footwashing was a remarkably

---

[1] This chapter began as a presentation to the Believer's Church Conference devoted to the Lord's Supper. As the title of this chapter conveys, this study seeks to explore the topic of footwashing in relationship to the Lord's Supper.

widespread practice in the ancient world and functioned in a variety of ways: as a sign of hospitality, for the purpose of comfort and/or hygiene, as a sign of servitude, and as a religious/cultic cleansing. In other words, footwashing was a part of everyday life. As such, footwashing came to be regarded as a sign of preparation in antiquity. It was so commonplace that to approach a task without adequate preparation could be described in a traditional saying as acting 'with unwashed feet'. Descriptions of footwashing most frequently occurred in banquet settings and/or before a meal of some type. In these situations a host would provide water, in some cases (if the home was an affluent one and the guest was deserving of special honor) spiced wine or ointments, for the guests to remove from their feet the dirt which had accumulated on their journey. Such a practice was commonplace and appears to be presumed. Most texts place the washing at the time the guests arrive.

When the commands of Jn 13.14-17 are read against the cultural context of western antiquity, it seems probable that the first readers (members of the Johannine community) would have taken vv. 14-17 as calling for compliance on their part. Given the extensive practice of footwashing in antiquity, it is reasonable to assume that the readers of the Fourth Gospel would have been familiar with footwashing of one kind or another through actual participation. These first readers were in a very different position than modern western readers, who, due to their unfamiliarity with the practice of footwashing, seem unable to take seriously that a literal fulfillment of the command is in view. The first readers' familiarity with the practice in general makes it likely that, after reading Jn 13.14-17, they would be inclined to carry out its literal fulfillment.

In addition to the evidence from western antiquity, the most natural reading of the text of Jn 13.14-17 is one that calls for a literal fulfillment of the commands. In v. 14 'therefore' (οὖν) serves to make clear the connection between Jesus' own actions in vv. 4-10 and the following commands. In the light of his actions, the disciples are instructed to wash one another's feet. The emphasis of his instruction is borne out by the appearance of 'also' (καί) and the emphatic use of the personal pronoun, 'you' (ὑμεῖς). The verb in this verse often translated as 'ought' (ὀφείλω) further highlights the mandatory nature of the act. Rather than a suggestion, this verb carries with it the idea of necessity and/or obligation. Its force can be seen from elsewhere in the Johannine literature. According to Jn 19.7, in an attempt to convince Pilate that Jesus should be crucified, the Jews say, 'We have (the) Law, and according to the Law he must (ὀφείλει) die.... In 1 Jn, the same verb is used to describe the mandatory nature of moral conduct (1 Jn 2.6 –

'The one who claims to remain in him ought himself to walk just as that one walked') and Christian service to other brothers and sisters (1 Jn 3.16 – 'In this we have known love, because that one laid down his life for us; we also ought to lay down our lives for the brothers'; 4.11 – 'Beloved, if God so loved us, we also ought to love one another'; 3 John 8 – 'Therefore, we ought to receive such ones as these, in order that we might be fellow-workers in the truth'). The only other time Jesus uses the term in the gospels is also in a context of mandatory service, that of a slave to a master (Lk. 17.10). Normally, in the other New Testament uses of this verb the nuance is that of:

> an obligation towards men which is deduced and which follows from the experienced or preceding act of God the Savior. In many instances the sentence construction indicates the connection between human obligation and the experienced act of salvation.[2]

Here, the disciples' directive to service is based upon the salvific action of the Lord and Master, for '... now that Jesus, their Lord and Teacher, has washed his disciples' feet - an unthinkable act! - there is every reason why they also should wash one another's feet, and no conceivable reason for refusing to do so.'[3] The disciples have received cleansing at the hands of Jesus. Now, they are instructed to preserve this practice. The stress of this verse lies upon washing one another's feet. Because of the connection of these verses with vv. 6-10 there is the implicit and contextual directive that the disciples receive this service/sign (from one another) as well as render it.

The force of Jesus' command for the disciples to practice footwashing among themselves in v. 14 is strengthened by referring to the footwashing as an example (ὑπόδειγμα) in v. 15. While a general call to humble service cannot be ruled out altogether, there are three reasons to think that the readers would see in ὑπόδειγμα a reinforcement of the direct command to wash one another's feet. The first consideration is the context of this verse. In v. 14, it has been clearly stated that the disciples are to wash one another's feet. Following so closely upon this explicit command, it is likely that ὑπόδειγμα would be taken in a specific fashion. Second, this is the first (and only) ὑπόδειγμα given by Jesus, which the readers encounter in the Fourth Gospel.[4] Third, the combination of 'just as ... also' (καθὼς ... καί) emphasizes the intimate connection between Jesus' action (washing the disciples' feet) and the

---

[2] F. Hauck, 'ὀφείλω,' *TDNT*, V, p. 563.
[3] D.A. Carson, *The Gospel according to John* (Grand Rapids: Eerdmans, 1990), pp. 467-68.
[4] J. Schultz, *The Soul of the Symbols* (Grand Rapids: Eerdmans, 1966), p. 62.

action of his disciples (washing one another's feet).⁵ They are to act precisely as he acted. The instructions to wash one another's feet are rooted and grounded in the actions of Jesus in vv. 4-10. Therefore, the footwashing is far more than an example. 'It is a definite prototype.'⁶ In all probability, the readers, as well as the disciples in the narrative, would take ὑπόδειγμα with reference to footwashing in particular, not humble service generally.

In v. 16 again there is an appeal to the person and status of Jesus as the basis of the command to wash one another's feet. This time it comes in the form of a saying that also appears in a Synoptic context (Mt. 10.24). The authority of the statement is understood by the double ἀμήν which precedes the rest of the saying. The ἀμήν ἀμήν formula denotes a particularly solemn saying which issues forth from Jesus' own authority. As Schlier concludes:

> The point of the Amen before Jesus' own sayings is: to show that as such they are reliable and true, and that they are so as and because Jesus Himself in His Amen acknowledges them to be His own sayings and thus makes them valid.⁷

Having already identified himself as Teacher and Lord (vv. 12-13), Jesus here expands upon the implication of his Lordship. Since as Lord he has washed the feet of his disciples, they have no choice but to take similar action, on account of their own position as slaves in relation to Jesus. Their own status and consequent actions cannot hope to be on a higher level than that of their superior. That identical action between Jesus and the disciples is being described is borne out by the use of this saying in Jn 15.20, where the world's hatred for Jesus and the world is said to be the same. Another maxim-like saying underscores the point. 'No one who is sent is greater than the one who sends him.' Again, the clear emphasis is upon the authority of Jesus' actions in relation to the similar activity of the disciples. This interpretation of the master-slave language, which agrees perfectly with the context, is much to be preferred over reading back service into v. 15 and thereby making it simply an ethical example. In any event, the full authority of Jesus is given to the injunction to wash one another's feet.

---

⁵ L. Morris, *The Gospel according to John* (Grand Rapids: Eerdmans, 1971), p. 621 n. 36.

⁶ H. Schlier, 'ὑπόδειγμα,' *TDNT*, II, p. 33. Apollonius of Citium uses ὑπόδειγμα on a number of occasions with the sense of 'illustration, (or) picture showing how something is to be done' (cf. H.G. Liddell & R. Scott, *A Greek-English Lexicon* (London: Clarendon Press, 1966], p. 1878). Cf. especially Apollonii Citiensis, *In Hippocratio De Articulus Commentarius* (ed. F. Kudlien; Berlin: Akademie-Verlag, 1965), pp. 38, 60-64, 112.

⁷ H. Schlier, 'ἀμήν,' *TDNT*, I, p. 338.

In v. 17 a final exhortation is given in order that the disciples might not fail to carry out the footwashing among themselves. This time the command takes the form of a blessing. It is not enough for the disciples to know what to do; they must actually do it in order to be considered blessed. The grammar of this verse bears out that the disciples possess some knowledge of the footwashing, now that Jesus has given this explanation, but must follow through with action. This contrast is accomplished by the use of a first-class conditional clause, which indicates a future possibility.

μακάριος normally implies 'an approving proclamation of fact, involving an evaluative judgement'.[8] The use of the term in this context clearly underscores the importance of acting out Jesus' commands to wash one another's feet. Such emphasis is similar to that of v. 8, where Peter is warned that μέρος with Jesus is dependent upon reception of the footwashing. Therefore, not only have the disciples received footwashing from Jesus as a sign of continued fellowship with him, but they are now also instructed to continue this practice. In the light of its earlier meaning, it is likely that the footwashing to be practiced by the disciples would convey a similar significance, continued fellowship with Jesus. Obedience to Jesus' commands to wash one another's feet results in a declaration of μακάριος.

In sum, the narrative contains not one, but three directives for the disciples to practice footwashing. It seems improbable that either the disciples (in the narrative) or the implied readers would understand such emphatic language as not having primary reference to the actual practice of footwashing. Or to put this in the form of a question, if the Johannine Jesus had intended to institute footwashing as a continuing religious rite, how else could he have said it to get his point across? When compared with the words of institution associated with water baptism and the Lord's Supper, the commands to wash feet appear to be the most emphatic of the three.

But support for taking vv. 14-17 as calling for a literal fulfillment is not limited to the evidence from western antiquity and our own reading of the text of the Fourth Gospel. For in the case of Jn 13.14-17, this interpretation may be tested by how actual readers in the early church understood these commands. A number of early Christian texts give evidence of the regularity with which a reading of Jn 13.14-17 resulted in the practice of footwashing. In these cases, the relationship of the practice to John 13 is explicit. Such evidence comes from Tertullian (*De Corona* 8), the Canons of Athanasius (66), John Chrysostom (*Homilies on John* 71), Ambrose (*Of the Holy Spirit* 1.15), Augustine

---

[8] R.E. Brown, *The Gospel according to John*, II (Garden City: Doubleday, 1970), p. 562.

(*John: Tractate* 58.4), the *Apostolic Constitutions* (3.19); John Cassian (*Institute of Coenobia* 4.19), Pachomias (*Rules* 51-52), and Caesarius of Arles (*Sermon* 202 and 86). In addition to these texts, others indicate that Christian footwashing was observed in a variety of contexts in the early church. Such evidence comes from 1 Timothy 5.10, Tertullian (*To His Wife* 2.4), Origen (*Genesis Homily* 4.2), Cyprian, the Synod of Elvira (Canon 48), Ambrose (*Sacraments* 3.4, 7), Augustine (*Letter* 55.33), Sozomen (*Ecclesiastical History* 1.11.10), John Chrysostom (*Genesis Homily* 46), Caesarius of Arles (*Sermon* 1, 10, 16, 19, 25, 67, 104, 146), and Benedict of Nursia (*Regula Monachorum* 35).

When the Fourth Gospel is taken as the starting point, there is every reason to believe that footwashing was practiced as a religious rite in the Johannine community. Not only does the literary and exegetical analysis reveal that the implied readers would have understood Jn 13.14-17 as calling for a literal fulfillment, but the cultural environment of western antiquity demonstrates that readers of the Fourth Gospel would have been predisposed to practice footwashing as a result of reading Jn 13.1-20. The evidence from early Christianity exhibits that a number of people read the text in just such a fashion. Not only is the geographical distribution of the evidence impressive, in that it comes from North Africa (Tertullian), Egypt-Palestine (Origen), Asia Minor (1 Timothy, John Chrysostom), Italy (Ambrose, Augustine), and Gaul (Caesarius), but the diverse contexts in which the commands were fulfilled are also noteworthy, in that they range from the church, to monastery, to the home. Enough examples have been given to show both that the implications of the reading of the Jn 13.1-20 were somewhat consistent and the practice of footwashing was widespread.

The evidence for the practice of footwashing based on John 13 is of sufficient strength to conclude that in all likelihood the Johannine community engaged in religious footwashing as the direct result of Jn 13.1-20, or the tradition that lies behind it. Indeed, those within footwashing communities would want to argue that instead of interpreters needing to demonstrate the probability of the practice in the Johannine community, the burden of proof is on those who would deny such a probability.

The Meaning of Footwashing

If there is sufficient reason to believe that Jesus, as depicted in John 13, desired that footwashing be practiced by his followers, what was the intended meaning of this act? Several aspects of the text point in the direction of an answer.

Footwashing and the Passion of Jesus

A variety of indicators in the text demonstrate that a close tie exists between the passion of Jesus and the footwashing. First, the reader is prepared for this connection in John 12 where Mary's anointing of Jesus' feet is said to be a preparation for his burial. Second, the location of the footwashing within the farewell materials (John 13-17) indicates that the footwashing, along with the rest of the materials, was intended to prepare the disciples for Jesus' departure. Third, the tie to the passion is made explicit in 13.1, which serves as the introduction to the entire Book of Glory (John 13-21), where the reader learns that Jesus' hour had come. Fourth, the statement that Jesus loved his own εἰς τέλος at least suggests to the reader that Jesus' 'end' is near. Fifth, the appearance of Judas in v. 2 ominously foreshadows the betrayal of Jesus. As Raymond Brown notes:

> The betrayal is mentioned in 2 precisely so that the reader will connect the footwashing and the death of Jesus. Jesus undertook this action symbolic of his death only after the forces had been set in motion that would lead to crucifixion.[9]

Mention of the betrayer will also be made in 13.11. Sixth, in v. 3 the return of Jesus to the Father is mentioned again. Seventh, more than one commentator has seen a reference to the death of Jesus when in v. 4 he is described as laying aside (τίθησιν) his clothing, since τίθημι has this meaning in over half its Johannine occurrences. Additionally, the mention of Jesus disrobing foreshadows in the footwashing the humiliation connected with the laying down of his life. The stark reality of nakedness presents a clear reference to the crucifixion. As P.G. Ahr concludes:

> The reference to the crucifixion is ever more clearly present in the statement about Jesus' nakedness: anyone familiar with the story of Jesus' death can grasp the reference to the removal of clothes, and, indeed, it is the very unexpectedness of this statement which points the reader to this reference.[10]

'All of this serves to relate the footwashing to the death of the Lord.'[11]

---

[9] Brown, *The Gospel according to John*, II, p. 563.

[10] P.G. Ahr, 'He Loved Them to Completion?: The Theology of John 13-14' in *Standing before God: Studies on Prayer in Scripture and in Tradition with Essays in Honor of John M. Oestereicher* (ed. A. Finkel & L. Frizzell; New York: Ktav, 1981), p. 77. M. Hengel, *Crucifixion* (trans. J. Bowden; Philadelphia: Fortress Press, 1977), pp. 29 n. 21 and 87 notes that often crucifixion victims died naked.

[11] Brown, *The Gospel according to John*, II, p. 551.

The Unusual Nature of this Footwashing

The reader learns in John 13 that this is no ordinary footwashing. The first indication that there is more to this footwashing than meets the eye is the fact that it is chronologically out of place. When footwashing occurs in the context of a meal, it precedes the meal, most often occurring at the door of the host. However, the footwashing which Jesus provides for the disciples interrupts rather than precedes the meal.[12] The Evangelist underscores the importance of the footwashing by its unusual placement.

Another indication that this footwashing is unusual is the highly deliberative way in which Jesus' actions are described. Instead of simply saying that Jesus washed the feet of the disciples, John methodically underscores the significance of Jesus' actions by specifically mentioning each element of the procedure.

In v. 7 Jesus himself indicates that this footwashing is no ordinary one when he informs Peter that he will not understand the significance of this action until 'after these things' (μετὰ ταῦτα). Just as the disciples are unable to comprehend other events in the Fourth Gospel fully until after the resurrection (Jn 2.22 and 12.16), so Peter (and the other disciples with him) are unable to understand the full significance of the footwashing until after the resurrection.

Responding to Peter's emphatic refusal of the footwashing Jesus informs Peter that this act is not optional and that its significance is far-reaching: 'If I do not wash you, you have no μέρος with me.' One of the first things the reader would see in μέρος with Jesus would no doubt be a share in eternal life. Not only has the prologue promised such to those who believe (1.12), but it has also been stated that Jesus bestows eternal life upon those who are placed in his hands (cf. 3.35-36; 6.40; 10.28-29). The immediate referent is found in v. 3, where the reader is reminded of Jesus' knowledge that all things were placed in his hands by the Father. This interpretation is supported by the many New Testament texts where μέρος appears in contexts which deal with issues of eternal life and/or punishment (cf. Mt. 24.51; Rev. 20.6; 21.8; 22.19). Therefore, it seems safe to assume that one idea μέρος with Jesus conveys in Jn 13.8 is eternal life. Yet, this understand-

---

[12] Despite some strong support for δείπνου γενομένου ('when supper had ended') δείπνου γινομένου is to be preferred as the original reading. This judgment is based upon (1) slightly better external evidence (ℵ* B W it[d] syr[pal] arm) and (2) internal coherence, for it is obvious from the context (v. 26) that the meal continues after the footwashing episode is complete. Cf. B.M. Metzger, *A Textual Commentary on the Greek New Testament* (London: United Bible Societies, 1971), p. 239. However, either reading demonstrates the point that Jesus washes the disciples' feet at an unusual time.

ing does not exhaust the significance of μέρος. The closest structural parallels to this verse, found in Mt. 24.51, Ignatius' Epistle to Polycarp 6.1, and the Martyrdom of Polycarp 14.2, suggest that to share a person's μέρος was to share his/her identity or destiny. Matthew (24.51) describes the unfaithful servant as being assigned:

> a place with the hypocrites (καὶ τὸ μέρος αὐτοῦ μετὰ τῶν ὑποκριτῶν), where there will be weeping and gnashing of teeth (par. Lk. 12.46).

In affirming the legitimacy of ecclesiastical offices Ignatius claims:

> Give heed to the bishop, that God may also give heed to you. I am devoted to those who are subject to the bishop, presbyters, and deacons; and may it be mine to have my lot with them in God (καὶ μετ' αὐτῶν μοι τὸ μέρος γένοιτο σχεῖν ἐν θεῷ). Labor with one another, struggle together, run together, suffer together, rest together, rise up together as God's stewards and assessors and servants.[13]

As part of his last prayer, Polycarp gives thanks:

> I bless thee, that Thou has granted me this day and hour, that I may share, among the number of the martyrs (τοῦ λαβεῖν με μέρος ἐν ἀριθμῷ τῶν μαρτύρων) in the cup of thy Christ, for the Resurrection to everlasting life, both of soul and body in the immortality of the Holy Spirit.[14]

If anyone has cast their lot with Jesus in the Fourth Gospel, it is the disciples. To have a share in his destiny includes not only eternal life, but also being sent as Jesus himself was sent (4.31-38; 20.21-23), resurrection at the last day (6.40), and the hatred of the world (15.18-16.4). Simply put, it appears that μέρος here denotes continued fellowship with Jesus,[15] and a place in his community which ultimately results in uninterrupted residence in the Father's house (14.1-14). Such a view of μέρος dovetails neatly with 15.1-17, where remaining in Jesus is the key to life. Without such remaining, one's fate is like unproductive branches which are cut off and cast out to be burned. Consequently, the footwashing is a sign which points beyond itself to some deeper meaning. Two things point to the crucifixion/exaltation as essential to that deeper meaning. First, the qualities represented by μέρος (eternal

---

[13] Cited according to the translation of K. Lake, *The Apostolic Fathers*, I (Cambridge: Harvard University Press, 1912), pp. 273-75.

[14] Cited according to the translation of K. Lake, *The Apostolic Fathers*, II (Cambridge: Harvard University Press, 1913), pp. 330-31.

[15] Cf. F.F. Segovia, 'John 13:1-20, The Footwashing in the Johannine Tradition,' *ZNW* 73 (1982), p. 43, '... an acceptance of that which the washing symbolizes grants the disciples continued union with Jesus'. The context of belief, the Book of Glory, demonstrates that the footwashing does not initiate fellowship, but continues it.

life, identity with Jesus, sharing his destiny, mission, resurrection, and martyrdom) are ultimately secured through Jesus' death. Second, Jesus' act of humiliation in washing the disciples' feet foreshadows his ultimate act of humiliation on the cross. These hints in the narrative make it easier to understand the importance of footwashing. By refusing the footwashing, Peter is ultimately refusing the effects of the cross. The emphatic language of v. 8 removes all doubt concerning footwashing's importance. Without it Peter will have no μέρος with Jesus.

Footwashing as a Sign of Cleansing

Without a doubt, the meaning of the footwashing is given in Jn 13.10, where in response to Peter's request for washings in addition to his feet Jesus says, 'The one who has bathed has no need to wash except the feet but is wholly clean; and you are clean, but not all of you.' In order to understand the function of footwashing one must accurately identify (a) the meaning of the two verbs used to describe a washing, (b) the bath to which Jesus makes reference, and (c) the kind of cleansing which it provides.

It should first be noted that John appears to intend a distinction between the two verbs 'to bathe' and 'to wash'. The former (λούω) always has reference to a bath when it is found in the same context with the latter (νίπτω), and is never used in extant Greek literature to refer to a footwashing. Therefore, Jesus views the footwashing as a supplement to or an extension of an earlier bathe.

Jesus' explanation, which uses these two verbs, draws upon the ancient custom of the day. A traveler or guest would bathe at home before leaving on a trip. During the course of the journey, dirt/dust would become attached to the feet. Upon arrival the host would offer water to remove that which accumulated on the way. There would be no reason to bathe again, only to wash those parts of the body which had become soiled. Jean Owanga-Welo affirms the proverbial/parabolic character of Jn 13.10a by pointing to a parallel found in Seneca (*Epistulae Morales* LXXXVI 12):

> It is stated by those who reported to us the old-time ways of Rome that the Romans washed only their arms and legs daily – because those were the members which gathered dirt in their daily toil – and bathed all over once a week.[16]

---

[16] J. Owanga-Welo, 'The Function and Meaning of the Johannine Passion Narrative: A Structural Approach' (PhD dissertation, Emory University, 1980), p. 241.

Together with the evidence mentioned earlier, this text demonstrates the common character of the practice. The analogy is used by Jesus to convey the deeper meaning attached to the action.

The initial question is, to what is Jesus alluding when he speaks of a complete bath that makes someone clean? For the disciples in the narrative there is one option that seems most likely, baptism. Not only do the first disciples come from the Baptist's circle (which would imply an acquaintance with and appreciation for baptism), but Jesus (3.22) and/or his disciples (4.2) are also said to have baptized others and to have been more successful in these endeavors than John. Regardless of the way in which the tension between 3.22 and 4.2 is handled, the implication is the same. Baptisms are either performed by Jesus or under his auspices. Whether John's baptism, which is of divine origin (1.33), is being exalted by the subsequent actions of Jesus and the disciples, or his baptism is subsumed by the later practice, the implication for 13.10 is the same. It is extremely likely that the disciples, who baptize others, would have experienced baptism themselves, either at the hand of Jesus or John.

The readers, while familiar with baptism and its role, might be able to discern another meaning for λελουμένος. On the basis of the post-resurrection perspective of several statements in the narrative, the reader may suspect that the bath which cleanses has reference to the death of Jesus. Other passages in the Johannine literature testify to the connection between Jesus' death and cleansing. Owing to the special qualities of Jesus' blood in Johannine thought (Jn 6.53-56; 1 Jn 1.7-9; Rev. 1.5; 5.9; 19.13), as well as the remarkable usage of water in the Fourth Gospel, it is difficult to avoid interpreting the water and blood which come from Jesus' side in 19.34 as having reference to the life-giving and cleansing qualities of his death. 1 John 1.7-9 gives clear evidence of the connection between cleansing from sin and the blood of Jesus:

> But if we walk in the light as he is in the light, we have fellowship with one another and the blood of Jesus his Son cleanses (καθαρίζει) us from all sin. If we say that we have no sin, we deceive ourselves and the truth is not in us. If we confess our sins, he is faithful and righteous to forgive us (our) sins and cleanse (καθαρίσῃ) us from all unrighteousness.

There can be little doubt that such statements are based upon reflection about the crucifixion of Jesus. In Rev. 7.14, one of the elders responds to John concerning the identity of certain ones who are dressed in white clothes:

> These are the ones who are coming out of the great tribulation, and have washed their clothes and made them white in the blood of the Lamb.

Again the cleansing efficacy of the blood should be noted. The readers, then, might already see the significance of λελουμένος in terms of Jesus' death, especially in light of μετὰ ταῦτα. But it is unlikely that the cleansing through baptism and through the blood would have been seen as mutually exclusive.[17]

It would appear then that λελουμένος most likely has reference to baptism (and Jesus' death). Several additional pieces of evidence tend to corroborate this decision. One of the reasons for this identification is the effects of the bathing. Jesus says, 'The one who has bathed (λελουμένος) ... is wholly clean'. In early Christian literature no rite signifies complete cleansing from sin as does baptism. Certainly, the crucifixion is that event which accomplishes the cleansing, but it is baptism which signifies the cleansing. The occurrence of λελουμένος fits well with such a theme. Second, Jesus declares that there is no reason to repeat the complete bath one has received. Likewise, baptism is a rite which is once-and-for-all. Additional support for this nuance is the tense of λελουμένος. In the light of the significance of the perfect tense, which designates a past action with abiding results, it is difficult

---

[17] One or both of the suggested meanings for λελουμένος are the only viable options for the disciples in the narrative or the implied readers. However, the author knows of another possibility which the reader will encounter in 15.3. In this verse Jesus tells the disciples, 'Already you are clean (καθαροί) because of the word which I have spoken to you.' If it were legitimate to take λελουμένος in 13.10 as the referent of τὸν λόγον in 15.3, then perhaps the difficulty would be solved. On one occasion in the LXX (Judg. 3.19), λόγος does refer to a 'prophetic' action, when Ehud told King Eglon that he had a λόγος for him in private and then killed the king. However, such a parallel (if it be a parallel) is far too removed to explain 15.3. In addition, it appears that the λόγος of 15.3 has reference to Jesus' collective teaching, not one specific event. Approaching 13.10 in the light of 15.3, Bultmann argues that cleansing comes on the basis of the Revealer's word and on that basis alone. Therefore, λελουμένος is used to describe the bath in the word which makes cleansing with water secondary at best.

However, one of the difficulties in explaining 13.10 on the basis of 15.3 is the difference in context. While 13.10 speaks of cleansing from some uncleanness or defilement, 15.3 uses cleansing in the sense of pruning the branches in order to produce good fruit. Although there does not seem to be sufficient evidence to demand that 13.10 must be interpreted by means of 15.3, there may be a deeper connection between cleansing by means of pruning and cleansing through washing. Rather than playing 13.10 and 15.3 off against one another, the two statements about cleansing should be allowed to speak independently, perhaps at different levels of meaning. Perhaps C.H. Dodd offers the best analysis through comparison with a similar dilemma found elsewhere in the Fourth Gospel:

> The disciples are καθαροί through washing with water; they are καθαροί, also, διὰ τὸν λόγον. Similarly, eternal life comes by eating the flesh and blood of the Son of Man (6.54) and also, τὰ ῥήματα ἃ λελάληκα ὑμῖν are ζωή. The treatment of the two sacraments is analogous.

So, for the evangelist, cleansing takes place through water and the word, and both are dependent on the cleansing effects of Jesus' death. Cf. C.H. Dodd, *The Interpretation of the Fourth Gospel* (Cambridge: Cambridge University Press, 1970), p. 402 n. 1.

to assign the choice of tense to coincidence. Finally, there is some philological support for taking λούω as a reference to baptism. In several New Testament passages λούω and its cognates are likely references to baptism (Heb. 10.22; Eph. 5.26) or are closely related to it (Acts 22.16; 1 Cor. 6.11; Tit. 3.5).[18] Therefore, it seems likely that the readers would make the connection between λελουμένος and baptism as most scholars believe.

By following the ancient banquet practice to its completion the deeper meaning of the footwashing comes into view. The one who travels any distance at all on the dusty paths in the ancient orient accumulates dust which must be removed. If, in the analogy Jesus uses, λούω represents baptism, then it makes best sense to take the function of the footwashing as an additional act of cleansing. Dodd concludes:

> In xiii 10 λούεσθαι, to take a bath, is contrasted with νίπτειν, to wash a part of the body. Baptism is a bath (λουτρόν, Eph. v. 26; Tit. iii, 5). The Christian reader is assured that having undergone the λουτρόν he is καθαρός, yet may need some kind of recurrent washing.[19]

More than one interpreter has seen in the footwashing an allusion to forgiveness of post-baptismal sin.[20] This association is due in part to the occurrence of καθαρός in this verse. A cognate of this term appears in later Johannine literature (1 Jn 1.7, 9) with explicit reference to forgiveness of sin through the blood of Jesus. In addition, a multitude of ancient texts use καθαρός (and its cognates) in contexts which describe the forgiveness of sins. The LXX (Lev. 16.30; Pss. 18.14 [19.13]; 50.4 [51.2]), and certain para-biblical literature (Sir. 23.10; 38.10; Josephus, *Antiquities* XII 286; *Testament of Reuben* 4.8) use καθαρός in such a fashion. Although καθαρός may designate other kinds of cleansing (cf.

---

[18] As P. Grelot concludes, 'When one gives thought to this background, it is difficult not to see a baptismal allusion in the declaration by Jesus....' (P. Grelot, 'L'interpretation penitentielle du lavement des pieds', in *L'homme devant Dieu I: mélanges offerts au père Henri Lubac* [Paris: Aubier, 1963], p. 86). Obviously, there are other passages that do not equate λούω with baptism. For example, cf. Acts 9.37 and 16.33.

[19] C.H. Dodd, *Interpretation of the Fourth Gospel*, p. 401 n. 3.

[20] B.F. Westcott, *The Gospel according to St John* (Grand Rapids: Eerdmans, 1975), p. 191; B.W. Bacon, 'The Sacrament of Footwashing', *ExpT* 43 (1931-32), p. 221; O. Cullmann, *Early Christian Worship* (ed. A.S. Todd & J.B. Torrance; London: SCM Press, 1953), pp. 108-10; Dodd, *Interpretation of the Fourth Gospel*, p. 401 n. 3; Hauck, 'καθαρός,' *TDNT*, III, p. 426; A.J.B. Higgins, *The Lord's Supper in the New Testament* (London: SCM Press, 1952), p. 84; W.L. Knox, 'John 13:1-30', *HTR* 43 (1950), p. 163; G.H.C. MacGregor, *The Gospel of John* (London: Harper, 1959), p. 76; A. Maynard, 'The Role of Peter in the Fourth Gospel', *NTS* 30 (1984), pp. 534-35; idem, 'The Function of Apparent Synonyms and Ambiguous Words in the Fourth Gospel' (PhD dissertation, University of Southern California, 1950), pp. 329-30; A. Oepke, 'λούω,' *TDNT*, IV, p. 306.

Jn 2.6), its frequent associations with forgiveness of sin make it likely that the readers of the Fourth Gospel would have understood καθαρός to have reference to forgiveness of sin. Thus, while sin is not explicitly mentioned in v. 10, its presence is implied. Such an interpretation fits well with Jesus' emphatic language in v. 8. On this view, Peter is told that he would have no μέρος with Jesus because of (post-baptismal) sin, which had not been removed by cleansing. This meaning would become clear to Peter μετὰ ταῦτα. Another point concerns the Book of Glory. This understanding of footwashing fits well within the context of belief, of which chapter 13 is a part. The disciples are not being initiated into belief in this passage, but are continuing in their belief. Their earlier baptism, which the community probably understood as being at the hands of John (1.19-39) or possibly Jesus (3.22; however cf. 4.1-2), would designate initial belief and fellowship with Jesus, while footwashing would signify the continuance of that belief and fellowship.[21] As a sign of preparation for Jesus' departure, footwashing signifies the disciples' spiritual cleansing for a continuing relationship with Jesus and taking on his mission in the world. Yet, another point concerns evidence from chapter 3 which demonstrates that footwashing could be used in a sacred/cultic way (Exod. 30.17-21; 40.30-32; 1 Kgs 7.38; 2 Chron. 4.6). For Jesus to treat footwashing as a religious rite would not be wholly without precedent. Finally, the efficacious nature of the washing is emphasized by the way the footwashing 'foreshadows the self-giving involved in Jesus' death on the cross'.[22] In the light of the preceding considerations, an identification of footwashing with the cleansing from the sin contracted through daily life in this world is an appropriate one. Just as a banquet guest would bathe at home and only wash the feet at the house of the host/hostess to remove the dust and debris accumulated on the road, so Peter (the believer) who experiences baptism (which signifies a complete cleansing from sin) does not need to be rebaptized, but undergoes footwashing, which signifies the removal of sin that might accumulate as a result of life in this sinful world. In a sense, footwashing is an extension of bap-

---

[21] Carson (*Gospel according to John*, pp. 465-66) remarks, 'In his first epistle, addressed to Christians, to people who have already believed (1 John 5:13) and received eternal life (2:25), John insists that continuing confession of sin is necessary (1:9), as is continued dependence upon Jesus Christ, who is the atoning sacrifice for our sins (2:1, 2). The thought of Jn. 13:10 is not dissimilar.'

[22] J.R. Michaels, *John* (New York: Harper & Row, 1984), p. 227. Cf. also G.R. Beasley-Murray, *John* (Waco: Word, 1987), p. 235; idem, 'Baptism', *DNTT*, I, p. 154; Brown, *The Gospel according to John*, II, p. 586; Bruce, *John*, p. 283; W.K. Grossouw, 'A Note on John XIII 1-3', *NovT* 8 (1966), pp. 129-30.

tism, for it signifies the washing away of post-baptismal sins in Peter's (the believer's) life.[23]

The Relationship of Footwashing to the Lord's Supper

While the Fourth Gospel does not make the connection of the footwashing to the Lord's Supper altogether clear, three things may be deduced about the community's practice.

1. Because of its placement in the Fourth Gospel the footwashing was probably observed in conjunction with the eucharist. If so, it is possible that the footwashing took place in the context of a meal (perhaps the Agape?) together with the eucharist. It cannot be determined whether every eucharistic celebration would involve the footwashing.

2. If the footwashing was observed in connection with the eucharist then in all probability it preceded the Lord's Supper. John 13.1-30 is certainly open to such an interpretation. Of particular relevance are v. 12, which describes Jesus as rejoining the meal, and v. 27, which records that the meal had been completed. In 1 Cor. 11.28, Paul admonishes the Corinthian believers to examine themselves before approaching the Lord's Table. According to the *Didache* (14), in some early Christian circles a period of confession of sin preceded the eucharist:

> 1. On the Lord's Day come together, break bread and hold Eucharist, after confessing your transgressions that your offering may be pure; 2. but let none who has a quarrel with his fellow join in your meeting until they be reconciled, that your sacrifice be not defiled. 3. For this is that which was spoken by the Lord, 'In every place and time offer me a pure sacrifice, for I am a great King,' saith the Lord, 'and my name is wonderful among the heathen.'[24]

If the Johannine community's eucharistic celebration was anything like that described in the *Didache* (or allowed for a period of self-examination), the footwashing would most easily fit at this point, serving as the sign that confessed sin was forgiven. The believer would then be able to sit at the Lord's table with a clear conscience.

3. More than likely the footwashing itself was carried out by all members of the community. Such participation would accord well with the commands of Jn 13.14-17 and also with the emphasis upon mutual intercession in 1 John. Since the confession of sin may have

---

[23] Such an interpretation dovetails neatly with the preoccupation with post-conversion sin in 1 John and the interpretation of footwashing in the early church. Cf. J.C. Thomas, *Footwashing in John 13 and the Johannine Community* (JSNTS 61; Sheffield: JSOT Press, 1991), pp. 149-72.

[24] Cited according to the translation of K. Lake, *The Apostolic Fathers*, I, p. 331.

been a public one to the community, the brotherly intercession could well have been quite specific in its petitions.

It is not too difficult to envisage a footwashing of this sort in the context of the house church of the late first century. The environment of the home, as well as the small number of people involved, would be conducive to such mutual confession and intercession.

Conclusion

In the first century church (as well as that of the protestant reformers), baptism and eucharist were regarded as having been established by Jesus himself, as being directly related to his atoning death, and as continuing in the worshiping community. In view of these attitudes, several reasons may be offered in support of the classification of footwashing as a sacrament for the Johannine community and, consequently, for the contemporary church. When John's account of the footwashing is examined, each of the above characteristics are present: (1) There is no question that as portrayed in the Fourth Gospel the footwashing is instituted by Jesus. (2) It is clear from a number of literary allusions in John's Gospel that the footwashing is viewed as rooted and grounded in Jesus' atoning death. (3) On the basis of vv. 14-17 it has been demonstrated that footwashing is to be continued in the Johannine community. (4) Verses 14-17, taken as words of institution, are as explicit in terms of perpetuation of the practice as the eucharistic words of institution. If the Johannine community is familiar with the Synoptic traditions, the comparison between the two sets of words of institution could hardly be missed. (5) Finally, by taking the traditional place of the eucharist in the passion narrative, the footwashing appears in a sacramental context. There are even some writers in the early church that use sacramental language in describing the footwashing.[25]

In conclusion, while there appear to me to be a number of appropriate contexts for the religious practice of footwashing, I am personally convinced that with regard to its relationship to the Lord's Supper, the Brethren tradition has gotten it just about right. Since the footwashing serves primarily as a sign of the continual forgiveness of sins available for the believer, its observance just before the Lord's Supper is most appropriate.

---

[25] Cf. esp. the remarks of Origen (*Genesis Homily* 4.2), Ambrose (*Mysteries* 6.31), and Augustine (*Homilies on John* 58.5).

13

Footwashing – A Bibliographic Essay

Among the canonical Gospels, only the Gospel according to John contains an account of Jesus washing the feet of the disciples. Owing in part to its unique character, this pericope has been the subject of surprisingly intense study. These investigations are varied in both content and scope. However, there is no readily available survey of the major works on this topic. This chapter has the modest goal of filling this lacuna by introducing the reader to the various categories of literature which are devoted to the subject of footwashing and to give a brief overview of some of the major works on this topic.

Commentaries

A plethora of commentaries on the Fourth Gospel examine John 13 in the course of their respective expositions. These commentators include a number of ancient writers as well as contemporary scholars. Ordinarily, commentaries address textual, literary, and theological issues, with an emphasis on the meaning of the text itself. Owing to the nature and purpose of the individual works, full explorations of the data are somewhat limited.[1] Oddly enough, three of the smallest commentaries on John contain some of the most promising explorations of the practice of footwashing in the Johannine church.[2]

---

[1] The major commentaries include: C.K. Barrett, *The Gospel According to St. John* (Philadelphia: Westminster Press, 1978); R.E. Brown, *The Gospel According to John* 2 volumes (New York: Doubleday, 1966-70); R. Bultmann, *The Gospel of John* (trans. G.R. Beasley-Murray; London: SPCK, 1972); R. Schnackenburg, *The Gospel according to St. John* 3 volumes (trans. D. Smith & D.A. Kon; New York: Herder & Herder, 1968-82); G.R. Beasley-Murray, *John* (Waco: Word, 1987); D.A. Carson, *The Gospel according to John* (Grand Rapids: Eerdmans, 1990).

[2] Cf. the works of L.W. Countryman, *The Mystical Way in the Fourth Gospel* (Philadelphia: Fortress Press, 1987), J.R. Michaels, *John* (New York: Harper & Row, 1984), and K. Quast, *Reading the Gospel of John* (New York: Paulist Press, 1991).

Periodical Literature and Chapter-Length Studies

A number of pieces of periodical literature have been devoted to some aspect of footwashing. These articles range from quite brief pieces[3] to rather extensive studies.[4] By their nature, most of these articles either address a particular aspect of the footwashing pericope,[5] introduce a new element into the discussion,[6] and/or advance a specific way of interpreting the passage.[7]

Two chapter-length studies devoted to the topic merit some comment. An extensive study of the footwashing pericope appears as a Festschrift contribution for I.H. Marshall by Ruth B. Edwards.[8] This investigation is divided into three major sections. In the first section, Edwards surveys and critiques what she deems to be the three major interpretations of the footwashing, namely: 'The Exemplary or Moral Interpretation', 'Sacramental Interpretations', and 'Christological and Soteriological Interpretations'. She concludes

> ... that both an exemplary and a christological/soteriological meaning was intended by the author of our final text of John. It is also possible, though not certain, that some kind of sacramental significance was implied, though probably not with reference to either baptism or the Eucharist or the forgiveness of postbaptismal sin (p. 376).

In the next section Edwards discusses the 'Interrelationship of These Interpretations', arguing that the moral interpretation (vv. 14-17) appears to be among the earliest ideas, while the christological or soteriological interpretation is the work of the Evangelist. Given these two

---

[3] Two of the shortest studies are: A. Friedrichsen, 'Bemerkungen zur Fusswaschung John 13', *ZNW* 38 (1939), pp. 94-96 and G.G. Nicol, 'Jesus' Washing the Feet of the Disciples: A Model for Johannine Christology?' *ExpT* 91 (1979), pp. 20-21.

[4] Cf. M.-E. Boismard, 'Le lavement des pieds', *RB* 71 (1964), pp. 5-24; J.D.M. Derrett, '"Domine, tu mihi lavas pedes" (Studio su Giovanni 13:1-30)', *BO* 21 (1979), pp. 12-42.

[5] F.M. Braun, 'Le lavement des pieds', *RB* 71 (1964), pp. 5-24; J.D.G. Dunn, 'The Washing of the Disciples' Feet in John 13:1-20', *ZNW* 61 (1970), pp. 247-52.

[6] W.L. Knox, 'John 13:1-30', *HTR* 43 (1950), pp. 161-63; A.J. Hultgren, 'The Johannine Footwashing (13:1-11) as Symbol of Eschatological Hospitality', *NTS* 28 (1982), pp. 539-46.

[7] R. Eisler, 'Zur Fusswaschung am Tage vor der Passah', *ZNW* 14 (1913), pp. 268-71; H. Weiss, 'Footwashing in the Johannine Community', *NovT* 21 (1979), pp. 298-325; F. Manns, 'Le lavement des pieds. Essai sur la structure et la signification de Jean 13', *RSR* 55 (1981), pp. 149-69; S.M. Schneiders, 'The Foot Washing (John 13:1-20): An Experiment in Hermeneutics', *CBQ* 43 (1981), pp. 76-92.

[8] R.B. Edwards, 'The Christological Basis of the Johannine Footwashing', *Jesus of Nazareth: Lord and Christ: Essays on the Historical Jesus and New Testament Christology* (I.H. Marshall FS; ed. J.B. Green & M. Turner; Grand Rapids: Eerdmans, 1994), pp. 367-83.

understandings of footwashing in the passage, Edwards concludes that footwashing functioned as a sacramental rite within the community signifying participation in Christ's service and death. A final section is devoted to exploring the implications of this understanding of the footwashing for Johannine Christology, where Edwards argues for the coherence of the two at very deep levels.

Another chapter-length study worthy of mention is the more recent study of the footwashing pericope by Richard Bauckham.[9] One of the major preoccupations of this study is to determine whether or not Jesus actually washed the feet of the disciples. To answer this question Bauckham begins with a brief survey of 'Footwashing in Antiquity' noting the social implications for an inferior social standing of one who performs the footwashing for another. This is followed by a discussion of 'The Johannine Interpretation of the Footwashing', where Bauckham affirms the close connection of the act to the cross, the two interpretations of footwashing contained within the pericope, and the fact that the commands of Jesus would in all likelihood meet with literal fulfillment on the disciples' part. The origin of the passage is sought by means of reflection upon the Johannine nature of this passage and a comparison of John 13 with the Synoptic tradition, where Bauckham concludes that the latter is not the source of the former. The study concludes with one of the more extensive examinations on the history of the practice of footwashing within the early church, where Bauckham argues for a practice well established independently of the influence of the Fourth Gospel. In conclusion, the author believes that the activity of Jesus more likely accounts for the origin of John 13 than do proposals which suggest that the account was inspired by 'sayings of Jesus which require his disciples to relate to each other by humble service rather than self-aggrandizing lordship' (p. 429).

Dictionary Articles

A third group of investigations consists of dictionary and encyclopedia articles. By far the most comprehensive piece in this group is the contribution of B. Kötting.[10] This article combines a number of significant aspects for the understanding of footwashing. Beginning with an examination of the place of footwashing in antiquity, Kötting uncovers an enormous number of references, although he seldom cites the original source material firsthand. His analysis presents the various functions

---

[9] R.J. Bauckham, 'Did Jesus Wash his Disciples' Feet?' *Authenticating the Activities of Jesus* (ed. B.D. Chilton & C.A. Evans; Leiden: Brill, 1999), pp. 411-29.

[10] B. Kötting, 'Fusswaschung', *Reallexicon für Antike und Christentum*, VIII (ed. T. Klausner; Stuttgart: Hiersemann, 1950-), pp. 743-59.

of footwashing in Egypt, Greece, and Judaism. Next, Kötting surveys the New Testament references to footwashing: Lk. 7.44, 1 Tim. 5.10, and Jn 13.1-20. The last major section of the study is an overview of footwashing in the history of the church, in particular the early church. These references to early Christian practice are arranged topically. This section concludes with attention given to the representation of footwashing as a work of art. Kötting's article is perhaps the best survey and introduction to the topic available.

Dissertations, Theses, and Monographs

A final major group of investigations consists of several monograph length works on the topic. These diverse studies illumine Jn 13.1-20 through rather extensive examinations of particular issues of interest. Owing to their peculiar nature and obvious value, a brief survey is here offered.

Apparently, the first dissertation on footwashing was written in 1898 by Plato G. Maness.[11] This work, handwritten with unnumbered pages, chronicles the nature and practice of footwashing in the New Testament and early Christianity. In particular, it examines the place of footwashing in general Christian social life, its connection with baptism, its place in religious social gatherings, and its practice on Maundy Thursday. Despite the fact that Maness's study is now over a century old, it is still the best survey of the practice of footwashing in the early church. Maness supplements his ThD dissertation with a volume of essays which seeks to demonstrate the continuation of the practice of footwashing in the history of the church.[12] In this work Maness surveys the practice of footwashing in the Mennonite Church, the German Baptist Brethren Church, the Church of God (Winebrenner), and the Baptists.

Hildegard Giess examined the footwashing episode in the light of its artistic representations during the fourth to the twelfth centuries.[13] As preparation for this investigation, Giess provides a very brief examination of John 13, a short survey of footwashing in the Jewish-Hellenistic world, and a bit more attention to the view of footwashing in the Patristic period. The text of the dissertation concludes with an enunciation of possible motives for the production of such art and an examination of the artistic representations in the fourth to twelfth cen-

---

[11] P.G. Maness, 'Feet Washing in the Early History of the Christian Church. A.D. 30–A.D. 694' (ThD dissertation, Southern Baptist Theological Seminary, 1898).

[12] P.G. Maness, 'Essays on Feet Washing' (Southern Baptist Theological Seminary, 1898).

[13] H. Giess, *Die Darstellung der Fusswaschung Christi in den Kunstwerken des 4.-12. Jahrhunderts* (Rome: Herder, 1962).

turies. Following the text, Giess includes a photographic catalog of the artistic depictions of footwashing.

In 1965, Bertrand Zweifel submitted a thesis on Jn 13.1-20 for the License in Theology at Lausanne University.[14] At the time of its completion, it was the most comprehensive study on the topic and still ranks as one of the more exhaustive treatments of the text of Jn 13.1-20. Beginning with a survey of (then) recent research, Zweifel reviews the work of H. Pernot, O. Cullmann, E. Lohmeyer, R. Bultmann, and C.H. Dodd. The major portion of the thesis is devoted to a textual examination of Jn 13.1-20 that is divided into two parts, literary criticism and the exegesis proper. In the section devoted to literary criticism Zweifel renders decisions on the relationship of John to the Synoptics, the Aramaic nature of John's text, the context of Jn 13.1-20, and the structure of the pericope. This critical investigation is followed by a rather traditional exegetical treatment, which occupies over half of the thesis.

Two German dissertations on footwashing appeared between 1965 and 1967. Georg Richter devotes his entire work to documenting the history of the interpretation of footwashing.[15] The materials are organized and examined according to the following time periods: the Fathers, the Middle Ages, the Reformation/Council of Trent, the Enlightenment, the age of Liberalism, modern exegesis, and the Eastern Church from the Middle Ages to the present. Within these broad timeframes the views of the various interpreters are arranged topically. In a final chapter, Richter offers his own thoughts on the footwashing pericope, arguing that Jn 13.1-20 contains two contradictory interpretations of the footwashing (vv. 1-11 and vv. 12-20) that have been brought redactionally together. Richter proposes that only the first, which has a Christological-soteriological emphasis, is in agreement with the aim of the Gospel.

Like Richter, Wolfram Lohse offers a history of the interpretation of footwashing.[16] However, this work differs from that of Richter in that Lohse begins his investigation with an examination of Jn 13.1-20, and footwashing in the ancient world. Following this section, Lohse presents the various interpretations of the passage topically, in two temporal groups: the pre-critical understanding and the modern understanding. As in Richter's work, a myriad of interpreters are cited. The dissertation concludes with Lohse's own attempt at an interpretation with a

---

[14] B. Zweifel, 'Jesus lave les pieds de ses disciples' (thesis, Lausanne University, 1965).

[15] G. Richter, *Die Fusswaschung im Johannesevangelium* (Regensburg: Friedrich Pustet, 1967). A helpful synopsis appears as 'The Washing of Feet in John 13.1-20', *TD* 14 (1966), pp. 200-205.

[16] W. Lohse, 'Die Fusswaschung (Joh 13:1-20): Eine Geschichte ihrer Deutung' (doctoral dissertation, Friedrich-Alexander-Universität zu Erlangen-Nürnberg, 1967).

somewhat systematic treatment of several key issues in Jn 13.1-20. These topics include tradition and redaction, John and sacramentalism, double-meaning and misunderstanding, as well as Lohse's proposed interpretation, which emphasizes the Christological and sacramental dimensions of footwashing.

A different kind of examination, offered by Wadie Farag, is a history of the practice of footwashing as a religious rite.[17] Although primarily devoted to footwashing as a Christian rite, the practice in Jewish antiquity and Islam is documented. Farag examines Jn 13.1-20 and 1 Tim. 5.10 in a rather superficial fashion, cites the opinions of several figures in the early church, and surveys those church bodies which have observed and/or continue to observe this rite. The work concludes with a chart listing the protestant religious bodies in the USA that practice footwashing as a communal rite.

The practice of footwashing on Maundy Thursday was the subject of a 1977 MDiv thesis submitted to St. Vladimir's Orthodox Theological Seminary. Following an examination of the development of Holy Week, Dennis Rhodes investigates the historical background and meaning of footwashing. Rhodes concludes that the footwashing on Holy Thursday has reference to baptism. Through it 'the penitents are reconciled to the church, one might say a form of second baptism'.[18] He proposes that the practice of footwashing should not be confined to cathedrals and monasteries, but extended into the local parish.

Jean Owanga-Welo offered a structural analysis of the footwashing text in 1980.[19] Chapter 1 is devoted to problems of interpretation, which includes a brief survey of the significant issues in Jn 13.1-20 as well as a sampling of scholarly opinion. An examination of the theories and methods of structural analysis of narratives comprises the second chapter. This is followed by a structural analysis of the passion narrative as a whole. The final chapter consists of a structural analysis and interpretation of Jn 13.1-20. Owanga-Welo concludes that the footwashing is a qualifying test for the disciples which on the 'surface level' is interpreted as an example of humility, while on the 'deep level' it should be understood as anointing and purification in preparation for the disciples' enthronement.

---

[17] W. Farag, 'Religious Footwashing in Doctrine and Practice with special reference to Christianity' (PhD dissertation, Dropsie University, 1970).

[18] D.R. Rhodes, 'The Service of the Washing of Feet on Holy Thursday' (MDiv thesis, St. Vladimir's Seminary, 1977).

[19] J. Owanga-Welo, 'The Function and Meaning of the Johannine Passion Narrative: A Structural Approach' (PhD dissertation, Emory University, 1980).

In 1984, a ThM thesis on Jn 13.1-17 was submitted to Dallas Theological Seminary by Douglas D. Clevenger.[20] This work seeks to overview the history of footwashing in the ancient east as well as to render an exegetical analysis of the passage. Clevenger, who demonstrates little knowledge of the many critical issues involved in the passage, concludes that the footwashing depicts humility demonstrated by lowly service. According to this writer, literal footwashing is not commanded in Jn 13.14-15.

Anthony Linzey has devoted a Grace Theological Seminary MDiv thesis to John 13.[21] After examining several issues pertaining to background, Linzey investigates a number of exegetically significant factors in Jn 13.1-16. The last two chapters seek to understand footwashing within its literary and historical context and to identify the significance of footwashing. Linzey concludes love is that which Jesus seeks to communicate through the footwashing.

The most recent major treatment of the footwashing pericope is by Christoph Niemand.[22] This volume, the published version of the author's *Habilitationsschrift* presented to the Katholisch-Theologische Hochschule in Linz and under the supervision of Albert Fuchs, is a meticulous and detailed study of this Johannine text. Given its obvious importance, a more detailed description is here offered.

The work is divided into four parts of varying lengths devoted to (1) Introduction, (2) Analytical Study of the Text, (3) Verification, and (4) Concluding Remarks and Appendices. Parts 2 and 3 constitute the bulk of the monograph, accounting for 322 of its 460 pages.

Niemand begins part 1 of his study with a statement of purpose. His research aim is *not primarily* a synchronic interpretation of the text of the footwashing pericope as it now stands in the Fourth Gospel. Rather, he desires to bring light to the tradition and redaction history of this narrative by investigating the form, intention, and origin of the tradition unit from its beginning to the final developed form found in the Fourth Gospel (p. 2).

After this statement of purpose, the author offers comments on the nature of Johannine exegesis; including 'stratum analysis', 'consistent redactional' approaches, and redaction critical studies which have interpreted the Fourth Gospel in the light of the Synoptic Gospels. These observations are followed by a survey of previous approaches to

---

[20] D.D. Clevenger, 'The Role of Footwashing in John' (ThM thesis, Dallas Theological Seminary, 1984).

[21] A. Linzey, 'The Significance of Feet Washing in John' (MDiv thesis, Grace Theological Seminary, 1985).

[22] C. Niemand, *Die Fusswaschungserzählung des Johannesevangeliums: Untersuchungen zu ihrer Entstehung und Überlieferung im Urchristentum* (Studia Anselmiana 114; Rome: Pontificio Ateneo S. Anselmo, 1993).

the footwashing pericope itself, focusing primarily on form and redaction critical investigations which seek to identify the various literary strata of this pericope. The remainder of part 1 offers a preliminary discussion regarding the origin of the footwashing tradition with special mention given to (a) the relationship of John 13 to Lk. 22.27, (b) John 13 as a redactional construction from the Synoptic Gospels, and (c) other recent approaches to the tradition history of the footwashing tradition.

In part 2 Niemand provides a thorough analytical investigation of the footwashing pericope in order to trace the oldest elements in the tradition. Beginning with a reconsideration of the 'accepted idea' that 13.12-20 contains the traditional footwashing interpretation, Niemand embarks upon an exhaustive source critical, verse-by-verse analysis of Lk. 22.24-27 and Jn 13.12-20, 'the second footwashing interpretation'. Niemand determines that the Lukan passage has no concrete point of contact with the Johannine one and is certainly no witness to the Jesus tradition which lies behind Jn 13.12-20. He also here concludes that no part of Jn 13.12-20 is traditional as it contains no pre-Johannine material.

The second major section of part 2 examines 13.6-11 in order to determine whether or not this portion of the pericope contains a pre-Johannine interpretation of the footwashing. In this section special attention is devoted to an examination of vv. 6-8, the nature of the footwashing's symbolic meaning or sense, as well as a close exegetical analysis of vv. 9-10abc. This detailed investigation leads Niemand to propose and offer evidence for the tradition history hypothesis that 13.9-10abc is the oldest footwashing interpretation to be found in John 13. He goes on to argue that these verses (including εἰ μὴ τοὺς πόδας in 13.10), along with vv. 4-5, form the text of the pre-Johannine footwashing narrative. The import of this conclusion for Niemand is that at the earliest stage of the tradition's history, footwashing functioned primarily as an action of religious cleansing and washing.

In part 3 Niemand proposes to define the meaning of this religious cleansing and washing by establishing the oldest footwashing tradition's milieu of origin as well as its original meaning and life setting. In order to aid in this attempt the author seeks to identify the relationship between purity, impurity, and washings in the religious environment of the New Testament by examining the following: (1) the Old Testament, (2) Jewish literature of the second temple period, (3) the attitudes of the Essenes and the writings found at Qumran, (4) the baptism of John and the baptism of the mightier one, and (5) the Mandean literature. He also includes brief discussions of proselyte baptism, other possible baptisms of the period, as well as religious washings in the Hellenistic mystery religions.

In the final section of part three it becomes clear that for Niemand the *Sitz im Leben* of the oldest footwashing tradition cannot be discerned apart from its relationship to John's baptism and, in turn, early Christian baptism. The investigation which results leads Niemand to conclude that a concrete connection exists between John's baptism and early Christian baptism so that it is possible to speak of the latter as a resumption and development of the former (Christian baptism was from the beginning an extended form of John's baptism with a post-Easter kerygmatic content). Owing to these two baptisms' fundamental similarities, those who came to believe in Jesus and had earlier received John's baptism had no need for rebaptism. But eventually a question arose with regard to the proper means of incorporating newcomers who knew only John's baptism into the Christian house church community, an issue to which Acts 18.24-28 testifies. It is within a context such as this that the *Sitz im Leben* of the oldest footwashing tradition is to be located. More specifically, the thrust of Niemand's thesis is that those disciples who had experienced the conversion baptism of John the Baptist before belief in Jesus were not in need of rebaptism, but rather in need of footwashing as a sign of initiation and integration. As such, footwashing also functioned as a sign of welcome to respect and honor new and unknown disciples upon their arrival in the community of faith. This specific use of footwashing was ordinarily in the context of a meal of celebration or wedding feast. In this way the connotations of footwashing in the ancient world as a sign of hospitality and honor converge with the eschatological emphases of Jesus and the early church in baptism to produce this understanding of footwashing.

This work has numerous strengths and weaknesses. First, Niemand's acquaintance with the major works on footwashing is excellent, although the omission of Bertrand Zweifel's 'Jésus lave les pieds de ses disciples' (thesis, Lausanne University, 1965) and Jean Owanga-Welo's 'The Function and Meaning of the Johannine Passion Narrative: A Structural Approach' (PhD dissertation, Emory University, 1980) is surprising. Second, the author's conclusions on the relationship of Lk. 22.27 to Jn 13.12-20 should give pause to scholars who are keen to assign the origin of the latter to the former. Third, his treatment of the Apollos passage (Acts 18.24-28) is stimulating and may have implications for other investigations as well. Fourth, Niemand deserves high marks for his assessment of the relationship between John's baptism and early Christian baptism, the baptismal sense of λελουμένος in 13.10, and his decision to include the reading εἰ μὴ τοὺς πόδας in that same crucial verse. Fifth, although painstaking in its method and possessing its own logic, the book's primary weakness is the speculative nature of the conclusions reached, specifically with regard to the major thesis.

For those pursuing matters of tradition history, Niemand will provide interesting, if not always convincing, reading. However, those interested in the meaning of the footwashing text in its final form will be less enthusiastic. Focused as it is upon issues of tradition history, this book comes at a time when many scholars are more interested in the final form of the text and its (contemporary) readers. Had Niemand's work appeared twenty years ago it would no doubt have gotten a warmer reception than perhaps it will today. However, given its many contributions, to ignore this monograph owing to recent paradigm shift(s) would be most unfortunate, both for its author as well as students of the Fourth Gospel. Needless to say, it is now must reading for present and future interpreters of the footwashing pericope.

Although numerous other works exist on the footwashing pericope, perhaps this essay provides an initial orientation to the literature on footwashing and might function as a helpful bibliographic introduction to the topic.

14

The Charismatic Structure of Acts[*]

Intensive study of the book of Acts continues to go forward in a variety of arenas. The book's on-going appeal in academic circles is evidenced in part by the fact that it has been the subject of multi-volume studies near the beginning and end of the twentieth century.[1] In addition, scores of monographs and even multi-volume commentaries[2] have recently appeared. At the popular level, the book of Acts is the object of intense study as believers of various confessions consult it in order to understand better matters such as early Christian history, church offices, church growth, healing and exorcism, and the work of the Holy Spirit. Despite increasingly detailed investigation, one aspect of Acts which has not yet received the attention it deserves is the structure of the book. While every commentator (and bible study group for that matter!) must make decisions with regard to structure (for the purpose of establishing an outline if for no other reason), there is as yet no clear consensus about the structure of Acts. However, as various literary approaches to the study of Scripture have shown, often the meaning of a book is closely connected to its structure. Therefore, energy expended on seeking to sort out the structure of any biblical book is energy well spent. As I hope to show, this is particularly true with regard to Acts.

When attempting to discern the structure of the book of Acts, at least four pieces of evidence must be taken into account. First, in terms of the Acts narrative, there is a clear geographical progression from

---

[*] An earlier draft of this chapter was presented to the joint meeting of the Society for Pentecostal Studies and the Wesleyan Theological Society at Asbury Theological Seminary in Wilmore, KY, March 2003. I am grateful to the delegates for the many helpful comments made in the ensuing discussion.

[1] Cf. F.J.F. Jackson & K. Lake, eds., *The Beginnings of Christianity: The Acts of the Apostles I-V* (London: Macmillan, 1920); B.W. Winter, et al., *The Book of Acts in First Century Setting I-VI* (Grand Rapids: Eerdmans, 1993-).

[2] For example, cf. the work of M.-É Boismard, *Les actes des deux apôtres* (Études bibliques; nouvelle série; Paris: J. Gabalda, 1990) and C.K. Barrett, *A Critical and Exegetical Commentary on the Acts of the Apostles*, I-II (Edinburgh: T & T Clark, 1994-98).

Jerusalem to Rome. Second, it is also clear that for the most part the book focuses attention upon two important characters, Peter and Paul. Third, there are not a few literary markers within the text that offer some guidance in discovering the structure of the text. Finally, the role of the Holy Spirit within the narrative of Acts is so significant that some interpreters have suggested the book might better be entitled, 'The Acts of the Holy Spirit'. While several proposals have been put forward which focus on other aspects of the text, most proposals regarding the structure of Acts are based upon one or more of these four textual characteristics. In this chapter, I seek to set forth a proposal for the structure of Acts which takes into account each of these elements.

Geographical Progression in Acts

One of the most common ways of understanding both the development and structure of Acts is to give pride of place to the geographical progression of the book. Often this geographical progression is seen as delineated in Jesus' words found near the beginning of Acts (1.8):

> But you will receive power after the Holy Spirit has come upon you, and you will be my witnesses in Jerusalem and in all Judea and Samaria and unto the ends of the earth.

The proposal of I.H. Marshall is representative of this approach.

1.1–5.42	Witnesses in Jerusalem
1.1–2.47	The beginning of the Church
3.1–5.42	The church and the Jewish authorities
6.1–11.18	Witnesses in Judaea and Samaria
6.1–9.31	The church begins to expand
9.32–11.18	The beginning of the Gentile mission
11.19–28.31	Witnesses to the Ends of the Earth
11.19–14.28	The mission from Antioch to Asia Minor
15.1–15.35	The discussion concerning the Gentiles in the church
15.36–18.17	Paul's missionary campaign in Macedonia and Achaia
18.18–20.38	Paul's missionary campaign in Asia Minor
21.1–28.31	Paul's arrest and imprisonment[3]

Clearly, the strength of Marshall's proposal is that it gives detailed attention to the geographical progression of Christianity. However, despite Paul's prominence in the final section of the outline, the leading characters do not receive appropriate attention. Interestingly, there is

---

[3] I.H. Marshall, *The Acts of the Apostles* (New Testament Guides; Sheffield: JSOT Press, 1992), p. 29. A similar suggestion is made by L.T. Johnson (*The Acts of the Apostles* [Collegeville, MN: Liturgical Press, 1992], p. 10), who proposes the following structure: Acts 1-7 – First Church in Jerusalem, Acts 8-12 – Evangelization of Judea and Samaria, Acts 13-28 – The Gospel Spreads to Asia Minor and Europe – Rome.

no mention of the activity of the Holy Spirit. Nor are the literary markers in the text reflected in the division of the text in this outline.

Another proposal for the structure of Acts which takes the geographical dimension as the dominant indicator is that set forth by J.C. O'Neill.[4] Noting the geographical and theological importance of Jerusalem and Rome, O'Neill proposes that the book be divided into the following five sections:

1.9–8.3	Jerusalem
8.4–11.18	From Jerusalem to Judea, Samaria, and Antioch (Peter, John, and Barnabas)
11.19–15.35	Gentiles between Jerusalem and Jerusalem
15.36–19.20	The Jerusalem Council and Beyond (James)
19.21–28.31	Paul's Decision to Return to Jerusalem and then to Rome[5]

O'Neill notes that Jerusalem has an important role in each section of the book and that this outline matches Luke's theological emphasis of following the Gospel from Jerusalem to Rome.

Clearly, O'Neill picks up on a dominant theme in Acts, underscoring the crucial geographical and theological role of Jerusalem. However, there are certain weaknesses with it as well. Little attention is paid to the importance of the literary markers in the text for the structure of the book. Though O'Neill is aware of attempts to structure the text in this fashion he rejects the idea that they are dominant.[6] While this proposal does pay some attention to the roles of Peter and Paul, it does not seem to give them their due weight. Unfortunately, the role of the Holy Spirit in Acts is not deemed important enough to merit a mention. Marshall's proposal is open to similar criticisms.

The Roles of Peter and Paul in Acts

Recognizing the important roles played by Peter and Paul in the Acts narrative, some scholars have suggested that their stories should form the basis for understanding the book's structure. For example, R.B. Rackham divides Acts into 'The Acts of Peter' (1.6–12.25) and 'The Acts of Paul' (13.1–28.31).[7] His detailed outline of the book reveals that he pays careful attention to the role of significant individuals as well as the geographical progression of the book. However, Rackham makes only passing reference to the Holy Spirit and appears to ignore the literary markers within the text. The artificiality of outlines, which

---

[4] J.C. O'Neill, *The Theology of Acts in its Historical Setting* (London: SPCK, 1970), pp. 59-76.
[5] These captions reflect my attempt to capture O'Neil's thought.
[6] O'Neill, *The Theology of Acts in its Historical Setting*, pp. 64-65.
[7] R.B. Rackham, *The Acts of the Apostles* (Grand Rapids: Baker, 1964), pp. cix-cxi.

so focus on Peter and Paul, have been rightly criticized by P. Menoud,[8] among others.

Charles Talbert also divides the book of Acts into the two sections of chapters 1–12 and 13–28. For Talbert, however, the reason for this structure is not so much that the former section of the book focuses upon Peter and the latter upon Paul, but rather it is owing to numerous literary parallels between these two sections of the book.[9] Talbert identifies seven major literary parallels that occur sequentially in these two sections of Acts.[10] He also identifies nine other parallels between these sections that do not appear to occur in any type of systematic order within the narrative.[11] This proposal, originally set forth in his PhD dissertation, becomes the basis for his later John Knox Preaching Guide on Acts.[12] In addition to the criticisms made by Menoud of this general approach, this proposed structure fails to take sufficiently into account the literary markers in the text and the role of the Holy Spirit. Oddly, in Talbert's Preaching Guide outline, neither Peter nor Paul is mentioned by name.

The Literary Markers in Acts

In a dictionary article now nearly a century old, C.H. Roberts notes that the book of Acts can be divided structurally into six panels each of which conclude with a summary statement describing the growth of the word of God, the church, and/or both.[13] The statements he identifies, found in 6.7, 9.31, 12.24; 16.5, 19.20, and 28.31, result in the following panels:

> *The First Period* – The Church in Jerusalem and the Preaching of St. Peter – 1.1–6.7
> *The Second Period* – Extension of the Church through Palestine – 6.8–9.31
> *The Third Period* – The Extension of the Church to Antioch – 9.32–12.24
> *The Fourth Period* – The Extension of the Church to Asia Minor – 12.25–16.5

---

[8] P. Menoud, 'Le plan des Actes des Apôtres', *NTS* 1 (1954), pp. 45-51.

[9] C.H. Talbert, *Literary Patterns, Theological Themes, and the Genre of Luke-Acts* (SBLMS 20; Missoula, MT: Scholars Press, 1974), pp. 23-26.

[10] The parallels identified by Talbert are found in 2.1-4 and 13.1-3; 2.14-40 and 13.16-40; 3.1-10 and 14.8-13; 3.12-26 and 14.15-17; 6.8-8.4 and 14.19-23; 10-11 and 13-21; 12 and 21-28.

[11] These suggested parallels are 8.9-24 and 13.6-12; 9.36-43 and 20.9-12; 10.25-26 and 14.13-15; 12.6-11 and 16.24-26; 8.14-17 and 19.1-6; 6.1-6 and 14.23; 5.34-39 and 23.9; 6.13-14 and 21.20-21, 25.8; 1.21-22 and 23.11, 26.16.

[12] C.H. Talbert, *Acts* (Atlanta, GA: John Knox Press, 1984).

[13] C.H. Roberts, 'Chronology of the New Testament', in *A Dictionary of the Bible Dealing with its Language, Literature, and Contents*, I (ed. J. Hastings; New York: Scribner's Sons, 1911), pp. 403-25 (cf. esp. 421).

The Fifth Period – The Extension of the Church to Europe – 16.6–19.20
The Sixth Period – The Extension of the Church to Rome – 19.21–28.31

While various individuals have acknowledged these summary statements, few have utilized them as foundational in determining the overall structure of the book. Notable exceptions include the commentaries by French Arrington[14] and David Gooding.[15]

However, as Arrington notes, Roberts's proposal overlooks the fact that there are two additional summary statements (2.47; 11.21) to which Roberts makes no reference, nor does he utilize them in his structure of Acts.[16] Also missing from this proposal is any indication of the significance of the Holy Spirit's role within the narrative. Absent as well is any acknowledgement of the importance of Peter and Paul within the book.[17]

The Role of the Holy Spirit in Acts

While an appreciation of the importance of the Holy Spirit in the narrative(s) of Luke–Acts is increasing among New Testament scholars, few have reflected upon its significance for the structure of the book of Acts. Pioneering work in this area comes from the pen of Roger Stronstad, a Pentecostal New Testament scholar known especially for his work on Lucan pneumatology.[18] Following up his earlier work Stronstad has recently argued that one of the dominant themes, if not *the* dominant theme, of Acts is 'the prophethood of all believers'.[19] So significant is this theme, Stronstad argues, that the entire book may be structured around the stories Luke narrates of charismatically anointed prophetic figures. For Stronstad the book takes the following shape:

The Disciples: A Company of Spirit-Baptized Prophets – 1.12–2.41
The Acts of the Community of Prophets – 2.42–6.7
The Acts of Five Charismatic Prophets – 6.8–12.24
The Acts of Stephen: A Charismatic Deacon – 6.8–7.60
The Acts of Philip: A Charismatic Deacon – 8.1–40

---

[14] F.L. Arrington, *The Acts of the Apostles: A Pentecostal Commentary* (Peabody, MA: Hendrickson, 1988).

[15] D.W. Gooding, *True to the Faith: a Fresh Approach to the Acts of the Apostles* (London: Hodder & Stoughton, 1990).

[16] Oddly enough, neither does Arrington.

[17] These weaknesses are not as pronounced in Arrington's outline, which mentions the Holy Spirit once and underscores Paul's importance in part by entitling the final section 'Paul Arrives in Rome'.

[18] Cf. R. Stronstad, *The Charismatic Theology of St. Luke* (Peabody, MA: Hendrickson, 1984).

[19] R. Stronstad, *The Prophethood of All Believers: A Study in Luke's Charismatic Theology* (JPTS 16; Sheffield: Sheffield Academic Press, 1999).

The Acts of Barnabas: A Charismatic Prophet
The Acts of Agabus: A Charismatic Prophet
The Acts of Peter: A Charismatic Apostle
The Acts of Paul: A Charismatic Prophet – 12.25–28.31

Among the strengths of this proposal are the following: First, it allows the pneumatology of Acts, which is perhaps the dominant theme in the book, to have the visibility its significance merits. Second, rather than artificially dividing the book around the activities of two of its dominant figures, it gives Peter and Paul the attention they deserve and at the same time reveals the significance of a number of other charismatically anointed individuals. Third, on occasion major transitions within the proposed outline coincide with literary markers in the text (cf. specifically 6.7; 12.24; 28.31). The proposal's major weaknesses are to be found in the fact that the importance of the geographical progression within the book is not reflected in the outline, nor does it take into sufficient account the book's other literary markers.

The Charismatic Structure of Acts

As the above survey reveals, each of these four views identifies one or more aspect(s) of the text that should be taken into consideration when attempting to discern the structure of Acts.[20] In the discussion that follows, I will seek to set forth a proposal that is informed by the insights of others and at the same time pushes the discussion forward in a constructive way.

In order to provide the interpretive context for the modest proposal that follows, I offer a word of testimony (as my Pentecostal tradition

---

[20] There are, of course, other proposals with regard to the book's structure that do not fit neatly with those described above. One example is the structure recently set forth by R. Wall (*New Interpreters Bible* X [Nashville: Abingdon, 2002], pp. 35-36), who divides the book into two major sections identified as 'Acts 2.14–15.12, PART ONE: A NARRATIVE OF CONVERSION' and Acts 15.13–28.28, PART TWO: A NARRATIVE OF CONSECRATION'. The geographical progression constitutes a major portion of Part 1. In addition, Wall is more successful than most in acknowledging the activity of the Holy Spirit in his proposal and is quite accomplished in identifying the significant characters within the Acts narrative. However, the literary markers are not determinative for his outline. B. Witherington III (*The Acts of the Apostles: A Socio-Rhetorical Commentary* [Grand Rapids: Eerdmans, 1998], pp. v-ix) proposes a rhetorical structure for the book which is successful in conveying the sense of geographical progression in the book as well as the importance of key characters. The presence of the Spirit in the outline is not as pronounced, nor are the literary markers sufficiently utilized, though he knows of their significance (cf. the discussion on p. 74).

would put it).²¹ My initial interest in this topic grows out of my efforts to develop a distinctively Pentecostal approach to teaching Biblical Studies in general and New Testament Introduction in particular.²² It is my conviction that among the things that students need in their initial graduate level encounter with the New Testament is to become acquainted with the Structure, Content, and Theological Emphases of a given document.²³ As I began to write my lectures anew, in the light of the paradigm I saw emerging, my challenge included focusing on the structure of the individual texts examined in the course. As I have made this interpretive journey I have been delighted to find that a variety of insights valuable for the interpretation of a text emerge as a result of deliberate focus on the structure and contours of that text. In setting forth my proposal with regard to Acts I shall attempt to share it as I experienced the journey, so that the study of this narrative will itself take somewhat of a narrative form.

My own methodological orientation, greatly informed by various literary approaches, led me to take my initial clues from the literary markers in the text. One of the things that immediately gained my attention was the fact that, as Roberts had pointed out, the Acts narrative is punctuated with a variety of summary statements that more or less chronicle the spread of the Gospel and growth of the church (Acts 6.7; 9.31; 12.24; 16.5; 19.20). It struck me that such periodic statements functioned somewhat as a refrain throughout the narrative and would not be lost on the hearer/reader. This refrain reminded me of the function of the summary statements which appear at the close of the major discourses in the Gospel according to Matthew (7.28-29; 11.1; 13.53; 19.1; 26.1) and are themselves not without structural significance.²⁴ I was puzzled by the fact that so few commentators followed this literary lead, but encouraged by the work of Arrington and Gooding. Of course, as I began to pursue this line of thought I soon discovered that Roberts had omitted two additional summary statements, those occurring in 2.47 and 11.21. Given their obvious connections to the other summary statements I included these two in my

---

²¹ For those unfamiliar with 'Pentecostal testimony', perhaps a functional equivalent would be the 'autobiographical' approach that has recently appeared in certain sections of the Biblical Studies guild.

²² Cf. Chapter 1 above and J.C. Thomas, '"Pentecostal Explorations of the New Testament": Teaching New Testament Introduction in a Pentecostal Seminary', *JPT* 11.1 (2002), pp. 120-29.

²³ Other aspects include familiarity with a given book's canonical context, original context, church context (*Wirkungsgeschichte*), and Pentecostal context.

²⁴ On this cf. D.R. Bauer, *The Structure of Matthew's Gospel: A Study in Literary Design* (BLS 15; Sheffield: Almond Press, 1989).

initial attempts to plot the broad contours of the text. I found that they contributed to the overall structure in a helpful way.

Before taking up the issue of the structure of Acts I had the opportunity to edit Roger Stronstad's *Prophethood of All Believers*. I must admit that I was quite taken by the way in which he saw the theme of charismatic anointing as not only a dominant one within the book but also that he structured the entire book around it. Given the fact that few scholars make more than passing reference to the Holy Spirit in discussing the structure of Acts, I was quickly convinced that Stronstad's insights merited consideration as I continued my reflection about the book's structure. Specifically, I began to explore the connections between the literary markers in the text and the theme of charismatic anointing. What I found was quite surprising and very encouraging.

It soon became clear to me that not only were these two ways of approaching the structure of Acts compatible with one another, but also that when interfaced they reveal even more clearly the charismatic emphasis of the book. By focusing on the major sections marked out by the summary statements and by giving adequate attention to the charismatic emphases of the text, the structure and content of the narrative clearly emerge. On this view, the narrative is divided into eight panels that chronicle the spread of the Gospel and the growth of the church by means of the direction and anointing of the Holy Spirit. The following tentative outline illustrates this point:

1.1-5 – The Prologue
1.6–2.47 – The Anointing of the Charismatic Community in Jerusalem
3.1–6.7 – The Acts of the Charismatic Leader Peter and Those of the Charismatic Community in Jerusalem
6.8–9.31 – The Acts of Certain Charismatic Leaders (and the Conversion of a Future One) in Jerusalem, Judea, and Samaria: Stephen, Philip, and Paul
9.32–11.21 – The Acts of a Certain Charismatic Leader in Lydda, Caesarea, and Jerusalem: Peter
11.22–12.24 – The Acts of Certain Charismatic Leaders in Antioch and Jerusalem: Barnabas, Agabus, and Peter
12.25–16.5 – The Acts of a Certain Charismatic Leader: Paul – From Antioch to Derbe and Back Again, From Antioch to Jerusalem and Back Again
16.6–19.20 – The Acts of a Certain Charismatic Leader: Paul – The Call and Journey to Macedonia
19.21–28.31 – The Acts of a Certain Charismatic Leader: Paul – To Macedonia, Jerusalem and Rome

The conclusion that the literary markers and the theme of charismatic anointing interfaced in such a remarkable fashion led me to a closer examination of the content in each panel of the text. What I began to see astounded me. For in each of the eight panels I saw that there was either a description of a charismatic anointing, reference to someone so anointed, or an account of the Spirit's charismatic activity! The examples are as follows:

2.1-4 – The Outpouring of the Holy Spirit on the Day of Pentecost
4.30-31 – The Jerusalem Believers Are All Filled with the Holy Spirit
8.14-17 – The Samaritan Believers Receive the Holy Spirit
10.44-48 – Cornelius and his Household Are Filled with the Holy Spirit
11.24-28 – Barnabas, Full of the Holy Spirit and Faith
13.9 – Saul/Paul, Full of the Holy Spirit
19.1-7 – The Disciples at Ephesus Are Filled with the Holy Spirit
20.22–21.11 – Spirit/Prophetic Activity in Paul and Agabus

This discovery served to confirm for me that the literary markers are important for determining the book's basic structure and that the charismatic emphasis of Acts is more dominant than even many Pentecostals have had the eyes to see. In other words, the charismatic dimension of Acts is part of the very fabric of the narrative.[25]

It is also readily visible from the interface between the literary markers and the theme of charismatic anointing that prominent characters within the narrative receive appropriate attention in the book's structure. However, such attention is not limited, as in some proposals, to the two major characters (Peter and Paul), but includes a number of other charismatically anointed individuals who play significant roles in the spread of the Gospel and the growth of the church.

Finally, this articulation of the book's structure also gives a sense of the geographical progression of the Acts narrative as it follows the various charismatically anointed individuals from Jerusalem to Rome. However, by giving due attention to the literary markers in the text the nature of the progression is more in keeping with the way in which the narrative describes this unfolding drama. For example, instead of appropriating extra-textual language like 'Paul's first, second, and third missionary journeys' to describe portions of Paul's activities, as is not infrequently done,[26] this approach allows the text to define the geographical progression in its own terms.

When all these factors are taken into consideration the following structure emerges:

---

[25] Other evidence of this emphasis might be found in the various references to the symbolic conquering of evil in Acts 5.1-11; 8.9-24; 13.4-12; 16.16-18; 19.11-20; 28.1-6. On this cf. Johnson, *The Acts of the Apostles*, p. 11.

[26] Cf. for example, W. Neil, *The Acts of the Apostles* (Grand Rapids: Eerdmans, 1981).

1.1-5 – The Prologue
1.6–2.47 – The Anointing of the Charismatic Community in Jerusalem
   [2.1-4 – The Outpouring of the Holy Spirit on the Day of Pentecost]
3.1–6.7 – The Acts of the Charismatic Leader Peter and the Charismatic Community in Jerusalem
   [4.30-31 – The Jerusalem Believers Are All Filled with the Holy Spirit]
6.8–9.31 – The Acts of Certain Charismatic Leaders (and the Conversion of a Future One) in Jerusalem, Judea, and Samaria: Stephen, Philip, and Paul
   [8.14-17 – The Samaritans Receive the Holy Spirit]
9.32–11.21 – The Acts of a Certain Charismatic Leader in Lydda, Caesarea, and Jerusalem: Peter
   [10.44-48 – Cornelius and his Household Are Filled with the Holy Spirit]
11.22–12.24 – The Acts of Certain Charismatic Leaders in Antioch and Jerusalem: Barnabas, Agabus, and Peter
   [11.24-28 – Barnabas, Full of the Holy Spirit and Faith]
12.25–16.5 – The Acts of a Certain Charismatic Leader: Paul – From Antioch to Derbe and Back Again, and From Antioch to Jerusalem and Back Again
   [13.9 – Saul/Paul, Full of the Holy Spirit]
16.6–19.20 – The Acts of a Certain Charismatic Leader: Paul – The Call and Journey to Macedonia
   [19.1-7 – The Disciples at Ephesus Are Filled with the Holy Spirit]
19.21–28.31 – The Acts of a Certain Charismatic Leader: Paul – To Macedonia, Jerusalem and Rome
   [20.22–21.11 – Spirit/Prophetic Activity in Paul and Agabus]

While other dimensions of the text no doubt merit consideration in discerning the structure of the Acts narrative, perhaps this modest proposal will serve to generate additional helpful discussions among those interested in this biblical text. It is my hope that this short study will contribute in some small way to a better understanding of the book of Acts.

15

Women, Pentecostals, and the Bible:
An Experiment in Pentecostal Hermeneutics

I

Perhaps few topics have generated more discussion among Pentecostal scholars over the past few years than that which has emerged around the issue of 'Pentecostal Hermeneutics'. Scholars who have entered into this debate range from those who deny the need for a distinctive Pentecostal hermeneutic, preferring to follow current evangelical models, to those who are in dialogue with a number of methodologies that have come to the forefront within the last two decades. While no consensus has emerged as of yet, it appears that many scholars working within the Pentecostal tradition are less content to adopt a system of interpretation that is heavily slanted toward rationalism and has little room for the role of the Holy Spirit.

Several reasons account for the desire on the part of some Pentecostal scholars to identify and articulate a hermeneutic that is more representative of the tradition and its ethos. Disappointment with the results of rationalism is one major factor in the emergence of this trend. Owing to the promises made for rationalism, growing out of the Enlightenment, many western thinkers became convinced that pure reason was the key to the interpretation of any literature, both biblical and non-biblical. But the results of an unbridled rationalism have been anything but uniform, as witnessed in the diversity of current theological thought, which in and of itself suggests that there is more to interpretation than reason.[1]

The dearth of serious critical reflection on the role of the Holy Spirit in the interpretive process has also whetted the appetite of several Pentecostal scholars for an approach which seeks to articulate what the Spirit's role is and how the Spirit works specifically. It is, indeed, one of the oddities of modern theological scholarship that both liberal and

---

[1] This assessment is true even of evangelical theology, where an extremely high view of Scripture has brought little consensus on a variety of interpretive matters.

conservative approaches to Scripture have little or no appreciation for the work of the Holy Spirit in interpretation.[2] Obviously, such a hermeneutical component is of no little interest to Pentecostal scholars.[3]

Another contributing factor to this recent surge of hermeneutical activity among Pentecostals is the belief of several scholars that the role of the community in the interpretive process is extremely important. Given the community orientation of Pentecostalism on the one hand and the excesses of a somewhat rampant individualism among interpreters generally (both liberal and conservative) on the other hand, reflection on the place of the community in the hermeneutical process would appear to be a natural next step in the development of a Pentecostal hermeneutic.

Finally, the recent paradigm shift(s) in the field of hermeneutics generally has suggested to some scholars that the time is right to enter into a serious discussion about Pentecostal hermeneutics. Not only have insights from recent hermeneutical discussions confirmed the appropriateness of certain Pentecostal interpretive emphases (such as the importance of experiential presuppositions in interpretation and the role of narrative in the doing of theology), but also the insights gained from a diversity of approaches to the biblical text have given some Pentecostals courage to believe that they too have some contribution to make to the current hermeneutical debate.

While it might sometimes be thought, or even charged, that Pentecostals desire to articulate their own hermeneutical approach merely to be distinctive, in point of fact, it would appear that just as Pentecostals have been able to help the church rediscover a number of biblical truths with regard to pneumatology, so they may also have gifts to give when it comes to the interpretive process itself.

But what would a Pentecostal hermeneutic look like and, more importantly, how would it function? What would be the essential components of such an interpretive approach and how would one settle on them? These are just the beginning of a multitude of questions that this topic raises.

This short study seeks neither to offer an exhaustive overview of the topic of Pentecostal hermeneutics, nor to articulate in a detailed fashion a sophisticated theory of interpretation.[4] Rather, it seeks to explore

---

[2] C. Pinnock, *The Scripture Principle* (San Francisco: Harper & Row, 1984), p. 155.

[3] One of the few serious treatments of this topic among Pentecostals is the work of J.W. Wyckoff ('The Relationship of the Holy Spirit to Biblical Hermeneutics' [PhD dissertation, Baylor University, 1990]), who after an historical survey proposes a model regarding the Spirit's role based largely on an educational paradigm of teacher.

[4] For some recent attempts at Pentecostal hermeneutics, cf. the following: G.T. Sheppard, 'Pentecostalism and the Hermeneutics of Dispensationalism: Anatomy of an Uneasy Relationship', *Pneuma* 6 (2, 1984), pp. 5-33; M.D. McLean, 'Toward a Pente-

one possible paradigm, which is derived from the New Testament itself. After a brief discussion of this interpretational paradigm, the approach will be tested by attempting to gain leverage on a particularly difficult issue by the use of insights derived from this biblical model.

II

It is possible, of course, to find a number of different hermeneutical approaches in the New Testament and several full-length studies have been devoted to the use of the Old Testament by various New Testament writers.[5] Of these many interpretive approaches, one in particular has had a special appeal for many Pentecostals, especially at the popular level, and has recently also shown up in certain academic discussions on Pentecostal hermeneutics.[6] This approach is that revealed in the deliberations of the Jerusalem Council as described in Acts 15.1-29.

As is well known, the Jerusalem Council came together to determine if Gentile believers in Jesus must convert to Judaism in order to become full-fledged Christians. Luke relates that when Paul and Barnabas arrived in Jerusalem with the report regarding the conversion

---

costal Hermeneutic', *Pneuma* 6 (2, 1984), pp. 35-56; H.M. Ervin, 'Hermeneutics: A Pentecostal Option', in *Essays on Apostolic Themes* (ed. Paul Elbert; Peabody, MA: Hendrickson, 1985), pp. 23-35; F.L. Arrington, 'Hermeneutics', *Dictionary of Pentecostal and Charismatic Movements* (ed. Stanley Burgess, Gary B. McGee; Grand Rapids: Zondervan, 1988), pp. 376-89; R. Stronstad, 'Trends in Pentecostal Hermeneutics', *Paraclete* 22 (3, 1988), pp. 1-12; R. Stronstad, 'Pentecostal Experience and Hermeneutics', *Paraclete* 26 (1, 1992), pp. 14-30; J.D. Johns & C. Bridges Johns, 'Yielding to the Spirit: A Pentecostal Approach to Group Bible Study', *JPT* 1 (1992), pp. 109-34; A.C. Autry, 'Dimensions of Hermeneutics in Pentecostal Focus', *JPT* 3 (1993), pp. 29-50; R. Israel, D. Albrecht, & R.G. McNally, 'Pentecostals and Hermeneutics: Texts, Rituals and Community', *Pnuema* 15 (1993), pp. 137-61; T.B. Cargal, 'Beyond the Fundamentalist-Modernist Controversy: Pentecostals and Hermeneutics in a Postmodern Age', *Pneuma* 15 (1993), pp. 163-87; R.P. Menzies, 'Jumping Off the Postmodern Bandwagon', *Pneuma* 16 (1994), pp. 115-20; G.T. Sheppard, 'Biblical Interpretation after Gadamer', *Pneuma* 16 (1994), pp. 121-41; J. McKay, 'When the Veil Is Taken Away: The Impact of Prophetic Experience on Biblical Interpretation', *JPT* 5 (1994), pp. 17-40; R.D. Moore, 'Deuteronomy and the Fire of God: A Critical Charismatic Interpretation', *JPT* 7 (1995), pp. 11-33; R.O. Baker, 'Pentecostal Bible Reading: Toward a Model of Reading for the Formation of Christian Affections', *JPT* 7 (1995), pp. 34-48; K.J. Archer, 'Pentecostal Hermeneutics: Retrospect and Prospect', *JPT* 8 (1996), pp. 63-81.

[5] On this topic cf. especially E.E. Ellis, *The Old Testament in Early Christianity* (Grand Rapids: Baker, 1992); R.B. Hays, *Echoes of Scripture in the Letters of Paul* (New Haven: Yale University Press, 1989); C.A. Evans & J.A. Sanders, *Luke and Scripture: The Function of Sacred Tradition in Luke-Acts* (Minneapolis: Fortress, 1993).

[6] Cf. the discussion by F.L. Arrington, 'Hermeneutics', pp. 387-88 and R.D. Moore, 'Approaching God's Word Biblically: A Pentecostal Perspective' (A Paper Presented to the Society for Pentecostal Studies, Fresno, CA).

of the Gentiles, certain believers who were members of the religious party of the Pharisees (τινες τῶν ἀπὸ τῆς αἱρέσεως τῶν Φαρισαίων) demanded that the Gentile believers (1) be circumcised and (2) keep the law of Moses. As a result of this report and its somewhat mixed reception, the apostles and elders gathered together to look into this matter (ἰδεῖν περὶ τοῦ λόγου τούτου).

The first person to speak, Peter, begins by noting the actions of God among them. It was *God* who chose to allow the Gentiles to hear the Gospel (through the mouth of Peter) and believe. It was the *God* who knows all hearts who testified as to the validity of their faith by giving them the Holy Spirit. *God* had made no distinction between Jew and Gentile either in the giving of the Spirit or in the cleansing of hearts. In the light of such experience, Peter reasons that to place the yoke (of the Law?) upon these Gentiles would be tantamount to testing (πειράζετε) God. In contrast to the bearing of this yoke, Peter says it is by faith that all are saved!

This speech is followed by a report from Barnabas and Paul, which also places emphasis upon God and the things that he did through them among the Gentiles, such as signs and wonders.

James now takes center stage and addresses the group. He not only interprets Peter's testimony to mean that God has received the Gentiles as a people unto his name, but he also goes on to argue that this experience of the church is in agreement with the words of the prophets, citing Amos 9.11-12 as evidence. Therefore (διό), in the light of what God had done and the agreement of these actions with the words of the prophets, James concludes that the Gentiles who are turning to God should not have their task made more difficult by requiring of them the observance of circumcision and the keeping of the Law of Moses. Rather, these Gentile converts are to be instructed to 'abstain from food polluted by idols, from sexual immorality, from the meat of strangled animals and from blood'. In the letter written to communicate the findings of this meeting to the church at large, the decision is described as resulting from the Holy Spirit, for v. 28 says, 'It seemed good to the Holy Spirit and to us not to burden you with anything beyond the following requirements.'

Several things are significant from Acts 15 for the purposes of this inquiry. First, it is remarkable how often the experience of the church through the hand of God is appealed to in the discussion. Clearly, this (somewhat unexpected?) move of God in the life of the church (the inclusion of the Gentiles) was understood to be the result of the Holy Spirit's activity. It is particularly significant that the church seems to have begun with its experience and only later moves to a consideration of the Scripture.

Second, Peter's experience in the matter of Gentile conversions has led him to the conclusion that even to question the Gentile converts' place in or means of admission to the church draws dangerously close to testing God. Apparently Peter means that to question the validity of the Gentile believers' standing before God, in the face of what the Spirit has done, is to come dangerously close to experiencing the wrath of God for such undiscerning disobedience. In this regard it is probably not without significance that earlier in Acts (5.9) Peter asked Sapphira how she could agree to test the Spirit of the Lord (πειράσαι τὸ πνεῦμα κυρίου) through her lie. The results of her testing are well known. Is Peter implying a similar fate for those who stand in the way of the Gentile converts?

Third, Barnabas and Paul are portrayed as discussing primarily, if not exclusively, their experience of the signs and wonders which God had performed among them as a basis for the acceptance of the Gentiles. That such a statement would stand on its own, says a great deal about the role of the community's experience of God in their decision-making process.

Fourth, James also emphasizes the experience of the church through the activity of God as a reason for accepting the Gentile converts. It is clear that Luke intends the readers to understand that James adds his own support to the experience of the Spirit in the church, for James does not simply restate Peter's earlier words, he puts his own interpretive spin upon them.

Fifth, it is at this point that Scripture is appealed to for the first time in the discussion. One of the interesting things about the passage cited (Amos 9.11-12) is that its appeal seems primarily to have been that it agreed with their experience of God in the church.[7] But how did James (and the church with him) settle on this particular text? Did Amos intend what James claims that the text means? Could not the believers from the religious party of the Pharisees have appealed with equal or greater validity to other texts which speak about Israel's exclusivity and the Gentiles' relationship to Israel (cf. esp. Exod. 19.5; Deut. 7.6; 14.2; 26.18-19)?

When one reads the Hebrew text of Amos 9.11-12, or a translation based upon the Hebrew text, it becomes immediately obvious that there is no explicit reference to the inclusion of Gentiles as part of the people of God. In point of fact, in the Hebrew text, Amos says that God will work on behalf of the descendants of David 'so that they may

---

[7] As L.T. Johnson (*Scripture and Discernment: Decision Making in the Church* [Nashville, TN: Abingdon, 1996], p. 105) observes, 'What is remarkable, however, is that the text is confirmed by the narrative [events previously narrated in Acts], not the narrative by Scripture.'

possess the remnant of Edom and all the nations, which are called by the name, says the Lord that does this.' Although it is possible to read the reference to Edom and the other nations in a negative or retaliatory sense, it is also possible to see here an implicit promise concerning how Edom (one of the most hostile enemies of Israel) and other nations will themselves be brought into the (messianic) reign of a future Davidic king.[8] Whether or not such a meaning was intended by Amos is unclear.

By way of contrast, the LXX rendering of Amos 9.11-12 seems to intend a message about the inclusion of other individuals and nations who seek to follow God. At this crucial point, the text of Acts is much closer to the LXX, which reads, 'That the remnant of men and all the Gentiles, upon whom my name is called, may seek after (me), says the Lord who does these things.' The difference in the Hebrew text and the LXX seems to have resulted, in part, from reading Edom (אדום) as Adam (אדם) and taking the verb 'they shall possess' (יירשו) as 'they shall seek' (ידרשו).[9] Whatever may account for this rendering,[10] it is clear that James, as described in Acts 15.17, shows a decided preference for the LXX's more inclusive reading.

But why did James choose this particular text for support when other Old Testament passages (cf. Isa. 2.3; 42.6; Mic. 4.2; and esp. Zech. 2.11) appear to offer better and clearer support for the inclusion of Gentiles within the people of God? Such a choice is difficult to understand until one views it within the broader context of the Lucan narratives. Specifically, Luke seems concerned to demonstrate that the promises made to David are fulfilled in Jesus and thus have implications for the church.

In the gospel, Joseph is identified as a descendant of David (1.27). The angel speaks to Mary regarding Jesus saying, 'The Lord God will give him the throne of his father David, and he will reign over the house of Jacob forever; his kingdom will never end' (1.32-33). Zecha-

---

[8] So argues W.C. Kaiser, 'The Davidic Promise and the Inclusion of the Gentiles (Amos 9:9-15 and Acts 15:13-18): A Test Passage for Theological Systems', *JETS* 20 (1977), p. 102.

[9] C.F. Keil, *Minor Prophets* (Grand Rapids: Eerdmans, 1975), p. 334 n. 1 and D.A. Hubbard, *Joel & Amos* (Leicester; IVP, 1989), p. 242.

[10] Some argue a Hebrew text that challenges the MT at this point lies behind the LXX. Cf. M.A. Braun, 'James' Use of Amos at the Jerusalem Council: Steps toward a Possible Solution of the Textual and Theological Problems', *JETS* 20 (1977), p. 116. R.J. Bauckham ('James and the Jerusalem Church', in *The Book of Acts in Its First Century Setting*, vol. 4: *Palestinian Setting* [ed. R.J. Bauckham; Grand Rapids, MI: Eerdmans, 1995), pp. 415-80) argues that the composition and interpretation of the Scriptural quotation in 15.16-18 is the result of 'the skilled use of contemporary Jewish exegetical methods and ...' (how) 'the quotation is exegetically linked with the terms of the apostolic decree' (p. 453).

riah (apparently) speaks of Jesus when he says, 'He has raised up a horn of salvation for us in the house of his servant David' (1.69). Joseph and Mary go to the city of David for the census because Joseph is of the house and line of David (2.4). Later, the angels direct the shepherds to the city of David to find Christ the Lord (2.11). In Luke's genealogy of Jesus, David is mentioned (3.31). In a dispute over the Sabbath Jesus appeals to the actions of David (6.3). The blind beggar near Jericho addresses Jesus as the Son of David when he calls for help (18.38-39). In a discussion with the Sadducees and teachers of the Law Jesus says that although the Messiah is called Son of David, David calls him Lord (20.41-44).

This same emphasis continues in the book of Acts. Peter states that the Holy Spirit spoke Scripture through the mouth of David (1.16). In the Pentecost sermon Peter attributes Scripture to David again (2.25) and says that he foretold the resurrection of Jesus (2.29-36). A little later in the narrative David is again identified as one through whom the Holy Spirit spoke (4.25). In Stephen's speech David is described as one who enjoyed God's favor (7.45). Several references to David are found in chapter 13 in Paul's sermon at Pisidian Antioch. David is said to have been a man after God's own heart whose descendant is the Savior Jesus (13.22-23). Jesus is said to have been given 'the holy and sure blessings promised to David' (13.34) and his death is contrasted with that of David (13.36).

That Luke would continue his emphasis on David should surprise no one. It would appear then, that part of the reason for the choice of this particular text from Amos is to continue the emphasis on the continuity between David and Jesus. It may also be significant that the first citation of Amos (5.25-27) in Acts (7.42-44) speaks of exile, while Acts 15 speaks of restoration.[11] Consequently, to cite the rebuilding of David's fallen tent as the context for the admission of Gentiles into Israel was perhaps the most effective way of making this point.

Sixth, James rather clearly speaks with authority as he discloses his decision. That the decision is closely tied to the previous discussions is indicated by the use of 'therefore' (διό). That James has the authority to render a verdict is suggested by the emphatic use of the personal pronoun I (ἐγὼ κρίνω). But as the epistle itself reveals (v. 24), the deci-

---

[11] For a comprehensive discussion of this approach cf. P.-A. Peulo, *Le problème ecclésial des Acts à la lumière de deux prophéties d'Amos* (Paris: Cerf, 1985). Cf. also J. Dupont, '"Je rebâtirai la cabane de David qui est tombée" (Ac 15, 16 = Am 9, 11)', in *Glaube und Eschatologie* (ed. E. Grässer & O. Merk; Tübingen: J.C.B. Mohr [Paul Siebeck], 1985), pp. 19-32. M. Turner (*Power from on High: The Spirit in Israel's Restoration and Witness in Luke-Acts* [JPTS 9; Sheffield: Sheffield Academic Press, 1996], pp. 314-15) argues strongly for an interpretation which emphasizes 'that Zion's restoration is *well under way* as a consequence of Jesus' exaltation to David's throne.'

sion was one that involved the whole group and the guidance of the Holy Spirit.

Seventh, several stipulations were imposed upon the Gentile converts. Most significant is the omission of a reference to circumcision. Aside from the directive to abstain from sexual immorality, the other commands refer to food laws. Although there is some evidence that their origin is in the regulations regarding aliens who lived among the Hebrews, as found in Lev 17-18, their intent is a bit puzzling. Are they to be seen as the lowest common denominator of the Torah's dietary laws or as the true meaning of the food laws? Are they intended to be seen as universally valid? The practice of the later church (and perhaps Paul's own advice in 1 Cor. 8.1-13) has not viewed the food laws as binding, however.[12] Perhaps it is best to view them as (temporary) steps to ensure table fellowship between Jewish and Gentile believers. When the composition of the church changed to a predominantly Gentile constituency, it appears that these directives regarding food were disregarded.

III

What sort of hermeneutical paradigm may be deduced from the method of the Jerusalem Council and what are the components of this model? Of the many things that might be said, perhaps the most obvious is the role of the community in the interpretive process. Several indicators in the text justify this conclusion. (1) It is the community that has gathered together in Acts 15. Such a gathering suggests that for the author of Acts it was absolutely essential for the (entire?) community to be in on the interpretive decision reached. (2) It is the community that is able to give and receive testimony as well as assess the reports of God's activity in the lives of those who are part of the community. (3) Despite James's leading role in the process, it is evident that the author of Acts regarded the decision as coming from the community under the leadership of the Holy Spirit. All of this evidence suggests that any model of hermeneutics which seeks to build upon Acts 15 cannot afford to ignore the significant role of the community in that process.

---

[12] There is some evidence that the decree regarding food was still followed as late as 177 CE in Gaul. Eusebius's report (*E.H.* V.1.26) of one female Christian's response to her tormenter, shortly before her martyrdom, illustrates this point. She said, 'How would such men eat children, when they are not allowed to eat the blood even of irrational animals?' Cited according to the translation of K. Lake, *Eusebius, Ecclesiastical History* I (London: Heinemann, 1926), p. 419.

A second element which must be mentioned at this juncture is the role the Holy Spirit plays in this interpretive event. In point of fact, appeal is made to the action of God and/or the Holy Spirit so often in this pericope that it is somewhat startling to many modern readers. For not only is the final decision of the Council described as seeming good to the Holy Spirit, but the previous activity of the Spirit in the community also spoke very loudly to the group, being in part responsible for the text chosen as most appropriate for this particular context. Such explicit dependence upon the Spirit in the interpretive process clearly goes far beyond the rather tame claims regarding 'illumination' which many conservatives (and Pentecostals) have often made regarding the Spirit's role in interpretation. While a model based on Acts 15 would no doubt make room for illumination in the Spirit's work, it would include a far greater role for the work of the Spirit in the community as the context for interpretation. While concerns about the dangers of subjectivism must be duly noted, the evidence of Acts 15 simply will not allow for a more restrained approach.

The final prominent component in this interpretive paradigm is the place of the biblical text itself. Several observations are called for here. First, the methodology revealed in Acts 15 is far removed from the historical-critical or historical-grammatical approach where one moves from text to context. On this occasion, the interpreters moved from their context to the biblical text. Second, the passage cited in Acts 15 was chosen out of a much larger group of Old Testament texts which were, at the very least, diverse in terms of whether Gentiles were to be included or excluded from the people of God. It appears that the experience of the Spirit in the community helped the church make its way through this hermeneutical maze. In other words, despite the fact that there were plenty of texts that appeared to teach that there was no place for the Gentiles as Gentiles in the people of God, the Spirit's witness heavily influenced the choice and use of Scripture. Third, Scripture was also apparently drawn on in the construction of certain stipulations imposed upon the Gentile converts to ensure table fellowship between Jewish Christian and Gentile Christian believers. This step seems to have been a temporary one and these stipulations in no way treat the Gentile converts as less than Christian nor as inferior to their Jewish-Christian brothers and sisters. These points unmistakably reveal that the biblical text was assigned and functioned with a great deal of authority in this hermeneutical approach. However, in contrast to the way in which propositional approaches to the issue of authority function, Acts 15 reveals that the text's authority is not unrelated to its relevance to the community, its own diversity of teaching on a given topic, and the role which the Scripture plays in the constructing of temporary or transitional stipulations for the sake of fellowship in the community.

In sum, the proposed Pentecostal hermeneutic built on Acts 15 has three primary components: the community, the activity of the Spirit, and the Scripture. In order to gauge the usefulness of this paradigm, it will now be tested by addressing a specific particularly difficult issue currently facing the church.

IV

One of the most significant current debates within the ecclesiastical world is that regarding the role of women in the ministry of the church. A number of problems complicate the issue, not least of which is the fact that the New Testament evidence ranges from texts that describe women as active participants in ministry to those that advocate the (complete) silence of women in the church. Although various approaches to these texts have been followed, for many interpreters the question comes down to one: did Paul (or someone writing in his name) mean what he said regarding silence? Normally, one of three interpretive decisions is made. (1) One possibility is that Paul intended for women to remain silent and, therefore, outside the ministry of the church. The passages which appear to advocate a leading role for women must mean something else or, at the least, be interpreted in a fashion that would not contradict the silence passages. (2) Another option is to say that Paul meant what he said regarding silence but did not intend these statements to be taken as universally applicable. Rather, they were directed to specific situations and have nothing, or very little, to contribute to the broader question. (3) Still another approach is to say that Paul simply did not mean what he seems to have said. Therefore, these texts do not contradict those which assign a leading role to women in the ministry of the church.

Each of these interpretive options, regardless of the theological orientation of the interpreters, is grounded in a somewhat rationalistic approach to the biblical text, which seeks to determine, primarily through historical-critical investigation, the meaning of these passages and how it is that they might fit together. For the most part, Pentecostals have followed the lead of others in attempting to come to a decision regarding this crucial issue. Unfortunately, there exists at present a logjam in most Pentecostal groups that shows few signs of breaking up. It is to this issue that the paradigm contained in Acts 15 is now applied.

The Pentecostal Community

As with the approach found in Acts 15, the appropriate place to begin this discussion is with the community in which this attempt at interpretation is to take place. Pentecostals should have little trouble with this component for the movement itself has been one in which community has played a leading role. For our purposes, the community is here defined as those individuals called out of the world by God who have experienced salvation through Jesus Christ and are empowered by the Holy Spirit to do the work of ministry in this present world. This community could be a single, local Spirit-filled body or a group (or denomination[s]) of such congregations. One of the crucial elements would be the presence of a sufficient level of knowledge of one another, accountability, and discernment within this community to safeguard against the dangers of an uncontrolled subjectivism and/or a rampant individualism. It would be a community whose shared experience of the Spirit would allow for testimony to be given, received, and evaluated in the light of Scripture. Therefore, as far as this issue is concerned, interpretation is no private affair, in the sole possession of scholars, but is the responsibility of the community. This observation remains valid even if, as in Acts 15, a group of leaders representing the larger group are called upon to perform such a function.

The Work of the Holy Spirit

It is within such a community that the experiences of the Spirit, or the acts of God, are manifested. As in Acts 15, the activity of God is made known to the larger community through testimonies about the work of the Holy Spirit. What sorts of testimonies would such a Pentecostal community hear regarding the role of women within the movement, and from whence would they come? The testimonies from the past found in the pages of publications like *The Apostolic Faith, Church of God Evangel, Pentecostal Holiness Advocate, Pentecostal Evangel, Latter Rain Evangel, Bridal Call,* the *Crusader* and many others from around the world would bear witness to the fact that God had gifted women to do the work of ministry in the Pentecostal revival. The ministerial records from various denominational archives would reveal the ways in which the Spirit has endowed sons *and daughters* with gifts for ministries that circle the globe and manifest themselves in the planting of churches, founding of schools and orphanages, publishing of newsletters and magazines, working with the poor and oppressed, as well as singing, preaching, teaching, and supporting the church financially. In addition to these forms of testimony, would not those converted, sanctified, Spirit Baptized, healed and called into the harvest through the ministries of our sisters join in the raising of their voices as to God's actions among us?

In the face of such powerful testimonies to the activity of God in the church, is a response like Peter's not appropriate – why do you wish to test God by placing restrictions upon the ministry of our Pentecostal sisters? If indeed God is giving gifts to women for ministry, are we not in danger of divine wrath if we test God by ignoring his actions? What if there are some in the broader community who object that *they* have not seen such ministry among women? One could only respond that most of those in Jerusalem had not seen Gentile converts with their own eyes, but in the end were willing to accept the testimony of others who had witnessed such conversions. At least within the Pentecostal community, the work of the Spirit would lead most to the conclusion that God does intend for women to take a leading role in ministry. But what about the biblical texts? Do they not, at least in some respects, contradict what the Spirit appears to be doing in the community? How should these texts be approached and what exactly do they tell us about women in ministry?

The Role of the Scripture

The dilemma at this point is the nature of the biblical evidence itself. For, in truth, the New Testament seems both to affirm and deny a leading role for women in the ministry of the church.

On the one hand, it must be acknowledged fully that there are passages which state that women are to remain silent in the congregation (1 Cor. 14.33b-35) and are not permitted to teach or have authority over a man but must be silent (1 Tim. 2.11-12). Both texts have proven to be notoriously difficult to interpret in part because they seem to be contradicted or at the least modified by other passages in the same epistle (1 Cor. 11.5) or group of epistles (Tit. 2.4).[13]

On the other hand, there are a number of texts that appear to assume a prominent role for women in the church's ministry. These texts indicate: (1) that it was expected that women had the gift of prophecy (Acts 21.9) and/or would pray and prophesy in the community's public worship (1 Cor. 11.3-16), (2) that women were regarded as co-laborers with Paul in ministry (Rom. 16.3, 12; Phil. 4.3), (3) that somewhat technical terminology for ministry functions could be assigned to women, particularly the term διάκονον (Rom. 16.1) and

---

[13] One Pentecostal scholar goes so far as to suggest that the passage found in 1 Cor. 14.33b-35 is a later interpolation into the text. This somewhat radical decision is based almost wholly on internal considerations. Cf. G.D. Fee, *First Corinthians* (Grand Rapids: Eerdmans, 1987), pp. 699-705.

perhaps even ἀπόστολος (Rom. 16.7),[14] (4) that a woman could take the lead in instructing a man more fully in the way of the Lord (Acts 18.26), and (5) that women hosted house churches (Acts 12.12; Rom. 16.3; 1 Cor. 16.19; Col. 4.15), which in all likelihood included more than simply providing space for worship.[15]

In the light of the experience of God in the community, there can be little doubt which texts are most relevant to Pentecostals in the question regarding the role of women in the ministry of the church. Simply put, it would appear that given the Spirit's activity, those texts which testify to a prominent role for women in the church's ministry are the ones which should be given priority in offering direction for the Pentecostal church on this crucial issue. To the objection that might be raised on the basis of the silence passages, one can only respond that this objection is quite similar to the one that some of those present in Acts 15 could have produced regarding the exclusion of the Gentiles from the people of God. Despite the fact that a couple of silence passages do indeed exist, the powerful testimony of the Spirit coupled with numerous New Testament passages that clearly support a prominent role for women in ministry necessitate a course of action which not only makes room for women in the ministry of the church but also seeks to enlist all the talents of these largely under-utilized servants of the Lord in the most effective way possible for work in the harvest.

A final way in which the Scripture might function in grappling with this issue concerns the possible need for the adoption of temporary stipulations in order to preserve the 'table fellowship' of the broader community. Whatever the precise nature of such stipulations, in keeping with the spirit of those adopted in Acts 15, these stipulations should (1) be grounded in the biblical tradition, (2) in no way serve to undermine the legitimacy of women as ministers, and (3) most likely be regarded as temporary stipulations for the sake of genuine sensitivity on the part of some, both male and female, in the broader community of faith. However, it must be stated in no uncertain terms that the spirit of Acts 15 would clearly be violated if discussion about what might be legitimate stipulations regarding women in the ministry of the church in a given situation were taken as opportunities to impose (in some cases existing) oppressive restrictions upon women under the guise of sensitivity.

---

[14] There may have even been an order of widows in the early church (1 Tim. 5.9, 10).

[15] Cf. the relevant discussions in D. Birkey, *The House Church: A Model for Renewing the Church* (Scottdale, PA: Herald Press, 1988) and V. Branick, *The House Church in the Writings of Paul* (Wilmington: Michael Glazier, 1989).

V

Several concluding observations are offered here in order to summarize the major results and implications of this inquiry.

First, this study suggests that there may indeed be a distinctive hermeneutical approach to Scripture, contained in the New Testament itself, that is more in keeping with the ethos and worldview of the Pentecostal community than are many of the interpretive approaches currently being employed by a number of Pentecostal interpreters. Three elements are crucial for this approach to Scripture: the role of the community, the role of the Holy Spirit, and the role of Scripture.

Second, the community functions as the place where the Spirit of God acts and where testimony regarding God's activity is offered, assessed, and accepted or rejected. It also provides the forum for serious and sensitive discussions about the acts of God and the Scripture. The community can offer balance, accountability, and support. It can guard against rampant individualism and uncontrolled subjectivism. A serious appreciation for the role of the community among Pentecostals generally, and Pentecostal scholars specifically, might perhaps result in less isolationism on the one hand, and a serious corporate engagement with the biblical text rather than equating a majority vote with the will of God, on the other hand.

Third, in this paradigm the Holy Spirit's role in interpretation is not reduced to some vague talk of illumination, but creates the context for interpretation through his actions and, as a result, guides the church in the determination of which texts are most relevant in a particular situation and clarifies how they might best be approached. Acts 15 suggests that the Spirit may also offer guidance in the community's dialogue about the Scripture.

Fourth, in this hermeneutical model the text does not function in a static fashion but in a dynamic manner, making necessary a more intensive engagement with the text in order to discover its truths in ways that transcend the mere cognitive.

Fifth, this approach clearly regards Scripture as authoritative, for ultimately the experience of the church must be measured against the biblical text and, in that light, practices or views for which there is no biblical support would be deemed illegitimate. Thus, there is protection from rampant subjectivism. But instead of understanding the authority of Scripture as lying in the uniform propositions to which Scripture is sometimes reduced, in this paradigm an understanding of authority includes a respect for the text's literary genre and the diversity as well as the unity of Scripture. Therefore, this method regards Scripture as authoritative but allows the form and the content of the canon to define the nature of biblical authority and, consequently, one might say that it approaches the issue of biblical authority more biblically.

Sixth, this interpretive model suggests a way forward for the church when faced with issues about which the biblical evidence is (or appears to be) divided. Just as the Spirit's activity in the community was able to lead the church to a decision regarding the inclusion of Gentiles, despite the diversity of the biblical statements on this topic, so it would seem that this paradigm could assist the (Pentecostal) church in grappling with significant issues that simply will not disappear (for example the issues of divorce and the relationship between the church and civil governments).

Seventh, this hermeneutical method has been tested by examining the role of women in the ministry of the church. The results of this brief analysis suggest that many Pentecostal churches have not paid nearly enough attention to the activity of the Holy Spirit in empowering women for a variety of ministries in the church, and as a result, have allowed one or two texts to undermine the balance of the biblical teaching on this topic, as well as the Spirit's own witness. If this paradigm proves to be one of which Pentecostals make use, then perhaps the Pentecostal church will be less inclined simply to follow others (whether liberal or conservative) on this topic and will have the courage, like the church in Acts 15, to make decisions which 'seem good to us *and the Holy Spirit*'.

This experiment, then, is offered with the hope that it might be of some assistance to Pentecostals in our attempt to articulate a Pentecostal hermeneutic.

16

The Order of the Composition of the Johannine Epistles

I

The advent of literary criticism and narrative analysis have resulted in the reading of familiar texts with new eyes, as readers seek to allow the text in its final form to have its say. Although literary analysis has often been done in some isolation from and/or in reaction to historical analysis, there are now indications of a willingness on the part of some scholars to explore the ways in which literary analysis and historical reconstruction may be used in a complementary fashion.[1] This short study, which is part of that larger endeavor, proposes that the order of the Johannine Epistles' composition may be clarified by approaching the topic via a literary analysis of the text of the epistles themselves.

My own efforts on this topic are the result of a pedagogical experiment and began quite by accident. In a recent graduate seminar on the Johannine Epistles, my students and I examined the epistles in the reverse order of their appearance in the canon. The very modest goal of this approach was simply to ensure that 3 and 2 John were read on their own terms, before being overshadowed by 1 John and skewed as a result. The only additional justification offered for this 'unorthodox' approach was the reminder that the canonical order of New Testament epistles was determined by length, with letters written by the same individual arranged in descending order, the longest letter standing first and the shortest letter standing last.[2]

However, as the term progressed it became more and more apparent that for many scholars 1 John had so overshadowed 3 and 2 John that their comments on and observations about the text of the two smaller

---

[1] For such attempts in Johannine studies cf. D. Rensberger, *Johannine Faith and Liberating Community* (Philadelphia: Westminster, 1988); J.C. Thomas, *Footwashing in John 13 and the Johannine Community* (Sheffield: JSOT, 1991); M.W.G. Stibbe, *John as Storyteller* (Cambridge: Cambridge University Press, 1992).

[2] Cf. the discussion in B.M. Metzger, *The Canon of the New Testament* (Oxford: Clarendon Press, 1987), pp. 295-300.

epistles were often determined by a prior study of 1 John. My seminar's reading of the epistles indicated that perhaps a number of points regarding the relationship between the epistles should be rethought, not least of which was the order of their composition.

It should, of course, be noted that there is little consensus about the order of the Johannine Epistles' composition, with nearly every conceivable order having been set forth. Scholars have argued that 1 John precedes 2 John,[3] that 2 John precedes 1 John,[4] that 3 John precedes 1 and 2 John,[5] and that the epistles were written at the same time.[6] Some

---

[3] Cf. A. Plummer, *The Epistles of St. John* (Cambridge: Cambridge University Press, 1886), pp. 28 and 58; J. Chaine, *Les Épitres Catholiques* (Paris: Gabalda, 1939), p. 240; R.K. Harrison, *Introduction to the New Testament* (Grand Rapids: Eerdmans, 1964), p. 426; A.M. Hunter, *Introducing the New Testament* (Philadelphia: Westminster, 1972), p. 182; R. Bultmann, *The Johannine Epistles* (trans. R.P. O'Hara, L.C. McGaughy, & R.W. Funk; Philadelphia: Fortress, 1973), pp. 1-3; K. Wengst, *Der erste, zweite, und dritte Brief des Johannes* (Würzburg: Echter Verlag, 1973), pp. 230-31; J.A. du Rand, 'Structure and Message of 2 John', *Neot* 13 (1979), p. 113; R.E. Brown, *The Epistles of John* (Garden City: Doubleday, 1982), pp. 31-32; G. Schunack, *Die Briefe des Johannes* (Zurich: Theologischer Verlag, 1982), pp. 108-109; K. Grayston, *The Johannine Epistles* (Grand Rapids: Eerdmans, 1984), p. 7; D. Guthrie, *New Testament Introduction* (Downers Grove: IVP, 1990), p. 885.

[4] Cf. G.W. Barker, W.L. Lane, and J.R. Michaels *The New Testament Speaks* (New York: Harper & Row, 1969), p. 424; F.-M. Braun, *Les Épitres de Saint Jean* (Paris: Cerf, 1973), p. 208; J.A.T. Robinson, *Redating the New Testament* (Philadelphia: Westminster, 1976), pp. 287-88; I.H. Marshall, *The Epistles of John* (Grand Rapids: Eerdmans, 1978), p. 10; P. Bonnard, *Les Épitres Johanniques* (Geneva: Labor et Fides, 1983), p. 119; B. Olsson, 'The History of the Johannine Movement', *Aspects on the Johannine Literature* (ed. L. Hartman & B. Olsson; Uppsala: Coniectanea Biblica, 1987), p. 34; G. Strecker, *Die Johannesbriefe* (Göttingen: Vandenhoeck & Ruprecht, 1989), pp. 26-28; C.H. Talbert, *Reading John* (New York: Crossroad, 1992), p. 9.

[5] C.H. Dodd, *The Johannine Epistles* (New York: Harper & Row, 1946), p. lxvii; Braun, *Les Epitres de Saint Jean*, pp. 202-203; Bonnard, *Les Épitres Johanniques*, p. 120; Olsson, 'The History of the Johannine Movement', p. 34.

[6] Cf. Robinson, *Redating the New Testament*, p. 288; D.W. Burdick, *The Letters of John the Apostle* (Chicago: Moody Press, 1985), pp. 417 and 444; R. Schnackenburg, *The Johannine Epistles* (trans. R. & I. Fuller; New York: Crossroads, 1992), p. 273. Some scholars argue that 2 and 3 John served as cover letters to 1 John. Cf. E.J. Goodspeed, *An Introduction to the New Testament* (Chicago: University of Chicago Press, 1937), pp. 319-24 and M.C. Tenney, *New Testament Survey* (Grand Rapids: Eerdmans, 1961), p. 375. Both L.T. Johnson (*The Writings of the New Testament* [Philadelphia: Fortress Press, 1986], pp. 503-10) and J. Reumann (*Variety and Unity in New Testament Thought* [Oxford: Oxford University Press, 1991], p. 204) believe that 3 John was a letter of introduction for Demetrius and that 2 John was a cover letter for 1 John. P. Perkins (*The Johannine Epistles* [Wilmington: Michael Glazier, 1984], p. 74) also suggests that 2 John was a cover letter for 1 John.

scholars have questioned whether there is enough evidence even to make a guess regarding the chronological order of the epistles.[7]

Of these many views, one particular approach should be mentioned briefly, owing to the stature and influence of its proponents. Recently, both Raymond E. Brown and Judith Lieu have argued that perhaps 2 and 3 John represent the last canonical evidence of the Johannine community's existence. Brown believes that 3 John logically comes after the other two epistles and reveals an emerging church structure that grew in reaction to the secession evidenced in 1 and 2 John.[8] For her part, Lieu sees evidence that in 3 John the party lines are hardening, with the Johannine concept of 'truth' becoming a mere slogan.[9] While Lieu makes clear her view that both 2 and 3 John follow 1 John, she seems to suggest that 2 John was composed after 3 John and represents a further stage in the entrenchment of the community against its opponents. Although denying that Diotrephes is to be identified as one of the 'false teachers', implicit in both positions is the idea that Diotrephes' hard-line approach concerning the reception of missionaries is in one way or another the result of the theological disruption of the Johannine community. But are such conclusions about 2 and 3 John the result of a careful reading of these texts, or that of an elaborate reconstruction based in large part upon 1 John? Birger Olsson warns of the circularity of all such assessments of the Johannine epistles by observing, 'The choice [of order] to a great extent depends on how one reconstructs the historical situation common to the Johannine writings about 100 A.D.'[10]

This essay attempts to break out of such circularity through approaching the historical issue of the order of the Johannine Epistles' composition by means of a brief literary analysis of the text and content of each of these epistles. As in the graduate seminar mentioned above, the epistles are examined in the reverse order of their appearance in the canon to ensure that 3 and 2 John receive as unprejudiced a reading as possible. The implications of this reading for the order of the Johannine Epistles' composition are given in the final portion of this study.

---

[7] Cf. the comments in P. Feine, J. Behm & W.G. Kümmel, *Introduction to the New Testament* (trans. A.J. Mattill, Jr.; Nashville: Abingdon, 1966), p. 316 and D.F. Büchsel, *Die Johannesbriefe* (Leipzig: A. Deichert, 1933), p. 92.

[8] R.E. Brown, *The Epistles of John*, pp. 31 and 107-108.

[9] Cf. J. Lieu, *The Second and Third Epistles of John* (Edinburgh: T. & T. Clark, 1986), pp. 148-65.

[10] Olsson, 'The History of the Johannine Movement', p. 34.

II

When 3 John is studied on its own terms, without the benefit or hindrance of reading it through the lens of 1 and 2 John, it becomes immediately apparent that 3 John has absolutely nothing that points to the false teaching which 1 and 2 John identify and combat. An examination of 3 John reveals that the epistle is devoted to an exhortation from the Elder to Gaius regarding the hospitable reception of Johannine emissaries. This exhortation includes a warning not to be influenced by the bad example of Diotrephes, who opposes the Elder at various points. However, there is no hint that Diotrephes is guilty of the kind of false teaching found in 1 or 2 John.

The absence of a reference to such false teaching implies one of four things: (1) either 3 John was written shortly before the outbreak of the false teaching described in 1 and 2 John, or (2) 3 John was written after the outbreak of the false teaching to a congregation within the community which had not yet been made aware of the theological deviation, or (3) 3 John was written after the outbreak of the false teaching but the Elder chose to make only extraordinarily subtle references to the false teaching, or (4) 3 John was written long after the theological controversy had passed.

The last option would appear to be ruled out owing to the several similarities between 2 and 3 John, which suggest that these two letters are not separated by a long interval of time. Concerning the second and third options, it is simply too difficult to believe that the same author who is so quick to discuss the dangers of false teaching in 1 and 2 John would write to a community and/or individual and not make the slightest reference to such false teaching. Even if the dominant theme in 3 John is the hospitable reception of missionaries, one would expect the Elder at least to mention the threat of the false teachers as an additional reason for Gaius to render support to the emissaries from the Elder. If, as most scholars believe, the problem with Diotrephes is unrelated to the false teaching, then a tension such as the one which exists between the Elder and Diotrephes (over leadership?) could have arisen at any time. If Diotrephes' exclusion of the Elder's emissaries was the result of the advice given in 2 Jn 10 to refuse those who bring false teaching,[11] it seems likely that the Elder would have drawn attention to his earlier instructions and/or reminded Gaius that such a course of action was to be taken because of heretical teaching, not lesser disagreements. In addition, it would be ill advised to conclude that it was the emergence of false teaching that prompted the initiation of sending emissaries from one congregation to another within the Johannine

---

[11] Lieu, *The Second and Third Epistles of John*, p. 164.

community. The mobility that existed in early Christianity generally argues against this idea, as does the fact that the Fourth Gospel itself contains mandates for missionary activity (cf. Jn 4.31-38; 20.19-23), which would have eventuated in the reception and sending of both missionaries and emissaries.

When approached on its own terms, 2 John reads very much like an initial attempt to warn a particular community, at some distance from the Elder, of the impending visit of false teachers. This short letter makes two basic points: (1) it warns the readers about the inevitable arrival of the deceivers and (2) it instructs them to take swift and decisive action if and when these deceivers arrive. The strict instructions given in vv. 10-11 read more like an initial emergency measure than the 'final' answer to the problem of false teachers. In all likelihood, the Elder wrote several other letters of warning to surrounding communities at the outbreak of this deception.[12] It appears that the threat of deceivers dividing the community in 2 John calls for much more severe measures than the Elder's approach in 3 John, which gives evidence of the extraordinary lengths to which he went in order to dialogue with and respond to his 'opponent' Diotrephes.[13]

In contrast, 1 John suggests that some time had transpired since the first appearance of the deceivers. This assessment is based, in part, on the fact that by the time 1 John was written the false teachers had left the Johannine community (1 Jn 2.18-27; 4.1-6) and had established an alternative community with its own distinctive interpretation of the Johannine Jesus traditions. But before these opponents left the Johannine community they had apparently caused such serious problems that a more comprehensive response was needed than that given in 2 Jn 10-11. It would appear that 1 John represents the result of the theological reflection generated within the community over the teaching of the

---

[12] M. Hengel, *The Johannine Question* (trans. J. Bowden; London: SCM Press, 1989), p. 39.

[13] Wengst (*Der erste, zweite, und dritte Brief des Johannes*, p. 230) argues that a progression is discernible from the Fourth Gospel, through 1 John to 2 John by tracing the way in which the love command is described. What in the Fourth Gospel (13.34) is described as a 'new command', is both an 'old and new command' in 1 John (2.7-8), and finally becomes an 'old command' in 2 Jn 5. For Wengst, this progression is an indication that by the time 2 John is written the command is no longer regarded as new. However, one must ask whether it is not more reasonable to see 1 Jn 2.7-8 as a theologically reflective conflation of Jn 13.34 and 2 Jn 5. For if 2 Jn 5 is in some way patterned after 1 John, one is hard pressed to explain why the writer would preserve only the claim that the command is old, when both John and 1 John describe it as new. More probably, the Elder in the heat of the moment describes the love command in 2 Jn 5 as old given the community's chronological distance from Jesus. In the light of later theological reflection the writer of 1 John seeks to preserve both the oldness and newness of the command. On this, cf. J.C. Thomas, *1 John, 2 John, 3 John* (PCS; London: T & T Clark, 2004), pp. 43-44, 102-104.

opponents. This epistle, then, was written to encourage those within the community to remain loyal to that 'which was received from the beginning' and in so doing responded to the views of opponents who wished to lead the faithful astray.

It might of course be objected that the non-epistolary form of 1 John indicates that it was a sermon designed for those congregations in close proximity to the Elder, implying that 2 John was written later for those congregations at some distance from the Elder.[14] However, this proposal fails to convince for several reasons. First, if 1 John was intended for those in close proximity to the Elder, one wonders why the letter would have been written in the first place, as the Elder would have been able to address these congregations firsthand. Second, this proposal fails to take into adequate account the similarities between 1 John and other 'sermons' which were apparently intended to function in some ways as an epistle (e.g. Hebrews). It is even possible that 1 John circulated among various congregations in the Johannine community with variable prescripts and greetings or several short personal notes to the different principals of the house church congregations,[15] although it must be admitted that there is no textual evidence for such a claim. Third, as has already been argued, when 1 and 2 John are approached independently it is 1 John, not 2 John, which shows signs of being the later of the two.

III

The reconstruction of the Johannine community's history is an extraordinarily complex and difficult task. The primary data from which the various hypotheses are constructed consist of the Fourth Gospel and 1, 2, 3 John. The way in which a particular vision of the community's history emerges is dependent in large part upon the way in which these texts are interpreted in relation to one another. The order in which the Johannine Epistles were composed is, therefore, an important part of such historical reconstruction.

Several suggestions regarding this task emerge from the analysis of the Johannine Epistles offered here. (1) Owing to the absence of any trace of the false teaching as found in 1 and 2 John, it is likely that 3 John was the first of these three epistles to have been written. This letter, devoted to the hospitable reception of the Johannine emissaries, probably was written just before the community was torn with the strife of false teaching. (2) It appears that 2 John was written shortly after the outbreak of the false teaching. The letter's general tone and its

---

[14] Brown, *Epistles of John*, pp. 31-32.
[15] Hengel, *The Johannine Question*, p. 48.

somewhat radical admonitions regarding those who bear the false teaching sound much more like an initial attempt to respond to the 'heresy' than a final desperate attempt to save the community. (3) In contrast to the thinking of many scholars, this study suggests that 1 John was the last of these epistles to have been written. The product of considerable reflection, 1 John appears to be a more comprehensive response to the false teaching of the opponents than that given in 2 John. It sought to expose the faulty interpretation of the Johannine Jesus tradition on the part of the opponents as well as to encourage the church to remain faithful to that 'which was received from the beginning'.

If these suggestions concerning the order of the Johannine Epistles' composition are anywhere near the mark then future readings of 2 and 3 John must be undertaken on their own terms, being examined for what they reveal about the community. In addition, certain aspects of the community's history may need to be rethought.

While certainty on such issues may forever be beyond the reach of the interpreter, perhaps the modest results of this short study will contribute to a better understanding of the community's history as well as suggest one of the ways in which literary analysis may be of service to historical concerns.[16]

---

[16] I would like to thank A.T. Lincoln and R.D. Moore for reading an earlier draft of this chapter.

17

The Literary Structure of 1 John

I

Students of 1 John are faced with a number of unique interpretive challenges, not least of which is the identification of the document's structure. The nature of this challenge is reflected by the lack of a true consensus among scholars with regard to the structure of 1 John and by the fact that some interpreters have given up altogether on the possibility of ever being able to identify a clear structure in the book. This observation should not be taken to imply that Johannine scholarship has shown no interest in the issue, on the contrary there has been (and continues to be) a plethora of proposals set forth.[1] However, most of the theories fail to convince owing to one of two weaknesses. On the one hand, they often do not pay sufficient attention to the clear literary markers that appear in the work, evidenced by various literary patterns in the text itself. On the other hand, it is not uncommon for interpreters to impose outlines on the book which show little regard for the actual contents of certain units in the text.

To illustrate this point the generally helpful bi-partite outlines of Raymond Brown and Stephen Smalley are briefly examined. Brown's proposal proves attractive because of its simplicity and because of the way it highlights the structural similarities between 1 John and the Fourth Gospel. Like the structure of the Fourth Gospel, the outline of 1 John picks up on two major divisions with a prologue and a conclusion.

> I. The Prologue (1.1-4)
>
> II. Part One (1.5–3.10): The Gospel that God is Light, and we must walk in the light as Jesus walked.

---

[1] For an overview of scholarly proposals on the structure of 1 John cf. the discussion in R.E. Brown, *The Epistles of John* (Garden City, NY: Doubleday, 1982), pp. 116-29 and Chart Five on p. 764. Cf. also the summary in P.J. van Staden, 'The Debate on the Structure of 1 John', *HTS* 47 (1991), pp. 487-502.

III. Part Two (3.11–5.12): The Gospel that we must love one another as God has loved us in Jesus Christ.

Conclusion (5.13-21): A statement of the author's purpose.[2]

While there are obvious benefits to Brown's observation about the similarities between the structure of 1 John and that of the Fourth Gospel, the more closely the text is examined, the less convincing this particular outline appears to be. One of the problems is that the two major divisions seem somewhat contrived. Brown bases his conclusion in part on the 'unique' nature of 1.5 and 3.11 which each contain the phrase 'This is the message'. Initially, this phrase seems to function as a structural marker. However, as one looks further, it appears that the phrase might not be able to bear such weight. First, if this phrase were intended to serve as a structural marker, the author misses a wonderful opportunity to underscore this function by not using the same word order in Greek on both occasions. Clearly, this criticism is a minor one, but does give one pause as to whether the proposed use of the phrase was intentional on the writer's part. Second, perhaps the exclusive claims made for the use of ἀγγελία in 1.5 and 3.11 should be modified somewhat in the light of 1 Jn 2.25 where 'This is the message' also occurs (although ἐπαγγελία is used in the latter passage while ἀγγελία appears in the former ones). Other 'formulae' ('This is the command' and 'This is the testimony') are also found in 1 John (3.23 and 5.11, respectively). Another weakness with Brown's suggestion is one common to many bi-partite divisions. If the author has deliberately divided the text into two sections, which are somewhat thematic in character, how are we to account for the repetition of major themes in the latter section that have previously appeared in the former?

Stephen Smalley has proposed a more detailed bi-partite outline. Smalley's division of the text revolves around the exhortations to live in the light and to live as children of God. Each of these exhortations is followed by several basic conditions for fulfilling the exhortations.

I. Preface (1.1-4) The Word of Life

II. Live in the Light (1.5–2.29)
   (a) God is Light (1.5-7)
   (b) First Condition for Living in the Light: Renounce Sin (1.8-2.2)
   (c) Second Condition: Be Obedient (2.3-11)
   (d) Third Condition: Reject Worldliness (2.12-17)
   (e) Fourth Condition: Keep the Faith (2.18-29)

---

[2] Brown, *The Epistles of John*, p. 124.

III. Live As Children of God (3.1–5.13)
   (a) God is Father (3.1-3)
   (b) First Condition for Living as God's Children: Renounce Sin (3.4-9)
   (c) Second Condition: Be Obedient (3.10-24)
   (d) Third Condition: Reject Worldliness (4.1-6)
   (e) Fourth Condition: Be Loving (4.7-5.4)
   (f) Fifth Condition: Keep the Faith (5.5-13)

IV. Conclusion (5.14-21) Christian Confidence [3]

One of the strengths of Smalley's outline is that it attempts to explain the thematic repetition found in the book. However, it also shows signs of being too forced. Two examples may be cited. First, despite Smalley's attempt to explain the cyclical nature of the work, 1 John itself refuses to cooperate fully, as the second exhortation has five not four conditions. Another problem with the outline is that it divides into two separate sections the three erroneous claims of the opponents cited by John in ch. 1, claims which rather clearly are intended to be taken together.

Despite the unlikelihood of a new proposal winning the day on such a complex issue, which many of the best Johannine scholars have addressed, there appears to be room for another proposal which seeks to identify the structure of 1 John without dividing the text into units that ignore the literary patterns contained in the work and without unduly forcing a unit into a structural division simply for the sake of an outline. This proposal, then, focuses attention on the structure of 1 John as revealed by the text itself and seeks, as far as possible, to allow the text to reveal its shape on its own terms.

II

A variety of literary indicators in the work reveal certain dimensions of the text's structure. Raymond Brown has identified several literary patterns in the text of 1 John which may serve as markers identifying specific literary units within the book. These include: (1) three occurrences of ἐὰν εἴπωμεν in 1.6–2.2; (2) three sentences which use the formula ὁ λέγων in 2.4-11; (3) seven clauses in 2.29–3.10 where the construction πᾶς ὁ is followed by a participle; (4) and the use of οἴδαμεν as the lead verb three times at the conclusion of the book (5.18-20). In addition to these textual markers, Brown notes there are a few portions of the text that interpreters never break up owing to

---

[3] S.S. Smalley, *1, 2, 3 John* (Waco, TX: Word, 1984), p. xxxiii.

their subject matter: 2.12-14; 2.15-17; 4.1-6.[4] Such clues, while not solving the puzzle of the structure of 1 John as a whole, do reveal something of the nature of the book's microstructure if not its macrostructure. To ignore clues like these would seem to ensure that the interpreter has little chance of identifying the broader structure of 1 John.

In addition to these hints, a careful reading of the content of the individual passages reveals broader indicators in the text, such as the book's flow and development of thought and especially its repetition of theme and vocabulary, which point to the work's structure. Specifically, it appears that 1 John has a concentric or chiastic structure. That is to say, the text seems to mirror itself, with the most important section standing at the center of the work.

It goes without saying that many 'alleged' chiastic structures are visible only to those scholars who propose them (perhaps this proposal will be so judged at the end of the day) and that numerous scholars doubt their existence altogether. Therefore, it is necessary to indicate what is and is not being claimed here. No claims are made for agreement in terms of length of individual passages nor for an exact mirroring of content in every case. But rather this proposal suggests that the use of similar catchwords/phrases and sections which parallel one another in terms of content indicate a desire for the reader to reflect upon the connections between different portions of the text.

With this disclaimer having been made, the basic structure of 1 John may be set forth as follows:

A – 1.1-4 – Prologue – Eternal Life

  B – 1.5–2.2 – Making Him a Liar (Walking)

    C – 2.3-17 - New Commandment

      D – 2.18-27 – Antichrists

        E – 2.28–3.10 – Confidence – Do not Sin

          F – 3.11-18 – Love One Another

        E' – 3.19-24 – Confidence – Keep the Commands

      D' – 4.1-6 – Antichrists

    C' – 4.7–5.5 – God's Love and Ours

  B' – 5.6-12 – Making Him a Liar (Testimony)

A' – 5.13-21 – Conclusion – Eternal Life

---

[4] Brown, *The Epistles of John*, p. 118.

Although this structure should become clear as the reader makes his or her way through the text of 1 John, limitations of space prohibit an exhaustive examination of the text here. Therefore, in what follows, brief comment is offered on several of the prominent features of the structure of 1 John, with comment first being offered on the structure's center.

Love One Another – 3.11-18
At the center of the book (section F)[5] stands a discussion of what might legitimately be called the most important commandment for the Johannine community, to love one another. The supreme love of Jesus and the corresponding love that believers are to have for one another are contrasted with the hatred of evildoers, the biblical example of Cain illustrating the point. The writer makes clear that this kind of love is closely connected to eternal life, while those who do not love remain in death. The kind of love advocated is one which is expressed not only in word but in deed – helping those which are in need, even to the point of laying down one's life. This passage then contains three ideas/terms that are very important in 1 John: love, eternal life, and remaining (μένω). The emphasis on love is also developed in sections C and C' and is mentioned in two other parts of the book (cf. sections E and E').

Confidence – 2.28–3.10 and 3.19-24
Standing on either side of this central pericope are passages which are connected to one another in several ways but most clearly by the use of the phrase 'confidence (before God?)'. Section E (2.28–3.10)[6] is

---

[5] 1 John 3.11-18 is identified as a major division within the book by C.H. Dodd, *The Johannine Epistles* (New York: Harper, 1946), pp. 81-82; G.P. Lewis, *The Johannine Epistles* (London: Epworth Press, 1961), p. 84; F.F. Bruce, *The Epistles of John* (Grand Rapids: Eerdmans, 1970), p. 32; C. Haas, M. de Jonge, & J.L. Swellengrebel, *A Translator's Handbook on the Letters of John* (London: UBS, 1972), p. 15; I.H. Marshall, *The Epistles of John* (Grand Rapids: Eerdmans, 1978), p. 188; P. Bonnard, *Les Épîtres Johanniques* (Geneva: Labor et Fides, 1983), pp. 73-74; K. Grayston, *The Johannine Epistles* (Grand Rapids: Eerdmans, 1984), p. 5; J.R.W. Stott, *The Letters of John* (Grand Rapids: Eerdmans, 1988), p. 61; D.M. Smith, *First, Second, and Third John* (Louisville: John Knox Press, 1991), p. 88; G. Strecker, *The Johannine Epistles* (ed. H. Attridge; trans. L.M. Maloney; Minneapolis, MN: Fortress Press, 1996), p. 107.

[6] For this division of the text cf. J.C. O'Neill, *The Puzzle of 1 John* (London: SPCK, 1966), pp. 31-32; Brown, *Epistles of John*, pp. 378-79; Bonnard, *Les Épîtres Johanniques*, p. 31; R.A. Culpepper, *1 John, 2 John, 3 John* (Atlanta: John Knox Press, 1985), p. 55; Stott, *The Letters of John*, p. 61; H.-J. Klauck, *Der erste Johannesbrief* (Zurich: Benziger Verlag, 1991), pp. 170-71; C.H. Talbert, *Reading John* (New York: Crossroad, 1992), pp. 28-29. Both N. Alexander (*The Epistles of John* [New York: Macmillan, 1962], pp. 75-76) and Dodd (*The Johannine Epistles*, p. 66) begin this section with v. 29 instead of v. 28.

marked off as a literary unit by the pericope's frequent use of the term τέκνα and the contrasting of those who are born of God with those born of the Devil. Additionally, there are seven occurrences of the construction πᾶς ὁ followed by a participle. There is also an emphasis in this text upon remaining (2.28; 3.6, 9). Clearly, one of the most important emphases of this passage is the correlation between confidence and moral purity. Specifically, in order to be confident (before God?) one must purify oneself as he (Jesus) is pure, practice righteousness, and not remain in sin. The pericope concludes by noting that the one who does not love his brother is not of God.

Although articulated somewhat differently, Section E' (3.19-24)[7] is also concerned with 'confidence before God'. Again, moral purity is very much in evidence, although this time the emphasis is upon whether or not the believer's heart condemns him or her. In this case 'confidence before God' leads to the believer's asking for whatever is needed. The heart does not condemn the one who keeps the commands, especially the commands to believe in the name of his son Jesus Christ and *to love one another*. Whereas moral purity indicates whether or not one is a child of God in section E, here keeping the commands indicates that one remains in God and God remains in him or her. In the former passage, the seed (σπέρμα) of God remains in the believer (3.9), in the latter it is the Spirit that has been given (3.24b).

Antichrists – 2.18-27 and 4.1-6

The two passages that border those devoted to confidence before God have a number of thematic similarities. The first of the two texts, section D (2.18-27),[8] opens with a discussion of the last hour and the

---

[7] The following identify 1 John 3.19-24 as a textual unit: B.F. Westcott, *The Epistles of St John* (Grand Rapids: Eerdmans, 1966), p. 115; Dodd, *The Johannine Epistles*, pp. 87-88; J. Bonsirven, *Épîtres de Saint Jean* (Paris: Beauchesne, 1954), pp. 172-74; Lewis, *The Johannine Epistles*, p. 88; Bruce, *The Epistles of John*, p. 32; Haas, de Jonge, & Swellengrebel, *A Translator's Handbook on the Letters of John*, p. 15; Marshall, *The Epistles of John*, p. 196; Grayston, *The Johannine Epistles*, p. 5; Stott, *The Letters of John*, p. 61; Smith, *First, Second, and Third John*, p. 93; Strecker, *The Johannine Epistles*, pp. 120-30. Slight variations are offered by O'Neill, *The Puzzle of 1 John*, pp. 42-43 (3.19b-24) and F. Vouga, *Die Johannesbriefe* (Tübingen: J.B.C. Mohr, 1990), pp. 58-59 (3.18-24).

[8] 1 John 2.18-27 is identified as a literary division by Dodd, *The Johannine Epistles*, p. 47; Bonsirven, *Épîtres de Saint Jean*, pp. 119-22; O'Neill, *The Puzzle of 1 John*, pp. 23-28; Bruce, *The Epistles of John*, p. 31; Haas, de Jonge, & Swellengrebel, *A Translator's Handbook on the Letters of John*, p. 15; J.L. Houlden, *The Johannine Epistles* (New York: Harper & Row, 1973), p. 75; R. Schnackenburg, *The Johannine Epistles* (trans. R. & I. Fuller; New York: Crossroad, 1992), p. 132; Marshall, *The Epistles of John*, pp. 147-48; Bonnard, *Les Épîtres Johanniques*, pp. 53-54; Culpepper, *1 John, 2 John, 3 John*, pp. 42-43; Stott, *The Letters of John*, p. 61; Vouga, *Die Johannesbriefe*, p. 62; Klauck, *Der erste Johannesbrief*, pp. 145-46; Smith, *First, Second, and Third John*, p. 71; Strecker, *The*

arrival of the antichrists, who were formerly part of the community. It continues by emphasizing the way in which the χρῖσμα they have received from the Holy One ensures that they know all things, the implication being that they should be able to discern the difference between truth and lies. The Liar denies that Jesus is the Christ; the antichrist denies the Father and the Son; those who deny the Son do not have the Father. Proper confession indicates that one has the Father and remains in that which was heard from the beginning. Such remaining is the promise: eternal life. In a final admonition the readers are warned about the deceivers and reminded that if they remain in the χρῖσμα they have received, they will need no teacher, for this χρῖσμα will teach them the truth. There they are to remain.

The parallel to this pericope, section D' (4.1-6),[9] is equally concerned about false teaching and begins with an admonition to test every spirit to determine its origin. Section D had indicated that many antichrists had gone out, now in section D' it is noted that many false prophets have gone out into the world. Like its parallel passage, this text also indicates that confession is an important aspect in discerning/testing the spirits. The one who confesses Jesus having come in the flesh is of God. The one who does otherwise is not only 'not of God', but is identified as the antichrist. Because the readers are 'of God', they hear him; whereas those who are not of God do not hear him. Discerning between the Spirit of God and the spirit of deception is made possible, in part, by the confession one does or does not make.

The New Commandment/God's Love and Ours – 2.3-17 and 4.7–5.5

The two texts which stand on either side of the antichrist passages are devoted to the command to love. In section C (2.3-17)[10] there is a very

---

Johannine Epistles, p. 61. Slight variations are offered by Lewis, *The Johannine Epistles*, p. 88 and Alexander, *The Epistles of John*, p. 65 (2.18-28).

[9] For this division of the text cf. Westcott, *The Epistles of John*, p. 139; C. Gore, *The Epistles of St. John* (London: John Murray, 1920), p. 164; Dodd, *The Johannine Epistles*, p. 97-99; Bonsirven, *Épîtres de Saint Jean*, pp. 185-86; Alexander, *The Epistles of John*, p. 101; O'Neill, *The Puzzle of 1 John*, p. 46; W. Thüsing, *Die Johannesbriefe* (Düsseldorf: Patmos-Verlag, 1970), p. 20; Haas, de Jonge, & Swellengrebel, *A Translator's Handbook on the Letters of John*, p. 15; Houlden, *The Johannine Epistles*, pp. 104-105; Schnackenburg, *The Johannine Epistles*, p. 197; Marshall, *The Epistles of John*, pp. 203-204; Brown, *Epistles of John*, p. 486; Grayston, *The Johannine Epistles*, p. 5; Smalley, *1, 2, 3, John*, pp. 215-17; Culpepper, *1 John, 2 John, 3 John*, pp. 77-78; Stott, *The Letters of John*, p. 61; Klauck, *Der erste Johannesbrief*, pp. 226-227; Smith, *First, Second, and Third John*, p. 97; Strecker, *The Johannine Epistles*, p. 131. Lewis (*The Johannine Epistles*, p. 93) offers a slight variation (3.24b–4.6).

[10] For this division cf. Alexander, *The Epistles of John*, p. 55 and Bruce, *The Epistles of John*, p. 31. Most scholars divide this portion of the text into two sections.

close connection between keeping the commands and loving as one ought. The text begins by asserting that the evidence (knowledge) of knowing God is the keeping of the commands. In contrast to the one who does not keep the commands and is a liar, the one who keeps his word is assured that the love of God has been perfected, which is itself evidence of knowing God. The keeping of the new commandment, to love one's brother, indicates that one walks in the light – for hating one's brother reveals that one walks in darkness. In vv. 12-14 are found six declarations (divided into two poetic sections), about forgiveness of sin, knowledge of the one from the beginning, and victory over the evil one for the young men, in whom the word of God remains. The writer closes this section by returning to a discussion of love, indicating the diametric opposition between love of the world and love of the father. The things of the world, which is fading, are contrasted with doing God's will, which remains forever.

Two things stand out about section C' (4.7–5.5).[11] First, the number of points of contact between this passage and section C are astonishingly high. Second, as 1 John nears its end, several terms that have appeared earlier in the book reappear in this passage. The primary theme of this section is love. The text contains a number of elements which make clear its major emphasis, beginning with a form of the word love (ἀγαπητοί) to address the readers. Following this are affirmations that God is (the origin of) love (vv. 7, 8, 16) and that he first loved us (vv. 10, 19), which resulted in the sending of his son into the world (vv. 9, 10, 14). The command to 'love one another' is never far from view, nor is the connection between loving God and loving one's brother. In point of fact, the evidence of knowing, remaining in, and being born of God is love for one's brother. Whereas in section C (2.4), the one who claimed to know God but did not keep his commands is called a liar, so in C' (4.20) the one who claims to love God but hates his brother is a liar. In the former section (2.5) the love of God has been perfected in the one who keeps his word, while in the latter the love of God has been perfected in those who love one another (v. 12) and remain in God (v. 17). Such perfect love casts out all fear of (the) judgement, while those who fear reveal a lack of such perfected love (v. 18). As in section C, there is a close tie between love and keeping his commands (5.2, 3).

---

[11] Cf. Stott, *The Letters of John*, p. 61. For a similar, though not identical, division of the text (most scholars conclude the section at 5.4 or 5.4a), cf. Alexander, *The Epistles of John*, p. 105; Haas, de Jonge, & Swellengrebel, *A Translator's Handbook on the Letters of John*, p. 15; Schnackenburg, *The Johannine Epistles*, p. 206; Brown, *Epistles of John*, pp. 512-23; Smalley, *1, 2, 3, John*, pp. 235-36; Strecker, *The Johannine Epistles*, p. 142.

But such parallels do not exhaust the ways in which these texts are intertwined. One finds an affirmation about the forgiveness of sins not only in section C (2.12), but also in section C' (4.10). In addition both passages contain declarations about 'overcoming'. In 2.12, 14, it is said that the young men overcome (νενικήκατε) the evil one, while in 5.4, 5 'our faith' is identified as the 'victory that overcomes' (ἡ νίκη ἡ νικήσασα). In section C (2.14) the children 'have known the Father', while in C' (4.7) 'the one who loves knows God'. In 2.14, the word of God 'remains' in the 'young men', while in 4.12, 13, 16 God 'remains' in us. Another point of literary affinity between these passages is found in the statements that concern the one who hates his or her brother (2.11 and 4.20). Both of these sections underscore clearly the fundamental connection between proper claims (belief) and proper conduct (actions).

Along with section F, these two parallel passages make clear that the command to love one another is an extremely important aspect of this work's message.

Making Him a Liar – 1.5-2.2 and 5.6-12

At first glance the texts that stand on either side of the passages devoted to the love command do not appear to be connected in any fashion. However, despite first impressions, there are several ways in which these texts are related. The most impressive similarity is the catchphrase to 'make him a liar'. God is the object in both occurrences of this phrase. This statement is made as a result of an improper claim regarding sinlessness in 1.10 and a lack of belief in God in 5.10. In both cases the veracity of God is being challenged: implicitly in the former, explicitly in the latter. It might not be going too far to say that in section B (1.5-2.2)[12] God is made a liar by an improper claim regarding one's walk, while in section B' God is made a liar by improper belief with regard to God's testimony.

In addition to the appearance of this catch phrase, each of these sections stresses the blood of Jesus. Although the term αἷμα appears only one time in section B (1.7), it clearly exerts a significant influence on the rest of the passage. The relationship of Jesus' blood to sin is that it cleanses the individual from all sin and/or unrighteousness. In section

---

[12] Several scholars identify 1 Jn 1.5–2.2 as a literary unit. Cf. Bonsirven, *Épîtres de Saint Jean*, pp. 83-84; Alexander, *The Epistles of John*, p. 105; Bruce, *The Epistles of John*, p. 31; Haas, de Jonge, & Swellengrebel, *A Translator's Handbook on the Letters of John*, p. 15; Marshall, *The Epistles of John*, p. 108; Brown, *Epistles of John*, p. 192; Culpepper, *1 John, 2 John, 3 John*, pp. 12-15; Stott, *The Letters of John*, p. 61; H.-J. Klauck, *Die Johannesbriefe* (Darmstadt: Wissenschaftliche Buchgesellschaft, 1991), p. 67. Cf. also Schnackenburg, *The Johannine Epistles*, p. 71, who sees 1.6-2.2 as dependent upon 1.5.

B' (5.6-12),[13] the double mention of the blood qualifies the way in which Jesus had come and is identified as one of three witnesses (to Jesus). For the reader of 1 John, the appearance of αἷμα in B' would scarcely be understood in any other fashion than as connected to the cleansing/forgiveness of sin as in section B.

A final point of contact is that both passages begin with similar statements: 'And this is the message...' in 1.5 and 'This is the one who comes...' in 5.6. Near the end of section B' (5.11), a similar phrase appears: 'And this is the testimony...'.

Eternal Life – 1.1-4 and 5.13-21
As might be expected, the beginning and conclusion of 1 John differ significantly in that they serve different purposes. Section A[14] introduces the readers to what follows, while section A'[15] appears to offer a conclusion which in some ways builds upon several themes that have appeared before and develops them further. Yet, despite such divergent aims, they too have something in common. Eternal life is identified in both sections as being central to the purpose of the work. Standing at the heart of section A (1.2-3) is a discussion of eternal life, which here, appears to be a reference to Jesus, and, consequently, the reason for writing. In the first verse of section A', the purpose of the writing is so that the readers would know they have eternal life (5.13). The final portion of this section (5.20) also makes a last reference to eternal life. Given the prominent positioning of eternal life in sections A and A', it

---

[13] Cf. Westcott, *The Epistles of St John*, p. 180; Bruce, *The Letters of John*, p. 32; Thüsing, *Die Johannesbriefe*, p. 21; Stott, *The Letters of John*, p. 61. For similar, though not identical, divisions (most scholars begin the section at 5.4b or 5.5), cf. Haas, de Jonge, & Swellengrebel, *A Translator's Handbook on the Letters of John*, p. 15; Marshall, *The Epistles of John*, p. 230; Bonnard, *Les Épitres Johanniques*, p. 106; Schnackenburg, *The Johannine Epistles*, pp. 230-31; Brown, *The Epistles of John*, p. 569; Talbert, *Reading John*, p. 44; Strecker, *The Johannine Epistles*, p. 181. Slight variations are offered by Bultmann, *The Johannine Epistles*, p. 79; Smalley, *1, 2, 3 John*, pp. 274-75 (5.5-13); Lewis, *The Johannine Epistles*, p. 116; Grayston, *The Johannine Epistles*, p. 5; Smith, *First, Second, and Third John*, p. 121 (5.6-13); Dodd, *The Johannine Epistles*, p. 106 (5.7-12).

[14] There is near unanimity that 1 Jn 1.1-4 is a distinct literary unit.

[15] Westcott, *The Epistles of John*, p. 188; Alexander, *The Epistles of John*, p. 124; Bruce, *The Epistles of John*, p. 32; Thüsing, *Die Johannesbriefe*, p. 21; Haas, de Jonge, & Swellengrebel, *A Translator's Handbook on the Letters of John*, p. 15; Houlden, *The Johannine Epistles*, p. 133; Marshall, *The Epistles of John*, p. 242; Bonnard, *Les Épîtres Johanniques*, pp. 111-12; Schnackenburg, *The Johannine Epistles*, pp. 245-46; Brown, *Epistles of John*, p. 607; Culpepper, *1 John, 2 John, 3 John*, p. 106; Vouga, *Die Johannesbriefe*, pp. 74-75; Klauck, *Der erste Johannesbrief*, p. 318; Talbert, *Reading John*, pp. 50-51; Strecker, *The Johannine Epistles*, p. 197. Slight variations are offered by O'Neill, *The Puzzle of 1 John*, pp. 61-62 (5.13b-21); Lewis, *The Johannine Epistles*, p. 199; Bultmann, *The Johannine Epistles*, p. 85; Smalley, *1, 2, 3, John*, pp. 293-94; Smith, *First, Second, and Third John*, p. 133 (5.14-21).

comes as no surprise to find the reappearance of this topic in sections D, F, and B'.

III

This proposal, then, argues that in contrast to many assessments, the text of 1 John has a rather clear literary structure that is concentric in form. This approach has sought to be respectful of both the literary markers in the text and the way in which content defines the boundaries of certain textual units. In doing so, this suggested outline not only avoids the problem of ignoring the textual indicators with regard to structure, but also goes some way toward explaining much of the book's thematic repetition. It also provides a basic outline that is faithful to the work's major Johannine emphases. As such, this proposal may aid the interpretation of 1 John in several ways.

First, by providing a broad framework in which the many individual units may be read, the reader is encouraged to appreciate the book's theological contribution as a whole, rather than as a series of unconnected blocks of teaching that tend to spiral in a somewhat haphazard fashion. Second, by identifying the arrangement of the book's thematic flow this proposal encourages the reader to pay careful attention to the way in which certain themes and terms appear and reappear throughout the work. By observing the development of these emphases the interpreter is in a better position to identify the theological heart of the work. Third, this proposal calls for additional exploration to determine the extent of the parallel passages' similarities and differences. Such activity cannot help but reveal more of the theological and thematic richness of this document. Fourth, this analysis of the text of 1 John indicates that many of the themes which Johannine scholars have identified as central to the thought of the document are, in many cases, revealed in the structure of the work itself. These include the emphasis on love, eternal life, antichrists, confidence before God, walking in the light, and receiving the testimony of God.

While this investigation has been primarily concerned with literary issues, the results of this literary analysis may have a modest implication for understanding the Johannine community's history a bit better. While debates about the document's literary genre continue among Johannine scholars, the structure here proposed suggests that it was important for the message of 1 John to be retained and perhaps memorized. To deduce that this structure would facilitate memorization appears valid whether 1 John is dependent on the Fourth Gospel or not. However, such a conclusion could support the majority view that 1 John is a commentary of sorts on the content of the Fourth Gospel, written to clarify those aspects of the Fourth Gospel that, in the opinion of the author of 1 John, were being misinterpreted by his opponents.[16] If 1 John were intended to function as a teaching document for the community, its concentric structure might serve to facilitate memorization, thereby enabling those in the community to retain much of this 'commentary' orally.

[16] Cf. esp. the discussion in Brown, *Epistles of John*, pp. 90-92.

Index of Names

Achtemeier, P.J. 70
Ahr, P.G. 203
Aker, B. 171, 172
Albrecht, D. 235
Albright, W.F. 49, 50
Alexander, K.E. 13, 18, 33, 42, 93, 94, 175, 176, 181, 188
Alexander, N. 259, 261, 262, 263, 264
Alexander, P.S. 130, 131, 132, 155
Allen, W.C. 49, 88
Allison, D.C. 51
Archer, K.J. 235
Arndt, W. 170
Arrington, F.L. 171, 227, 235
Aulén, G. 188
Aune, D. 65, 66, 72
Autry, A.C. 235

Bacon, B.W. 209
Baker, R.O. 235
Barker, G.W. 249
Barrett, C.K. 117, 118, 119, 120, 121, 122, 128, 191, 192, 213, 223
Barth, H.M. 97, 98
Barth, K. 17
Bauckham, R.J. 46, 215, 238
Bauer, D.R. 28, 229
Bauer, W. 84, 117, 170
Beare, F.W. 51
Beasley-Murray, G.R. 117, 119, 121, 122, 128, 210, 213
Becker, J. 158

Behm, J. 250
Bell, E.N. 21, 100, 103
Bergman, J. 25
Bernard, J.H. 117, 122, 195, 196
Best, E. 70, 71, 73
Betz, O. 157
Bietenhard, H. 64
Billerbeck, P. 131
Birkey, D. 245
Blass, F. 137, 150
Boer, H. 165
Boismard, M.-E. 121, 214, 223
Bonhoeffer, D. 17
Bonnard, P. 51, 249, 259, 260, 264
Bonsirven, J. 260, 261, 263
Botterweck, G.J. 25
Bowdle, D.N. 164
Branch, R.G. 27
Branick, V. 245
Brassac, A. 106
Braun, F.-M. 214, 249
Braun, M.A. 238
Breck, J. 157
Broadus, J.A. 105
Brown, C. 68
Brown, R.E. 60, 117, 118, 119, 120, 121, 122, 125, 126, 127, 128, 129, 134, 157, 164, 171, 172, 191, 193, 201, 203, 210, 213, 249, 250, 253, 255, 256, 257, 258, 259, 261, 262, 263, 264, 266
Brown, S. 60

Bruce, F.F. 196, 210, 259, 260, 261, 263, 264
Büchsel, D.F. 250
Bultmann, R. 63, 87, 117, 118, 119, 120, 122, 123, 124, 125, 126, 128, 159, 191, 192, 194, 195, 213, 217, 249, 264
Burdick, D.W. 249
Burge, G.M. 111, 157, 161, 163, 171, 172
Busemann, R. 71
Butler, A.H. 97

Callahan, A. 18
Cargal, T.B. 235
Carson, D.A. 51, 52, 125, 164, 173, 196, 199, 210, 213
Chaine, J. 249
Charette, B.B. 17, 30, 115, 184
Chevallier, M.-A. 171, 172
Clemmer, W.M. 85
Clevenger, D.D. 219
Coenen, L. 68
Coggins, R.J. 143
Conybeare, F.C. 105
Corell, A. 121
Countryman, L.W. 213
Cranfield, C.E.B. 68, 72
Crawford, F. 102
Crossan, J.D. 90
Cullis, C. 17, 94
Cullmann, O. 65, 195, 209, 217
Culpepper, R.A. 158, 259, 260, 261, 263, 264

Dana, H.E. 150
Danby, H. 183
Danker, F.W. 85, 88, 170
Daube, D. 138, 139
Davey, F.M. 117, 118, 192, 193
Dautzenberg, G. 65
Davies, W.D. 51
Dayton, D.W. 19, 23, 176
De Jonge, M. 259, 260, 261, 262, 263, 264

De la Potterie, I. 160, 168, 172
Debrunner, A 137, 150
Derrett, J.D.M. 214
Dodd, C.H. 118, 208, 209, 217, 249, 259, 260, 261, 264
Du Rand, J.A. 249
Dugas, P.D. 102
Dunn, J.D.G. 45, 51, 54, 57, 65, 171, 172, 191, 192, 214
Dupont, J. 239

Ebrard, J.H.A. 105
Edwards, R.B. 214, 215
Eisler, R. 214
Elliot, J.K. 77, 80, 81, 82, 83, 106
Ellis, E.E. 63, 235
Ervin, H.M. 164, 171, 235
Evans, C.A. 235

Farag, W. 218
Farmer, W. 79, 80, 81, 82, 83, 92, 111
Fee, G.D. 244
Feine, P. 250
Filson, F.V. 50
Foerster, W. 70
Fortna, R.T. 124, 125, 128
France, R.T. 52, 57, 62, 71
Frank, E. 157
Freyne, S. 69
Freer, C.L. 103, 104
Friedrich, G. 65
Friedrichsen, A. 214
Frodsham, A. 103, 104
Fuchs, A. 219
Fuller, R. 65
Funk, R.W. 150

Gaechter, P. 51
Gause, R.H. 161, 173
Gerhardsson, B. 63
Giess, H. 216, 217
Gingrich, F.W. 170
Gnilka, J. 52

Godbey, W.B. 102, 104
Godet, F.L. 118
Goldstein, A. 66
Gooding, D.W. 227
Goodspeed, E.J. 249
Goppelt, L. 51, 65
Gordon, A.J. 94, 95
Gore, C. 261
Gortner, J.N. 104
Gould, E.P. 81, 82
Goulder, M.D. 52
Grant, F.C. 51
Grayston, K. 249, 259, 260, 261, 264
Green, J.B. 35
Gregory, C.R. 79, 83, 84
Grelot, P. 209
Grossouw, W.K. 210
Grundmann, W. 51, 52
Gummerie, R.M. 195
Gundry, R. 52
Guthrie, D. 173, 249

Haas, C. 259, 260, 261, 262, 263, 264
Haenchen, E. 117, 118, 119, 120, 122, 196
Hammond, C.H. 106
Harder, R. 85
Harrison, R.K. 249
Hauck, F. 184, 195, 199, 209
Hays, R.B. 235
Haywood, G.T. 101, 102
Heil, J.P. 171
Hengel, M. 57, 64, 66, 67, 71, 72, 75, 129, 155, 203, 252, 253
Hicks, R. 183
Higgins, A.J.B. 209
Hill, D. 51, 53
Hinnebusch, P. 75
Hodges, Z.C. 160
Holman, C. 57
Holwerda, D. 165, 169, 172
Hort, F.J.A. 103

Horton, S.M. 172
Hoskyns, E.C. 117, 118, 191, 192, 193
Houlden, J.L. 260, 261, 264
Hubbard, D.A. 238
Hug, J. 109, 110
Hultgren, A.J. 214
Hunter, A.M. 128, 249
Hunter, B.M. 95
Hunter, H.D. 4, 171

Irvin, D.T. 21
Israel, R. 235

Jackson, F.J.F. 223
Jensen, P. 41, 180
Jeremias, J. 66, 88
Johns, C. Bridges 3, 13, 235
Johns, J.D. 12, 235
Johnson, L.T. 224, 237, 249
Johnson, S.E. 84
Johnston, G. 157, 164
Jones, L.P. 161

Kaiser, W.C. 238
Katz, P. 87
Keil, C.F. 238
Kelhoffer, J.A. 108, 109, 111
King, M.L. 17
Klauck, H.-J. 259, 260, 261, 263, 264
Knox, W.L. 84, 209, 214
Kötting, B. 215, 216
Kümmel, W.G. 250
Kydd, R.A.N. 4
Kysar, R. 121, 155

Ladd, G.E. 167, 173
Lagrange, M.-J. 52, 128
Lake, K. 205, 211, 223, 240
Land, S.J. 3, 4, 8, 10, 19, 22, 23, 176
Lane, W.L. 68, 89, 249
Lee, E.L. 96
Lemcio, E.E. 16

Letourneau, P. 158, 170, 171, 172
Lewis, G.P. 259, 260, 261, 264
Lieu, J. 250, 251
Lightfoot, R.H. 84, 118
Lincoln, A.T. 30, 254
Lindars, B. 117, 118, 119, 120, 121, 122, 125, 127, 128, 129, 190, 191, 192
Linnemann, E. 81, 83
Linzey, A. 219
Locher, G.W. 157
Lohmeyer, E. 217
Lohse, E. 65
Lohse, W. 192, 217, 218
Luther, M. 17
Luz, U. 17
Luzarrage, J. 85
Lyonnet, S. 160

Macchia, F.D. 21
MacDonald, W.G. 158
MacGregor, G.H.C. 209
MacMullen, R. 45
Maier, G. 52
Maness, P.G. 216
Mann, C.S. 49, 50
Manns, F. 214
Manson, C. 17
Mantey, J.R. 150
Marsh, J. 184, 191
Marshall, I.H. 214, 224, 225, 249, 259, 260, 261, 263, 264
Martin, J.P. 57
Martin, L.R. 182
Martin, R.P. 68
Martyn, J.L. 156
Marx, W.G. 58
Mason, C.H. 21, 96
Maynard, A. 209
McComisky, T. 69
McDowell, D.H. 186
McLean, M.D. 234
McKay, J. 235
McKay, M.L. 72

McNally, R.G. 235
McNeile, A.H. 51, 52, 53, 54
Mealand, D.L. 58, 59
Meeks, W.A. 156
Meier, J.P. 52, 60
Menken, M.J.J. 163, 164
Menoud, P. 226
Menzies, R.P. 44, 175, 188, 235
Metzger, B.M. 64, 75, 78, 83, 84, 87, 107, 110, 111, 119, 137, 138, 193, 194, 195, 196, 204, 248
Meye, R.P. 70, 88, 89
Michaelis, W. 50
Michaels, J.R. 119, 210, 213, 249
Miles, B. 18
Mix, S. 17
Mollat, D. 184
Moloney, F.J. 193
Montague, G.T. 57
Montgomery, C.J. 94, 100, 185
Moore, G.F. 131
Moore, R.D. 3, 4, 24, 27, 182, 235, 254
Morgenthaler, R. 80, 81
Morris, L. 117, 118, 119, 121, 128, 196, 200
Moule, C.F.D. 64, 85, 91
Mounce, R. 51
Müller, U.B. 157
Murray, A. 94
Mussner, F. 157

Neil, W. 231
Neusner, J. 64, 131, 132, 133, 134, 135, 136, 137, 139, 140, 141, 143, 144, 145, 146, 147, 148, 149, 150, 151, 152, 153, 155, 156
Nicol, G.G. 214
Nicol, W. 124
Niemand, C. 196, 219, 220, 221, 222
Nuzum, C. 185, 186

O'Callaghan, J. 48
O'Neill, J.C. 225, 259, 260, 261, 264
O'Reilly, L. 44
Oepke, A. 195, 209
Olshausen, H. 105
Olsson, B. 249, 250
Owanga-Welo, J. 194, 195, 206, 218, 221

Palma, A.D. 164
Pamment, M. 49
Patte, D. 50
Penney, J.M. 44
Perkins, P. 249
Pernot, H. 217
Perry, S.C. 99, 100
Petersen, N. 90, 91, 92
Petts, D. 173, 175, 176
Peulo, P.-A. 239
Pinnock, C.H. 159, 234
Plummer, A. 117, 249
Porsch, F. 157, 162, 164, 171, 172
Powery, E.B. 17
Purvis, J.D. 138

Quast, K. 213

Rackham, R.B. 225
Radl, W. 115
Reedy, C.J. 86, 87
Rengstorf, K. 62
Rensberger, D. 156, 160, 248
Reumann, J. 249
Rhodes, D.R. 218
Richter, G. 217
Roberts, C.H. 226, 227, 229
Robinson, J.A.T. 118, 130, 155, 195, 196, 249
Roebuck, D. 21
Rowley, H.H. 138
Ruckstuhl, E. 117, 127, 128
Ruddi-Weber, H. 72

Salmon, G. 105
Sanders, J.N. 196, 235
Sawders, J.E. 97
Schiffman, L.H. 138
Schlatter, A. 50, 117
Schlier, H. 200
Schmidt, T.E. 58, 59
Schnackenburg, R. 51, 117, 118, 119, 121, 122, 127, 128, 137, 157, 172, 213, 249, 260, 261, 262, 263, 264
Schneiders, S.M. 214
Schniewind, J. 50
Schultz, J. 199
Schunack, G. 249
Schweizer, E. 51, 57, 67, 73, 127, 159
Scott, J.J. Jr. 53
Scrivener, F.H.A. 105
Segovia, F.F. 196, 205
Sevrin, J.-M. 41, 180
Sexton, E. 97
Seymour, W. 18
Shearer, W.C. 106
Shelton, J.B. 36, 44
Sheppard, G.T. 234, 235
Simpson, A.B. 94, 187
Smalley, S.S. 117, 119, 121, 123, 128, 130, 156, 255, 256, 257, 261, 262, 264
Smith, D.M. 123, 124, 128, 259, 260, 261, 264
Smith, R.H. 52, 57, 58
Solivan, S. 9
Spurling, R. 21
Stagg, F. 52, 72
Staley, J.L. 158
Stibbe, M.W.G. 248
Stott, J.R.W. 259, 260, 261, 262, 263, 264
Strachan, R.H. 128
Strack, H.L. 131
Strecker, G. 249, 259, 260, 261, 262, 264

Stronstad, R. 4, 44, 227, 230, 235
Suess, Dr. 94
Swellengrebel, J.L. 259, 260, 261, 262, 263, 264
Swete, H.B. 78, 107
Synan, V. 4

Talbert, C.H. 226, 249, 259, 264
Tannehill, R.C. 90, 91, 92
Tasker, R.V.G. 191
Taylor, C. 109
Taylor, G.F. 103
Taylor, V. 68
Teeple, H.M. 124, 128
Temple, S. 124
Tenney, M.C. 249
Theissen, G. 67
Thomas, J.C. 3, 4, 15, 17, 21, 22, 23, 24, 33, 40, 41, 93, 157, 158, 161, 176, 179, 180, 195, 211, 229, 248, 252
Thüsing, W. 261, 264
Thyen, H. 117
Tolstoy, L. 17
Tomlinson, A.J. 21, 99, 100, 103
Tregelles, S.P. 106
Trilling, W. 53
Trompf, G.W. 85, 86
Turner, M. 44, 158, 172, 173, 176, 239
Twelftree, G.H. 179

Urshan, A. 101

Van der Horst, P.W. 84, 85
Van Staden, P.J. 255
Vellanickal, M. 160
Vermes, G. 65, 142, 143
Von Harnack, A. 118
Von Tischendorf, C. 102
Von Wahlde, U. 124
Vouga, F. 260, 264

Waddell, R.C. 183
Walker, W.O. 51
Wall, R.W. 16, 33, 228
Walvoord, J.F. 54
Weeden, T. 89, 91
Weiss, H. 214
Wengst, K. 249, 252
Wesley, J. 17
Westcott, B.F. 103, 117, 209, 260, 261, 264
Wheeler, T. 187
Whitney, S.W. 105
Wilkens, W. 127
Williamson, W.P 100
Wilson, M.R. 182
Windisch, H. 157, 172
Winter, B.W. 223
Witherington, B. III 228
Wyckoff, J.W. 234

Zahavy, T. 147
Zweifel, B. 217, 221

Index of Biblical and Other Ancient References

BIBLICAL REFERENCES
(WITH APOCRYPHA)

Genesis
12.1-3 25
18-21 26
20 26
24.58 68
25.21 26
30.22-24 26
34.25 147
48.14 153
48.18 153
49.26 153

Exodus
1.18 68
4.6-8 26
4.29-31 26
12.21 68
15 94
15.26 26, 185
19.5 237
19.7 68
20.4-6 182
20.8-11 141
29.8 153
30.17-21 210
40.30-32 210

Leviticus
8.12 153
11.29-38 133
12.3 146
16.30 209
17-18 240
23.38 142

Numbers
9.10-12 153
12 26
15.35 143
21 26, 185, 186, 187
21.4-9 181, 187
21.9 42, 181, 182, 186
35.30 148

Deuteronomy
7.6 237
8.15-16 164
14.2 237
19.15 148
21.23 72
26.18-19 237
32.39 27

Joshua
7.6 153

Judges
3.19 208
3.28 66
12.1 68
13 26

1 Samuel
1 26
10.1 153
12.6 68

2 Samuel
1.10 153
3.29 153

1 Kings
7.38 210
12.21 68
13.33 68
17 27
17.24 27

2 Kings
4 26
4.29 85
5 27
5.15 27
5.17 27
17 138
18.4 182

2 Chronicles
2.18 68
4.6 210
7.13-14 28
7.20 28

Nehemiah
9.1 153
13.19 142

1 Maccabees
2.27-28 66
6.1-2 138

Psalms
18.14 209
19.13 209
50.4 209
51.2 209
103 94

Wisdom
16.5 13

Sirach
23.10 209
38.10 209
50.25-26 138

Tobit
7.9 195

Isaiah
2.3 238
19.22 27
38 26
42.6 238
53 94
53.4 29, 95

Jeremiah
17.21-22 141

Lamentations
2.10 153

Ezekiel
33.4 153

Joel
2.28 98
3.4 153
3.7 153

Amos
5.25-27 239
8.15 67
9.9-15 238
9.11-12 236, 237, 238

Obadiah
15 153

Micah
4.2 238

Zechariah
2.11 238

Matthew
3.7-11 60
4.8-10 58
4.18-22 58
4.23-25 28, 29
4.24 56
5-7 28, 29
5.1 63
5.3-10 60
5.20 56, 59
6.1-4 58
6.17 153
6.19-24 58
6.25-34 58
7.15-23 57, 60
7.15-20 46
7.21 56, 59
7.22 57
7.28-29 229
8-10 29
8-9 28, 29
8 94
8.16-17 29, 175, 176, 188
8.16 56
8.17 95
8.18-22 58
8.23-27 29
8.28-34 56
9.8 38
9.9-13 58, 59
9.32-34 56
9.33 38
10 28
10.1 29, 185
10.3 59
10.5-15 57
10.5 29
10.7-8 114
10.7 29
10.8 29
10.9-10 58

10.24 200
10.41 57
11.1 229
11.18-19 59
12.9-14 29
12.22-37 56
12.22-32 29
12.22 56
12.28 48, 49, 51, 52, 54, 55, 56, 57
12.33-37 60
12.43-45 57
13 28
13.44-46 58
13.53 229
14.35-36 29
15.1-20 151
15.21-28 29, 56
15.31 38
16.1-4 115
16.24-28 58
17.14-20 29
17.14-18 56
17.19-22 57, 58
17.24-27 58
18 28
18.3 56, 59
18.21-35 58
19.1 229
19.16-22 58
19.23-30 58
19.23 56, 58, 59
19.24 48, 52, 54, 55, 56, 58, 59
20.1-16 58
20.29-34 29
21.11 65
21.12-17 58
21.18-22 60
21.23-46 55
21.23 60
21.31 48, 52, 54, 55, 56, 59, 60
21.32 59
21.43 48, 49, 52, 53, 54,

55, 56, 60
21.45 60
22.15-22 58
23 18, 55
23.5-12 60
23.14 56, 59
24-25 28
24.23-28 57
24.45-51 58
24.51 204, 205
25.14-30 58
25.31-46 60
25.37-46 58
26.1 229
26.6-13 58
26.14-16 58
26.17 153
27.1-10 58
27.38-44 58
27.57-61 58
28.11-15 58
28.16-20 29
28.17 114
28.18-20 95, 114
28.19 114
28.20 95

Mark
1.1-16.8 81, 82, 83
1.1 30
1.2-13 30
1.4 82
1.14-15 30
1.16-20 30, 67
1.17 70
1.21-28 31
1.21 81
1.27 85
1.29-34 31
1.30-2.4 81
1.35-39 31
1.35 81
1.40-45 31
1.45 32
2.1-3.6 31

2.1-12 31, 33
2.7-8 31
2.12 38, 85
2.13-14 67
2.28 64
3.1-6 31, 143
3.6 31
3.7-12 31
3.10-11 31
3.13-6.13 31
3.13-19 68, 70
3.13-14a 31
3.13 68
3.14b-15 31
3.14 68
3.15 69
3.16 68
3.20-30 31, 69
3.31-34 31
3.31 81
4.1-34 31
4.35-41 31
4.41 85
5.1-20 31, 70
5.15 89
5.20 32, 38, 81
5.21-43 31, 70
5.33 89
5.34 33
5.36 89
5.42-43 85
6.1-6a 31, 69
6.1 63
6.2 85
6.4 65
6.6b-13 69
6.7-13 70
6.7 31, 69
6.12-13 32
6.12 114
6.13 22
6.14-29 32
6.15 65
6.30 32, 70
6.50 89

6.52 85
7.1-23 151
7.3 151
7.31-37 32
7.37 85
8 70
8.11-12 115
8.11 81
8.22-10.52 70
8.22-26 70
8.27-28 65
8.31-11.10 86
8.34-38 70, 73
8.34 71, 72
8.35-38 74
9.5 63
9.6-7 85
9.6 89
9.30 81
9.32 89
10.1-12 63
10.1 185
10.32-33 85
10.33 82
10.46-52 70
10.52 33
11.18 85
11.21 63
11.30 81
12.2 81
12.4-5 82
13.35 81
14-15 90
14.3 153
14.28 82
14.43 81
14.45 63
14.64 82
15.1 81
15.44 85
16 95, 96, 97, 98, 100, 101, 102
16.1-8 89
16.2 81
16.5-6 85

16.8 77, 79, 80, 81, 83, 84, 85, 87, 88, 89, 90, 91, 92, 93, 105, 106, 108, 111
16.9-20 18, 33, 77, 79, 80, 81, 83, 86, 91, 92, 93, 94, 95, 102, 103, 105, 106, 108, 109, 110, 111, 112, 114, 115
16.9-14 33, 83, 112
16.9 80, 81, 83, 108, 114
16.10 81, 83, 87, 91, 112, 113
16.11 81, 82, 83, 112, 113
16.12-13 110, 114
16.12 81, 82, 83
16.13 83, 112, 113
16.14 34, 77, 82, 83, 106, 113
16.15-20 81, 83
16.15-18 34, 96, 112
16.15 34, 81, 82, 83, 113, 114
16.16 82, 83, 113, 114
16.17-20 103
16.17-18 34, 96, 113
16.17 83, 113
16.18 83, 100
16.19-20 34, 112, 113
16.19 83, 108
16.20 34, 80, 81, 83, 96, 108, 109, 113, 114

Luke
1.27 238
1.32-33 238
1.69 239
2.4 239
2.11 239
3.31 239
4 35, 36
4.16-30 63
4.18-19 35
4.25-26 27
4.35 83
5.17 36
5.25-26 37
6.3 239
6.17-49 36
6.18-19 36
6.38 184
7.16-17 38
7.22 35
7.44 216
7.46 153
8.2 110, 114
8.46 36
8.48 37
9.1-6 37
9.1-2 37
9.6 37
9.8 81
9.10 37
9.43 38
10.1-24 37
10.4 85
10.9 37
10.17 37
10.19 115
10.25-37 139
11.37-54 151
12.46 205
13.17 38
13.32 36
17.10 199
17.11-19 37
17.14 37
17.19 37
18.35-43 37
18.38-39 239
18.42-43a 37
18.43 38
20.41-44 239
21.28 111
21.38 116
22.24-27 220
22.27 220, 221
22.51 35
24.13-35 114
24.13-32 110
24.50-53 115

John
1-12 163
1.1-18 117
1.1 159
1.2 159
1.3-4 162
1.4 39, 118, 178
1.7 118
1.9 118
1.10-11 167
1.10 118
1.11-12 118
1.12-13 160
1.12 159, 165, 204
1.13 160
1.14 118, 159, 161, 167
1.16 161
1.17 161
1.18 159
1.19-39 210
1.29 159
1.32-33 158, 159, 160
1.32 162
1.33 162, 166, 173, 207
1.35-51 123
1.38 137, 168
1.39 41, 63, 180
1.41 137
1.46 41, 180
1.49 63
2.1-12 123
2.1-11 120, 133
2.5 39, 178
2.6 133, 210
2.11 38, 39, 123, 124, 177, 178
2.22 168, 204
2.24 38, 177
3 159, 161, 162, 181, 187

Index of Biblical and Other Ancient References

3.2 63, 168
3.3 159, 160
3.5 48, 126, 160, 165
3.6-8 160
3.7 160
3.14-15 42, 160, 181, 185, 186, 187, 188
3.14 42, 165, 181, 185, 186
3.15 42, 181
3.15-16 39, 178
3.16-21 160
3.16 184
3.17 120
3.18-19 120
3.21 161
3.22-30 119
3.22 119, 207, 210
3.24 126, 137
3.26 65
3.31-36 127
3.34 160, 162, 166
3.35-36 204
3.36 39, 178, 184
4-7 121
4 137, 160, 165
4.1-42 123
4.1-2 210
4.1 119
4.2 119, 126, 207
4.8 137, 138
4.9 137
4.10 160
4.14 39, 161, 165, 178
4.21 161
4.22 161
4.23-24 165
4.23 41, 120, 161, 162, 167, 180
4.24 162
4.25 40, 137, 179
4.27 138
4.29 41, 180
4.31-38 43, 205, 252
4.31 63

4.36 39, 178
4.39-42 162
4.42 38, 177
4.43-54 123
4.44 137
4.46-54 38, 177
4.50 39, 178
4.51 39, 178
4.53 39, 178
4.54 121, 123, 124
5 121, 122, 145, 148
5.1-18 38, 39, 143, 177, 178
5.1-16 124
5.1 121
5.6 39, 178
5.9 143
5.14 40, 179
5.15 40, 179
5.24-25 120
5.28-29 120, 126
5.30 169
5.31-47 147
5.33-35 147
5.36-44 147
5.40 184
5.45 147
5.46-47 147
6 121, 122, 124
6.1-30 124
6.1-15 184
6.1-14 124
6.1 121, 137
6.2 38, 40, 177, 179
6.4 121
6.12 184
6.13 184
6.16-26 124
6.22-59 165
6.25 63
6.33 184
6.35 184
6.39-40 120, 126
6.40 204, 205
6.41-58 184

6.44 120, 126
6.48 184
6.51-58 126
6.51 184
6.53-56 207
6.53 162
6.54 120, 208
6.59 168
6.63 162
6.68 162
6.71 137
7 119
7.1-13 124
7.1 121
7.3 119
7.8 119
7.10 119, 120
7.14-24 146
7.14 168
7.21-23 147
7.21 38
7.22 137
7.28 168
7.33 169
7.35 168
7.36 111, 116
7.37-39 163, 167, 171, 172
7.37-38 164
7.37 163
7.38-39 166
7.38 163, 164, 165
7.39 163, 165, 166, 173
7.44 111
7.52 111
7.53-8.11 116
8 148
8.13 147
8.14 169
8.15 120
8.16 120
8.20 168
8.21 169
8.31 171
9 41, 145, 180

9.1-41 38, 178
9.2 63
9.3 40, 41, 179, 180
9.6-7 145
9.7 40, 137, 179
9.11 40, 145, 179
9.15-17 179
9.15 145
9.17 40,180
9.24 41,169, 180
9.25-33 41,180
9.27 41,180
9.28 41,180
9.34 41,180
9.39-41 41,180
10.10-22 124
10.10 183, 184
10.17-18 170
10.28-29 204
10.28 184
11 41, 180
11.1-57 38,178
11.1-44 124
11.4 41,180
11.8 63
11.12 41,180
11.15 41,180
11.20-27 41,180
11.28 168
11.33 166, 170
11.34 41,180
11.41b-42 42,181
11.45 42,181
12 203
12.16 168, 204
12.31 170
12.37 38, 177
12.47 120
12.48 120
13-21 203
13-17 203
13 122, 201, 202, 204, 210, 213, 215, 216, 219, 220
13.1-30 211
13.1-20 202, 216, 217, 218
13.1-17 219
13.1-11 217
13.1-6 219
13.1 203
13.2 203
13.3 169, 203, 204
13.4-10 198, 200
13.4-5 220
13.4 203
13.6-11 220
13.6-10 199
13.6-8 220
13.7 168, 204
13.8-9 150
13.8 191, 196, 201, 204, 206, 210
13.9-10 220
13.9 151, 192
13.10 190, 191, 192, 194, 195, 206, 207, 208, 209, 210, 220, 221
13.11 203
13.12-20 127, 217, 220, 221
13.12-17 196
13.12-13 200
13.12 211
13.13-14 168
13.14-17 197, 198, 201, 202, 211, 212, 214
13.14-15 219
13.14 198, 199
13.15 199, 200
13.16 200
13.17 201
13.21 166, 170
13.27 211
13.33 169
13.34 252
14-16 166, 173
14 122
14.1-14 205
14.4 169
14.6 161, 162, 167
14.12-13 43
14.13-14 167
14.15-31 166, 167
14.16 167
14.17 165, 167, 173
14.22 137
14.26 168
14.28 169
14.31 122
15-17 122, 129
15.1-16.33 127
15.1-17 205
15.3 208
15.18-16.4 205
15.20 200
15.26-16.4 43,172
15.26 168, 169
15.27-16.4 168
16.4-15 169
16.5-6 169
16.5 169
16.7 169, 172, 173
16.8 169
16.9 169
16.10 169
16.13-15 40, 179
16.13 170
16.15 170
17.5 172
17.13-21 43
18.1 122
18.9 126
18.10 137
18.20 168
18.28 153, 155
18.32 126
19.7 198
19.13 137
19.17 137
19.26-27 170
19.30 170
19.34-35 126
19.34 42, 164, 171, 181,

Index of Biblical and Other Ancient References

207
19.35 128, 129
19.38 38, 177
20.9 137, 164
20.16 137, 168
20.19-23 43, 171, 252
20.21-23 173, 205
20.22 171, 172, 173
20.24 137
20.26 172
20.30-31 38, 116, 124, 177
20.30 117, 123
20.31 117
21 116, 117, 124, 127, 129
21.2 137
21.7 137
21.20-23 129
21.20 137
21.24 116, 128, 129
21.44 111

Acts
1-12 226
1-7 224
1.1-6.7 226
1.1-5.42 224
1.1-2.47 224
1.1-5 230, 232
1.1 43, 115
1.6-12.25 225
1.6-11 115
1.6-2.47 230, 232
1.8 44, 95, 224
1.9-8.3 225
1.12-2.41 227
1.16 239
1.21-22 226
2 114
2.1-4 15, 44, 226, 231, 232
2.14-15.12 228
2.14-40 226
2.17 98

2.19 44
2.22 44
2.25 239
2.29-36 239
2.38 114
2.42-6.7 227
2.43 44
2.47 15, 227, 229
3.1-6.7 230, 232
3.1-5.42 224
3.1-10 44, 226
3.12-26 226
4.25 239
4.29-30 44
4.30 44
4.30-31 15, 44, 231, 232
5.1-11 231
5.9 237
5.12 44
5.14 45
5.15-16 44
5.34-39 226
6.1-11.18 224
6.1-9.31 224
6.1-6 226
6.7 15, 226, 228, 229
6.8-12.24 227
6.8-9.31 226, 230, 232
6.8-8.4 226
6.8-7.60 227
6.8 44
6.13-14 226
7.17 184
7.38 44
7.42-44 239
7.45 239
7.54 115
7.56 43
8-12 224
8.1-40 227
8.4-11.18 225
8.6-7 44
8.9-24 226, 231
8.14-17 15, 44, 226, 231, 232

9.1-19 43, 115
9.31 15, 226, 229
9.32-12.24 226
9.32-11.21 230, 232
9.32-11.18 224
9.33-34 44
9.34 43
9.36-43 226
9.36-42 44
9.37 209
9.42 45
10-11 226
10 114
10.25-26 226
10.44-48 15, 44, 231, 232
11 114
11.19-28.31 224
11.19-15.35 225
11.19-14.28 224
11.21 15, 227, 229
11.22-12.24 230, 232
11.24-28 15, 44, 231, 232
12 226
12.6-11 226
12.12 245
12.24 15, 226, 228, 229
12.25-28.31 228
12.25-16.5 226, 230, 232
13-28 224, 225, 226
13-21 226
13.1-3 226
13.4-12 231
13.6-12 226
13.9 15, 44, 231, 232
13.12 45
13.16-40 226
13.22-23 239
13.34 239
13.36 239
14.3 44
14.8-13 226
14.8-10 44

14.13-15 226
14.15-17 226
14.19-23 226
14.23 226, 240
15 236, 239, 240, 241,
    242, 243, 245, 246,
    247
15.1-35 224
15.1-29 235
15.12 44
15.13-28.28 228
15.13-18 238
15.16-18 238
15.17 238
15.24 239
15.28 236
15.36-19.20 225
15.36-18.17 224
16.5 15, 226, 229
16.6-19.20 227, 230,
    232
16.7 43
16.16-18 231
16.24-26 226
16.33 209
18.6 153
18.18-20.38 224
18.24-28 221
18.26 245
19 114
19.1-17 15
19.1-7 44, 231, 232
19.1-6 226
19.11-20 114, 231
19.11-12 55
19.17-18 45
19.20 15, 226, 229
19.21-28.31 225, 227,
    230, 232
20.7-12 55
20.9-12 226
20.22-21.11 15, 44, 231,
    232
21-28 224, 226
21.9 244

21.11 226
21.20-21 226
22.6-16 43
22.16 209
23.9 226
23.11 226
25.8 226
26.12-18 43
26.16 226
28.1-6 115, 231
28.3-9 44
28.3-6 99
28.31 15, 226, 228

Romans
3.24 186
15.19 45
16.1 244
16.3 244, 245
16.7 245
16.12 244

1 Corinthians
2.4-5 46
6.11 209
8.1-13 240
11.3-16 244
11.5 244
11.28 211
12 114
12.9 45
12.28 45
12.30 45
14 114
14.33-35 244
16.19 245

Ephesians
5.26 209

Philippians
2.6-7 82
4.3 244

Colossians
4.15 245

1 Thessalonians
1.5 46

1 Timothy
2.11-12 244
5.9-10 245
5.10 202, 216, 218

Titus
2.4 244
3.5 209

Hebrews
10.22 209
12.2 115

James
5 22
5.14-18 47
5.16 17

1 Peter
2.24 175, 188

1 John
1 257
1.1-4 255, 256, 258, 264
1.2-3 264
1.5-3.10 255
1.5-2.29 256
1.5-2.2 258, 263
1.5-7 256
1.5 40, 179, 256, 263,
    264
1.6-2.2 257, 263
1.7-9 207
1.7 209, 263
1.8-2.2 256
1.9 209, 210
1.10 263
2.1-2 210
2.1 167

2.3-17 258, 261	4.12 262	21.4 46
2.3-11 256	4.14 262	21.8 204
2.4-11 257	4.16 262, 263	22.19 204
2.4 262	4.17 262	
2.5 262	4.18 262	
2.6 199	4.19 260	OTHER ANCIENT
2.7-8 252	4.20 262, 263	REFERENCES
2.11 263	5.2-3 262	
2.12-17 256	5.4-5 263, 264	*Acts of John* 83
2.12-14 258, 262	5.5-13 257	
2.12-13 263	5.6-12 258, 263, 264	Ambrose
2.13 263	5.6 264	104
2.14 263	5.7 111	
2.15-17 258	5.10 263	*Of the Holy Spirit*
2.16 263	5.11 256, 264	1.15 201
2.18-29 256	5.13-21 256, 258, 264	
2.18-27 252, 258, 260	5.13 210, 264	*Mysteries*
2.25 210, 256	5.14-21 257	6.31 212
2.28-3.10 258, 259	5.18-20 257	
2.28 260	5.20 264	*Sacraments*
2.29-3.10 257		3.4 202
2.29 259	2 John	7 202
3.1-5.13 257	5 252, 254	
3.1-3 257	10-11 252	*Apostolic Constitutions*
3.4-9 257	10 251	3.19 202
3.6 260		
3.9 260	3 John	Augustine
3.10-24 257	17, 127, 248, 249, 250,	104
3.11-5.12 256	251, 252, 253, 254	*Homilies on John*
3.11-18 258, 259	8 199	58.5 212
3.11 256		
3.16 199	Jude	*Letter*
3.19-24 258, 259, 260	3 18	55.33 202
3.23 256		
3.24 260	Revelation	*John: Tractate*
4.1-6 252, 257, 258, 260, 261	1.4-5 161	58.4 202
	1.5 207	
4.7-5.5 258, 261, 262	5.9 207	Benedict of Nursia
4.7-5.4 257	7.14 207	*Regula Monachorum*
4.7-8 262	7.17 46	35 202
4.7 263	9 18	
4.9-10 262	13.3 46	Caesarius of Arles
4.10 262, 263	13.12 46	*Sermon*
4.11 199	19.13 207	1 202
4.12-13 263	20.6 204	10 202

16 202
19 202
25 202
67 202
86 202
104 202
146 202
202 202

Canons of Athanasius
66 201

Citiensis, A. 200

1 Clement 112

Cyprian, The Synod of Elvira
Canon
48 202

Chrysostom 104

Cyril of Jerusalem
Lecture
13.20 183

Didache
14 211

Epistle of Barnabas 112
12.5-7 183

Eusebius
Eccl.Hist.
V.1.26 240

Hippolytus
Refutation of all Heresies
11 183

Ignatius
Epistle to Polycarp
6.1 205

Martrydom of Polycarp
14.2 205

Irenaeus
Against Heresies
3.10.5 108

Jerome
104

John Cassian
Institute of Coenobia
4.19 202

John Chrysostom
Genesis Homily
46 202

Homilies on John
71 201

Josephus
Antiquities
IX, 291 138
XII, 286 209

Wars
II, 131 151

Justin Martyr
104

Apology
I.45.5 80, 109

Dialogue with Trypho
41 183
44 183

Lactantius
The Divine Institutes
26 183
51 183

Midrashim
130

Mishnah
130, 131, 132, 133, 183
Berakoth
7.1 140
8.8 139

Shebiith
8.10 141

Shabbat
7.2 145
11.1-2 143-44
19.1 146
19.3 147
19.4 147
22.5-6 145

Pesahim
6.2 146

Rosh Ha-Shanah
3.8 183

Hagigah
2.5 153

Besah
2.2. 135
2.3 135

Yebamot
15.1-2 148-49

Ketubot
1.6-9 149-50

Eduyoth
3.2 153

Kelim
5.11 134
25.7-8 135

Oholet
18.7-9 154

Parah
3.2 136
Niddah
4.1 140

Yadayim
3.1 153
3.1-2 151-52

Origen
Genesis Homily
4.2 202, 212

On the Passion
14-15 183

Pachomias
Rules
51-52 202

Philo
Allegory
2.19-21 183
2.76-81 183

Plotinus
Treaties
30-33 84

Plutarch
Moralia
958B 195

The Shepherd of Hermas
112

Seneca
Epistulae Morales
LXXXVI, 12 195, 206

Sozomen
Ecclesiastical History
1.11.10 202

Talmud
130, 131

Tatian
Diatessaron 108

Tertullian
De Corona
8 201

On Idolatry
5 183

To His Wife
2.4 202

Testament of Issac
1.7 51
2.8 51
8.5-6 51

Testament of Jacob
2.25 51
7.11 51
7.19-20 51
7.23 51
7.27 51
8.3 51

Testament of Levi
9.11 195

Testament of Reuben
4.8 209

www.ingramcontent.com/pod-product-compliance
Lightning Source LLC
Chambersburg PA
CBHW032002220426
43664CB00005B/110